Libr@ries:

*Changing Information Space
and Practice*

Libr@ries:
Changing Information Space and Practice

Edited by

CUSHLA KAPITZKE
University of Queensland

BERTRAM C. BRUCE
University of Illionis, Urbana-Champaign

 LAWRENCE ERLBAUM ASSOCIATES, PUBLISHERS
2006   Mahwah, New Jersey   London

Lawrence Erlbaum Associates, Inc., Publishers
10 Industrial Avenue
Mahwah, New Jersey 07430
www.erlbaum.com

Cover design by Tomai Maridou

Library of Congress Cataloging-in-Publication Data

Libr@ries : changing information space and practice / edited by Cushla Kapitzke and Bertram C. Bruce.
    p.   cm.
Includes bibliographical references and index.
ISBN 0–8058–5481–9 (alk. paper)
    1. Libraries—Information technology. 2. Library science—Technological innovations. 3. Digital libraries. 4. Libraries and society. 5. Information society. 6. Information technology—Social aspects. I. Kapitzke, Cushla. II. Bruce, Bertram C.
Z678.9L51135   2006
025'.00285—dc22   2005050743

Books published by Lawrence Erlbaum Associates are printed on acid-free paper, and their bindings are chosen for strength and durability.

Printed in the United States of America
10 9 8 7 6 5 4 3 2 1

Dedicated to our mothers

— Iris Lucy —

grace, peace, protection, *parrhesia*.

Macushla

— Catherine Eva —

whose willingness to take the @ into her life
is only one of many ways in which she has remained
inquisitive and continued to grow.

Chip

Contents

Foreword: Information Politics in Education   ix
  Michael A. Peters

Preface   xiii

Illustrations, Figures and Tables   xvii

About the Contributors   xix

Introduction   xxv
  Cushla Kapitzke and Bertram C. Bruce

I Arobase Space

1 Digital Libraries as Virtual Spaces   3
  Nicholas C. Burbules

2 Literacy Spaces—Library Design   17
  Susan Boyce

3 Ordered by Desire: School Libraries in Past and Present Times   37
  Mark Dressman and Sharon Tettegah

4 From Library to Cybrary: Changing the Focus   57
  of Library Design and Service Delivery
  Janine Schmidt

5 Surrogation, Mediation and Collaboration: Access to Digital   73
  Images in Cultural Heritage Institutions
  Abby A. Goodrum

II Arobase Knowledge

6 Next Generation Metadata Tools: Supporting   91
  Dynamic Knowledge Spaces
  Jane Hunter

7 Knowledge Management and Research in Cybraries   113
   David Rooney and Ursula Schneider

8 Cybraries in Paradise: New Technologies   133
   and Ethnographic Repositories
   Linda Barwick and Nicholas Thieberger

9 Redefining Libr@ries by Rethinking Research   151
   Cushla Kapitzke

III Arobase Capital

10 The Scholarly Wing of the Public Cybrary   179
   and the Right to Know
   John Willinsky

11 The Politics and Philosophy of E-text: Use Value, Sign Value,   197
   and Exchange Value in the Transition from Print
   to Digital Media
   Timothy W. Luke

12 Alternatives to Pay-for-View: The Case for Open Access   211
   to Historical Research and Scholarship
   Mark Lawrence Kornbluh, Melanie Shell-Weiss,
   and Paul Turnbull

13 Search Engine Anatomy: The Industry   229
   and Its Commercial Structure
   Bettina Fabos

14 Monopoly, Monopsony, and the Value of Culture   253
   in a Digital Age: An Axiology of Two
   Multimedia Resource Repositories
   Phil Graham

15 Structuring Open Access to Knowledge: 271
   The Creative Commons Story
   Brian Fitzgerald

16 The Arobase in the Library—The Libr@ry in Society   281
   Bertram C. Bruce and Cushla Kapitzke

Author Index   295
Subject Index   305

Foreword:
Information Politics in Education

Michael A. Peters

That information is the vital element in a "new" politics and economy linking space, knowledge, and capital is the central theme and premise of this provocative and compelling volume. The chapters focus on the information utility, as they carefully style it—*libr@ries*—a neologism that speaks of the ways in which virtualized libraries blend place and space, transforming social practices of information use. They adopt an approach to the changing role and function of libr@ries in the emerging "global information infrastructures" that firmly resists the easy temptation, characteristic of much literature in this area, to reify technology, setting it free in the abstract as a set of technical innovations and forces that drives all social change. By contrast, drawing on poststructuralist approaches, the editors, Cushla Kapitzke and Bertram C. Bruce, want to emphasize the embeddedness, contextual, and cultural craftedness of information use as a set of social practices, and to insist, as they put it in their Introduction: "No (informational) text is free of politics." This is to underline the specific politics and eco-cybernetic rationalities that accompany an informational global capitalism comprised of new multinational edutainment agglomerations capable of colonizing the emergent ecology of info-social networks, in part, through notions of information literacy (see Kapitzke, 2003).

The choice of language to describe the library as an informational utility (see Taylor, 2004) is no accident: It is a deliberate recombinant coding of the language of practice and of ecology. This twofold aspect is worthy of further reflection.

The language of practice taken primarily from Foucault and applied within discourse provides both a materialist and historicist understanding of information use and user, emphasizing its contingent status as networked practices (of the self). This understanding, which characterizes the editors' Foucauldian approach, avoids the essentialization of information as either a third dimension of matter, or its use as a necessary and universal feature of being human, which is common to Heideggerian-inspired philosophies. Instead, Kapitzke and Bruce reposition practices of information networking and information users as variable, contingent, and local (self)-constructions that can be revealed through empirical investigation. In this the editors clearly identify themselves with the contemporary turn to practices (Schatzki, Knorr Cetina, & Von Savigny, 2001)—which privileges practical reason and the practical over the theoretical, based on a return to Aristotle, to the continuing influence of Marx, and to the currency of both Heidegger and Wittgenstein—a turn that clearly influenced both Foucault and Bourdieu. In this approach, theory of practice is embedded in the priority of practical engagement with the world, a materialist social ontology, and a view of language as practice based.

Turning to ecology, some theorists claim that the network is a pattern common to all life. The concept of the network was developed in the 1920s to describe communities of organisms linked through food webs, and its use was extended to all systems levels: cells as networks of molecules, organisms as networks of cells, ecosystems as networks of individual organisms (Barabási, 2002; Capra, 1996). The notion of networks has recently been used to describe society and to analyze a new social structure based on networking as a new form of organization (Castells, 1996). Whereas the network pattern is a basic organizational pattern of all living systems (Capra, 2004, p. 29) whose key characteristic is self-generation—the continual production, reproduction, repair and regeneration of the network—the critical question is whether there is a basic unity integrating biological, cognitive, and social dimensions, or whether there are significant and irreducible differences between biological and info-social networks, as suggested by the analysis of practices.

On the strong view held by Capra, social networks are self-generating networks of communication that, unlike biological networks, operate in the nonmaterial realm of meaning rather than matter, and are produced for a purpose according to some design. Like biological networks, as they develop they form multiple feedback loops that become self-generating, producing a shared or common context of meaning, which we call culture. Capra argued that it is through this networked culture that individuals acquire their identities as members of the social network. Social networks emulate this feature in that all living organisms have a physical boundary that discriminates between the system, the "self," and the environment.

If we accept the strong version, then we might argue with Capra (2004, p. 33) that "the key challenge of our new century—for social scientists, natural scientists and everyone else—will be to build ecologically sustainable communities." As he argued: "A sustainable community is designed in such a way that its technologies and social institutions—its material and social structures—do not interfere with nature's inherent ability to sustain life. In other words, the design principles of our future social institutions must be consistent with the principles of organisation that nature has evolved to sustain the web of life" (Capra, 2004, p. 33). But what does it mean to build ecologically sustainable informational communities that are not dominated, distorted, or deprived by the demands of global capital?

Kapitzke and Bruce (Introduction, this volume) provide us with some guides to answer this complex question. They provide clues, for instance, in their cultural history of time and space as basic referential categories for the contemplation of newly spatialized practices of libraries and they talk of the commodification of space and time, and of informational space under the combined pressures of globalization and corporatization. They also embrace the idea of an informational commons based on open source and freedoms of content, code, and infrastructure. Perhaps, most importantly for them, and as if to underline the cultural diversity of information practices, they choose and reinvent the French concept of *arobase* and propose *arobase space* as "sets of discursive practices shaped by the affordances and constraints of digital technologies which simultaneously manifest the historically constituted facets of place" (p. xxxiii) to provide a nondeterministic, dynamic, and socially embedded understanding of technologies that must be appreciated in terms of the "material, social and cultural contexts of use."

Castells (2004) also identified society through its specific social structures—"the networks powered by microelectronics and software based information and communication technologies" (p. 222), which he suggested have the following consequences: "the network society expands on a global scale" without borders; "networked organisations outcompete all other forms of organisation" (p. 222) in business, bureaucracy and education; "the networking of political institutions is the de facto response to the management crisis suffered by nation states in a supranational world" (p. 223); "civil society is reconstructed at the local and global level through networks of activists, often organised and debated over the internet, which form and reconfigure depending on issues, on events, on moods, on cultures" (p. 223); "sociability is transformed in the new historical context, with networked individualism emerging as the synthesis between the affirmation of an individual-centred culture, and the need and desire for sharing and co-experiencing" (p. 223); "the whole range of social practices, both global and local, communicates in the media space" (p. 223);

and finally, as if in confirmation of the approach taken by Kapitzke and Bruce, he concluded "in this network society, power continues to be the fundamental structuring force of its shape and direction" (p. 234). He elaborated: "But power does not reside in institutions, not even in the state or in large corporations. It is located in the networks that structure society. Or, rather, in what I propose to call the 'switchers'; that is, the mechanisms connecting or disconnecting networks on the basis of certain programmes or strategies" (p. 234). Surely, the libr@ry, as understood by Kapitzke and Bruce, is precisely that utility "switcher" capable of mediating and, to some extent, controlling the connections between the media, the market, the political, and the educational.

This is a vital collection to be read not only by teachers, librarians, and academics of all persuasions, but also, more broadly, by the general reading public.

—*Michael A. Peters*
College of Education
University of Illinois, Urbana-Champaign
Champaign IL
USA

REFERENCES

Barabási, A-L. (2002). *Linked: The new science of networks*. Cambridge, MA: Perseus.

Capra, F. (1996). *The web of life*. London: HarperCollins.

Capra, F. (2004). Living networks. In H. McCarthy, P. Miller, & P. Skidmore (Eds), *Network logic: Who governs in an interconnected world?* (pp. 25–34). London: Demos.

Castells, M. (1996). *The rise of network society*. Oxford, England: Blackwell.

Castells, M. (2004). Afterword: Why networks matter. In H. McCarthy, P. Miller, & P. Skidmore (Eds.), *Network logic: Who governs in an interconnected world?* (pp. 221–225). London: Demos.

Kapitzke, C. (2003). (In)formation literacy: A positivist epistemology and a politics of (out)formation. *Educational Theory, 53*(1), 37–53.

Schatzki, T. R., Knorr Cetina, K., & Von Savigny, E. (Eds.). (2001). *The practice turn in contemporary theory*. London: Routledge.

Taylor, J. (2004). The information utility. In H. McCarthy, P. Miller, & P. Skidmore (Eds.), *Network logic: Who governs in an interconnected world?* (pp. 179–188). London: Demos.

Preface

> *Henceforth, the visionary experience arises from the black and white surface of printed signs, from the closed and dusty volume that opens with a flight of forgotten words; fantasies are carefully deployed in the hushed library, with its columns of books, with its titles aligned on shelves to form a tight enclosure, but within confines that also liberate impossible worlds.*
>
> —Foucault (1977, p. 90)

In this, the age of global competition for national economies and educational systems alike, some would say that nothing is more crucial than a well-funded library replete with café au lait, or even, as in the institution where Cushla works, a 10-meter stream with real goldfish, vines, and trees, traversing the ground floor. In contrast, others say that in the current age of technologized disembodiment, nothing is more passé than having to front up physically to the library and a living human being with whom one must engage. Given this paradox, what are we to make of libraries today after some six millennia of use?

In some ways, Umberto Eco's stagnant monastic library and Ben Franklin's iconic civic institution have transmogrified into the infinite, chaotic, and ultimately useless Library of Babel, which Borges (1941) described so presciently long before the Internet. And yet, in other ways, little has changed in the world and the ways of libraries. In a prophetic style similar to that of Borges, Foucault's *Fantasia of the Library* cited earlier sought a new imaginary space in which reason and erudition fuse with unreason, fancy, and fantasy to disturb and disrupt the control and order of modernity and the positivist epistemologies epitomized for so long by the theory and practice of libraries. Yet, despite Foucault's vision and the panoply of digital technologies that theoretically make his dream possible, nonpositivist meaning and information spaces remain tantalizingly close and frustratingly far off.

This book has been written to explore tensions and contradictions that currently occur in, through, and around libraries. Virtual libraries, interactive digital museum objects, mobile phone access to scholarly databases, blogs and vlogs, Wikipedia, and so on, are just some of the developments with which library professionals and users are currently confronted. Written for practitioners and scholars alike, it seeks to provide theorized analyses of the shift from print-bound places to digital environments, logics, and cultures in and through what we call, libr@ries.

For millennia, libraries have functioned as repositories of social memory and cultural capital, comprising key sites for learning. In mutually beneficial synergies, literati and librarian produced, preserved, and distributed valorized texts and knowledges, and thereby played key roles in the interconnected political economies of society and schooling. But access to information resources and services is now losing its ties to time, place, face-to-face social interaction, and the micropolitics of institutional mediation. Bit by bit and brick by brick, online technologies and new media are disassembling the institutional spaces, privileges, powers, and practices of libraries.

Libr@ries: Changing Information Space and Practice addresses the current historical moment in which digitization and virtualization are transforming that traditional cultural icon, the library, into market-driven libr@ries. It brings together a distinguished group of scholars from a range of disciplinary backgrounds who variously interpret and problematize the increasing dematerialization and commodification of knowledge spaces and practices.

We open the book with an explanation of the term *arobase,* which is used to conceptualize the mutual infusion of social activity with technology, and which is changing libraries, knowledge, space, and capital so dramatically. Part I explores the notion of arobase space through chapters by Nicholas C. Burbules: Susan Boyce; Mark Dressman and Sharon Tettegah; Janine Schmidt; and Abby A. Goodrum. Part II turns to arobase knowledge through chapters by Jane Hunter; David Rooney and Ursula Schneider; Linda Barwick and Nicholas Thieberger; and Cushla Kapitzke. The chapters in Part III by John Willinsky; Timothy W. Luke; Mark Lawrence Kornbluh, Melanie Shell-Weiss, and Paul Turnbull; Bettina Fabos; Phil Graham; and Brian Fitzgerald consider the paradox of arobase capital and argue that the emergence of the libr@ry is emblematic of widespread change in public access to information, education, literacy, and intellectual property. We conclude with reflections on space, place, and the impact of the arobase.

ACKNOWLEDGMENTS

As just one manifestation of the great ongoing human conversation in a multitude of forms and modes of communication, this book is the product of many influences, inputs, and energies. We gratefully acknowledge the contribution made by Australian Research Council Discovery Funding for the project, *Multiliteracies, School Libraries, and Cybraries,* which provided a basis for the work. We especially thank Emma Charlton, Mark Bahr, Sharon Comstock and others—including teachers and librarians of various schools in Queensland and Illinois—who contributed to that project.

The School of Education at the University of Queensland supported Cushla during a semester of Special Study Program (sabbatical) leave. Chip and Susan Bruce, and the faculty of the Graduate School of Library and Information Science at the University of Illinois, Urbana-Champaign, graciously hosted Cushla during her visit to the United States in March 2004.

Chip would like to thank the Graduate School of Library and Information Science at the University of Illinois, Urbana-Champaign, as well as his colleagues and students there, for providing a stimulating and supportive environment for thinking about issues of new libraries and knowledge spaces. He also expresses appreciation for the 2004–2005 sabbatical year support from the university, which allowed a dedicated portion of time to produce the book.

Allan Luke and Carmen Luke suggested we send the prospectus to Naomi Silverman at Lawrence Erlbaum Associates, and we thank them for that. From the outset, Naomi supported the idea and helped bring the project to fulfillment through helpful suggestions and the right balance of flexibility and encouragement for us to stay more or less on schedule. Erica Kica at Lawrence Erlbaum Associates also was consistently helpful. Dawn Butler provided valuable editorial assistance locally. Ross Kapitzke, as always, afforded a keen and critically constructive eye, and Susan Bruce read and made suggestions for the introduction and conclusion.

We thank the contributors for submitting excellent chapters in a timely fashion, and for responding to detailed queries from us and Lawrence Erlbaum Associates. It is challenging to write in a rapidly changing context and for a multidisciplinary audience. Their chapters show that they successfully met that challenge.

The ghost of Mato and many like him haunt these pages (see chap. 16). Yet, as the opening quote from Trifonas in chapter 9 reminds, the "specter of the past" contains within it "a dream of the future." Family and friends constitute the physical point, place, and purpose of that dream for Cushla. In particular, Dan, Katrina and Julian—like their partners and friends— embody the amity, optimism, courage, and commitment needed to realize that future. Cushla thanks them for the fun, the fear, the frustration, the conversation, and the inspiration.

REFERENCES

Borges, J. L. (1998). Library of Babel. In *Collected fictions* (A. Hurley, Trans.), pp. 112–118. New York: Penguin.

Foucault, M. (1977). Fantasia of the library. In D. F. Bouchard (Ed.), *Michel Foucault: Language, counter-memory, practice: Selected essays and interviews* (D. F. Bouchard & S. Simon, Trans.; pp. 87–109). Ithaca, NY: Cornell University Press.

Illustrations, Figures, and Tables

FIG. I.1.   The arobase in a Parisian cityscape.   xxvii

FIG. 2.1.   Mininarratives for literacies.   28

FIG. 2.2.   Mininarratives for contextual surfaces and spaces   29
of the library.

FIG. 9.1.   Sculpture by Petrus Spronk outside the Victorian   153
State Library (Melbourne, Australia) that is based
on a feature of the Library's portico.

FIG. 9.2.   Homepage for Infocus Web site.   167

FIG. 16.1.   "Executive of the Dalmatian Peasants Party 1904."   290
Mato Drvenica, middle row 2nd from right. Josip
Smodlaka, middle row 3rd from right. Yele Drvenica's
brother, Machune Yerenich, back row 3rd from right.

TABLE 3.1.   Librarian practice and student response in three   40
school libraries, c. 1993

TABLE 3.2.   Librarian practice in three technologically equipped   48–49
school libraries, c. 2004

TABLE 14.1.   Sources of communications industry revenues   264

About the Contributors

LINDA BARWICK is a Senior Research Fellow in the Department of Music, University of Sydney, and is currently Director of PARADISEC (Pacific and Regional Archive for Digital Sources in Endangered Cultures), a collaborative cross-institutional initiative established in 2003 by the Universities of Sydney, Melbourne, and Australian National University for digital preservation and access to Australian researcher field recordings of endangered languages and musics of the Asia-Pacific region. Linda has research interests in Italian traditional music, Australian indigenous music, and music technology. Now based at the University of Sydney, she has published widely on theoretical matters and on field research in Australia, Italy, and the Philippines, and has collaborated in the recording and production of a number of CDs of Australian Indigenous music. She is an advocate for collaborative community-based research and the importance of intangible cultural heritage.

SUSAN BOYCE is currently Head of Library at the secondary Caulfield Campus of Caulfield Grammar School, an independent coeducational school in Melbourne, Australia. As part of her master's and doctoral studies, Susan has explored the sociopolitical implications of new communications technologies on changing literacy practices and spatial relations within the situated and networked spaces of two school communities.

BERTRAM (CHIP) BRUCE is a Professor of Library and Information Science, Curriculum and Instruction, Bioengineering, Writing Studies, and the Center for East Asian and Pacific Studies at the University of Illinois, Urbana-Champaign. Before moving to Illinois, he taught Computer Science at Rutgers (1971–1974) and was a Principal Scientist at Bolt Beranek and Newman (1974–1990). He received a BA in Biology from Rice

University in 1968 and a PhD in Computer Sciences from the University of Texas, Austin, in 1971. His central interest is in learning—the constructive process whereby individuals and organizations develop as they adapt to new circumstances. This work draws on ideas such as John Dewey's theory of inquiry, as well as on action research and situated studies. Much of it has focused on changes in the nature of knowledge, community, and literacy, as discussed in *Literacy in the Information Age: Inquiries into Meaning Making with New Technologies*, and other recent writing.

NICHOLAS C. BURBULES is the Grace Wicall Gauthier Professor in the Department of Educational Policy Studies at the University of Illinois. He has published widely on issues of educational philosophy, new technologies in education, and critical social and political theory. His most recent publications include *Watch IT: The Risks and Promises of New Information Technologies for Education* (Westview Press: 2000), with Thomas A. Callister, Jr., and more recently, *Pragmatism and Educational Research* (with Gert Biesta) and *Poststructuralism and Educational Research* (with Michael Peters), both forthcoming with Rowman & Littlefield Publishers.

MARK DRESSMAN is an Associate Professor in the Department of Curriculum and Instruction at the University of Illinois, specializing in the area of secondary literacy and literature instruction. His current research focuses on adolescents who struggle in school and the uses of theoretical frames in literacy research. Mark can be contacted at mdressma@uiuc.edu.

BETTINA FABOS teaches in the Department of Communication Studies at the University of Northern Iowa. She has written extensively about the role of the Internet in education, and has published articles about media representations in popular culture. Fabos is author of *Wrong Turn on the Information Superhighway: Education and the Commercialism of the Internet* (Teachers College Press), and is coauthor of *Media and Culture: An Introduction to Mass Communication* (Bedfords/St. Martin's). She received her MA from the University of Michigan, and her PhD from the University of Iowa, where she was awarded an Iowa Presidential Fellowship and a Spencer Fellowship. Fabos is also an award-winning video maker and former print reporter.

BRIAN FITZGERALD is a well-known intellectual property and information technology lawyer. He is coeditor of one of Australia's leading texts on E Commerce, Software, and the Internet—*Going Digital 2000*—and has published articles on law and the Internet in Australia, the United States, Europe, Nepal, India, Canada, and Japan. His latest (coauthored) books are *Cyberlaw: Cases and Materials on the Internet, Digital Intellectual*

Property and E Commerce (2002); *Jurisdiction and the Internet* (2004); and *Intellectual Property in Principle* (2004). His current projects include work on digital copyright issues across the areas of open content licensing and the Creative Commons, free and open source software, fan based production of computer games, licensing of digital entertainment, and anticircumvention law. In 2002, Brian was appointed as Head of the School of Law at Queensland University of Technology in Brisbane, Australia.

ABBY A. GOODRUM is the Velma Rogers Graham Research Chair in News Media and Technology and an Associate Professor in the School of Journalism, in association with the Edward S. Rogers Sr. Graduate school for Advanced Communications at Ryerson University. She holds a B.S. and M.S.L.I.S. from the University of Texas and a PhD in Information Science from the University of North Texas. Dr. Goodrum's research addresses the relation of various aspects of emerging information and communications technologies to information seeking, retrieval, and access.

Prior to coming to Ryerson University, Dr. Goodrum was on the faculty at Syracuse University in the School of Information Studies as well as a research scientist at the Information Institute of Syracuse and research associate with the Convergence Center for Communication and Media Studies. While on leave in 2004/05 she was a visiting research professor at the Canadian Centre of Arts and Technology, University of Waterloo.

Dr. Goodrum has authored or coauthored a book and more than 35 book chapters, journal articles, and refereed conference papers. She also serves on the editorial boards of the Journal of the American Society for Information Science & Technology and the Annual Review of Information Science & Technology.

PHIL GRAHAM is Associate Professor in Communication at the Business School, University of Queensland, and Canada Research Chair in Communication and Technology at the Faculty of Arts, University of Waterloo. He is coeditor of *Critical Discourse Studies,* and is widely published in the areas of new media, political economy of communication, discourse analysis, and media history.

JANE HUNTER is a Distinguished Research Fellow at the Distributed Systems Technology CRC. For the past 5 years, she has been project leader of the Multimedia Access for Enterprises Across Networks and Domains (MAENAD) project, which is developing data models, ontologies, metadata standards (Dublin Core, MPEG-7, MPEG-21), schemas, software tools and query languages to enable the indexing, archival, analysis, integration, and management of large multimedia collections. Over the past 5 years, she has published 1 book chapter, 10 (peer-reviewed) international journal papers, and 20 (peer-reviewed) international conference papers in the area of multimedia digital libraries. She has also been an editor of MPEG-7, Head of Australia's Delegation to MPEG, Chair of a number of MPEG Working groups, and PI on the Harmony International Digital Library project. She was an inaugural Smithsonian-Qld Fellow in 2001. She is currently the liaison between MPEG (Moving Pictures Experts Group) and W3C (World Wide Web Consortium) on the Editorial Board of the Elsevier Journal of Web Semantics.

CUSHLA KAPITZKE teaches in the School of Education at the University of Queensland, Australia. Her publications include *Literacy and Religion* (John Benjamins) and an edited volume, *Difference and Dispersion: Educational Research in a Postmodern Context* (PostPressed). She has published in *Educational Theory, Teachers College Record, Journal of Adolescent & Adult Literacy,* and *Educational Technology & Society.* Current research interests focus on the social and educational implications for Australia of intellectual property rights law as framed by the bilateral Australia/U.S. Free Trade Agreement.

MARK KORNBLUH is Professor of History and Director of the MATRIX Center for Humane Arts, Letters and Social Sciences at Michigan State University. He is also Executive Director of H-Net, Humanities and Social Sciences Online, and one of North American's leading researchers in the field of history in networked digital media. His publications include, *Why Americans Stopped Voting: The Decline of Participatory Democracy and the Emergence of Modern Electoral Politics, 1880–1918* (New York: New York University Press, 2000). Mark can be contacted at mark@mail.matrix .msu.edu

TIMOTHY W. LUKE is University Distinguished Professor of Political Science at Virginia Polytechnic Institute and State University in Blacksburg, Virginia. He also is the Executive Director of the Institute for Distance and Distributed Learning, and he serves as Codirector of the Center for Digital Discourse and Culture in the College of Arts and Sciences at Virginia Tech. His most recent books are *Capitalism, Democracy, and Ecology: Departing from Marx* (University of Illinois Press, 1999); *The Politics of Cyberspace* (ed. with Chris Toulouse; Routledge, 1998); and *Ecocritique: Contesting the Politics of Nature, Economy, and Culture* (University of Minnesota Press, 1997). His latest book, *Museum Politics: Powerplays at the Exhibition,* was published in Spring 2002 with the University of Minnesota Press.

DAVID ROONEY'S principle research and teaching interests are in knowledge policy, knowledge management, creative industries, and change management. He supervises research students with interests in creative industries, knowledge management, and change management. His PhD was based on historical studies of the relationship between technology and various levels of organization in the Australian music industry. David has published extensively in relation to knowledge-based economies, knowledge management, change management, and creative industries. He has won in the vicinity of $1 million in competitive research and teaching grants. He is currently Associate Director of the Center for Social Research in Communication and the Australian Creative Resources Archive, and is formerly Director of UQ Business School's Business Communication Program.

JANINE SCHMIDT is University Librarian at the University of Queensland. She took up this post 10 years ago and is responsible for a network of 13 branch libraries located at the three campuses of the university—St Lucia, Gatton, and Ipswich—and in the teaching hospitals. Also included within the responsibilities of the university librarian are the university archives and e-zones providing over 1,300 computers and an *Ask*IT computer training and help service for all students. She has also been responsible for calling a library a cybrary, denoting the combination of physical space and cyberspace in its facilities and service provision, its real and virtual collections, and its in-person and online information assistance. The library is the largest in Queensland and has over 2 million volumes, 13,000 print journal subscriptions, 18,000 e-journals, 135,000 e-books, 25,000 videos, and 650 networked databases, as well as pictorial and manuscript collections. The library employs 245 staff and has an annual budget of $26 million. All services and facilities design are focused on the library's clients. Janine is a graduate of the University of Queensland and has a master's degree in Librarianship from the University of New South Wales. She has published widely and speaks regularly at conferences.

URSULA SCHNEIDER is Professor and Head of the Department of International Management, Karl-Franzens Universität, Resowi-Zentrum G1, Universitätsstrasse 15, A-8010, Graz, Austria. She can be contacted at ursula.schneider@kfunigraz.ac.at

MELANIE SHELL-WEISS is Assistant Professor of History at Johns Hopkins University, and Assistant Director of H-Net, and works extensively with issues surrounding Multimedia and Teaching, as well as creating Multimedia classroom tools. She is currently revising her dissertation on immigration and 20th-century Miami, Florida, for publication. Melanie can be contacted at melanie@mail.h-net.msu.edu.

SHARON TETTEGAH is currently a faculty member in the Math, Science, and Technology Division of Curriculum and Instruction at the University of Illinois, Urbana-Champaign. She also holds a zero time appointment in Educational Psychology in the Cognition, Learning, Language, Instruction, and Culture (CLLIC) Division and is a faculty affiliate of the African American Studies and Research Program. She teaches courses on technology integration, identity and cyberspace, development of online instruction, and equity issues and technology (digital divide). Her current research interest is on teacher attitudes and perceptions using technology as a medium to understand behaviors.

NICHOLAS THIEBERGER is a Postdoctoral Fellow in Linguistics at the University of Melbourne and project manager of the Pacific and Regional Archive for Digital Sources in Endangered Cultures. His PhD dealt with documentation of a language of Vanuatu. His current interest is in developing methods for representation of ethnographic material based on reuse of the products of primary research and the implications that has for our ordinary practice as ethnographers.

PAUL TURNBULL is Professor of History and Historical Informatics at James Cook University, and an Adjunct Professor at the Center for Cross-Cultural Research at the Australia National University. He is Australia's leading researcher in the field of history in networked media and creator of South Seas, a web-based hypermedia companion to James Cook's momentous first Pacific voyage (1768–1771). He is a past President of H-Net, Humanities and Social Sciences Online. Among his recent publications is the coedited collection, *The Dead and Their Possessions: Repatriation in Principle, Policy and Practice* (Routledge, 2002).

JOHN WILLINSKY is currently the Pacific Press Professor of Literacy and Technology and Distinguished University Scholar in the Department of Language and Literacy Education at the University of British Columbia, and a Fellow of the Royal Society of Canada. He is the author of *Learning to Divide the World: Education at Empire's End* (Minnesota), which won Outstanding Book Awards from the American Educational Research Association and *History of Education Society*, as well as the more recent titles, *Technologies of Knowing* (Beacon) and *If Only We Knew: Increasing the Public Value of Social Science Research* (Routledge).

Introduction

Cushla Kapitzke
University of Queensland

Bertram C. Bruce
University of Illinois, Urbana-Champaign

> *Libraries contain gold, pure gold. The gold that banks contain is worthless compared to the contents of scientific libraries . . . and it's all free!*
>
> —Daniel, postgraduate science student

> *I don't have to go to the library anymore. If it's not on the Net, I don't want it.*
>
> —Sophie, Information Environments student

Foregoing the customary opener—something profound from philosopher or poet—we chose the previous comments made by students in the course of casual conversation. We did this for two reasons. First, they give voice to the raison d'être of educational institutions and their libraries, namely, learners all. And, second, their startling differences of viewpoint capture the continuities and contradictions, the politics and possibilities of emergent libraries and other forms of information organization and access. Daniel's fervent appreciation of his university library resonates with some of our own experiences of libraries as familiar places where people go for a range of different reasons. As symbols of institutional and community support, they are deemed variously friendly, safe, and helpful places to go not only for information per se, but also for community, colleagues, and a place to work, learn, and engage with culture. Part of what we want to do in this book is to examine the notion of library in all its richness as implied by Daniel's comment.

Sophie's quote, however, represents a different perspective. For those like her, the library lacks capital in the image stakes and is, quite simply, not relevant. Rather than reveling in the riches that libraries have to offer, she sees them as outmoded, difficult to use, and inadequate to the fast-paced information environments of today. Sophie views the traditional library as a constraining *place*, and she seeks a *space* of new possibilities. Her experiences of information and learning are tied to a web of hyper-linked multimedia, rather than to "bricks and mortar" and physical docu-ments. For some of us, Daniel's enthusiasm for the library as place invokes fond memories of our experience of libraries, but at the same time Sophie's fascination with the Internet resonates with a different set of experiences in which we see the virtual world playing a bigger role in our lives. In fact, as many librarians and library users are discovering, there may not be a simple choice of place versus space.

The purpose of this book is to explore the tension between Daniel's place and Sophie's space, as it is reflected in the new libr@ry. As editors, we set ourselves the challenge of exploring the multiple ways in which physical libraries are assimilating virtual libraries, and vice versa. That is, we sought to understand how library as place and library as space blend together in ways that may be both contradictory and complementary, a blending revisited in the concluding chapter. In turn, this exploration pro-vides opportunity to examine community, culture, and history, as they have been conceived in traditional libraries, to inform conceptions of vir-tual space. Seeking a suitable term to designate this rapidly evolving and much contested object of study, we devised the word *libr@ry* and employ the term *arobase* to signify the conditions of formation of new libraries within contexts of space, knowledge, and capital.

THE AROBASE IN THE LIBR@RY

We began the project using the word *cybrary* (from *cybernetics* and *library*) as a generic expression encapsulating the range of terms commonly used to denote new library and information forms. After the realization that notions of digital libraries and hybrid libraries did not sit comfortably together within the semantic parameters of the term *cybrary*—which had an established history and quite specific application—we subsequently devised the term *libr@ry*. Whereas some contributors chose to continue using the term *cybrary*, we adopted *libr@ry* to avoid privileging technolog-

FIG. I.1.   The arobase in a Parisian cityscape.

ical aspects of shifts in library and information practice. The symbol "@" that was inserted within the word *library* is used to indicate that technological mediation has a history, an established set of practices, and a political economy, which the technology may alter but not fully supplant. It is offered here as a semiotic space, deliberately speculative, variable, and open to be rejected, or adopted and co-constructed by those envisioning a different discursive and disciplinary field for libr@ries of the future.

This rhetorical device is used to convey two things. First, digital tools and new media are part of the current practice of traditional libraries. Second, "new" cannot be understood merely in technical terms, but must be considered within the context of long-standing questions around who has access to materials, how they are used, and who has control over them. We avoid the convenient phrase "new" because it tends to allude to improvement or advancement of the old, and to support teleological approaches assuming social progress through technological development. These approaches ultimately generate either naïve celebration or condemnation of technological innovation. In relation to space, for example, we refrained from adopting the terms *digital space, virtual space,* and *cyberspace* because they too privilege *techné* and invite a decontextualized understanding of technological affordances and constraints. This disembedding of techné from the social creates simplistic and unhelpful dichotomies between old and new, technical and nontechnical, virtual and real, and so on. Alternatively, the term *libr@ry* represents and foregrounds the incorporation of change in information use as ongoing social practices.

As used here, the symbol "@" refers to evolving discursive practices that are infused with—and which in turn infuse—technological values and logics. This familiar sign is used in e-mail addresses and is seen in the streets of major cities to identify Internet cafés. For example, the image in Fig. I.1 of a café in Europe used by one of us author during the writing of this chapter contains no less than 9 @s.

The symbol "@" has had a long and somewhat confused history (*Bibliothèque Nationale de France*, 2004; Herron, 1997; *Le dictionnaire encyclopédique de la langue française du XXIe siècle*, 2004; *Le 'pataphysicien Net*, 2004; Quinion, 2002; Tallmo, 1995). This history is emblematic of the ambiguous and often conflicting aspects of technology developments today. Both the symbol itself and the words used to describe it have evoked diverse responses in the realms of commerce, diplomacy, technology, art, and humor, and these reflect the multiple ways in which new information and communications technologies (ICTs) are entering into our daily lives in every way.

For example, the sign was used in commerce to indicate prices, and to denote locations long before the advent of e-mail. In 1896, the surrealist playwright Albert Jarry used it on the costume of Père Ubu in *Ubu Roi*. The words for the symbol are as diverse as the cultures using it. Finns use the term "miau" (cat), Germans say "Klammeraffe" (monkey's tail), Italians say "chiocciola" (snail), Israelis say "strudel," Americans say "at," Swedes say "Snabel-a" (elephant trunk), and Czechs say "rollmop." All of these words metaphorically signify nonlinearity and open circularity. Rather than employing the somewhat awkward symbol "@," or the English preposition "at," we deliberately sought a non-English term that would flow better and evoke the global dimensions of the processes under investigation. We therefore chose the French term *arobase*, and use it here to signify the recursive processes by which digital technologies are assimilated into existing material conditions and social relations through space, knowledge, and capital.

LIBR@RIES: SPACE, KNOWLEDGE, AND CAPITAL

Libraries often have been framed in terms of places, as mere repositories of organized collections. Birdsall (1994), Nardini (2001), and M. L. Radford and G. P. Radford (2001) showed the power of metaphors of place and their related assumptions and social values through which industrial age libraries were experienced and interpreted. Contemporary libraries, however, comprise increasingly complex informational networks and diverse ecologies providing access to online services and resources within global information infrastructures.

Our position on this complexity is that, irrespective of what physical forms these entities take, what counts epistemologically as a library or other knowledge resource is a product of discursive practice. That is, whereas information materials and services exist as objects and processes in the world, they have no *social meaning* outside of language, location, history, and culture. Library resources and services are understood and used within the meaning making of their designers, creators, managers, and users.

Following theorists like Foucault (1973) and Fairclough (1995), *discourse* is used here to refer to a rule-directed set of statements that enables and constrains what can and cannot be thought, said, and done in and through sites of social and pedagogical activity like libraries. We assume a genealogical approach in which technological innovation is viewed in relation to a field of forces. It is disruptive of these forces, and replete with possibilities for both emancipatory and oppressive social practices and relations. This follows the premise that no (informational) text is free of politics because, irrespective of whether it is part of an inquiry exchange at a reference desk or national policy formulation, all semiosis is awash with agendas, interests, values, and ideologies. Regardless of the context—real, virtual, or the conflated "real/virtual"—information work spaces are not outside of the logics and politics of text (i.e., language and image). Library buildings and their virtual counterparts alike can be viewed as texts that tell stories about their historical times, social powers, and political economies. Because the most successful ideological effects are those "that have no need for words, and ask no more than complicitous silence" (Bourdieu, 1977, p. 188), no building or byte is free of ideology, namely, free of meaning in the service of power.

Starting from this premise, the scholars herein were asked to explore developments in contemporary forms of information storage, sharing, and service for educational contexts. From different disciplinary perspectives, they variously, and on occasion divergently, interrogated and interpreted what they saw as key issues around change in libraries.

Three themes—*space, knowledge,* and *capital*—bubbled out of the chapter content and are used to structure the volume into three subsections. In Bakhtin's (1981, p. 84) terms, they "thickened, took on flesh, and made artistically visible" the social, economic, and political dimensions of libr@ries and new knowledge spaces. The first theme, space, encapsulates the *where* of the library, usually indicated by its name (e.g., Peaceville Public Library). The name tells perhaps where the building itself is located, how it is structured and organized spatially according to rooms, which objects are within which rooms and on which shelves, whether the information is open or closed stack, and whether there is a reference librarian available to assist. The second theme, knowledge, is the *what,* and refers to what the collection is, and what kinds of knowledge are valued and represented in that physical space. The third theme, capital, is less visible, but equally important nonetheless. It concerns *how* the library works socially in terms of internal and external policies and budgets. This includes who decides which materials to purchase, how and to whom support services are provided, and other issues that connect the library to users and to the outside world. These three dimensions, which are crucial in understanding the traditional library, afford a means of organizing the chapters as we examine the ways that the arobase enters into, suffuses, engages, and changes the library. In what follows, we look at the where, the what, and the how—the space, knowledge, and capital—of libr@ries.

Core questions addressed include the following. Considering the shift from print-based information to online modes and texts, what is the ongoing role of that once powerful mediatory institution, the library? What spatiotemporal sensibilities enable and constrain what can be thought, said, and done in relation to library practices and cultures within fast capitalist nation-states? What role does policy making in the related fields of information, technology, intellectual property, and so on play in these developments? How can librarians and cognate professionals extend the terrain of their everyday work beyond conventional parameters of dominant languages and knowledges, canons and cultures, texts and technologies? How can we imagine and practice libr@ries to better reflect and refract the highly complex and differentiated times and spaces of postmodernity? What kinds of textual and pedagogical spaces are libr@ries and new knowledge spaces framing for learners, young and old, to develop the literate sensibilities required by symbol-saturated and mediatized communities and economies of the 21st century?

AROBASE SPACE

Theories of virtual culture have tended to emphasize the disconnectedness of online experience from the embodied, emplaced world of "real" life. Enthusiasts and critics alike stressed the "extra-territorial" conditions of life online. As human subject and cultural artifact have become increasingly separated from the physical world, contemporary knowledge too is considered *de-referentialized,* and the spaces of its location ever more *de-territorialized* (Robins & Webster, 1999). It is argued here that although it is important to recognize the ways in which new media and communications technologies disembed and displace knowledge from local, cultural, and national roots, this exercise, of itself, is not enough. Instead, the focus is on ways in which information occurs in particular kinds of social, symbolic, and semiotic spaces that are constructed by discourse through the production and consumption of knowledge. It seeks to understand how knowledge is not outside of space, but is variously spatialized through discursive practice. The reason for this focus is that differential discursive practices entail disparities of access to social and cultural capital and, hence, to material wealth.

How then can we examine and understand this interface of discourse and space within the theory and practice of libr@ries? Space and time are fundamental categories of ontological contemplation because all human knowing and knowledge is *referential*. That is, things are typically understood *relatively*: Objects are here or there; moments are now or then (Munt, 2001). In "Western" ways of knowing, positivist epistemologies and objectivist positions on knowledge purged space of the pollution of materiality through excluding reference to agency and place. That is, the messiness of action and social agency and the unpredictable sentiment-based politics of place were removed, thereby reducing space to a spaceless abstraction.

Crang and Thrift (2000), for example, showed that space is not prior to, or separate from, social practice. It is not an inert container for things, thought, or action, but is better conceived as "*process* and *in process*," that is, "space and time combined in becoming" (p. 3). This assumption recognizes that *being* and *learning about being*—of self, others, and the world—is experienced as *practice* in and through space and time. Because space occurs in and through different institutional and discursive contexts (capitalism, ethnicity, gender, media, etc.), it creates different objects of knowledge, different ontologies, and different epistemic parameters. To begin to explore such "becomings" of social life, Crang and Thrift developed a number of "species" of space, some of which are the spaces of language and writing, spaces of self (interiority) and other (exteriority), and spaces of experience. More recent work on "timespace" (J. May & Thrift, 2001) avoids the prioritization of space over time by recognizing their indivisibility. May and Thrift conceded nonetheless that, because we exist within it, theorizing timespace requires "conceptualizing at the limits of representation" (p. 20). They then begin to do so by examining the spatial metaphors of 20th-century theorists.

Dominant images—mostly from the work of Bergson, Merleau-Ponty, Bachelard, and Heidegger—are those of energy, dynamism, and motion. Unprecedented global movements of people, capital, and trade, combined with the uptake of new media and virtual technologies, generated interest in metaphors of flow. Within a technocultural paradigm, however, this notion of flows views the source of philosophical understanding—cognition and intuition—as separate from the instant and the context. Yet, any separation between the organic and inorganic is untenable (Bentley, 1941; Haraway, 1994). Deleuze (1991) used the "rhizome," comprising "directions in motion" rather than separate units to overcome these unhelpful dualisms. He conceived "rhythm" as orders of ceaseless connection and reconnection comprising circulations rather than entities, or essences. Lefebvre (1991) similarly argued that the lifeworld is "folded into rhythms" through the textures of everyday time and space. Feminist theorists also have used metaphors of rhythm to disrupt what they called the "sexualization of space" and the commodification of time by the forces of capitalist labor (cf. Clément, 1994).

In summary, May and Thrift showed how social time, like space, is contingent, multiple, and heterogeneous because it is experienced according to an individual's social positioning. Time is, in effect, tied to the spatial constitution of society, and vice versa. There can, then, be no singular universal social theory that accounts for the timing and spacing of social life, or the social experience of, for example, information access within online environments. Knowledge may have been de-territorialized and notions of "place" long since lost their usefulness for understanding libraries and information work. Yet, being "extra-territorial," or outside of place, does not signify outside of social orders and their discursive practices and meanings. A timespace perspective on literate and pedagogical work occurring with and through online information activities recognizes, for example, that thought about theory is not outside of material, historical, cultural, or institutional space. It acknowledges that authorship and authority, knowing and knowledge, are spatially and temporally bound because neither theory nor space are empty of ideological effect: Both emplace and impart social practices and their associated discursive and political effects.

What, then, are these new species of informational space that are emerging out of, and yet enfold within themselves, the physical place of the traditional library? Through what textual genres and their associated literacies are libr@ries manifesting the blended cultures, communities, and economies of a globalized world? Given the disparities of wealth generated by the combined forces of increasing corporatization and globalization, as key knowledge institutions, do libr@ries critically reflect on their roles in either exacerbating or ameliorating differential access to the codes and symbols through which work, identity, and citizenship occur today?

The array of individual national and international programs around formal institutional libr@ries and other information initiatives are too numerous to mention here. This discussion focuses, therefore, on four informal spaces of informational practice that are making significant contributions to the emerging information commons. These include online libraries and archives, collaborative online initiatives, open source software, and the peer-to-peer revolution (the latter two are discussed in the section on capital later). The first online library, *Project Gutenberg,* was established in 1971 as a private initiative to republish out-of-copyright articles and books of interest. Because its goal was simply to establish a collection of materials for public use, *Gutenberg* comprised a continuation of traditional library values and practices. It has since been superseded by a more socially interactive project called *ibiblio.* Hosted by the University of North Carolina, *ibiblio* uses Linux software to archive public domain documents, text, audio, and databases that are contributed by users. The social impact of these kinds of projects can be judged partially by the extent of their use: the *ibiblio* servers, for example, respond to an average of 1.5 million information requests each day (Bollier, 2003). Large corporations have entered the field of digitizing texts: Google, for example, has teamed with university libraries to digitally scan books from their collections (Markoff & Wyatt, 2004).

The operating principle of these kinds of collaborative initiatives differs from the centralized social relations of conventional public knowledge. The notion of a center, or even the possibility of a number of centers, was demolished some four decades ago by the rhizomatic structure of the Internet. New information spaces typify the increasingly eccentric state of the open source information universe in that collections like *ibiblio* are managed by volunteer contributors with special knowledge or interest in the subject matter they catalogue. Like the many distributed proofreading projects, inclusive approaches to content building mean that material is organic, evolving, and relatively up to date. The open source software documentation section of *ibiblio,* for example, is widely regarded as the world's best source for this kind of material. This principle of democratic, two-way interaction, which is global in scope, embodies a different library–user relation from conventional one-way library transactions, and is generating a plethora of new information genres that are increasingly multimodal and intercultural in form and scope. It facilitates what Eglash, Crossiant, Di Chiro, and Fouché (2004) called "appropriating technology," rather than being a passive recipient, or victim, of it.

Arobase space—space infused with new technologies and their requisite literacy and information literacy practices—is a product of these developments. We therefore propose *arobase space* as:

> sets of discursive practices shaped by the affordances and constraints of digital technologies which simultaneously manifest the historically constituted facets of place.

This definition implies that, whereas the virtual, cyber, and digital has important social implications, it is not outside of the space of discourse, or inseparable from discursive practices that are materially, historically, and culturally constituted.

There are three key aspects of this conception. First, we explicitly avoid determinism in either direction—that is, we seek to avoid viewing technology as a novel, independent, or determinate factor in social relations and outcomes. At the same time, the notion of arobase space allows for the influence of technology while avoiding the converse determinism in which social relations are seen as totally determinate of the use of technology.

The second aspect is that it conceives of the relations between technology and the larger social system as dynamic, one in which both existing social relations and forms and uses of technology are under continual processes of change akin to Giddens' (1979, 1984) notion of structuration. The third aspect is that this conception denies the existence of autonomous technology, that is, technologies whose properties, operations, and effects can be meaningfully discussed outside of the consideration of material, social, and cultural contexts of use.

Nicholas C. Burbules taps into this two-way principle of interactivity in chapter 1, and makes a theoretical case for rethinking digital libraries beyond simple collections of textual content. He argues that what is most exciting about digital libraries is not their low cost, high volume storage capacity, but their potential as virtual spaces of shared inquiry and learning. His focus is, therefore, squarely on the social rather than the technical or informational. Consistent with Crang and Thrift's notion of space as constructed and experiential, the virtual for Burbules is not merely something online, but rather comprises social meaning that is mediated by a range of technological and nontechnological means, including film, music, daydreams, or even an intense conversation. This resonates with our notion of infused arobase space. Virtual spaces involve structures that are commonly classified as *architectures* and *maps*: both of which digital libraries have. Burbules argues, therefore, that exploring the architectural configurations of digital libraries can help us to understand how these new (arobase) spaces interact with human desire, meaning, and imagination. When the processes needed to generate these configurations are made explicit, they can be applied elsewhere to minimize constraints and exclusions that typify other spaces, virtual and otherwise.

The notion of blended human and technological space is explored at some length in geographic "mappings" of cyberspace (Dodge & Kitchin, 2001). Drawing from theories of cartography, computer-mediated communications, information visualization, literary theory, cognitive psychology, and cultural studies, Dodge and Kitchin argued that long-standing dichotomies between present–future, real–virtual, place–space, public–private, and the industrial–informational are worn down. Within the philosophical arena, feminist social and literary theory similarly has shown how dualities and binarisms structure difference, inequality, and oppression. In the world of everyday material experience, for those with access to them, convergence of the real, the unreal, the surreal, and the hyperreal has diminished the divide between organ and machine, reality and simulation, nature and culture, and thereby afforded an array of unprecedented timespaces of human engagement with each other through text.

As described by Susan Boyce in chapter 2, school libraries of today are one such hybrid timespace. Through a case study methodology, Boyce examines the cultural construct of one school library and the persistent power of metaphors of print and place in that library. She argues that the way school media center specialists and librarians represent their libraries online as virtual instantiations of a "place" to be visited is evidence of the enduring power of "territoriality" within de-territorialized contexts. These long-standing values and concepts deny the possibility of rethinking library and information services in ways that are more closely aligned to the potentials of distributed spatial flows and the different kinds of social relations these afford. She laments that a sincere desire for innovation has been hijacked by the potency of long established institutional discourses, and explores the possibilities for educational change by examining the social and spatial implications of literacy experiences in hybrid library environments. By mapping the surface traces of library spaces and literacy spaces; by evaluating the social logics of their designs; and by aligning spatial design with new cultural identities, forms of textual surfaces, and their attendant multimodal literacies, Boyce recontextualizes the "place" of the school library.

The subtle but powerful forms of racializing and classing discourses within institutional spaces of school libraries is the focus of Mark Dressman and Sharon Tettegah's analysis in chapter 3. Since its emergence in North America, the library profession has consistently asserted a value-free stance toward the promotion of access to information and literacy. Library procedures for selecting and organizing materials, and normative pedagogical practices like the ritual of "story time," embody this philosophical assumption. Dressman and Tettegah juxtapose past and present contexts, showing how these fuse in current discourses of North American school librarianship. They examine the history of those discourses and their implications for the patrons of three school libraries that served children of different ethnic and social class backgrounds a decade ago, and then consider the implications of computerized technologies and the Internet for challenging and/or extending those discourses today and into the foreseeable future. In a nondeterminist approach to space similar to that of May and Thrift, they show how authority, enculturation, seduction, and suppression are embedded within everyday routines and practices like the regulation of time and knowledge and the social relations that the spaces of built forms mediate.

Like those of schools, libraries of higher education institutions are undergoing tremendous change in design, construction, and pedagogical relationship to learners and users. In chapter 4, Janine Schmidt explores the blending of modernist and postmodernist educational discourses within higher educational library provision. In her examination of current trends in library design, she explains how libraries are redressing the lack of functionality and "use-friendliness" of traditional university libraries as they morph into hybridized physical and online cultural spaces. The need to improve "services to clients" has replaced the emphasis on institutional and procedural outcomes such as how to house physical collections and to seat readers. In the current fast capitalist consumerist moment, many see the key challenge for the library profession as that of attracting clients through "value-adding" and "branding." As noted in the discussion of capital later, the incursion of market values from global discourses of human capital theory and managerialism into library practice manifests as "client-centered" experiences and services that take the form of new pedagogies around information literacy.

Abby Goodrum's work on cultural heritage institutions closes this section. Chapter 5 pulls back from libraries per se and reminds the reader that whereas physical constraints that have historically separated libraries from other key cultural heritage players—namely, museums and archives—are dissolving, philosophical differences remain. Goodrum uses the issue of patron demand for better access to visual material within and across these institutions to rethink traditional, discrete logics of practice, and to enhance exchange and collaboration at national and international levels. We would argue that an understanding of arobase space is crucial to this understanding and to the continuation of their curatorial roles.

AROBASE KNOWLEDGE

For thousands of years, epistemological inquiry has pondered the nature of knowledge, the justification of its truth value, and rules for its orderly production, organization, and dissemination. It is widely accepted today that there is nothing natural or neutral about what counts as knowledge, or about the way it is accessed and used. Irrespective of its physical locus— whether in the ceremony of oral culture, the book of print culture, or the interface of digital culture (Kapitzke, 2001)—knowledge is and always was a much contested terrain. This is more so since the ascendance of scientific knowledge and recognition of its commercial value.

Recurring themes on the *postmodern* condition of knowledge and the *information revolution* include changes in the methods and locations of knowledge production, distribution, and application; the impact of new information technologies on knowledge acquisition and knowledge management; new classifications of knowledge; and changes in the relation between knowledge and wealth creation (Boekema, 2000; Bowker & Star, 1999; Evans & Wurster, 2000; Johnston, 1998; Shapiro & Varian, 1999; Wenger, McDermott, & Snyder, 2002).

Questions of knowledge in librarianship are typically conceived in terms of the agentive function of the library. That is, which aspects of knowledge reified in collections of materials does the library select and organize? But we can flip the issue and ask: Which new forms of knowledge are colonizing, domesticating, and changing the library? These new knowledges and their associated "digital epistemologies" (Lankshear, Peters, & Knobel, 2000) are afforded, in part, by the multimodal texts and literacies of online and mobile communications technologies. Fanfiction and fanzines, gaming and blogging, animé and relay chat, and text and video messaging are some of the textual practices that young people, in particular, engage in and that constitute contexts for significant informal learning. Empirical work by Bruce (2003); Frechette (2002); Goodson, Knobel, Lankshear, and Mangan (2002); Holloway and Valentine (2003); Lankshear and Knobel (2003); and Livingstone (2002) confirms the impact of new media on the lifeworlds of children and young people. For instance, the power of peer-to-peer sharing (P2P) such as the popular music file-swapping service Kazaa, has influenced government policy and legislation on issues of intellectual property and contributed to scientific and industry applications of considerable social and economic significance.

The work cited previously documents the power of consumerist texts through "pedagogies of everyday life" (Luke, 1996), and it highlights a shift from educational institutions to informal learning by doing on the part of young people. There are three educational corollaries to this social and cultural trend that have implications for educational libraries. First, the hierarchical relationship between teacher and learner—and therefore between learner and librarian—has diminished, as power to assert what is "most worth-while culturally and the means to get it have slipped away from the traditional gatekeepers and cultural transmitters— schools, teachers, universities, books, libraries" (Smith & Curtin, 1998, p. 225). Second, this erosion of authoritative status tends to devalue conventional transmission models of teaching and to stimulate more problem-based inquiry through learner-centered search, critique, and the integration of ideas. Lexical changes in the everyday language of libr@ries reflect this pedagogical shift. Common examples are the substitution of *database* for *catalogue*, *descriptors* for *subject headings*, *tags* for *fields*, *originator* for *publisher*; and *creator* for *author*, all of which signify a change in the author–user relation (cf. McLean, 2000). A third corollary is the move from acquiring information for some future use to *just-in-time* learning through researching, namely, learning to learn about information and through information.

As libr@ries adopt online media, questions regarding the production, organization, and dissemination of knowledge need to be reframed and reconsidered. As argued earlier in the discussion of arobase space, we want to avoid reductive terms such as new knowledge and digital knowledge. Instead, we suggest a term that implies both changes in knowledge formation and the grounding of existing discursive practices. We therefore propose *arobase knowledge* as:

> sets of discursive practices around sense-making and sharing that are imbued with the affordances and constraints of digital technologies.

In the second section, authors explore arobase knowledges from a variety of perspectives. Having established the social and economic underpinnings of the technological, it is important nonetheless to understand how these forces and practices manifest at a micro, technical level. In chapter 6, Jane Hunter introduces the world of information "ontologies" and "interactive annotations." There are two things that strike us about this chapter. The first is the blurring of boundaries between creativity and consumption, and between production and publication through the reciprocal merging of human being and machine. This convergence of *techné* and *soma* is represented in Hunter's language in terms like "human understandable" and "machine readable." A second distinctive thing is the new forms of language use from the application of artificial intelligence to knowledge management. "Ontology," for Hunter, means something entirely different from how we have used it thus far in this introduction. Another noteworthy development is the use of metaphorical language deriving from domains like mining and the military. What do phrases like "knowledge extraction" and "knowledge capture" say about how we think about knowledge? Is it of concern that, as humanity has exploited and depleted the earth's natural resources, we may well be following a similar principle—not of depletion with the abundance of information, but of exploitation—in relation to the resources of an information commons?

Hunter describes innovations of "third generation" knowledge management, and describes how she expects the field to evolve over the next few years. David Rooney and Ursula Schneider provide a foil and cautionary note to this approach in chapter 7. They claim that librarians have been "seduced" by the rhetoric of knowledge management, and argue that, as it is understood and practiced in industry, knowledge management is not helpful to libr@ries. Two arguments support this contention: namely, that library "collections" are not the locus of knowledge, and sophisticated information technology systems do a poor job of managing knowledge. They then propose a framework for conceptualizing knowledge in a way that would enable libraries to go beyond industrial applications of knowledge management and the limitations of information technology. Similar to Burbules, Rooney and Schneider argue that knowledge is a system of phenomenological qualities, or emergent properties of relations that interplay with and within individuals, groups, times, places, and the physical objects of those places. In what they call an "ethics or virtue epistemology," the authors conclude that a focus on, and understanding of, the fluid and social aspects of knowledge systems would enhance the role information professionals play as facilitators of communication, relationships, and transcendent intellectual work.

Experimentation with new curricula at systemic levels provides evidence of social acceptance of alternative knowledges and epistemologies. The New Basics curriculum of the education system of Queensland, Australia, is one such example (see Education Queensland, 2000). As well as the standard disciplinary curriculum organizers such as English and science, this futures oriented, non-Aristotelian curriculum moves beyond status quo knowledges to clusters of essential practices that students require to thrive in present and future social conditions. Key features of this curriculum are its mainstreaming of previously marginalized community and cultural knowledges, and the placing of intercultural understanding at the heart of curriculum, pedagogy, and assessment.

Print-based libraries have historically performed poorly at providing for cultural and linguistic diversity but techniques of multimodal archiving are now making this possible. Linda Barwick and Nicholas Thieberger provide an example of this in chapter 8. Drawing on their experience in establishing the Pacific and Regional Archive of Digital Sources in Endangered Cultures (PARADISEC), Barwick and Thieberger explore the potential of networked digital systems in indexing and making accessible audiovisual research recordings of the languages and performance traditions of Pacific and Southeast Asian people groups. They provide critical historical and contemporary perspectives on their own research experience, and consider past and present convergences and tensions between the complex and often conflicting agendas of researchers, technologists, and local cultural centers in the region.

In a post-9/11 context, the notion of "fugitive" knowledges needs mention. These have emerged in the United States in particular with the Bush administration's will to power through legislation such as the 2001 Patriot Act, the Total Information Awareness initiative, and the Attorney General's 2003 Domestic Security Enhancement Act (cf. Kellner, 2003). "Illegal" knowledges are viewed by many as intrusions of privacy: for example, into one's reading fare as part of the government's agenda on public search and surveillance that comes masked under the banner of "security for the homeland." For instance, Section 215 of the Act allows FBI agents to obtain a warrant from a secret federal court to scrutinize library and/or bookstore records of anyone connected to an investigation of international terrorism or spying. Unlike conventional search warrants, however, there is no need for agents to show that the target is suspected of a crime, or possesses evidence of criminal activity.

This situation has brought some activists to the place where they are considering disengaging with the mainstream media and developing communication channels of their own. Simon (2003) and Halleck (2003), for example, show how, in this post-Patriot Act era, social repression is the visible manifestation of layers of self-censoring by a public who understands full well the message of the state: Citizens may be subjected to ostracism, inconvenience, and possibly arrest should they express pro-privacy and pro-peace sentiment. Nonetheless, some like Bousquet (2003, p. 5) courageously assert that silence becomes "common sense," and the "most pervasive form of surveillance generated by the Patriot structure of feeling is 'Watch Yourself.'" Consistent with the theme of opening spaces for innovative and transgressive arobase knowledges, in chapter 9 Cushla Kapitzke seeks to influence the research trajectory by mapping the extant field of libr@ry studies, identifying gaps and silences, and providing suggestions for alternative theoretical and empirical directions.

AROBASE CAPITAL

Educational libraries have always been bit players in the political economy of book publishing. Apple (1989, 2001) documented recurring struggles over questions of authorized school curricula and authoritative textbooks in the (re)production of social orders along the axes of philosophical, classed, and religious difference. There are, nevertheless, several schools of thought on the political economies of emergent technologies, information, and education.

Critical theorists of the left (e.g., Adorno & Bernstein, 1991; Barber, 1995; Chomsky, 1999; Harvey, 1993; Nobel, 1979; Schiller, 1989) are mostly structuralist and strongly antimarket in perspective. Typically, this scholarship draws from Marxian and neo-Marxian theory to present massified analyses focused on producers and publishers and to express moral outrage that technologies like the Internet represent the interests of capital. These authors might argue, for example, that increases in the cost of printed materials accompanied by improved accessibility and affordability of new communications technologies compel libraries to automate and move online. Indeed, Baker (2001) and Wisner (2000) documented the wide-scale destruction of print journals and newspapers during the 1990s, and provide evidence of the deleterious effects of this trend on print collections. The recent outsourcing of the Educational Resources Information Center (ERIC), its subsequent downsizing through elimination of clearinghouses and the automation of materials indexing are developments that might justifiably concern critical theorists (see American Educational Research Association, 2003).

Alternatively, researchers who draw from postmodernist ideas (cf. Lash, 2002; Poster & Aronowitz, 2001; Robins & Webster, 1999) acknowledge the decentralization, disorganization, and uncontrollability of online environments and their user economies. This work considers not only the military/industrial complex but also a spectrum of governmental, institutional, and communal interests and ideologies that compete for visibility and influence in the field.

There is no doubt, however, that the Digital Millennium Copyright Act (DMCA) enacted by the U.S. Congress in 1998 exceeds traditional copyright principles. One means of doing this has been to make it illegal to circumvent technological devices restricting access to digital materials, or illegal even to share information about how to overcome technological locks (Lessig, 2004). Technolocks provide a means for extending property rights over information, consumers, and competitors by controlling what can and cannot be done with cultural products. Within this context, there is the possibility that business interests will use encryption and licensing to revoke freedoms that have traditionally been associated with books and libraries. For instance, corporations currently making handheld appliances for e-books are invoking the DMCA to "lock" text and diminish public access and the fair use rights of readers.

Groups advocating for the legal protection of public information employ the metaphor of the "commons." This term typically refers to tangible assets like water and forests, as well as to intangible capital (e.g., patents, copyrights) and cultural resources (e.g., broadcast airwaves, public spaces) (Bollier, 2003). Being inherited freely, these resources traditionally were shared and held in trust for future generations. As a provision of state funding, public libraries were an integral part of the industrial era social capital, or knowledge commons (Kranich, 2004). Because a healthy public domain was considered fundamental to creativity, culture, science, education, democratic governance, and industry, the courts and social policy historically protected it.

The role played by market values is dependent, to a lesser or greater extent, on public policy. Policy scholarship from a sociological perspective views policymaking as one of the many rationalities of social regulation and governance. Policy theorists currently recognize three main paradigms in social policy studies: positivist, postpositivist, and poststructuralist. Whichever approach to information policy is taken—whether the emphasis is on social problems and their "solution" through policy implementation, or alternatively, on the social construction of the issues and policy directions "selected" to "fix" them—information policy studies typically use two broad concepts to frame developments in the field. These are neoliberalism and *dirigisme* (Moore, 1998). A neoliberal framework emphasizes the value of private capital and market principles in social services, and is the model adopted by the G8 nations, the European Union, and other fast capitalist economies such as Australia. Alternatively, dirigiste approaches refer to those in which the state plays more of an interventionist role, as in many East Asian countries. Clearly, there are benefits and drawbacks to both approaches, but a considerable body of research argues that a moderately interventionist policy context, which views the public as an involved critical citizenry rather than simply as *consumers* or *laborers,* is better equipped to cope with structural change and its social costs (C. May, 2002; OECD, 1997, 2001). Nevertheless, in the West, a new relation of state and capital to knowledge has emerged with a deregulated policy context gradually transferring control of information and communication products and services to private providers and the market (cf. Cooper, 2002; McChesney & Schiller, 2003).

Conventional economic models that pit the state against the market (e.g., either public libraries or privatized information) do not accurately portray current realities. Vaidhyanathan's (2003) notion of the "anarchist in the library" provides a more useful metaphor for the complex political economies of emergent knowledge spaces. Efforts on the part of corporations to limit access and constrain the many literate practices and textual economies with which people are currently engaging comprise just some of many less formalized strategies on a spectrum of struggles ranging from private initiatives to those that are formal and highly structured. Despite the language of warfare used to describe these developments (see Benkler's, 2003, "battle over the information ecology"), the gift economy constituting many forms of civic and professional activism and creativity is one that is frequently overlooked in market-centric research and literatures.

Tensions between public–private and benefit–control all point to the need for a reconsideration of political economy. Once again, this may be framed not as an entirely new social field, but more as forms and practices that extend existing conceptions. Arobase capital therefore comprises

> sets of discursive practices imbued with digital technologies that intersect with and co-constitute economic power.

The chapters in this third section explore the ways in which arobase capital intersects with libr@ries as information spaces, providers, and services. It opens with chapter 10, in which John Willinsky makes an elegant appeal to educational and research communities, and to library bodies and government agencies to forego self-interest in the struggle to maintain open and fair access to the scholarly archive. By drawing on parallels with the public library movement of the 19th century, Willinsky provides a compelling case for how this will benefit the research community and, more importantly, the broad civic body. Willinsky examines historical analogies of the public library's principles of the right to knowledge, literacy as a cornerstone of democracy, the enlightenment of the people, and the support of the public sphere. Nonetheless, in fine *parrhesiastic* form (see Bruce & Kapitzke, chap. 16), his analysis is refreshingly "fearless" and honest about the more contentious dimensions to the case for public libraries, including as he does, their didactic and morally censorious function, and their reflection of class, gender, and ethnic biases. Willinsky's study of lessons to be had from comparable efforts in the 19th century connects the past and the present to the future as he encourages the academy to recognize its responsibilities for the greater circulation of knowledge at the beginning of the 21st century.

In chapter 11, Timothy W. Luke similarly examines the values and politics of knowledge as they are transformed by the transition to digital modes of communication and scholarship. He shows how many of the "standards" used by society and scholars to judge the quality, utility, and durability of knowledge derive from print forms, and argues that, despite the residuals of print literacy, the cybrary and its educational counterparts are important generative sites for new approaches to knowledge.

As noted earlier, open source software and peer-to-peer revolutions are central factors in the establishment and maintenance of arobase space and knowledge. These loosely organized, nonhierarchical communities of literate practice play significant roles in the public interest agenda by helping to preserve the open Internet agenda and to maintain a commons of information that fuels the humanities, education, government, science, and culture. Chapter 12, by Mark Lawrence Kornbluh, Melanie Shell-Weiss, and Paul Turnbull, regrounds the issues through a practical example of innovation around open resource networks specifically for the humanities. Humanities scholarship is an important cultural resource, and the authors argue that the social and economic benefits to be gained from its free and wide circulation outweigh what scholars stand to gain from allowing their work to be locked within online pay-for-access publication systems. They make a convincing case that scholars in the humanities would do well to follow the lead of the growing number of scientific research communities who have opted to share information openly, not just between peers, but also with the many constituencies that stand to benefit from open online access to high quality information.

A decade ago, the Internet itself was touted as an *agora* for virtual communalism and democratic participation. That is, until it too was colonized by the corporate sector. Chapter 13, by Bettina Fabos, focuses on the commercialization of search engines through consolidation of the industry, and examines the implications of this trend for education and academic research. With large portals like Yahoo! buying up smaller search engine providers to better influence and profit from commercial searches, Fabos details how commercially stacked Internet search processes tend to marginalize nonprofit and academic sites. Because commercial search engines have largely replaced libraries as sites for student research, Fabos argues the need for a comprehensive digital archive movement and tools for cross-searching subject directories. These are the exciting alternatives to commercial search engines.

Much has been written about the drawbacks and disadvantages of the expansion and consolidation of mass media monopolies to consumers. Philip Graham turns this argument on its head in chapter 14 by examining the issue from the perspective of the creator/producer through the concept, *monopsony*. He contends that new media provide new opportunities, and shows how technological potential to store and redistribute large amounts of cultural "junk" creates space for more people to participate in the production of local and global cultural forms. Two related initiatives illustrating such innovation are the multimedia repository building projects, the Australian Creative Resources Archive (ACRA) and the Canadian Center for Cultural Innovation (CCCI), described by Graham.

Issues of copyright are central to the success of initiatives like the aforementioned. In chapter 15, Brian Fitzgerald discusses the open content licensing model as an alternative to the conventional "all rights reserved" approach. He describes the Creative Commons movement from an Australian context and legal perspective, and assigns to libr@ries a key role in the accomplishment of this important cultural means of revolutionizing information management.

Chip Bruce and Cushla Kapitzke close the book with chapter 16 by grounding their conceptual formulations in a biographical narrative. Titled *Mato's Fez*, this historical cameo shows how place and space, technology and practice, are woven not only throughout the ideas presented by the authors of the volume but also into the lives of ordinary people, and espeically those who work with and through contemporary libr@ries.

CONCLUSIONS

As Daniel's quote asserts, there is much about libraries of the past and the present that is positive and worth preserving. Sophie's rejection, however, highlights the reality that as spaces of social and educational practice through the ordering of knowledge and knowing, there are things about libraries that are not so useful, upbeat, or, in some circumstances, welcoming. The historical ground of their roots has shifted. As lovers of books and libraries—and critical technophiles too—this volume hopefully contributes in some way to the revisioning and renewal of libr@ries and the information profession. We invite you, reader, to enter and contribute to this important conversation.

REFERENCES

Adorno, T. W., & Bernstein, J. M. (1991). *The culture industry: Selected essays on mass culture.* London: Routledge.

American Educational Research Association (AERA). (2003). *AERA comments on ERIC statement of work: Association letter to Secretary of Education.* Retrieved from http://www.aera.net/communications/news/030509.htm

Apple, M. W. (1989). The political economy of text publishing. In S. de Castell, A. Luke, & C. Luke (Eds.), *Language, authority and criticism: Readings on the school textbook* (pp. 155–169). London: Falmer.

Apple, M. W. (2001). *Educating the "right" way: Markets, standards, God, and inequality.* New York: Routledge.

Baker, N. (2001). *Double fold: Libraries and the assault on paper.* New York: Random House.

Bakhtin, M. M. (1981). *The dialogical imagination* (C. Emerson & M. Holquist, Ed. and Trans.). Austin: University of Texas Press.

Barber, B. R. (1995). *Jihad vs. McWorld.* London: Corgi Books.

Benkler, Y. (2003). Freedom in the commons: Towards a political economy of information. *Duke Law Journal, 52,* 1245–1276.

Bentley, A. F. (1941). The human skin: Philosophy's last line of defense. *Philosophy of Science, 8*(1), 1–19.

Bibliothèque Nationale de France. (2004). *L'histoire de l'arobase.* Retrieved December 17, 2004, from http://expositions.bnf.fr/utopie/pistes/ateliers/image/fiches/arobase.htm

Birdsall, W. F. (1994). *The myth of the electronic library: Librarianship and social change in America.* Westport, CT: Greenwood.

Boekema, F. (Ed.). (2000). *Knowledge, innovation and economic growth: The theory and practice of learning regions.* London: Edward Elgar.

Bollier, D. (2003). *Silent theft: The private plunder of our common wealth.* New York: Routledge.

Bourdieu, P. (1977). *Outline of a theory of practice.* Cambridge, England: Cambridge University Press.

Bousquet, M. (2003). Section 1: Beyond the voting machine. In M. Bousquet & K. Wills (Eds.), *The politics of information: The electronic mediation of social change* (pp. 3–6). Stanford, CA: Alt-X Press.

Bowker, G. C., & Star, S. L. (1999). *Sorting things out: Classification and its consequences.* Cambridge, MA: MIT Press.

Bruce, B. C. (2003). *Literacy in the information age: Inquiries into meaning making with new technologies.* Newark, DE: International Reading Association.

Chomsky, N. (1999). *Profit over people: Neoliberalism and global order.* New York: Seven Stories Press.

Clément, C. (1994). *Syncope: The philosophy of rapture* (S. O'Driscoll & D. Mahoney, Trans.). Minneapolis, MN: University of Minnesota Press.

Cooper, M. (2002). *Cable mergers and monopolies: Market power in digital media and communications networks.* Washington, DC: Economic Policy Institute.

Crang, M., & Thrift, N. (2000). Introduction. In M. Crang & N. Thrift (Eds.), *Thinking space* (pp. 1–30). Routledge: London.

Deleuze, G. (1991). *Bergsonism.* New York: Zone Books.

Dodge, M., & Kitchin, R. (2001). *Mapping cyberspace.* New York: Routledge.

Education Queensland. (2000). *New Basics: Curriculum organizers.* Brisbane: Education Queensland.

Eglash, R., Crossiant, J., Di Chiro, G., & Fouché, R. (Eds.). (2004). *Appropriating technology: Vernacular science and social power.* Minneapolis, MN: University of Minnesota Press.

Evans, P., & Wurster, T. S. (2000). *Blown to bits: How the new economics of information transforms strategy.* Boston: Harvard Business School Press.

Fairclough, N. (1995). *Critical discourse analysis: The critical study of language.* New York: Longman.

Foucault, M. (1973). *The order of things: An archaeology of the human sciences.* New York: Vintage.

Frechette, J. D. (2002). *Developing media literacy in cyberspace: Pedagogy and critical Learning for the twenty-first-century classroom.* Westport, CT: Praeger.

Giddens, A. (1979). *Central problems in social theory: Action, structure, and contradiction in social analysis.* Berkeley, CA: University of California Press.

Giddens, A. (1984). *The constitution of society.* Cambridge, England: Polity Press.

Goodson, I., Knobel, M., Lankshear, C., & Mangan, J. M. (2002). *Cyber spaces/social spaces: Culture clash in computerized classrooms.* New York: Palgrave Macmillan.

Halleck, D. D. (2003). The censoring of burn! In M. Bousquet & K. Wills (Eds.), *The politics of information: The electronic mediation of social change* (pp. 18–44). Stanford, CA: Alt-X Press.

Haraway, D. (1994). Manifesto for cyborgs: Science, technology, and socialist feminism in the 1980s. In S. Seidman (Ed.), *The postmodern turn: New perspectives on social theory* (pp. 82–115). New York: Cambridge University Press.

Harvey, D. (1993). Class relations, social justice and the politics of difference. In M. Keith & S. Pile (Eds.), *Place and the politics of difference* (pp. 41–66). New York: Routledge.

Herron, S. (1997). *A natural history of the @ sign.* Retrieved December 17, 2004, from http://www.herodios.com/herron_tc/atsign.html

Holloway, S. L., & Valentine, G. (2003). *Cyberkids: Children in the information age.* London: Routledge Falmer.

Johnston, R. (1998). *The changing nature and forms of knowledge: A review.* Canberra, ACT: Dept. of Employment, Education, Training, & Youth Affairs.

Kapitzke, C. (2001). Ceremony and cybrary: Digital libraries and the dialectic of place and space. *Social Alternatives, 20*(1), 33–40.

Kellner, D. (2003). *From 9/11 to terror war: The dangers of the Bush legacy.* Lanham: Rowman & Littlefield.

Kranich, N. (2004). Libraries, civil society, and the public sphere. In D. Schuler & P. Day (Eds.), *Shaping the network society: The new role of civil society in cyberspace* (pp. 279–300). Cambridge, MA: MIT Press.

Lankshear, C., & Knobel, M. (2003). *New literacies: Changing knowledge and classroom learning.* Philadelphia: Open University Press.

Lankshear, C., Peters, M., & Knobel, M. (2000). Information, knowledge and learning: Some issues facing epistemology and education in a digital age. *Journal of Philosophy of Education, 34*(1), 17–40.

Lash, S. (2002). *Critique of information.* Thousand Oaks, CA: Sage.

Latour, B. (1993). *We have never been modern* (C. Porter, Trans.). New York: Harvester Wheatsheaf.

Le dictionnaire encyclopédique de la langue française du XXIe siècle (2004). *Arobase.* Retrieved December 17, 2004 from http://www.encyclopedie-universelle.com/

Le 'pataphysicien Net (2004). *Arobase et gidouille.* Retrieved December 17, 2004 from http://www.h27pataphysicien.net/histoire.htm

Lefebvre, H. (1991). *The production of space* (D. Nicholson-Smith, Trans.). Oxford, England: Blackwell.

Lessig, L. (2004). *Free culture: How big media uses technology and the law to lock down culture and control creativity.* New York: Penguin.

Livingstone, S. M. (2002). *Young people and new media: Childhood and the changing media environment.* London: Sage.

Luke, C. (1996). *Feminisms and pedagogies of everyday life.* Albany: State University of New York Press.

Markoff, J., & Wyatt, E. (2004, December 14). Google is adding major libraries to its database. *The New York Times*. Retrieved December 17, 2004 from http://www.nytimes .com/2004/12/14/technology/14cnd-goog.html

May, C. (2002). *The information society: A skeptical view.* Cambridge, England: Polity Press.

May, J., & Thrift, N. (Eds.). (2001). *Timespace: Geographies of temporality.* London: Routledge.

McChesney, R., & Schiller, D. (2003). *The political economy of international communications: Foundations for the emerging global debate about media ownership and regulation.* Geneva: United Nations Research Institute for Social Development.

McLean, J. (2000). Cyberseeking: Language and the quest for information. In D. Gibbs & K. L. Krause (Eds.), *Cyberlines: Languages and cultures of the Internet* (pp. 79–101). Albert Park: James Nicholas.

Moore, N. (1998). Policies for an information society. *Aslib Proceedings, 50*(1), 20–24.

Munt, S. R. (2001). Technospaces: Inside the new media. In S. R. Munt (Ed.), *Technospaces* (pp. 1–18). New York: Continuum.

Nardini, R. F. (2001). A search for meaning: American library metaphors, 1876–1926. *Library Quarterly, 71*(2), 111–140.

Noble, D. F. (1979). *America by design: Science, technology, and the rise of corporate capitalism.* Oxford, England: Oxford University Press.

Organisation for Economic Co-operation and Development. (1997). *Towards a global information society: Global information infrastructure, Global information society: Policy requirements.* Paris: Committee on Information, Computer and Communications Policy.

Organisation for Economic Co-operation and Development. (2001). *Education policy analysis: Education and skills.* Paris: Centre for Educational Research and Innovation.

Poster, M., & Aronowitz, S. (2001). *The information subject.* Amsterdam: G+B Arts International.

Quinion, M. (2002). *Where it's at.* Retrieved December 17, 2004, from http://www .worldwidewords.org/articles/whereat.htm

Radford, M. L., & Radford, G. P. (2001). Libraries, librarians, and the discourse of fear. *Library Quarterly, 71*(3), 299–329.

Robins, K., & Webster, F. (1999). *Times of the technoculture: From the information society to the virtual life.* London: Routledge.

Schiller, H. I. (1989). *Culture, Inc.: The corporate takeover of public expression.* New York: Oxford University Press.

Shapiro, C., & Varian, H. R. (1999). *Information rules: A strategic guide to the network economy.* Boston: Harvard Business School Press.

Simon, B. (2003). Illegal knowledge: Strategies for new-media activism. In M. Bousquet & K. Wills (Eds.), *The politics of information: The electronic mediation of social change* (pp. 55–65). Stanford, CA: Alt-X Press.

Smith, R., & Curtin, P. (1998). Children, computers and life online: Education in a cyberworld. In I. Snyder (Ed.), *Page to screen: Taking literacy into the electronic era* (pp. 211–233). New York: Routledge.

Tallmo, K.-E. (1995). @—a sign of the times. Retrieved December 17, 2004, from http://art-bin .com/art/asignoftimes.html

Vaidhyanathan, S. (2003). *The anarchist in the library: How peer-to-peer networks are transforming politics, culture, and information.* New York: Basic Books.

Wenger, E., McDermott, R., & Snyder, W. (2002). *Cultivating communities of practice: A guide to managing knowledge.* Boston: Harvard Business School Press.

Wisner, W. H. (2000). *Whither the postmodern library? Libraries, technology, and education in the information age.* Jefferson, NC: McFarland.

I

Arobase Space

1

Digital Libraries as Virtual Spaces

Nicholas C. Burbules

In this essay I reflect on some things that other educators can learn from librarians, from the emergence of digital libraries, and from the transformation of traditional libraries into technology centers that provide access to a universe of information resources and opportunities for online communication and interaction within a virtual space. Librarians have long considered themselves to be educators, of course, and libraries have long been learning spaces for young people and adults; yet the form that these technological developments are taking in libraries provides a set of conceptual resources and ways of thinking about education that teachers, I will argue, have been slower to pick up as relevant to *their* institutional context.

My discussion begins by re-examining some of the metaphors we use to describe the online space, metaphors which often inhibit our ability to recognize its distinctive character and possibilities. I then examine the nature of *spaces* and *places*, and what it means to think of digital libraries and other institutions as places, and not only as spaces; here I argue that spaces become places largely through two kinds of practice that transform them—mapping and architecture. These transformative practices take on special significance in the context of *knowledge* spaces/places (as libraries and schools are), and they present designers with a set of difficult tradeoffs to negotiate. Such design decisions express particular judgments and values—including assumptions about the nature of knowledge itself. I conclude that one of the prime potentials of virtual knowledge spaces is in fostering a distinctive *publicity of practice;* a publicity that directly affects

our ways of thinking about and practicing collaborative inquiry, accountability, and ownership of knowledge.

RE-EXAMINING OUR METAPHORS

To begin, I want to re-examine some of the metaphors and casual ways of
speaking that have dominated the ways educators and others talk about
the possibilities of these digital technologies—not just computers, but
the way that *networked* computers constitute a dynamic and distributed
knowledge space. Why is the term "space" important here? Because even
now the dominant modes of talking about these networks rely on terms
like "medium," "pipeline," or "delivery system." This way of talking
manages to be simultaneously an under-theorized description of what a
networked space is and how it works, while at the same time—and more
seriously—expressing a thin and instrumentalist conception of teaching,
which can in very few circumstances be thought of merely as the delivery
or transfer of information. In opposition to this way of talking, I will rely
here on describing teaching and learning environments as *spaces*, spaces
within which people *move, act, interact,* and in a significantly nonmeta-
phorical sense, *live*.[1]

This brings up the second key term I will rely on here, the *virtual*. Standing outside the specific example of "virtual reality" systems for a moment,
the term has generically come to mean simply "computer-mediated" (a
virtual conversation, a virtual conference, a virtual classroom); in such
contexts it means little more than "online." Yet it also carries a separate
connotation, largely derived from the "virtual reality" context, namely,
virtual as artificial, simulated, or almost-but-not-quite-real. Here too a
number of superficial assumptions are being made (not the least of which
is the presumed gulf between the "virtual" and the "real," which is becoming increasingly problematic). But here I mean only to invoke the idea that
a *virtual space* is not a substitute for the "real thing," but a distinct experiential domain itself, real in its own way—certainly real in its effects—
and having the capacity to support significant educational possibilities
once we regard it seriously *as* a space, and not just as a delivery system
or second-best compromise when you cannot occupy a "real" space. For
example, in my own online teaching, I have increasingly found that these
classes develop their own personalities, compared with face-to-face teaching in traditional classrooms, and that it is pointless to try to evaluate globally which is "better" than the other: they each have their advantages and
disadvantages, and each needs to be evaluated and understood on its own
terms. An online class, its communications, its productions, its syllabus,
readings, and other learning resources, together comprise a virtual space

in which a wide range of interesting and surprising things happen that do not happen, or do not happen in the same way, in an ordinary classroom. "Virtual" does not mean artificial or second-best in such settings.

The third metaphor I want to rely upon is *mobility* as a way of thinking about learning. It is worth noting how the names of most of the popular web browsers—Explorer, Navigator, Safari—denote journeys, travel, and exploration. Like other kinds of movement, navigating the Web may involve serendipitous discovery, risk, and even getting lost. As I have argued elsewhere, the HTML links that constitute the Web *as* a web comprise both semantic and navigational properties: they allow us to move between web pages, but they also express, implicitly or explicitly, relations of meaning. Hence moving across links is a connective process as well as one of meaning-making—and hence potentially one of learning. As an example, consider what is happening when I build a web page collecting and linking to various other political sites: the decisions I make about which ones to include, which to exclude, the order in which they are listed, the commentary I may add, even in the text or graphics I choose to animate as links, all express a nascent political philosophy. By using this page, other people may make different associations from the ones I make; but their processes of interpretation and movement among the resources I have provided is structured in part by what I have linked together (and what I have left out). One is not simply *accessing* information in these more complexly structured contexts; one is moving within a knowledge space.

Spaces, virtuality, movement. These ways of thinking about networked systems open up a new vocabulary for talking about education, in contrast with more commonly invoked terms. They take us beyond an information-driven conception of knowledge and a mercly connectionist theory of how meanings are related; they provide a better framework for talking about the activities of shared inquiry and learning that can take place in collaborative spaces. They are not new or original terms, I suspect, for how most librarians think about their domains; but they are strikingly different from the dominant vocabularies that have emerged, thus far, for ways of talking about online teaching and learning (where, as I have said, people commonly think of networks merely as delivery systems for providing access to information).

FROM SPACES TO PLACES

The next step in my argument is to explore how *spaces* become socially significant *places*. A place is a socially or subjectively meaningful space. It has an objective, locational dimension: people can look for a place, find it, move within it. But it also *means* something important to a person or a group of people, and this latter, more subjective, dimension may or may not be communicable to others. When people are in a *place*, they know where they are, what it means to be there, and at least some of what they are expected to do there. Place also has an important temporal dimension because places emerge, change, and develop diachronically: a space may be a place at one point in time, but not earlier or later; or it may change into a different place.[2]

This transformation of space into place is sometimes intentional. We might not just visit a space; after a while we move in, start to rearrange the furniture, so to speak, and make it comfy. Spaces are transformed by such activities. And this is not necessarily an individual endeavor, but can be a collective one—indeed, it is often the quality of a space as a *shared space* that plays a crucial role in its development into a *place*. Things happen there, memorable things (whether pleasant or unpleasant, but *important*), which mark the space as a place ("this is where it happened"). Places become familiar, acclimated to us as we are to them. They become marked by various social conventions (rules, norms, customs, vocabularies). They become, in many cases, a locus of community. In all of these respects a relatively objective space and time, a pre-transformative given, becomes something marked, signified, *important* through human practices; and in this both the space and those inhabiting it are changed in relation to each other. A place is a special, important kind of space; but those occupying it also stand in a different relation to the space, and to each other, because they are there. In this description I have purposely not emphasized whether these must be specifically *virtual* spaces; this dynamic is true of spaces and places generally (a crossroads, a battlefield, a classroom, a lovers lane). Or perhaps it is more accurate to say that insofar as spaces become places there is *always* an element of the virtual to them.

There are two distinctive ways in which we turn spaces into places.[3] One is by *mapping:* by developing schemata that represent the space, identify important points, and facilitate movement within it. A map is never an exact replica (as the story goes, the only map that would be identical would be an exact copy of the original, which would be useless as a map)—a map always simplifies, selects from, and schematizes the original, and it is the particular way in which this simplification, selection, and schematization occur that makes this version of the space a place. These are practical activities; we make certain, and not other, choices because they allow us to do things in the space that are meaningful and important to us. There can be multiple maps, and in this sense they may constitute different *places*, even when they refer to the same space.

There are also maps that represent patterns of use. Trails that are worn by many feet tramping through forests, or across campus greens, are maps of a sort. Again, they simplify, select from, and schematize a space: they identify what is important to people, they mark out key spots, they facilitate movement. Trails also indicate another important characteristic of maps: how their use can also shape and transform the space they represent. By modifying the space, and providing explicit paths of direction, they turn the space into its own map. This process can be seen at work in the World Wide Web, for example through frequency indicators: page counters as well as ratings of "most frequently visited" sites. Such representations tend to influence patterns of future use, because they influence how search engines pick out and identify sites, which sites get selected for indexes, and so on. Viewed pragmatically, the representation (or map) is not discrete from the thing represented; it acts upon and is acted upon by it—and like other trails it actively influences the choices of later participants.

Yet another kind of map is one showing relations of relative centrality and relative periphery, from some point or points of reference. The repetitiveness of "relative" here is not accidental: there can be no absolute center of a space that is any more necessary than any other—in fact, it is as true to say that a center is *defined by* the map, as to say that the map begins from a center. In at least one important phenomenological sense, the Ptolemaic map of the solar system, with the earth at the center, was correct (although it was clearly wrong in an objective, physical sense). And a more rhizomic map may have no single center at all. But a map of relative centrality and periphery can still provide a way of simplifying, selecting, and schematizing the pragmatic relation of what is more or less useful or relevant to a given purpose, or set of purposes. This sort of endeavor can be highly beneficial even though there is nothing necessary about this particular mapping, even if others would map it differently—indeed, we should expect this to be true in order for such maps of relative centrality and periphery to be useful to different people (because their purposes and criteria will differ). Some classification systems, as in libraries, can be thought of as maps in this sense.

In sum, a map does two things at once: it marks significant places, and it makes places significant by marking them.

The second important way in which spaces become places is through *architecture*. A space becomes a place when we build into it enduring structures. Often we live in these structures, work in them, study in them, observe or admire them. We are changed by these things we create as we change them—the relation runs both ways. Architecture here is not only the initial design or building, but the transformation of it over time; in this sense, we always help build the structures we occupy, through our practices, and the structures are not fully finished until they have been used for a while (in one sense, then, they are never "finished"). Here I do not mean architecture only in the literal sense of buildings and bridges and so on;

there are architectures also of language, of customs, of complex practices and activities (games, for example)—all of these can play a role in transforming a space into a place.

Architectures transform not only a space but the patterns of activity for those who occupy them. These patterns can be viewed along five polarities:

(1) movement/stasis
(2) interaction/isolation
(3) publicity/privacy
(4) visibility/hiddenness
(5) enclosure/exclusion

These interrelated dynamics shape the ways in which participants operate within a space, and the particular constellation of them gives a space its distinctive character as a certain kind of place: for example, structures along the polarity of isolation, hiddenness, and privacy, versus those emphasizing visibility, interaction, and publicity.

(1) Structures facilitate, direct, or inhibit movement. They anticipate the way in which people are likely to navigate a space, but by making this assumption they also tend to direct it. In an art museum, for example, this is reflected in choices such as what exhibits to put near each other, and where to put doorways. Where will people want to pause, and which paintings will they want to linger over? Yet there are substantive assumptions at work here as well: say one wants to learn about historical periods in art, but finds that the rooms have been organized by subject matter or styles of painting; all the information is there the visitor might want, but not in a pattern of mobility that supports the inferences he or she is trying to make. Which room to start with? Where to go next? How much zig-zagging between rooms or retracing of steps is necessary? The visitor's confusion and uncertainty may also produce a kind of paralysis, even though the design of the museum is, on its own terms, quite clear and easily navigated.

(2) The design of spaces also communicates assumptions and expectations about social interaction. Architectures, by directing movement, create avenues to bring people together or barriers to keep them apart. Where will crowds tend to congregate, for example? Architectures also make assumptions about the kinds of things which people will be doing in a space, and whether they want to be doing it with others or alone. Again, these assumptions also shape behaviors: if a telephone booth is only big enough for one person, three girl friends can't all talk to their friend at the same time; they have to decide who gets to talk first, which may start an argument.

(3) Publicity and privacy constitute a slightly different issue, which is the extent to which an architecture allows or inhibits the disclosure of the participants' selves, their activities, and not only their words and ideas, to others (and vice-versa). Are walls transparent; or are there walls at all? Can you be seen, or do you always know you might be seen, and how does this tend to encourage or discourage certain things you might do? Can you *choose* when you can be seen, and when you do not want to be?

(4) Visibility and hiddenness, here, refer to the transparency of architectures, to what they disclose or conceal within, and to what they disclose or conceal about themselves. This is not quite the same as publicity and privacy, because here what is exposed or hidden are characteristics of the architecture itself. Does a wall close off a room that only some people know how to get to? Where does this doorway lead, and who is allowed through it?

(5) Architectures thus also operate through enclosure and exclusion; what (or who) is counted in and what is counted out. Some structures are intended to define a community made special in its own eyes by its privileged access and made to feel secure so that others viewed as less worthy will not interfere. The very attractions of such a partitioned space give rise to its limitations: the risk of complacency and numbing homogeneity. If we assume that certain kinds of change and development can only come from encounters with new and challenging ideas, this architecture of enclosure and exclusion may seem less like a protective shell, and more like a self-built prison.

There is much more to be said about architecture and the dynamics of shaping spaces into places; but here again I want to return to the dynamics of virtuality. I have tried to indicate in a general way how specific design features express assumptions about social dynamics and practices, about values, about knowledge and substantive subject matter; in this, I have tried to enlarge the concept of "architecture" to mean much more than just the design of rooms and buildings. Architectures reveal and conceal; they facilitate and discourage; they welcome and exclude; they direct and redirect and inhibit certain choices. In all this, architectures assume particular modes of activity and interaction—and in these assumptions tend to bring them about (or to suppress other modes).

In summary, I have explained two different ways in which spaces become places. The first is mapping, which is in some ways a more reactive process; a process of representing a space in order to be able to move and work within it. A mapped space takes on the character of a place for those who understand and can use the map. It reflects, in some respects, the perspective of the patron, the learner, the visitor. The second way in which spaces become places is through architectures: enduring structures that reconfigure spaces. This is in some ways a more active process, in which the space is not only represented (mapped) but directly shaped and transformed. There are at least five ways, I have suggested, in which this transformation affects not only the configuration of space, but the activities of the persons who operate within it. These dimensions determine the kind of place it is. Architecture reflects more the perspective of the librarian, the teacher, the conscious designer of a learning space.

I do not mean to argue that these activities of mapping and architecture are utterly unrelated or dichotomous: sometimes a map is prefatory to designing a structure (a blueprint is a kind of map, in fact); sometimes a large, complex architectural layout includes maps or directional markers within it as a way of helping people get around; trails, as I describe them here, have features of both. In the case of libraries their intimate relation can be seen clearly: the classification systems that organize materials within a library are typically reflected directly in the configuration of the building or structure itself. While the ways in which mapping and architecture influence navigation and meaning-making may be different, the ways in which they facilitate and direct movement within knowledge spaces may express common assumptions about learning. Indeed, in a *digital* library the activities of mapping and architecture become in certain respects indistinguishable.

KNOWLEDGE SPACES/PLACES AND KNOWLEDGE PRACTICES

The design of knowledge spaces, which turns them into knowledge *places*, involves these processes of architecture and mapping: these twin processes shape the contexts in which activities get directed and given meanings of certain sorts. They strongly influence, if not determine, patterns of movement; they provide choices, but choices between options which are themselves *not* chosen; they guide practices of interaction among people and other practices particular to the domain that is being designed (a kitchen, a park, a web site, a course syllabus, a library). This close link between spaces/places and practices gives neither one priority: spaces become places in regard to the practices that happen to occur there, but they also anticipate and to this extent influence the practices that do occur. The example of trails as a kind of "map" shows how practices transform a space and give it shape and structure; while, on the other hand, the five polarities just discussed as dimensions of architecture clearly anticipate, and to this extent shape, the actual practices that are and are not likely to develop within a space. Furthermore, consider how the development of maps influences the later practices that occur within a space, but *in a way* that is distinctive to the kind of map it is (a topographical map of hills, valleys, and rivers may cover the same space as a tourist map of sightseeing attractions and shops, but each reflects a different set of assumptions about what people will use the map to do, and in so doing they give rise to different *places* within the same *space*). Hence the design of spaces and the development of practices is a dynamic relation, each affecting the other, and the consequently emergent *places* are constituted in this interaction.

Knowledge places, then, are knowledge spaces that have become familiar for the people who explore, discover, and collaborate within them: they are not just archives or receptacles for information. Designing these with an eye toward making them places, and not just spaces, involves a number of decisions and balancing acts. First, there is the tradeoff between expert organizations of knowledge and organizations of knowledge conceived with learners in mind: the first provides the most complete and orderly system of interrelations, but this may be of little use to those first learning or exploring the domain; the latter may provide some latitude of choice and exploration for novices, but at the cost that their idiosyncratic organizations of understanding may be partial and in some respects inaccurate. The literature in science education on "misconceptions," however, has made clear that even these partial and inaccurate understandings can provide a basis for further learning; while these misconceptions may constitute impediments to learning later on, they typically incorporate substantial, if incomplete, understandings. Hence many prefer the term "partially correct conceptions." This shift in orientation, from evaluating learner development not directly by comparison with expert knowledge, but in terms of a developmental model, seeing the glass of understanding as half full and not only half empty, provides an important corrective to views oriented solely around whether learners can give the "correct" answer under certain circumstances (such as when taking a timed test).

Again, much of this is not news to librarians, who frequently struggle with the issue of designing a learning space in such a way that it is attractive and useful to diverse patrons (and not simply in terms of their own convenience and sensibilities). Schmidt (Chapter 4 of this volume) addresses this issue of library design. Other educators, I must say, often seem to forget this lesson.

A second tradeoff is between what could be called localized and general knowledge. Knowledge that is of very significant relevance and usefulness in one context may be utterly useless in others; conversely, more general knowledge, without being interpreted and framed appropriately may be—while true in one sense—irrelevant and useless to certain specific contexts and practices. Educators, teachers and librarians alike, work in a system that tends to privilege more general knowledge; while for many of their patrons or clients, it is the local and personally salient that matters most. How are these competing values reflected in the design of knowledge spaces, and how are the choices and practices of participants directed and constrained as a result?

A third tradeoff is in terms of establishing common standards and classification schemes. The idea of effective movement within a space requires markers that are recognizable and consistent; otherwise each space is *de novo*. In the case of physical libraries, this means things like classification systems and other conventions, so that someone walking into any library still has a sense of familiarity and recognizable order. Hunter (Chapter 6 of this volume) discusses how these standards and classification systems can be machine-generated. In the case of subways, anywhere in the world, this means standard conventions, such as color coding different lines, and prominently marking the points of transfer between them. In the case of the World Wide Web, it means things like standardizing domain names and URLs, and how hyperlinks work. The very freedom of movement one is seeking to provide depends on some constants. But such conventions and standards are not neutral: a library classification system incorporates countless assumptions that from certain points of view might be appear as biases or lacunae. This does not argue against classification systems; any alternative would simply raise different points of criticism on the same grounds. But it does lay clear the need for being reflective about the non-neutrality of such systems—and in some cases for making their limitations apparent to participants, so that participants have some options in thinking outside those structures.[4]

How does this play out in the context of virtual spaces/places? I have been arguing here for an educational philosophy built around concepts like mobility, inquiry, and collaboration, and for design principles—both in the architecture and the mapping of knowledge spaces—that are self-conscious about the knowledge practices one wants participants to engage in, individually and collectively (practices that, I have stressed, also reflect back upon and transform the space, turning it into a place). In the context of standard libraries, these choices are fairly well conventionalized: classification systems, shelving and display markers, diagrams and maps of the layout of the library, and so on. Many of these conventions are spatial in the sense of being bounded by physical limits (for example, how big a room is, or how many books a shelf or set of shelves will hold without collapsing); but also by practices (such as patrons who remove books to examine them but often replace them in the wrong location—sometimes intentionally in order to prevent others from finding them) which over time compromise the usability of the resource for future patrons. Some of these sorts of limitations and problems would not arise with the design of digital libraries, for reasons spelled out well by other papers in this book; but new ones will arise, some of which are impossible to predict in the long run.

In the short run, however, one trend can already be seen, which raises some cause for alarm: if the design decisions that are made in building digital libraries are driven primarily by commercial values, they may foster the development of knowledge spaces and practices that are more oriented toward proprietary interests, rather than in supporting virtual places and communities that better serve the needs of diverse constituencies. Worst of all, this trend may exacerbate a problem that is already present in current educational discourse, namely, an overemphasis on instrumentalist, information-driven conceptions of knowledge itself.

CONCLUSION: HOW WE THINK ABOUT KNOWLEDGE

In the course of this chapter I have addressed a number of impediments to achieving this vision of virtual learning spaces/places. Often these are instantiated in the metaphors and analogies through which people try to make sense of these complex and challenging new spaces. But in some ways the central barrier is the way we think about knowledge itself: knowledge as a set of facts, knowledge as expert understanding, knowledge as authorized tradition, knowledge as questions that have been settled with finality, knowledge as a property of individual minds, and so on. In this final section I want to explore how a reflection on virtual knowledge spaces and knowledge practices challenges these sorts of assumptions about knowledge. Examining where, how, and by whom knowledge comes to be established and authorized changes the way we think about the knowledge that results—as dynamic, provisional, subject to renegotiation; as socially distributed, not just residing in individual brains; and as necessarily tailored to the social and psychological spaces that must accommodate knowledge, and to the practices that authorize it as such.[5]

By all of this I mean to highlight the quality of spaces as *shared* spaces, an intersubjective process that is part of how they become places (this is especially, though not uniquely, true of knowledge spaces/places). This shared quality grants to the activities that occur there a degree of publicity; and in the case of knowledge spaces/places specifically this publicity of practice involves processes of collective adjudication, critique, and collective "ownership" that belie the Cartesian model of knowledge as a property of entirely egoistic thought and introspection. The degree to which one wishes to foster publicity and shared participation in certain practices is, you will recall, among the chief decisions made in the architecture of spaces. In the case of physical spaces, such publicity comes at the expense of certain costs and compromises. In the case of virtual spaces/places, the same is true, but (1) the possibilities of publicity and shared participation are on a much wider scale, (2) one is offered the prospects of multiple "publics," with some choice among them, and (3) *virtual* spaces/places provide a distinctive set of options in choosing or not choosing public-ity, at least in certain respects (for example, whether one participates in an anonymous fashion or not; whether one fashions a virtual identity that is significantly different from one's "real life" identity, and so on).[6] Yet, given the collaborative nature of knowledge I am sketching here, choices against the value of publicity and shared participation also carry costs and com-promises: what one may gain in "ownership" one loses in a lack of con-structive feedback from others; what one may gain in personal notoriety or credit one loses in a lack of collegial feeling and involvement; what one may gain in terms of local salience may be lost in more general relevance; and so on.

What is most striking to me about virtual spaces/places today is the tre-mendous impetus they have given to commons-oriented thinking about intellectual property and ownership.[7] Fitzgerald (Chapter 15 of this vol-ume) also addresses this issue. From Linux, to weblogs, to open directory archives, new knowledge spaces/places have gained value as a knowl-edge resource largely through the efforts of uncredited groups of people contributing knowledge and expertise to collective undertakings. Many have commented on the implications of this shift for copyright law, or for other institutional practices (such as tenure in universities, which is typ-ically based upon measures of individual scholarly productivity within narrowly controlled and sanctioned venues). Here I am focusing on the implications of this shift for thinking in new ways about the design of knowledge and knowledge spaces/places as environments for learning. And, to return to my opening theme, it is noteworthy that while most libraries have long been committed to these notions of the publicity of knowledge, open access, and the commons, schools for the most part still seem wedded to the conception of knowledge as an individual possession. The emergence of the digital library is potentially a huge step forward in making new knowledges and participation in new knowledge practices available on a massive scale, and often at little or no cost; will digital class-rooms and schools be designed with similar imperatives in mind?

NOTES

1. Some of the following discussion draws from Burbules (Forthcoming).
2. On "place" as an educational concept see, for example, David Gruenewald (2003), which includes an excellent bibliography; Jane McKie (2000); and David Kolb (2000). For important theoretical work on space and place more generally see Michel de Certeau (1984, especially pp. 117–118 ff.—although de Certeau's rela-

tion of "space" to "place" is the exact opposite of mine); David Harvey (1990, especially chapter 13); and Henri Lefebvre (1991).

3. Some of these ideas were first explored in the last chapter of Nicholas C. Burbules and Thomas A. Callister, Jr. (2000). See also Martin Dodge and Rob Kitchin (2001).

4. See the discussion of "critical hyperreading" in "Rhetorics of the Web."

5. On the topic of "distributed knowledge," I am grateful to my colleagues in the Distributed Knowledge Research Collective, a National Science Foundation funded collaboration which primarily included Geoffrey Bowker, Bertram C. Bruce, Caroline Haythornthwaite, Alaina Kanfer, Joseph Porac, and James Wade. Its web site is: www.dkrc.org.

6. This topic is discussed at some length in "Rethinking the virtual."

7. See Yochai Benkler, "Coase's Penguin, or Linux and the Nature of the Firm" for a very revealing analysis of this trend (http://www.benkler.org/CoasesPenguin.html).

REFERENCES

Burbules, N. C. (1997). Rhetorics of the Web: Hyperreading and critical literacy. In I. Snyder (Ed.) *Page to Screen: Taking Literacy Into the Electronic Era* (pp. 102–122). New South Wales: Allen and Unwin.

Burbules, N. C. (2000). Aporias, webs, and passages: Doubt as an opportunity to learn. *Curriculum Inquiry, 30*(2), 171–187.

Burbules, N. C. (2002). The Web as a rhetorical place. In I. Snyder (Ed.) *Silicon literacies* (pp. 75–84). London: Routledge.

Burbules, N. C. (2003). On virtual learning environments. Invited lecture, Wisconsin Library Association annual meeting, Autumn.

Burbules, N. C. (Forthcoming). Rethinking the virtual. In J. Weiss, J. Nolan, & P. Trifonas (Eds.) *The international handbook of virtual learning environments.* Dordrecht: Kluwer.

Burbules, N. C. (Forthcoming). Navigating the advantages and disadvantages of online pedagogy. In C. Haythornthwaite and M. M. Kazmer (Eds.) *Learning, culture and community in online education: Research and practice.* New York: Peter Lang.

Burbules, N. C., & Callister, T. A., Jr. (2000). *Watch IT: The promises and risks of information technologies for education.* Boulder, Colorado: Westview Press.

Burbules, N. C., & Linn, M. C. (1988). Response to contradiction: Scientific reasoning during adolescence. *Journal of Educational Psychology, 80*(1), 67–75.

de Certeau, M. (1984). *The practice of everyday life.* Berkeley: University of California Press.

Dodge, M., & Kitchin, R. (2001). *Mapping cyberspace.* New York: Routledge.

Gruenewald, D. (2003). Foundations of place: A multidisciplinary framework for place-counscious education. *American Education Research Journal, 40*(3), 619–654.

Harvey, D. (1990). *The condition of postmodernity.* London: Blackwell.

Kolb, D. (2000). Learning places: Building dwelling thinking online. *Journal of Philosophy of Education, 34*(1), 121–133.

Lefebvre, H. (1991). *The production of space.* London: Blackwell.

McKie, J. (2000). Conjuring notions of place. *Journal of Philosophy of Education, 34*(1), 111–120.

2

Literacy Spaces—Library Design

Susan Boyce
Deakin University, Melbourne, Australia

> *Spatial codes are frequently the primary medium for ideological statements . . .*
>
> —Hodge and Kress (1991, p. 61)

Digital communications have now settled with a degree of familiarity in school libraries, but the location and arrangement of computers in library spaces often appear as a new communications "overlay," subject to the same long-standing, print-based assumptions that have governed traditional library spaces. I make this observation because I believe it is important to note how established cultural assumptions continue to regulate both professional and spatial conventions in the school library, despite more than a decade of integrating digital communications technologies and online information services. Note, for example, how the propensity for locating computers in "information" areas rather than "reading" areas mirrors persistent, 19th-century patterns for organizing knowledge and texts (e.g., "fact" and "fiction" bays). Recall, as well, how the spatial configuration of computers in school libraries satisfies the supervisory desire for unobstructed observation of monitor screens, realizing long-standing school library preoccupations with discipline and surveillance. These examples show the ongoing influence of print literate values and judgments on professional library practice. They confirm the enduring agency of established cultural assumptions, whose strength continues to mediate professional perceptions about spatial relations and literacy experiences, and to overshadow recognition of new patterns for communications sociality.

This chapter intends to bring attention to what appears to be an evasion on the part of the school librarianship profession of the social and political implications inherent at the intersection of two major modes of communication and information. Rarely, if at all, does the professional writing of librarianship acknowledge the moments of conflict, irony, and paradox accompanying the coming together of print and digital communications cultures. Located in this transitional territory, and confronted with the technological complexities of information and communications technologies (ICTs), school librarians have experienced significant, if unrecognized, contradictions associated with issues of text, technology, and spatiality. By discussing these issues, later illustrated in case studies, this chapter explains how such instances challenge established power-based ideologies that are operative in the production of cultural identity and social relations within institutional practices. Historical moments such as these hold the potential to transform the discourses of literacy, libraries, and schooling. The challenge confronting school librarians lies in recognizing the anomalies that exist between the cultures of print and digital literacies.

Beginning with a review of the ideological foundations underpinning the traditional spatial paradigm for Australian school libraries, this challenge is addressed by examining the spatialities and literacies that intersect within the convergence of communications cultures in school libraries. Then the discussion moves to how recent understandings about post-print literacies, emerging from the domain of literacy education, run counter to the values endorsed by this spatial paradigm. To illustrate this argument, two case studies drawn from a recent study of a secondary school library are presented. These depict transitions in both literacy practices and spatial relations in a school community adapting to the impact of new communications technologies. Both the discussions and case studies are offered here to contribute further understanding of the social and political relations at stake in the transformation from library to cybrary.

SOCIAL SPATIALITY IN AUSTRALIAN SCHOOL LIBRARIES

This first discussion registers the important historic liaison between public and school library movements in the United States and Australia because this connection had significant repercussions in the later development of school libraries in both countries. In a study of three American school libraries, Dressman (1997a, 1997b; and see Dressman & Tettegah, chap. 3, this volume) informed us of the close, if short-lived, association established by the American public library movement with school libraries, so that "school libraries in their present form are the direct descendants of early public librarians' missionary incursions into the public schools" (Dressman, 1997b, p. 15). By the turn of the 20th century, school libraries in the United States were well established and, more often than not, they were managed by women trained in library science education rather than in teachers' college programs. Significant to the present discussion, Dressman noted that, as a consequence, these libraries "carried all the organizational markings of the public library" (p. 15).

The early growth of public library movements in both the United States and Australia was partly shaped by discourses of social justice and the public good. Assisted by philanthropic support and public funding, public library movements achieved institutional status as they strove to provide the masses with opportunities for personal empowerment through self-education, the promotion of literacy, and free access to information. It should not be overlooked, however, that the motivating forces of social justice and the public good, actualized and regulated through library discourses, also contributed to the production of particular forms of cultural subjectivity and social order, which were congruent with the prevailing political interests of social integration, regulation, and compliant citizenship.

In the latter half of the last century, school libraries in Australia received their most significant boost through the efforts of the Australian public library movement. Bundy (2001) spoke of the long-standing alliance of school and public library movements in Australia. He paid tribute to Sara Fenwick, who visited Australia in 1964 at the invitation of the Library Association of Australia. Her work in Australia had the effect of improving children's library services in schools and the public library movement (see Fenwick, 1966). Notably, it contributed to the success of the 1968 campaign for Commonwealth funding for school libraries, and, in this way, affected the transfer of public library paradigms, and the politics of public spatiality, into the domain of schooling and educational librarianship.

The spatial configuration of public libraries, already fixed in public consciousness as an accepted cultural model for library space, shaped standards for the iconic place and social spaces of school libraries. In public libraries, conventions for spatial ordering were originally governed by discourses supporting social discipline and control. The open plan of their internal public spaces was arranged for the purposes of administrative surveillance and for the cultural conditions and social relationships associated with print readership—expectations of silence and individual readership. Finding affinity with the social regulation of schools and schooling, these assumptions also framed perceptions about the school library, despite the fact that school and public libraries served different contexts. Public space within a school community is less likely to achieve the disaffecting, institutional anonymity of a public library space, and more likely to be perceived as a shared space within a far more tightly cohesive community.

Differences between patterns of sociality in public and school libraries are marked. As shared "common" spaces, public libraries are visited and occupied by separate individuals with discrete and disparate purposes. School libraries, on the other hand, may be visited simultaneously by two or more class groups of 30 plus students—all of whom know each other, and many of whom might be engaged in the pursuit of similar research tasks. "Commonsense" assumptions, the legacy of conventions and expectations about decorum in large enclosed public spaces, call for behavior that serves the common good of all library users (e.g., thoughtfulness and respect) so that everyone may achieve their different ends. Although this is achievable in the circumstances of the public library where patrons are unlikely to know each other, and have separate interests, it is less realistic in the school library, whose social groupings are differently constituted. Although school libraries are communal libraries, they are not "public" libraries, despite their derivation from the historic liaison between school and public library movements.

This backward glance at the social and political genealogy of school library spaces serves to remind us of the powerful assumptions that continue to underwrite the conceptual and material constructs of the school library, despite the changing social, economic, and communications climate of the 21st century. We continue to see evidence of this—most particularly, for example, in construction of virtual library spaces where hierarchical relationships order the architecture of library web pages. It is also evident in the physical spaces of the "real" library, where the distribution of computers is largely confined to nonfiction areas, reproducing and reinforcing traditional, print-based codes and values about genre, information, and literacy. Although school librarians may be familiar with the notion that the transition from library to cybrary involves a shift from "place" to "space," they may also need to review how the cultural logics of two different communications systems have been orchestrated in library spaces.

Castells (1996, pp. 448–449) declared the future likelihood of architecture and design to be redefined by the dominant form of "space of flows." This suggests looking to a different social logic from that of print literacy, which continues to affirm the iconicity of the situated "place" of the library. Recent understandings about the production of space in relation to social practice (Lankshear, Snyder with Green, 2000) confirm the interrelatedness of communications practices and spatiality. By maintaining awareness of the ongoing effects of embedded and active practices on the production of social spaces, we may be able to bring this understanding to bear on the architectural design of virtual and material structures, and thus achieve greater congruence between cultural practice and spatial design. Remaining conscious of the relation between communications practices and social spatiality, next consider changing notions about literacy education.

POSTMODERN PERCEPTIONS OF LITERACY

This discussion begins by acknowledging the notion of "multiliteracies" as referring to practices evolving from hybrid cultures, diverse modes of communications, and new sets of social relations. The New London Group's (1996) *A Pedagogy for Multiliteracies: Designing Social Futures* is representative of work in this field. The intention of the New London Group was to address the gap between what is taught in schools and what students experience in the lived world outside of schools. They identified fundamental disparities in educational outcomes, and revised the premises of literacy pedagogy by developing "a series of hypotheses about the directions literacy pedagogy might take in order to meet the radically transformed communication demands our students are likely to encounter in their near futures" (Cope & Kalantzis, n.d.). They nominated the most notable conditions of social change as the ever-increasing significance of cultural differences and linguistic diversity, and the potential for making meaning in multimodal ways through new communications technologies. Their work proposes an "epistemology of pluralism which provides access without having to erase or leave behind different subjectivities." It addresses the effects of changing economies, politics, and culture on the circumstances of people's private, public, and working lives.

Secondly, further to the idea of multiliteracies, recent insights explain new literacies in relation to the surface logics of text, especially in terms of time and space. Johnson-Eilola (1997) and Wysocki and Johnson-Eilola (1999) explained the surface of print text as a spatial interface that privileges the social logic of linear time and chronological "depth," whereas the social logic of an electronic interface is organized around a spatially organized sequence of surfaces and screens. Consequently, in conditions where we are simultaneously connected to multiple screens, reading across an interface of multiple surfaces, multiple strands of information rather than in-depth, time and space collapse into each other so that "past and future can only merely be other locations in space" (Wysocki & Johnson-Eilola, 1999, p. 363).

Their work does not construct a strictly dichotomous comparison between the social logics inherent in communications technologies, but rather offers these two paradigms as different ways of experiencing communication spaces. Wysocki and Johnson-Eilola's explication of subjectivity in relation to new forms of literate identity suggests "a radical unbinding of history from subjectivity." This makes it "impossible to believe in the unity of a single, stable subject"—particularly that of the print literate subject constructed in earlier versions of literacy (p. 365). Unbinding or opening offer opportunity for remaking cultural meanings and new social identities. Wysocki and Johnson-Eilola assisted here by providing a geopolitical understanding of digitally networked textual spaces as interface spaces, which are contingent on constructed relationships:

> If we understand communication not as discrete bundles of stuff that are held together in some unified space, that exist linearly through time, and that we pass along, but as instead different possible constructed relations between information that is spread out before us, then . . . living becomes movement among (and within) sign systems. (p. 365)

Kress (1999, p. 68) also discussed literacy in terms of space and time, referring to the shift from a "temporal-sequential logic of spoken (and to a lesser extent written) language to the spatial-simultaneous logic of the visual."

These ideas have circulated through the domains of literacy education, but have been less evident in the professional discourses of school librarianship. In coming to grips with changing conditions, librarians have established virtual library services and automated systems. They have also integrated digital texts into their resources and rearranged spatial configurations to accommodate the apparatuses of digital technologies. But these arrangements may be superficial traces, which do no more than gloss the dominance of established print library discourses. I submit that the politics of print-based concepts of "place" and social spatiality continue to regulate conventions for coordinating information and texts, library demeanor, cultural subjectivity, and sociospatial relations. School librarians have yet to come to terms with the changing politics of new communications practices and social change, and to make the break with long-standing interests that continue to shape professional concepts.

To support these claims, the discussion now reflects on the way that school librarians, on the whole, have tended to construct online virtual library and information services. Here, they have brought a characteristically ordered mind-set to representing the library in cyberspace and replicating their material domain. Despite the immediacy of networked delivery to desktops, the design of library home pages often emulates the social ordering of knowledge in the "real" library. In many cases, in fact, cybrary

web pages are no more than a digital reconstruction of 19th-century institutional print library mores—a "place" to be visited—a cultural match
for mind-sets produced throughout a conscientiously print-oriented experience of schooling. These constructions make use of digital space as a
means for "*representation*," reproducing existing sets of social relations
rather than exploiting the digital flow of networked space as "*interface*,"
as a means of distributive delivery to points of need.

As a strategy, on the part of cybrarians, this might seem fair enough,
given the unresolved politics of technology, information, and communications practices in school communities. Within these conditions, the
temptation to inscribe the library's services as an impressively large and
helpful presence on the school network seems understandable. Nevertheless, I suggest it should be equally tempting not to overlook opportunities open for exploration and innovation in this new communications
environment.

Local area networks propose rich possibilities for doing things differently, particularly in the service of contained, "known" communities such
as school communities. In such situations, it may be possible to re-devise
digital library services in a way more in keeping with the social logic, ecology, and culture of online, networked space. In my own workplace, we
have come to speculate on the possibility of a more imaginative delivery
of information services. The postmodern cybrary may come to shed its
earlier, institutional, corporate identity and to morph instead into a more
anonymous omnipresence—anticipating and delivering specifically "just-
in-time" requirements triggered by the prompt of predesigned structures.
Here, we advocate a less situated, but more spatially simultaneous presence—"creating an electronic text requires deciding not just *where*, but
when the text will be displayed" (Reinking, 1995, p. 25). This shift represents a move against replicating the iconic status of the library as a place in
an overt colonization of cyberspace, which may be perceived as advancing professional status as much as serving the community.

How else, other than by experiment and exploration, can we begin to
chart digital territory in new imaginative ways for both schooling and
library services—to create and shape the architecture of new spaces, new
environments? Too often the lack of time, skills, and resources leads us to
opt for ready-made solutions. Commercial software packages for network
management and course delivery offer easier, homogenous solutions. As
an option, however, they encourage us to forego the opportunity to design
our own spaces. Heedlessly, we are invited to succumb, yet again, to the
imposition of an imported cultural paradigm, a commercial system that
offers to homogenize and program our local cultures with new sets of reg-
ulating conventions that impose predefined forms of subjectivity within
new forms of prescribed enclosure.

When formulating policy and decisions about the use of networked space, we would do well to remember the inherited paradigm resulting from the public library/school library liaison. The system we incorporate today may achieve transparency through familiarity, leaving us with the persistent legacy of these decisions. Now, during this transitional period of changing communications and social orders, it is useful to evaluate both existing policies and practices, and new technologies for what they propose for the future and for their potential to perpetuate, if not amplify, the status quo.

SPATIAL RELATIONS IN LITERACY SPACES
AND LIBRARY DESIGN

Two instances drawn from a recent case study of a secondary school library build on these discussions. The study focused on issues surrounding the transition of the library, including its systems and management practices, as staff strove to understand the implications of cybrary status. The accounts offered here amplify themes raised in the preceding discussions by depicting how literacy practices and social spatiality intersected at the research site during this period of transition.

During the study, as a member of the library staff, and a researcher, I noted some of the frequently unacknowledged political and cultural inconsistencies that permeated the integration of print and digital communications. The first account describes ways in which ambiguity and paradox accompanied students' experience of "reading" in the library. The second documents the recursive effects, between digital and print cultures, on perceptions of situated spatiality at the research site.

Dressman's study (1997a, 1997b) addresses the geopolitics of school libraries, revealing the ambiguities lying between ideology and practice. Speaking as an advocate for nascent, autonomous literate subjectivities, he endorsed the value of ambiguity and ambivalence because they allow space in which to

> negotiate a compromise between reinvention and reproduction, between one's desires and the exigencies of one's moment . . . between concrete and abstract conceptualizations of space and their relation to human agency, which lies at the center of . . . the political geography of school libraries. (Dressman, 1997b, pp. 168–169)

In both accounts, I examine instances of such ambivalence by exploring cultural conflicts arising in perceptions about literacy and spatiality as the school community negotiated the conventions of established literacy practices across print and digital modalities. My perspective in this study was also assisted by the work of spatial theorists, including de Certeau (1984, 1986), Foucault (1984, 1986), Lefebvre (cited in Soja, 1996), and Paulston and Liebman (1994). These theorists' work heightened my awareness of the politics of social spatiality by bringing attention to the potential for public space to be characterized by existential qualities of cultural ambivalence and contestation. Dressman (1997a) designated these less acknowledged, abstract aspects of public space as "liminal spaces"—open to the struggle between control and subversion. Liminality, then, might be described as an existential dimension of spatiality, which is open to subversive reinterpretations, and refuses the imposition of prescriptive construction. From this perspective, liminal spaces can be understood as sites for paradox, contestation, and ideological disjunction. As such, however, they also yield rich evidence of emergent trends, imaginative subversion, and creative possibilities for future directions.

This discussion makes use of the term *liminality,* as used by Dressman, but does so conscious of the existential concepts of social spatiality also afforded by other spatial theorists mentioned earlier. Their concepts were especially useful in discerning the cultural anomalies arising between the spatial design of school libraries and recent notions about literacy education, as they are explored in the following case studies.

CASE STUDY 1: "READING" ACROSS TWO MODES OF COMMUNICATIONS

In this case study, the community's notions about the value of literary reading and the sanctity of the library's Reading Room, as an exclusively print literacy space, were staunchly maintained despite the current emphasis on information and ICTs. Teachers—but notably, not students—unanimously rejected the possibility of incorporating facilities for digital texts into this room.

Many researchers have explicated the ways that the culture of print literacy has worked to create a sense of individuated self and compliant self-discipline through the experience of private reading (cf. Green, 1997; Lanham, 1993). It should not be surprising that these ways of "being" have had particular appeal in schools, especially in school libraries where class groups exceeding 30 students visit for extended periods of time. Neither should it be overlooked that the practice of literary reading as a class group represents a deeper cultural investment, as a means of social integration and social discipline compatible with institutional requirements for the management of whole-school social events such as assemblies, chapel, and guest speakers.

Originally, time-tabled class reading sessions in our library were a regular component of the English curriculum for Years 7–9. The intention of these sessions was to encourage and promote reading with the purpose of improving literacy and a range of other less mentioned qualities such as concentration, imagination, the ability to "lose one's self" in a book, perseverance, and self-discipline. With these in mind, English teachers and librarians worked together to introduce students to a variety of texts following which, students were expected to settle in comfortable chairs for a period of sustained reading. This reading was understood to be an individual, silent, still activity under the supervision of the class teacher. But the 40 minutes dedicated to this event frequently proved to be too long for some readers to sustain the required decorum, so this conflict was resolved by devising an alternative solution. This involved dividing the lesson time into 20-minute periods and rotating groups of students into the reference area of the library where they used computers to work through prescribed, online, book-related programs.

"Reading" in the Reading Room was emphatically understood and practiced as an activity separate from computers and digital text. Yet, "screen" reading (and writing) was exactly what students engaged in when they took a break from their book reading to work on computers in the reference area. Two sorts of reading, valued but quite different, emerged. This represented an ideological paradox between the singular, print-oriented notion of literacy intended by the English curriculum policy and the diversity of multimodal literacies with which some students were more comfortable. Officially, according to the school timetable, the library's booking sheet, and the English curriculum, the class was in the Reading Room, developing sound print literacy reading habits. Unofficially, all stakeholders (i.e., teachers, students, and librarians) had, in fact, conspired to devise a pragmatic reinterpretation of curriculum policy and "reading."

The strategy served several purposes and resulted in some interesting effects in that the overt, primary desire to accommodate students' literacy preferences also conveniently eased the supervisory obligations and supported expectations for library order within the Reading Room. Perhaps more significantly, it reinterpreted existing library spaces, obliterating the spatial boundaries between the clear decorums of print and digital reading practices, between books and computers, and between forms of texts and technologies. By expanding "reading" to include less recognized forms of reading in the computer areas of the library, we had negotiated the spaces between "order and desire" (Dressman, 1997b), and conferred those areas with liminal dimensions in relation to the Reading Room and the English curriculum.

The irony of this instance, however, was that despite evidence of new literacy patterns emerging from the English/Library paradox, our community continued to differentiate between "real reading" and digital reading. This was possibly because getting lost in a digital text does not replicate the same sense of surrender, of losing oneself in print text. Although it is possible to be deeply absorbed while engaging with digital text, readers in this medium need to keep their wits about them, engaged as they are in the metacognitive process of navigation, as well as pursuing the substantive content of text. While at a computer, mind and body—or at least, mind and hand—work together executing autonomous choices, engaging, disengaging and re-engaging, reading in a different fashion, absorbed (lost?), but in control. For this sort of reading, readers negotiate the course of their reading, possibly changing directions, or adding to the text, and most likely engaging in verbal interaction with other students as they do so.

Aware of the ideological disjunctions involved in this experience, I explored and mapped all the possible contingencies involved in the experience of "reading" in the library with the intention of developing a more honest account of how technologies mediate literacy experience. I wanted to show how, in the case of reading across more than one mode of communication, experience might be characterized by multiple, and sometimes paradoxically oppositional, possibilities. The investigation was informed by the recent understandings relating to time and space explained earlier (Johnson-Eilola, 1997; Kress, 1999; Wysocki & Johnson-Eilola, 1999) and by awareness of the liminal ambiguities/possibilities now evident in "reading."

With the purpose of bringing attention to the availability of a wider and more complex range of potential literacy attributes, as they might occur across two modes of communications, I drew on Star's rules (cited in Paulston & Liebman, 1994, p. 218) for the study of invisible things. These emphasize the continuous, multilayered quality of phenomena, the multidirectional standpoints of social experience, and "the fundamental pluralism of human interaction." They cautioned that power is exercised by the "imposition of a position" and that "every stand-point has a cost" (p. 218).

I also drew on Star's (in Paulston & Liebman, 1994, p. 227) heuristic device to create a spatial schema for adapting attributes of text with mininarratives for literacies. To construct a set of interleaving strata for my model (See Fig. 2.1), I used the domains of Subjectivity, Social Relationships, Semiotic Coding, and the Social Logics of Textual Surfaces as themes to frame potential mininarratives. These themes allow a more comprehensive, more pluralist overview of literacy experience. Each strata, separately and together, proposes the potential for mapping multiple pathways and diverse dispositions for the "literate subject," contingent on the social and cultural contexts of experience.

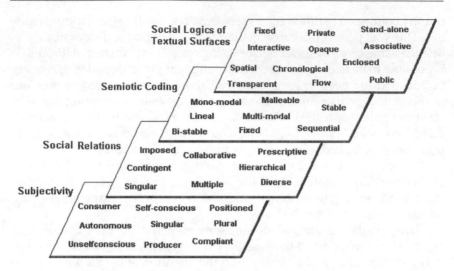

FIG. 2.1.   Mininarratives for literacies.

The strata of Fig. 2.1 should be understood as interpenetrating, that is, as simultaneous dimensions of literacy experience, without hierarchical or sequential order. Any number of these attributes might come into play simultaneously with varying degrees of congruency during a literacy experience. Teasing out the mini-narratives of literacy, *contextualized* as experience, contributed to our understanding of literacies and communications practices as inclusive of diverse social and cultural positions and interpretations, which exceed conventional school literacies. New understandings of literacies are inclusive of the predictable, and of hybrid possibilities. The logic of the multiliteracies pedagogy refuses prescribed pathways, thus inviting "pluralism which provides access without having to erase or leave behind different subjectivities" (Cope & Kalantzis, n.d.).

As our perceptions about the "contextuality" of literacy experience expanded, we came to perceive other environmental characteristics as contextual surface spaces. The delineation of floorspace, the arrangements for seating and shelving, the distinctive distribution of computers and books, and the generic categorization of texts all could be equated with page and screen as contextual surface spaces for literacy experience.

With this understanding in mind, I devised the map in Fig. 2.2, which builds on the previous model by adding more specifically contextual aspects of spatiality.

This mapping in Fig. 2.2 shows that a number of the multiple possibilities available for Contextual Surfaces and Spaces correspond with those mapped in the similar domains for Literacies (see Fig. 2.1), therefore identifying the coincidence of similar sets of spatial relations that were operative

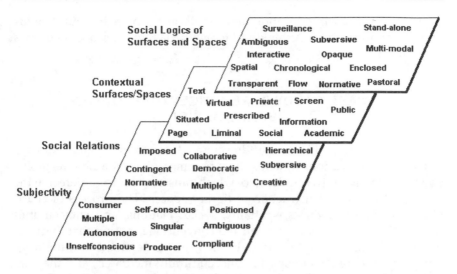

FIG. 2.2.   Mininarratives for contextual surfaces and spaces of the library.

in both. These simultaneous coincidences support perceptions discussed earlier (see Wysocki & Johnson-Eilola, 1999), namely, that the coordinates of textual practices and literacies are *spatial* as much as *temporal*.

The mappings provide a means of registering and elaborating possibilities for the enactment and experience of literacies across social, cultural, and technological contexts. Indeed, plotting such diversity helped us to understand the extent to which modes of communications and contextual surfaces are, in fact, imbued with political dynamics and with the propensity for imposing cultural dispositions and social relations—that literacies are value laden and contribute to shaping cultural identities and environments. Read against the earlier account of "reading" across two modes of communications, these mappings unravel both the ideological paradox and the political irony of that scenario.

Within the domains of new and diverse communications media, "reading," "writing," and enacting curriculum are different cultural acts compared to performing the same tasks within the culture of print communications. In the previous account, I have mapped evidence of the less-spoken spectrum of dispositions and attributes available within, and across, more than one mode of communication to bring attention to their absence (evasion?) in curriculum policies and conventional perceptions of literacy. Until this issue is addressed in pedagogy and curriculum design, students' literacy experiences oscillate between the values of two communications eras—between compliance to print literacy assessment criteria and the actualization of their own cultural technological communications identities. I believe that the political import of this situation is not readily recognized in education and the library profession, but it holds urgent implications for rethinking literacy pedagogy in school cybraries and schools.

CASE STUDY 2: RECONCEPTUALIZING LIBRARY DESIGN

As the librarians in this case study operated across the spatial domains of two communications systems, they became aware of a new recursive dynamic at work between the two, which caused them to re-perceive the social and political construction of library spaces. The process of charting attributes of literacies, spatiality, social relations, and subjectivities (Figs. 2.1 and 2.2) took us beyond the conventional notion that "virtuality" related solely to cyberspace. Instead, we understood that literacy/library spaces are technologically and culturally mediated, and they are imbued, therefore, with the potential for different sets of social relations and cultural subjectivities—conventional, virtual, and liminal. This perspective assisted in diminishing the construct of oppositional relationships between the real and the virtual. Understanding both situated spaces and online spaces as *contextual literacy interfaces* brought them into closer alignment in our perception. We reassessed the open plan of our situated library, believing this paradigm to be in need of a change more in keeping with both the economies and the ambient ecologies of various and multiple sociotechnological literacy practices.

With familiarity, the purposes and effects of established library ordering on social, physical, and intellectual ways of being had settled to the point of unnoticed transparency. Now, we needed to reconsider how our policies and practices supported the life of these norms in the conditions of new communications and social orders, to question the extent to which the local area network now fulfilled, if not amplified, a number of characteristically "library" obligations. Take, for example, the long-standing library practices of surveillance and censorship. The principle of panoptic surveillance, a determining factor in architectural design for school libraries, was now partially fulfilled through the administration of the school network. School spaces necessarily carry the obligation for supervision and care, but under new and different conditions of spatial occupation and literacy practice, the dynamic of supervision had also changed. Similarly, electronic network filters provided a means of reenacting forms of cultural censorship, previously exercised by selective, library acquisition policies.

Furthermore, the new logics of semiotic coding and the immediacy of key word searching facilities in digital systems now made other categories of ritualized library conventions seem questionable. These included differentiating between fact and fiction, the taxonomies of the Dewey Decimal system for clumping "knowledge" into certain cultural paradigms, the ponderously arcane rules for cataloguing and Subject Headings hierarchies, and (perhaps most significant of all) the dominance of the printed word.

These cultural conventions no longer hold for the post-postmodern subjectivities of our student population who read and write with intense concentration, ear-phoned with a deluge of noise pouring through their heads, for whom a space is *their* space because their presence defines it. A decade had passed since digital information and communications systems had revolutionized library information management systems, but, coordinated by the agenda of historic conventions and the ideology of library discourses, the physical spaces of our library still bore the imprint of the open plan, public library space. Our challenge was to reconceptualize the place and spaces of our library in a way that was compatible with changing communications technologies, multiliteracies practices, and emergent literate identities.

Seeking solutions, we visited other school libraries. Some schools had created spaces outside of the library to accommodate adolescents' hybrid social/academic experiences of school life. These spaces offered online facilities in a social space for autonomous purposes. We also visited a library class in a laptop school where students sat in a state of divided/ dualistic being—bodies captured by network connection points, minds released into the flow of their local area network—and further. The factory-like impression did not seem very removed from the classrooms of the last two centuries. The difference here was that new technologies seemed so overt, whereas time and familiarity have endowed the physical implications of print artifacts with transparency. The paradox of communications technologies lies in their potential to both liberate and regulate as their effects mediate mind, body, and environment. We realized that even the "space of flows" (Castells, 1996, p. 448) was subject to forms of boundedness and enclosure.

Now, considering our library as a site in which the situated and the virtual—the stand alone and the distributed—might find greater congruence, the challenge lay in acknowledging the full sociocultural context (Bigum & Green, 1993; Lankshear, Snyder, with Green, 2000) by making provision for the multiplicity of relationships possible within the combined dimensions of time and space.

We considered dissecting the open floor plan of our library, creating diverse, discrete spaces as a pragmatic solution. Having moved well beyond perceiving literacy as a singular, individual practice of perceiving students solely as consumers of texts, we now made provision for multiple forms of textual production, for diverse spatial configurations, and for pluralist forms of sociality. Given the various technologies required for multiliteracies, the differing degrees of public and private activities, and the validity of variable forms of literate sociality, reorganizing the open spaces of the library into discrete, customized literacy areas held practical and ideological appeal.

Nevertheless, notions about enclosure and definition ran counter to established critical-emancipatory discourses of literacy and librarianship. At a time when metaphors for libraries hinged on perceptions of "flow" and "everywhere and nowhere" (Luke & Kapitzke, 1999, p. 476), the prospect of drawing lines on an open library space brought issues of openness and boundedness into question. I recalled Massey's explanation that:

> All attempts to institute horizons, to establish boundaries, to secure the identity of places, can . . . be seen as *attempts to stabilize the meaning of particular envelopes of space-time.* They are attempts to get to grips with the unutterable mobility and contingency of space-time. Moreover, however common, and however understandable they may be, it is important to recognize them as such. For such attempts at the stabilization of meaning are constantly the site of social contest, battles over the power to label space-time, to impose the meaning to be attributed to a space, for however long or short a span of time. (Massey, 1994, p. 5, italics in original)

I pondered the binary opposition between openness and enclosure. Wrought in the current discourse of digital communications, perceptions about networked space, communications, and information flows favored the notion of openness as desirable. By comparison, forms of enclosure— the book and even the walls of the print-based library—seemed ideologically unfashionable. The established "open-floor plan" model for library design came as close as was possible within print-based culture to suggesting transparency and uninhibited access to information. Yet, here was the deceptive paradox of library design. The real purpose of spatial openness did not so much fulfill these emancipatory purposes as it did those of surveillance and discipline.

I decided that, among the numerous forms of enclosure and entrapment associated with the spatial conditions of communications, the creation of microworlds in our library was relatively innocuous. The idea of differentiated spaces resonated with the ideas of Brawne (1997, p. 8), who recommended that a "family of spaces" allowing for the small within the larger whole might be achieved by "place-making through structure, levels, materials and degrees of openness and closure." Concern about the binary opposition between openness and enclosure was resolved by our understanding of the latent (virtual?) potential of spatial liminality— that space is the product of intersecting social relations—and is, therefore, always in the process of construction. From this perspective, it seemed entirely plausible then that these microlibrary-world spaces might be perceived as approaching something Aleph-like, "whose center is everywhere and circumference is nowhere" (Borges cited in Soja, 1996, p. 55).

LITERACY SPACES—LIBRARY DESIGN:
CONDITIONS OF TRANSITION

The convergence of print and digital communications cultures has involved adjustments, adaptations, and redefinition of the social significance of the place and spaces of the school library. The conditions of this transformation, as described in the previous case studies, can be read as preemptive moments of cultural transition, rich in potential liminalities. These provide scope for renegotiating the territory between the long-standing norms that regulate profession and practice on the one hand, and the possibilities evidenced by postmodern identities and new understandings on the other.

In the past, the material status of the school library signified a singular cultural representation of text, literacy, knowledge, and information within the school. Now, within a new set of communications conditions, major shifts in perceptions of literacy and spatiality give rise to reconceptualizing both the place and the spaces of the school library. The adaptations described in this chapter may be noted as symptomatic of the current transitional shift from the iconic "place" of the traditional print library to the more diverse distribution of socioliteracy spaces—real and virtual—which constitute a postmodern cybrary. Consequently, I suggest that the significance of the contemporary school cybrary might be more usefully gauged by the provision of diverse, multimodal spaces, whose contextual *interfaces*, both real and virtual, enable the intersection of new generation social subjectivities with various forms of text and information.

The ideas explored in this chapter are offered as ground from which to review the professional discourses of both school librarianship and school library design, noting that neither can be separated from the politics of literacy and text. My perspective has paid particular reference to the social and political relations inherent in literacy practices and social spatiality. If architectural form and spatial design can be read as "ideological statements" (Hodge & Kress, 1991, p. 61), then the school library can be read as a site wherein spatial codes particularly reveal the ideological underpinning of cultural practices. Understanding literacies and modes of communication as social practices—"the mediated expression of deeper tendencies of society" (Castells, 1996, p. 448)—brings established preconceptions about library spaces and literacy practices into question, especially within the cultural context of converging modes of communications.

REFERENCES

Bigum C., & Green, B. (1993). Technologizing literacy: Or, interrupting the dream of reason. In A. Luke & P. Gilbert (Eds.), *Literacy in contexts: Australian perspectives and issues* (pp. 4–28). St Leonards, NSW: Allen & Unwin.

Brawne, M. (Ed.). (1997). *Library builders.* London: Academy Editions.

Bundy, A. (2001, September/October). Essential connections: School and public libraries for lifelong learning. Paper presented at *Forging Future Directions,* Conference of the Australian School Library Association, Sunshine Coast, Queensland, Australia.

Castells, M. (1996). *The rise of the networked society: Vol. 1. The information age: Economy, society and culture.* London: Blackwell.

Cope, B., & Kalantzis, M. (n.d.). Multiliteracies: Pedagogy at a glance. Retrieved October 2004 from http://www.edoz.com.au/educationaustralia/archive/features/mult4.html

de Certeau, M. (1984). *The practice of everyday life* (S. F. Rendall, Trans.). Berkeley, CA: University of California Press.

de Certeau, M. (1986). *Heterologies: Discourse on the other.* Berkeley, CA: University of California Press.

Dressman, M. (1997a). Congruence, resistance, liminality: Reading and ideology in three school libraries. *Curriculum Inquiry, 27*(3), 267–315.

Dressman, M. (1997b). *Literacy in the library: Negotiating the spaces between order and desire.* Westpoint, CT: Bergin & Garvey.

Fenwick, S. (1966). *School and children's libraries in Australia: A report to the children's libraries section of the Library Association of Australia.* Melbourne, Australia: Cheshire.

Foucault, M. (1984). *The Foucault reader* (P. Rabinow, Ed.). New York: Pantheon.

Foucault, M. (1986). Of other spaces. *Diacritics, 16*(1), 22–27.

Green, B. (1997, July). Literacy, information and the learning society. Keynote address at *Language, Learning and Culture: Unsettling Certainties,* first national conference of the Australian Association for the Teaching of English, Australian Literacy Educators' Association & the Australian School Library Association, Darwin, Australia.

Hodge, R., & Kress, G. (1991). *Social semiotics.* Cambridge, England: Polity Press.

Johnson-Eilola, J. (1997). Living on the surface. In I. Snyder (Ed.), *Page to screen: Taking literacy into the electronic era* (pp. 185–210). St. Leonards, NSW: Allen & Unwin.

Kress, G. (1999). English at the crossroads: Rethinking curricula of communication in the context of the turn to the visual. In G. Hawisher & C. Selfe (Eds.), *Passions, pedagogies and 21st century technologies* (pp. 66–88). Logan, UT: Utah State University Press.

Lanham, R. A. (1993). *The electronic word: Democracy, technology and the arts.* Chicago: University of Chicago Press.

Lankshear, C., Snyder, I., with Green, B. (2000). *Teachers and technoliteracy: Managing literacy, technology and learning in schools.* St. Leonards, NSW: Allen & Unwin.

Luke, A., & Kapitzke, C. (1999). Literacies and libraries—Archives and cybraries. *Pedagogy, Culture & Society, 7*(3), 467–491.

Massey, D. (1994) *Space, place and gender.* Cambridge, England: Polity Press.

New London Group. (1996) A pedagogy for multiliteracies: Designing social futures. *Harvard Educational Review, 66*(1), 60–92.

Paulston, R. G., & Liebman, M. (1994). An invitation to postmodern social cartography. *Comparative Education Review, 38*(2), 215–232.

Reinking, D. (1995). Reading and writing with computers: Literacy research in a post-typographic world. In K. Hinchman, D. Lees, & C. Kinzel, (Eds.), *Perspectives in literacy research and practice* (pp. 17–33). Chicago: National Reading Conference Inc.

Soja, E.W. (1996). *Thirdspace: Journeys to Los Angeles and other real and imagined places.* Oxford, England: Blackwell.

Wysocki, A., & Johnson-Eilola, J. (1999). Blinded by the letter: Why are we using literacy as a metaphor for everything else? In G. Hawisher & C. Selfe (Eds.), *Passions, pedagogies and 21st century technologies* (pp. 349–368). Logan, UT: Utah State University Press.

3

Ordered by Desire: School Libraries in Past and Present Times

Mark Dressman
Sharon Tettegah
University of Illinois

Surely one of the most paradoxical issues in librarianship is the question of how to organize the texts of a library *rationally* (i.e., systematically, in ways that place related texts within close proximity or accessibility and in a system that can be easily understood by users) and yet not *ideologically* (i.e., in ways that subtly or not-so-subtly convey relations that privilege a particular worldview and its patrons). Prior to industrialism and the printing press, when texts were handwritten, few in number, or accessible only to narrow, close-knit groups of users, it is unlikely that anyone noticed or cared that this paradox existed. Historical accounts of textual order in ancient, medieval, and even early Enlightenment times indicate that often no rational order was placed on texts at all, whereas in other cases, the indexing of volumes was done idiosyncratically in ways that reflected the interests and needs of a particular group of users, who often were also the only users of that collection of texts.

During the 19th century, the rise of large urban areas made order and control of the masses an important issue within society. Major public institutions were mandated to serve the public interest challenging librarians with the paradox of devising an organizational system that would permit easy but nondirective access to libraries' texts (Foucault, 1979; see Willinsky, chap. 10, this volume). Yet, even then, the paradoxical nature of this issue, particularly among the early developers of library classification systems, remained largely unacknowledged. According to Garrison (1979), when Dewey devised his system in the 1870s he was apparently quite sure that in organizing "all human knowledge into ten tight holes" (p. 37), he had solved forever the question of how to classify and sort all texts (worthy of inclusion) within public libraries. Indeed, his hubris extended even further than this, because Dewey apparently was also quite sure that his system reflected a sort of "natural order" of textual knowledge—an order without political, economic, or cultural bias that brought librarians and users alike into a kind of harmony with the greater natural order of the universe itself.

Yet, no sooner was Dewey's system installed in public libraries (or "working men's universities," as their advocates marketed them) across the United States than the completeness of its order was challenged, not on the basis of theory but on the basis of its users' desire for books and forms of text outside the parameters of what Dewey and the almost all-male, university-educated founders of the public library movement deemed worthy of purchase and inclusion in public libraries (see Kapitzke, chap. 9, this volume). The books in question were popular fiction—not Shakespeare or the literature of the ancients or even the folk literature of early Britain or Europe or the folktales of more exotic cultures—all of which would have found a place in the Dewey 800s as "literature" or in the late 300s as "folklore," but books written for a mass audience that used contemporary fiction and whose attraction was as much their contents as a particular author's own style, and that were ostensibly meant to be read (or consumed) and discarded, rather than preserved and studied more than once. Again, according to Garrison (1979), it was only when working men failed to appear at libraries in the numbers predicted and the patronage of women and children dropped off, that pragmatic head librarians across the United States condescended to purchase popular novels and open children's rooms. They did so in sections that were segregated from the Dewey-ordered texts of the library's main collection, and in keeping with the presumed subjectivity of their readers, more "personally"—that is, by authors' last names, rather than by topic.

In this way, an ordering of textual knowledge based on a bifurcated, gendered politics of desire—in which women and children's putatively *subjective desire for diversion* was accommodated but at the same time carefully differentiated from men's putatively *objective need for knowledge* (later reconceived as "information")—was established in public, school, and university libraries across the United States. So deeply entrenched in the psyche of educated, literate citizens and librarians has this arrangement become that it continues in unquestioned and ubiquitous practice throughout most school and small town public libraries in the United States today, even though since the 1970s most major university and public libraries have abandoned Dewey's classifications for the more inclusive and complex system of the Library of Congress.

This chapter undertakes an exploration of this paradox for the users of school libraries in most parts of the United States. The first part of this chapter examines, through an ethnographic investigation conducted just prior to the advent of cybertechnology in 1993, the practices of librarians in three schools that served socioculturally distinct student populations. The second part examines, through a series of interviews, the practices of three different school librarians who, in 2004, were in the process of adapting to new possibilities for school librarianship and patron use prompted by burgeoning information technologies such as the Internet and the World Wide Web—practices (e.g., keyword searches, hypertextuality, and Boolean logic) that, in theory, may be counterhegemonic to the gendered and social class values embedded within the order of school libraries of the Deweyan period. In the conclusion, we will interrogate these counterhegemonic promises, and consider some enduring practical issues that need to be resolved before the full potential of cybertechnology within school libraries is realized.

Before proceeding, however, we need to offer a word of caution about the implications and generalizability of the data and analysis presented in this chapter. Although we have ordered our presentation in a way that suggests that the three libraries and librarians of 1993 and 2004 are "mirror images" of each other, they are, in fact, images reflected through two different mirrors (i.e., two different sets of data collected at different times by different individuals; Mark in 1993 and Sharon in 2004) and in different contexts. Rather than characterize the arguments and claims we make here as grounded mainly in the empirical evidence of school libraries and librarianship, the work of this chapter is predominantly theoretical and is couched in modals such as *could* and sometimes *should*, rather than in declarative statements of fact about what is. This chapter, then, looks at ways in which, in the past, the capacity of library patrons to make use of texts was constrained in principle by the physical and organizational need to place books on shelves in rooms systematically. It then alternately considers ways in which, through the possibilities of cybertechnology and cyberspace, in the present or near future the capacities of library patrons to make use of texts may, in principle if not always in practice, be freed from past constraints.

LOOKING ACROSS THREE SCHOOL LIBRARIES, CIRCA 1993

The three school libraries that serve as illustrations of Dewey's historical legacy were located in three very different neighborhoods within a major

TABLE 3.1

Librarian Practice and Student Response in Three School Libraries, c. 1993

Librarian and School	School Demographics	Librarian's Perception of Students and School	Library Program	Observed Student Response
Mary Strauss, Chavez Elementary	Working poor, inner-city neighborhood 90%+ Mexican American student population; many bilingual Spanish speakers	Like Mary as a child, students are "not readers" Teachers do not instill a "love of reading" Families, community do not value literacy or education as Mary does	Reading incentive programs to instill "a love of fiction" through rewards for reading series books and passing tests Students discouraged from browsing or reading nonfiction Dewey seldom taught	Resistance: Students sneak into library at odd times to check out informational books Find loopholes in reading programs that allow more choice Show a great interest in using the card catalogue but are unsuccessful
Barbara Henry, Crest Hills Elementary	Affluent professional neighborhood Majority of students are White, but there are some international students of color from a nearby university housing complex for married graduate students	Like Barbara as a child, students are expected to "pick up" reading and library skills through school projects, peers, and siblings during public library visits, and through reading at home Open library, browsing allowed	Weekly story times, grades k–6, are central to library program Students punish others who deviate or challenge norms Students are expected to "pick up" Dewey and the catalog on their own	Conformity: Students do "pick up" system and complete classroom assignments in conventional ways
Louise Currie, Roosevelt Elementary	Working-class urban neighborhood Predominantly White and Mexican American student population with some African Americans	Like Louise as a child, students are "really poor kids with a lot of inner motivation, who need a library where children can feel it is warm," and "they love me, and I am free to do some things on my own."	Weekly storytimes, grades k–2 Open library and browsing encouraged Elaborate narrative of a cave man who "discovers" Dewey system and explicit catalogue instruction	Negotiation: Students challenge, play with, cave man and other didactic narratives about the library as an ordered system Students are enthusiastic browsers throughout the library

city in the southwestern United States. Table 3.1 presents background information for each library and its program. Because housing and population within the city were highly segregated with respect to social class and ethnicity, each school served a demographically different, and very distinct, student population. Although data for the study were collected in the early 1990s (see Dressman, 1997, for a full account), the libraries themselves and their organization, as well as the demographics of the students served by them, remain much the same more than a decade later.

These three libraries also serve as excellent examples of the practices of school librarianship as it was practiced from the early to late 20th century. For example, each library observed a strict organizational bifurcation and physical segregation of fictional (i.e., novels and picture books) and nonfictional, or "factual" texts. At Crest Hills, the nonfictional texts were located to the right of the library entrance, whereas picture books were located to the left, in a "story corner" area delineated by an aisle and several bookcases; all fiction was located in a back room, connected to the main room of the library by a narrow hallway. At Roosevelt, librarian Louise Currie liked to stand in the center of the main room of the library and, with a motion of her arm that followed the central beam of the ceiling, declare that "all the books on the left are fiction, and all the books on the right are nonfiction." At Chavez, all books were located in one large room, with picture books and fiction in the central part of the room, the Dewey 000s to 800s along the far right wall, and the 900s along the far left wall. But the main technology for maintaining the distinction between fictional and nonfictional texts at Chavez was not their physical arrangement but librarian Mary Strauss' motivational reading programs. These programs actively discouraged checkout or even browsing within the nonfiction sections of the library on the grounds that informational texts did not provide the same sort of pleasure, and therefore did not lead to the same "addiction" to reading as fictional texts.

The librarians in each school also shared similar professional backgrounds. Each had a master's degree in school librarianship from the same state university, and each had more than 20 years of experience in the school district. These librarians differed, however, in the stories they told of their own family and educational histories, and in the ways they applied lessons from their own life experience to understanding the needs of their student patrons and adjusting their practices accordingly. Perhaps the most significant *differing* factor was the social class background of the librarians and the impact that background had on the ways that each librarian interpreted her own experience vis-à-vis the assumed social class experiences of the students she served.

At Chavez, for example, the lessons Mary Strauss took from her own life story led her to impose her own taste for fiction—a taste with ironic historical antecedents in the rise of "women's professions" (see Baym, 1978; Douglas, 1977)—as the antidote for the perceived lack of literate culture in the working poor, Mexican immigrant homes of her clientele in ways that, according to Garrison (1979), closely paralleled the practices of public and school librarians among the urban immigrants of the late 19th and early 20th centuries. "Kids are not readers by nature," Mary Strauss once noted as she told the story of her own education and professional development as a librarian. During each weekly class visit, Mary Strauss would exhort the students about the need to "exercise their brains" by reading through one of many such programs that were in operation for different grades. These programs and their accompanying evangelism culminated in a fever pitch during the day-long, schoolwide Reading Rally Day, which featured a Reading Robot, Read-Out Work-Out conducted on the front steps of the school by the school's physical education teacher, who would lead the students in a set of physical exercises that mimicked the physical motions of reading, so that, as Mary Strauss defiantly stated, the community would "see what's going on here."

At Crest Hills, middle-class Barbara Henry, who "picked up" reading as a child and "fell into" librarianship as an adult, offered no program of formal instruction in the Dewey system or the use of the card catalogue. However, students began using the card catalogue on their own initiative as early as the second grade, and had little problem locating books on their favorite topics on the shelves—a skill they "picked up," according to the librarian and the students themselves in interviews, through trips to the local public library with parents and older siblings.

Gender was the central principle by which not only the librarian but the students who used the library ordered their activities. In several weeks of observation, for example, every male student beyond the first grade who entered the library to browse went directly to the nonfiction section of the library, whereas every female student beyond grade 1 headed straight for the backroom to browse in the fiction section. Students of both genders might eventually circulate throughout the library (in fact, an inventory of the books students actually checked out revealed no gendered pattern), but the first stop for boys was always nonfiction and the first stop for girls was always fiction.

Barbara Henry also unconsciously encouraged "girls to be girls" and "boys to be boys" in her privileging of male protagonists, boy's responses, and "male" (fact-based, "objective") responses to narratives during story times. The protagonist of every story read by Barbara Henry during the several dozen story times that were observed over a 1-year period was a male—until the researcher asked her about this one day. The front row of each story time, and often the second row, was all male. Although nearly all the books the librarian read were fictional, the conversation she engaged them in—conversation dominated, again, largely by the boys in any group—pivoted on the exchange of informational facts related to the narrative of the book. Moreover, in focus interviews conducted with small groups of students by the researcher, a strict hierarchy prevailed in which the "coolest" (best dressed, most athletic) boys in the class dominated both the girls and other, "less cool," boys.

At Roosevelt, Louise Currie interpreted her own working-class background and early experience of the library as the template for her interactions with the working-class students during explicit skills lessons that offered a narrative of the library's order as a template for self-improvement through self-study. For example, in the story and accompanying posters that Louise Currie used to explain the logic of the Dewey system, a caveman stumbles into the light of day and asks himself, "Who am I?" Because this question is so basic and foundational to all other knowledge, books dealing with identity, philosophy, and ethics, come first in the Dewey system, in the 100s. Next, the caveman asks himself, "Who made me?," and so the 200s in Dewey's system are reserved for books dealing with religion. As the caveman progresses, he becomes more social in nature, asking questions about his neighbor (and so, the devotion of the 300s to social sciences), how to communicate with that neighbor (and so the 400s, for languages), how the world works (500s, for natural science), how to harness its resources for work (600s, for applied sciences) and pleasure (700s, for fine arts), and so on, through literature (800s) and, in recapitulation of all he has learned and achieved, history (the 900s). When not in use, the posters that accompanied the lecture were hung on the sides of the bookshelves that corresponded to the Dewey classification of the books they housed.

The story of the caveman, an autodidact who pulls himself up from ignorance to become a cultured, accomplished, and reflective being by the end of the story, was a motif that was frequently echoed in the stories that the librarian read to students during their library visits—of humble, plucky field mice who struggle to reach their goals, or of orphans who find unexpected ways to capitalize on their adversity and so raise themselves to prosperity and a secure social standing. This was also the story that Louise Currie told of herself as a child and a reader—of being the only child of two lower middle-class parents who were themselves both orphans: A child who learned to take the bus downtown to the public library, where she was befriended by a sympathetic librarian who encouraged her to "read anything I wanted to read, and read widely." These experiences weighed heavily on Louise Currie's sense of mission as a librarian. In reflecting on her own experience, she remarked, "You see kids who are really poor kids who achieve a whole lot because they have a lot of inner motivation; I was one of those . . . I want (the students) to be able to go away from this school with the feeling 'that was the place where it was warm, and they loved me, and I was free to do some things on my own.' "

An even more important factor contributing to the extent to which the structure of the library shaped the ways that students made sense of the library as a resource, however, seemed to be the social class backgrounds and agency—the socially and culturally produced and enacted *desire*—of the students themselves. At Chavez, the utilitarian, practical value that students placed on the library's texts as well as their own resourcefulness often placed them in direct conflict with the librarian's evangelism and leisure reading programs. The result of this conflict was that although students were frequently successful in upending the program and gaining access to the texts they wanted to read and use, they were also effectively prevented from gaining full access to the order of the library's texts or developing any real proficiency at accessing information, with long-term consequences that were likely to be socially, economically, and culturally more reproductive than productive for them.

By contrast, the congruence of the social class values of home, school, and librarian at Crest Hills produced conditions in which the gendered structure of the library aided and abetted the promotion of gendered social class values toward literacy and future careers in both positive (through the development of proficiency in the use of the library as an informational system) and negative (by concealing, denying, and sometimes punishing alternative, critical perspectives) ways that were ultimately as socially, economically, and culturally more reproductive than productive for both males and females.

Although all the students spoke of going to college, the girls in the class also spoke of "marrying up" (i.e., marrying a doctor, lawyer, or son of a wealthy family). In focus interviews with the students in this class, 23 of 25 students announced that they were going to attend one of three major, prestigious public universities in the state. One exception was Emily, a student whose parents were (Asian) Indian graduate students at the local state university, and who was ostracized by her peers for expressing an interest not in marriage but paleontology (the students announced with scorn that she was "going to Harvard"). A second was J.C., a boy whose family had publicly fallen from social grace in a financial scandal, and who had announced that he'd rather go to a technical school. For this announcement, J.C. was publicly ridiculed by the other boys in the class, who laughed that when he was 19, he'd be "hanging out with his friends at the alley, drinking beer." Given the level of ridicule and scorn suffered by any student who dared to deviate even slightly from the norm at Crest Hills, it is little wonder then that when boys dared to visit the backroom for chapter books they frequently "hid" behind a free-standing corner book rack. Similarly, when a group of three girls volunteered in an interview that they enjoyed the *An American Girl* series not for the characters or plots of the books' narratives but for the information about how people lived in particular historical periods that was provided in the appendix at the back of each book, they did so in whispers, and after looking around to see if anyone else was listening. Clearly, although students at Crest Hills possessed an enviable level of literacy and "bright" futures, they were still not free, in the sense of being able to make sense of texts or of their own lives outside the gendered boundaries of their homes, their school, and their library.

Only at Roosevelt, where gendering and social class practices were also observable, but where the crossing of gendered lines and the questioning of the library's order were respected by teachers and librarians, did the library seem to be a site in which student readers were allowed to make sense of the library on their own terms, even as they acquired a working knowledge of the library as an information system. During lessons, Louise Currie consistently remained open to the students' (sometimes misguided) questions and observations, always doing her best to respond to their developing understanding of how the library and its texts worked as an information system. When students asked a seemingly irrelevant question during a lesson or when they gave an answer to a question that at first seemed not to make sense, the librarian asked for clarification before she responded with a clarifying comment herself.

If students at Roosevelt did not consistently read or use the card catalogue with the same facility as at Crest Hills, they were, at least, able to do so in a way that "left (them) free to do some things on (their) own." To be sure, gender, assisted by the division of the library into fiction and nonfiction, was in force at Roosevelt: By a six to one ratio, more boys could be observed browsing in the Dewey sections than girls, whereas girls predominated by a similar ratio in the fiction side of the library. But there was, as at Crest Hills, no discernable difference in the rate of check out of fiction and nonfiction between the boys and the girls. Unlike at Crest Hills, however, in the third grade class that was the focus group of students for the study, there was no gender bias toward males in class participation. Moreover, whenever fiction figured into the class' work, it always involved a content and sometimes politically related topic, as when their teacher walked her students through a viewing of the movie *Jaws*, pointing out not only the biology and zoology that informed the plot, but deconstructing for the students the political subplot, in which the town's mayor and business community scheme to keep the town's beaches open despite the continued threat of a great white shark.

In summary, then, one might conclude on the basis of the three illustrative examples and discussion of the history and order of school libraries presented thus far that school libraries are almost inevitably spaces in which the desire of student patrons is continually subordinated to the structural demands of the library's textual order and librarians' own reading of that order, their own life histories, and the presumed needs of students based on their social backgrounds—a space in which it is only through the ironic subversion of the order of library programs that students might find opportunities to read whatever and however they desired. Yet that judgment overlooks a broader view of the school library as a cultural space and its historical relation to the primary educational spaces of schools, classrooms. Again, according to Garrison (1979), school libraries originally developed within elementary schools not as extensions or curricular support systems for classrooms, but as extensions of local public libraries, and in response to—or, rather, *in reaction to*—the emphasis on rote learning and stilted mechanical exercises that characterized much of urban classroom life in the late 19th and early 20th centuries. School libraries, then, were designed as spaces that were in some critical ways oppositional, or "other," to the spaces of classrooms. Whereas classrooms had individual or two-student desks arranged in rows that were often bolted to the floor, textbooks were uniform and drab, and teachers focused on a prescribed curriculum, libraries had tables and chairs, texts were selected for their variety and ostensible aesthetic appeal, and the prescribed activity included story times and free browsing.

The historical relation of school libraries' otherness to classrooms was also very much in evidence at Chavez, Crest Hills, and Roosevelt Elementary Schools. This was true not only in the ways that the three librarians described their programs' relation to the primary literacy curriculum of their schools (of which they were often critical), but also in the insistence of some students (particularly those at Chavez), against the reading programs of its librarian, that they should be allowed to check out whatever books they wanted to from the library (i.e., that the library was there to meet their desire and their needs, rather than the needs of any program or curriculum). This condition of spatial otherness to the primary, or institutional, spaces of society such as the home, the school, or the church, is the central characteristic of important cultural and geographic spaces termed *heterotopias* by the French cultural historian and philosopher Michel Foucault. Foucault (1986) offered an antidote or at least an apparatus for resistance to the vision of total determinism that had characterized the description of social structures in much of his work. Foucault (1986) imagined a geography of social space constructed of primary institutional spaces where the main work of reproducing society would be done (e.g., the home, church, or school), juxtaposed against an almost infinite and historically changing number of "other" spaces (e.g., gardens, zoos, libraries, cemeteries, and even motel rooms and Persian carpets) in which some aspect of the external world was schematically represented in microcosm, and into which individuals, in time of need or crisis, might retreat. There, and in relative privacy (or at least removed from external public inspection), individuals would have the chance to move about under their own agency, or "to do some things on their own," as Louise Currie said, and in the process to reconstruct a sense of oneself within the world at large, as well as some strategies for resistant or reconstructive play within the primary structures of the social world. Thus, at the end of the 20th century, we imagine the traditional school library to remain heterotopic, or "other," to the primary educational space of the classroom, and, despite all its historically and structurally determining features, to offer its patrons a microcosmic view of the academic world in which to refresh themselves.

This brings us, in the wake of dramatic technological advances in the fields of information science and librarianship, to ask how the paradox of the library as an ordered system that we described in the introduction to this chapter and illustrated in our discussion of three traditional school libraries might be altered by its integration with what we imagine to be yet an "other" space of almost infinite heterotopic possibility: a personal computer connected to a server containing information on all the texts of the library, activated by keyword searches, or connecting its visitor beyond to the resources of the Internet and the World Wide Web. Within such a space, users might escape the gendered order of fiction and nonfiction; they might evade the directives of Dewey's "ten tight categories" or overzealous librarians' reading programs; and they might find the means to move beyond the confines of the information contained within the carefully selected and written texts of the library itself to an infinite variety of texts with infinite and conflicting points of view or even misinformation—that is, to move into domains of social and political activity and exercises in citizenship and creative use of knowledge only suggested by the libraries of the 20th century.

THREE SCHOOL LIBRARIES IN THE AGE OF CYBERTECHNOLOGY, CIRCA 2004

It is with these possibilities in mind for heterotopic transformation of the school library in the 21st century that we undertook our investigation of three additional school libraries, during the 2003–2004 school year, in a period of rapid technological expansion of information resources. The three school librarians interviewed worked in K–6 elementary schools located within the school district of a small midwestern U.S. city. As Table 3.2 indicates, Joan Harrison (pseudonym) was the librarian for Simon Elementary, a new and relatively small elementary school of 264 students located

TABLE 3.2
Librarian Practice in Three Technologically Equipped School Libraries, c. 2004

Librarian and School	School Demographics	Traditional Library Program	Cybertechnology Resources	Uses of Technology
Joan Harrison, Simon Elementary	264 students, 30% White, 64% African American, 2.3% Latino, 3% Asian American 82% low income (based on school lunch eligibility) This school has a history of low performance on state achievement tests	No Dewey—Uses Library of Congress Classification; instructs all grades in LC Works to collaborate with teachers on units of study Open library program Occasional story times for primary grades students	Four desktop computers in library Access to electronic databases (e.g., Encarta™) through computer lab Filter systems for pornography, etc. No instruction in keywords, or use of search engines; librarian researches Web sites for units of study and posts URLs on the library link to the school Web site for students to access in the computer lab	Librarian routinely relies on searches of the World Wide Web for teacher-generated units Students take notes, produce written reports; some but not extensive use of PowerPoint Students use computer lab, not library, for word processing Librarian uses videoconferencing to conference with other librarians statewide
Julie Thomas, Reynolds Elementary	496 students, 69% White, 24% African American, 4% Latino, 6.5% Asian American 29% low income (based on school lunch eligibility) Students at this school perform at levels close to average on state achievement tests	Instruction for students in Dewey through weekly scheduled visits for all grades No open library; scheduled browsing times Students learn to use traditional card catalogue Story times for primary grades students	Two computers in library Access to electronic databases through computer lab; Accelerated Reader™ managed by teachers in lab Filter systems used Winnebago Spectrum™ used for cataloguing, student check-in/out by librarian	No use by students of any online cataloguing system Teachers and computer lab instructor works in computer lab with students on classroom research projects under teacher direction Students print out Web site info supplied by computer lab instructor for use in written reports, some using PowerPoint

School	Library programs	Technology	Student use
Alice Jacobs, Benton Elementary	Weekly story time for primary grades, used puppets, taught students sign language	Computer lab instructor researches Web sites for units of study, posts URLs on desktops for students to access in computer lab	No use of online catalog by students
465 students; 64% White, 28% African American, 0% Latino, 6% Asian American, 1% Native American	Readers Theater program for upper elementary classes	Two computers in the library; complaints about instability of technology	Students used search engines for classroom research in computer lab; no instruction in keywords, use of engines apparent
22% low income (based on school lunch eligibility)	Motivational reading program, "Battle of the Books" with competition between classes	Winnebago Spectrum™ used for cataloguing, student check-in/out by librarian	Student searches limited to topics nominated by the classroom teacher
Students at this school perform at levels that meet or exceed state achievement averages	Taught Dewey system using a bingo-type game; traditional card catalogue used	Filter systems used	Students used word processing for reports, writing; no apparent use of PowerPoint
		Databases available through computer lab, not library	
		Accelerated Reader™ through computer lab; librarian marks spines of AR books in the library	

in one of the oldest neighborhoods in the city. The overwhelming majority of Simon's students came from low income homes: 64% were African American and 30% were White (compared to figures for the school district as a whole, which was 31% African American and 60% White), with small percentages identifying as Latino and Asian/Asian American. Julie Thomas was the librarian for Reynolds Elementary, which was located in a well-established, predominantly middle-class neighborhood. Reynolds was a larger school, with nearly 500 students: 69% were White and 24% were African American, with small percentages identifying as Latino and Asian/Asian American. The third librarian worked at Benton Elementary, a new school (built as the architectural "twin" of Simon Elementary) with 465 students located in the newest part of the city: 64% White, 28% African American, with small percentages identifying as Latino/Hispanic and Asian/Asian American.

Data collection for these libraries included a series of interviews and member checks conducted with each librarian, as well as visits to each school library. These libraries were selected to provide a range of demographic and socioeconomic data within this city, just as the libraries in the 1993 study were selected. The lack of extended ethnographic data for these libraries, in comparison to the data for the three earlier libraries, does not provide the same opportunity as in 1993 for a fine-grained analysis of gender and social class practices within these libraries; however, in 2004, our interview data and observations do provide us with a comprehensive view and basis for comparison of the use of computer technologies within them.

Based on our own knowledge and appreciation of currently available technologies and prior knowledge of librarian practices, we imagined that we might find multiple elements being used in combination within the libraries, with the librarians coordinating their use in conjunction with teachers. Internally, we assumed the possibility of at least five elements:

1. The presence and routine use of banks of multiple computers that would be networked to each other, to a school or library server, and with high speed Internet connections
2. The possibility of a wireless environment, in which students would either check out or use wireless-enabled laptops within their classrooms to access texts and other graphic and audio materials stored on the library server, as well as search the World Wide Web
3. The use of an online catalog (supported by software programs for electronic check-in/out of materials) by students, teachers, and librarians

4. Multiple child-friendly databases (e.g., Encarta™), stored either on DVD and CD-ROM disks or on the library's server, and/or the frequent use of web-based information portals (e.g., NetSchools Orion™) by teachers, students, and librarian
5. Access to electronic books with text, graphics, sound, and animation

In terms of using technology to connect to resources external to the library, we imagined/assumed the presence of at least four elements:

1. Frequent extension of the informational resources of the library into the World Wide Web through work with students on identification of keywords and the use of search engines for web-based research projects
2. Instruction by librarians and teachers in the electronic importation of graphics, sound, and other noncopyrighted materials from the World Wide Web, as well as some instruction in how to synthesize these resources within multimedia presentations/text formats
3. Use of e-mail and videoconferencing to connect students with experts and classrooms across or within the United States and internationally
4. Some use of filtering programs on computers for pornographic and other objectionable materials

Finally, as an interface between the internal and external resources available, we imagined that each student might be provided an account, or space on the library or school server, in which they would store the graphics, texts, and other materials they had downloaded from their information searches, as well as writing and multimedia texts they had produced on their own.

However, interviews with all three school librarians produced a very different picture of the use of computer-based information technologies within their schools. As Table 3.2 indicates, none of the schools made use of a wireless environment of laptops, or of e-mail or videoconferencing (except by Joan Harrison at Simon Elementary, who reported videoconferences with other librarians around the state), and none provided space on a server for students to store electronic text and graphics. Moreover, none of the libraries contained the "banks" of computers for work within the library that we envisioned, or the use of an online catalog by the students; instead, each library had two to four computers with no online catalog search capability for the libraries' collections, although two librarians reported using Winnebago Spectrum™, a program that allowed them to catalog and check-in/out books electronically, and presumably also provided an online catalog function.

All three librarians told us that although students at their schools did have access to the World Wide Web, that access was provided not through the library but through banks of computers located in "labs" that were in rooms separate from the library and were coordinated by paraprofessional technicians who might or might not have a degree in education (but school librarianship). Alice Jacobs at Benton Elementary complained about the instability of the Internet connection at her school. By district policy, these computers did use filtering systems, as we assumed, but there was little direct use of search engines or of the World Wide Web anyway; instead, students used the computers in the labs to access predetermined Web sites that were searched either by the librarian (at Simon) in response to teachers' requests for information on teacher-nominated topics, or by the teachers themselves in collaboration with the lab technicians. Moreover, in none of the schools were students given instruction in how to use keywords or search engines; and whereas students at all three schools used computers for word processing, when they "imported" graphics or made use of information from the Web, they typically printed out the Web site and took notes from the hard copy, or physically cut out and pasted graphics onto the hard copy of their written reports. Finally, although reading programs such as Accelerated Reader™, which keeps track electronically of students' reading of fiction books gotten largely through the library, were in use in all three schools, these activities were also managed largely through the computer labs (where students went to take comprehension tests on the books they'd read) or individual classrooms. Only Alice Jacobs at Benton Elementary reported marking the spines of books in the library used in the Accelerated Reader™ program.

DISCUSSION

In summary, then, the picture that emerged of the integration of computer-based technologies within these three schools and their libraries was largely a picture of some professional/clerical integration. Librarians were using computer programs to ease the tasks of cataloguing and book check in/out, search the World Wide Web, and at one school keep apprised of professional developments. But, at the level of student use, there was little or no integration, with students instead going to spaces that were geographically and culturally separate from the library, and where their experiences in computer- and web-based information retrieval and knowledge production were mediated not by their librarians, but by their teachers, with some assistance by the lab paraprofessional. In these spaces, their capacity to browse the World Wide Web and to use the internet as they desired were truncated by a lack of instruction or opportunity to do anything but visit predetermined Web sites of the teachers' or paraprofessional's choosing; thus, any chance that the computer screen might function in Foucauldian (Dressman, 1997; Foucault, 1986) terms as a heterotopia, where students would "be free to do some things on their own" seems highly unlikely as well.

As for the libraries themselves as cultural and educational spaces and for the practices of librarianship within them, on first appraisal these would seem to be little changed in tenor or goals from the practices of librarianship described by librarians and observed in 1993. As Table 3.2 indicates, traditional practices such as story times and (relatively minimal) instruction in the use of the Dewey (or at Simon Elementary, the Library of Congress) system and card catalogue, with traditional issues such as whether or not the library should be "open" (i.e., free for browsing by all students all day) or "scheduled" for browsing and check out by classes, predominated within each library program.

However, we would argue that as much as these libraries might seem to be unaffected or unchanged by the advent of computer-based information technologies, something very quiet and drastic has been inadvertently changed for them, perhaps forever. And, we suspect, there will be long-term negative consequences for the future of school libraries and librarianship within the school district. That change is the effective shift, or even removal, of its function as the central repository within these schools of information and "hard" knowledge, and of the role of curator and expert in knowledge storage and retrieval, from these school libraries and their librarians to the space of the computer lab and the person of the paraprofessional technician who serves as its overseer.

Thus, we see the (gendered) bifurcation of reading-for-work and of reading-for-pleasure that began in the earliest years of school and public libraries with the separation of spaces and systems for organizing "books that are true" ("nonfiction") according to the Dewey system from spaces and systems for organizing "stories that are made up" ("fiction") by authors' last names (Dressman, 1997). It continued in these three schools in 2004 with the bifurcation of information retrieval and knowledge production within the space of the computer lab and the storage of storybooks and promotion of reading as an abstract cultural good remaining within the space of school libraries. To be sure, school libraries may retain their card catalogues and their collections of informational texts for some time; but, as these become increasingly expensive and laborious to maintain relative to the infinite variety and renewability and relative cheapness of computer databases and the World Wide Web, we suspect that their functionality, utility, and attraction to teachers and students will, over time, be likely to decrease, along with the significance of the role of the librarian within school contexts.

Moreover, given the very low level of instruction in the use of keywords and the general level of control by adults that characterized the use of computer-based resources by students at these three libraries, we also see a growing exacerbation in the quality and quantity of access to information between students from upper income and professional homes and students from lower income working-class homes within, if not also across, schools. Whereas in the past all students in a school had access to the same texts within the library—albeit access that differed across schools and sometimes teachers and librarians—today access to cyber-information and texts is largely mediated by one's access to, and expertise in the use of, the technology itself. Students from more affluent homes today are likely to have greater access to computers and the World Wide Web through high speed connections at home and more time to explore the technology on their own than their less affluent peers, and to receive more instruction in its use through informal scaffolding by more knowledgeable siblings and adults. Given the short time frames of most visits to computer labs (typically less than an hour at a time and perhaps only a few times a week), as well as the highly structured nature of those visits as they were described to us by the librarians we interviewed, these differences are unlikely to be compensated for at school. Moreover, students from more affluent homes are likely to have better access to, and instruction in, the production of knowledge gotten from cybertechnologies. For example, second-grade students and faculty at Reynolds Elementary were very impressed by a student's presentation on the author of the *Amelia Bedelia* (Parish, 2002) storybook series, which a parent whose professional area of specialization is instructional technology helped to scaffold, through multiple web searches and lessons in cutting and pasting from the World Wide Web. This was compared to presentations given by other students whose only access to information came through their teacher and a few sessions in the computer laboratory. Thus, it seems likely that if the practices of the librarians we interviewed continued, in time those students with home access to computer-based information technologies would acquire literacies in information retrieval and knowledge production that far exceeded the literate proficiencies of their less affluent peers in the same classrooms and schools.

CONCLUSIONS

We conclude our report and its analysis with a number of important qualifications. First, note how recent the advent of access to computer- and web-based technologies is within this school district. The librarians we spoke with complained of continuing problems, not only with a lack of hardware, but with the instability of the connection to the Internet in their schools. We also suspect that the relegation of Internet and web access to computer labs is a function of the history of the introduction of computer technology to these schools and the district prior in the mid- to late 1980s, when computer hardware was still very expensive and required much expertise to maintain, and when the use of computers was limited to word processing and some programmed instructional activities. The lack of technology within these libraries may also be a function of a lack of clerical help in these libraries, a factor that would mitigate against librarians welcoming "one more thing" into their libraries when they were already overburdened with story times and the clerical tasks involved in keeping track of their collections. Moreover, when librarians received their professional education may also be a factor; for example, Joan Harrison, at Simon Elementary, was most welcoming of technology in her school and was also the most recent graduate of a school of library science.

Thus, we can imagine that in time, as computers and Internet access become cheaper and more reliable and as librarians become more adept at using cataloguing software that would provide online searches of the materials in their libraries, the number of computers located in these libraries might increase, students might learn to retrieve books on topics using online searches, and the function of information retrieval and knowledge production might once again shift back to the space of the school library. Or, in another scenario, we might imagine well into the future that the functions of the computer lab might disappear as a wireless computing environment develops and as librarians assume the role of instructional leader in the retrieval of information and knowledge production throughout the school. Finally, we can imagine that in time as home access to the Internet and the Web become as ubiquitous as telephone and cable television service, the differences in literate proficiency with these technologies would be reduced.

Our second qualification is to note that our sample of three libraries located in one district of the United States does not begin to sample the possible scenarios for the use of cybertechnology within school libraries in the United States or internationally. More affluent districts or districts with differing histories of computer technology might well not have computer labs or might have already integrated technology into their school programs to an extent that school librarianship has already transformed itself and the library into a space quite different from its traditional form. Or, a lack of funding might actually have required the consolidation of computer- and Internet-based resources into one central space in the school—the library.

Clearly then, and as was acknowledged at the outset of this chapter, this comparative analysis of school libraries and librarianship before and after the advent of computer- and Internet-based technologies should not provide any basis for generalization about the current state of such technologies in school libraries in the United States. However, we do believe that the issues raised by this study (of the lack of openness allowed students access to the Internet and the World Wide Web in schools and its impact on their future literacies, of the level and quality of assistance provided to them in accessing cyber resources and using them to "do some things on their own," and of the growing disparity in access and literate proficiency that we see between students whose families have access to high-speed connections to the Internet and World Wide Web at home and those that do not) are worth further theoretical and empirical investigation.

REFERENCES

Baym, N. (1978). *Woman's fiction*. Ithaca, NY: Cornell University Press.

Douglas, A. (1977). *The feminization of American culture*. New York: Knopf.

Dressman, M. (1997). *Literacy in the library: Negotiating the spaces between order and desire*. Westport, CT: Bergin & Garvey.

Foucault, M. (1979). *Discipline and punish: The birth of the prison* (A. Sheridan, Trans.). New York: Vintage.

Foucault, M. (1986). Of other spaces. *Diacritics, 16*(Spring), 22–27.

Garrison, D. (1979). *Apostles of culture: The public librarian and American society, 1876–1920*. New York: The Free Press.

Parish, H. (2002). *Calling Doctor Amelia Bedelia*. (L. Sweat, Illus.). New York: Greenwillow Press.

4

From Library to Cybrary: Changing the Focus of Library Design and Service Delivery

Janine Schmidt
McGill University

Libraries have changed significantly over the last 20 years. Changes in the design and presentation of library facilities have matched changes in the information and communications technology environment. In the educational environment, teaching and learning practices have changed considerably. Library design in the educational environment has therefore reflected the changes in teaching and learning. Client behavior has also changed and library design and service delivery have responded to the new client needs that have become apparent. Various words have been used to describe the types of libraries that have emerged—learning resource centers, digital libraries, hybrid libraries, and e-libraries. At the University of Queensland, the term *cybrary* has been used to describe the combination of cyberspace and physical space in service delivery. The impact of changes in the information and communications technology environment, teaching and learning, and user behavior are outlined and the resulting model of service delivery and design is described.

CHANGING INFORMATION AND COMMUNICATIONS TECHNOLOGY ENVIRONMENT

New information and communications technologies have brought information readily available to the desktop and changed the nature of work

everywhere. Libraries first used computers to automate their lending operations. Next came Online Public Access Catalogues (OPACs) and library
holdings were listed in online databases. Card catalogues gradually van-
ished. The formats stored by libraries also changed. Initially, paper-based
abstracting and indexing services went online and were accessed remotely
by specialist librarians. These then became available in CD-ROM versions
and were brought in-house to libraries for use by all clients. Improvements in communication meant that electronic resources could be stored
remotely and accessed—any space, any pace, any place, any time.

The emergence of the Internet meant that many information resources,
previously known to only a few, and stored in libraries accessible only
to those able to visit them, opened a whole world of information access
and use to the wider community. The tyranny of distance was removed.
Increasingly, more and more information became available in electronic
format as the move to electronic formats hastened rapidly. Many journals went online. Although most journals are currently available in both
print and online versions, increasing numbers of titles are now "born digital." Many research libraries boast more journal titles available electronically than in print. The stalwart holdings of libraries—books—have also
become available electronically, although less successfully and in fewer
numbers than scholarly journals. Newspapers are available online. Digital videos are replacing analogue. Educational libraries have reserve collections of high use material and recommended readings available online.
Examination papers have gone digital in their storage. Higher degree
students are producing theses in digital formats. Libraries are no longer
storehouses and repositories for just books and journals. Vast repositories
of online materials exist—learning objects and research papers. Pictorial
and manuscript materials are being digitized. The Internet has become a
publication medium and vast quantities of information created by widely
disparate sources are available. School assignments, government reports,
research results, and polemic rantings are all available for public consumption. Libraries have become the online doorway to information in
any format stored at many different locations.

The consequences of these developments are considerable. Some saw
the developments as heralding the demise of the physical library. Others
saw an enhanced role for libraries. The Web site became critical to service
definition and delivery. Gateways and portals became important to ensure
both effective access and some form of control of the plethora of available information. Physical facilities required in this new environment are
vastly different. Vast numbers of computers must be provided in libraries
to facilitate access to and use of information in online formats. Sophisticated software is also required. Varying types of networked printers and
other devices are also required to ensure effective information access.

The digital divide is apparent in all communities and most libraries have provided computers for their communities to use, no matter what community that is. In some universities, the library often plays a support role for staff and students in the provision of computers and appropriate software to assist them with research, examination and assignment preparation, and general study. Equity of access to computing facilities has become a major consideration in any service design.

What also emerged was that much of the new information and communications technology developments rendered resource discovery and access more difficult. In particular, students returning to study who had not benefited from the use of information and communications technology from an early age were forced to acquire new skills and knowledge in the appropriate use of information resources. Information literacy programs already provided by libraries were strengthened. Library provision of information skills programs expanded to ensure students were able to use the technology effectively and to access online information successfully.

An associated concern with the growth of information and communications technology use has been misuse and, indeed, abuse. Protecting both the users and the library can be problematic. Whereas authentication regimes provide some of the answers to monitoring who users are and what they access, physical design strategies have also emerged to deal with some of the concerns. Security has always been an issue for libraries—protection of the collections has affected library design, as has protection of clients and of staff. The new issues emerging merely add another dimension.

CHANGING TEACHING AND LEARNING ENVIRONMENT

Most universities are now multi-million dollar enterprises and conduct themselves like businesses. In response to funding pressures and claims for accountability, universities have developed strategic plans that identify priorities, and operational plans to ensure their implementation. Clear strategies in relation to research imperatives are identified in these plans. Teaching and learning goals are also articulated. University teaching and learning enhancement plans recognize the centrality of campus facilities in meeting staff and student needs and the significance of appropriate physical facilities is highlighted in the plans.

As universities compete with each other for quality students, staff of excellence, and research funding, the resources and facilities on which the universities base both their bids and marketing activities have become more important. The importance of excellent teaching and learning spaces, as well as appropriate information and communications technology infrastructure have been highlighted as central to successful teaching and learning outcomes. The library has become crucial to research universities in achieving desired goals, and both collection content and facilities design are strategic components of effective libraries. The Australian Universities Quality Agency (AUQA) emphasized the need for excellence in universities' research and teaching and learning outcomes. Universities are benchmarking themselves against each other and facilities form a significant component of the benchmarking mix.

Teaching methods are changing. Collaborative learning, distant and remote learning, flexible learning, hands-on capabilities, simulated learning, resource-based teaching and learning, and multidisciplinary and mobile technologies are new modes of teaching and learning being adopted, or expanded. Virtual learning systems, or learning management systems (e.g., Blackboard or WebCT), are being used to create interactive online learning experiences for students. Online discussion and bulletin boards are enhancing, and in some cases replacing, in-person discussion or tutorial groups. These changes have contributed to rethinking the notion of a library. As teaching and learning have become more resource based and student centered, use of libraries has become more focused. Learning is becoming more personalized (Leadbeater, 2004). Students have long used the library as a learning laboratory. Libraries have provided copies of texts, recommended readings, and additional materials that expand the knowledge base provided by teaching staff. E-learning has led to changes in library requirements, but m-learning (mobile learning) is now impacting as well. Use of personal digital assistants (PDAs) has been trialed (Heath, Kruesi, Lasserre, Todd, & Thorning, 2004). Learning resources are loaded on to PDAs that can be carried around. Mobile learning also involves the use of mobile phones (McLean, 2003). With increasing amounts of electronically published and disseminated materials, learners regard the concept of place in their use of libraries differently. Knowledge is no longer confined to the walls of a building (Edwards & Fisher, 2001). The library may well be the contents of a palm pilot. The use of m-learning poses quite different challenges for resource and facility support.

The library has responded to increasing group work by students, either in small rooms or larger open spaces. Video streaming and multimedia formats are increasingly being used in academic programs. The library has provided alternative forms of storage for these resources, as well as appropriate hardware for viewing the material. Specialized computers provide for multimedia manipulation and production. Sophisticated printing and copying facilities are required for the creation of digitized formats and for their effective use.

Although it is changes in teaching and learning that have impacted most strongly on library design, changes in research from both the perspective of the topics studied and the methods used have also driven new approaches to library design. In universities with strong research outcomes, teaching is underpinned by research activity. The library remains a major source of inspiration for the humanities and social science researcher, but, increasingly, research outcomes are delivered to the desktop. Research libraries have changed significantly (Pradt-Lougee, 2002) and design must change to meet stated new goals and aspirations.

WHAT DO CLIENTS WANT?

Academic library clients are varied. They include undergraduate students, postgraduate students, teaching and support staff, researchers, administrators, students and staff from other universities, as well as members of the community. They can be segmented using market research strategies by age, discipline of study, origin, ability (or special need), and differential services have been developed by libraries to meet the various needs identified. Clients range from self-confident school-leavers skilled in playing computer games and communicating via Short Message Service (SMS) and e-mail to those returning to study after several years of absence from education who have had little contact with computers and need learning support. Both the total numbers and the percentages of postgraduate, mature age and international students are much greater than in previous years. Their information needs have also increased.

Hughes, Atkins, and Ng (2002) defined technology users in five broad categories: switched-on cybers, digital absorbers, tech pragmatics, techno learners, and digi-nots. These definitions can be applied to the modern users of academic libraries. A useful approach to using facilities results from thinking about clients from this perspective. Switched-on cybers in the library are enthusiastic about using information technology for learning, but this does not always equate to being information literate. In research conducted by Jones and Madden (2002), the Internet has become an essential tool for college students for communicating, accessing library materials, and performing research for assessment. If the results from this survey were translated to undergraduate students around the world, then 72% of students use e-mail daily and 73% use the Internet more than the library for research. Students are familiar with the use of general search engines and these have been the main means of retrieving information during their school years (Jones & Madden, 2002). Study of citations used by students for assignments might, however, put the lie to the extensive use of the Internet for source material. Where students know how to use tried and true trusted literature, they do use it.

The digital absorbers are keen to use technology, but they often need some instruction and assistance in doing so. They tend to form the bulk of library users. Digi-nots do not adopt new technology and have a passive lifestyle. They are the most difficult for libraries to serve but in the academic environment comprise only a small percentage of users. They require detailed and repeated instruction. Print guides can be useful, but the reluctance of this group to use information and communications technology is a great and time-consuming challenge for librarians and leads to different demands on use of facilities.

Most users have in common the immediacy in their need for information—they want the information here and now. Accessibility and ease of use of information resources are essential. This places great demands on library services and staff. In formulating the new library model, mapping user actions is important. The most heavily used resources and services should be identified, as well as the relationships of resources and services to each other. The levels and type of help or assistance required by clients must also be identified before the new model can be fully understood. In summary, approaches to library design must move from a collection and place focus, to a client and experience focus.

INFORMATION LITERACY

The changes in teaching and learning and in the client base have led to a greater emphasis on information literacy. The librarian has become a trainer and is ensuring that information skills are inculcated. Within Australia, there has been an acceptance by all Australian universities operating through the Council of Australian University Librarians (CAUL) of a framework for the provision of information skills or information literacy programs. Standards have been developed, modeled on some developed by the Association of College and Research Libraries (ACRL) in the United States. The Australian and New Zealand Institute for Information Literacy (ANZIIL) (Bundy, 2004) revised the standards that were initially developed by CAUL (2001). To provide for the increased training demand, many university libraries have created training rooms or refurbished existing spaces to include multiple computer terminals for student use, data projectors and screens for instruction, and ample desk space for writing and research. Many training rooms have come at the expense of floor space but have proved a worthy addition to the library.

These spaces are either enclosed or open and have been variously named—computer laboratories, information commons, ezones, or col-

laborative learning centers. They have become essential to the successful functioning of academic libraries. Appropriate software must be available, allowing students to fulfill all requirements to complete their tertiary
studies—word processing, spreadsheets, graphics software, bibliographic
referencing, and specialist applications software must all be installed.
To accommodate international students, multilanguage and multiscript
software are also provided. Computers with particular software can be
arranged in varying combinations. Some computers include all applications and access to all networks as computer workstations become the student working spaces. In many instances, express terminals with catalogue
only or e-mail only capabilities are provided. Connection to the Internet
and access to e-mail facilities are essential communication tools that help
students with both their academic and social life at university.

Librarians are the custodians of the information they provide and to
which they have access and have an important role in helping clients to
find and navigate print and electronic resources. Electronic literacy goes
hand in hand with information literacy (Jones, 1997).

WHAT IS A CYBRARY?

Libraries first used the new information and communications technology
for internal operations, management, and information access but were
slower to understand and initiate the changes required in information service delivery and design and architecture. Terms like *digital library* and
hybrid library were used partially to recognize the changes in the nature of
service delivery, but these failed initially to impact on design. New libraries were still designed to hold vast print collections, house readers in ser-
ried rows, and provide inquiry services from desks strategically located
near "reference" collections.

Some librarians did begin to respond to the changes. As early as 1997,
some called themselves "cybrarians," or librarians who "can maneuver
through cyberspace with ease, plucking information from its farthest
reaches" (Online, 1997). At the University of Queensland in Brisbane, Australia, the term *cybrary* was first used in 1997 to describe the library as a
way of persuading both library staff and clients to think and behave differently about both the library and information services they provided
and the services they used. The cybrary was defined in this context as
"a combination of real and virtual information resources, physical facilities and cyberspace and service delivery in person and online" (Schmidt,
2002). Its initial focus was to accommodate new thinking about service
delivery, staff perceptions of client services, as well as the physical design
of libraries. Others have defined the cybrary as a representation of "both a

conceptual and a structural change in traditional library design" (Boone, 2002, p. 232) and neither "'pure' libraries in the traditional sense of offering collections and a staff of librarians, nor technology centers that focus just on providing labs and other computing facilities" (Boone, 2001b), but a combination of the two.

A search on Google on July 14, 2004, found 50,300 references to "cybrary," with the University of Queensland Library/Cybrary appearing as number 13, although its page on National Library Catalogues Worldwide appeared as number 5. The same search on Yahoo retrieved 60,900 references, with the University of Queensland Library/Cybrary as number 3. A search on "cybrarian" retrieved 23,800 references on Google, with the interesting check at the beginning of the page: *Did you mean librarian?* The same search on Yahoo retrieved 44,000 references. Use of the term has shaped both service delivery provided by libraries and the design of the facilities.

Boone (2001a) developed his own criteria for the design of a cybrary. It should be intelligent with smart technology and ICT infrastructure. It should include both people and "thing" spaces in the right proportions. Flexibility and adaptability to changes in the delivery of information are essential. A balance between housing print and providing services in relation to electronic information resources must be achieved. Varied study environments and work spaces are required for new modes of teaching and learning currently seen in academic communities. Support and infrastructure for multimedia services is required. Facilities provided must serve collaborative learning among students, as well as collaboration between the teaching faculty and the library.

At the University of Queensland, the design focus was primarily on the user and on the kinds of interactions required with both collections and staff. The analysis of existing successful commercial service providers such as banks, telecommunication providers, video retailers, other retail outlets, and cafés proved most helpful. Despite research in other service industries, the final model is still a library, but one that responds directly to client needs with technology, not merely another library service but a tool seamlessly integrated into the user's acquisition of information. When developing the new library model, the nature of the service and levels were defined: standard—expected by all clients; specialist—targeted to a specific group; and value-added—an enhanced service where the user might pay. The levels of client assistance were also defined: one-on-one assistance with general and information inquiries and information skills training; lending and loans inquiries; and technical assistance. A working model of the library was developed (Schmidt & Wilson, 1998) by evaluating the relation between these levels of client assistance and service provision.

The World Wide Web and the use of technology will never replace the experience the library offers to its clients (Williams, 2002). The "google-ization" of resource discovery by students has already been referred to. Most students prefer to use that which is easy (Online Computer Library Centre, 2002). However, the place in which they conduct their activities is still very important and most libraries have seen little reduction in visitation rates. Cables and computers have been added and placed stress on existing physical facilities, but the physical facilities themselves have remained important in their enhancement of teaching, learning, and research experiences.

The change in library design and layout has not happened overnight. Rising costs in information access and the hardware to deliver it have not always allowed available funds to be spent on library design. The new cybrary is a hi-tech environment with computers networked to printers, providing clients with fast information downloads, enabling access from home or office. It is also high touch in that personalized assistance is still provided to ensure that clients find what they need and use information effectively.

LIBRARY AS EXPERIENCE

The library has long been the repository of knowledge, housing and protecting vast collections, seating readers, organizing access, and providing enough workspace for staff. The written word developed as a means of preserving events, stories, and ideas. Libraries were defined as collections of books used for reading or study or the buildings of rooms in which such collections were kept. Most library buildings were—and still are—large, intimidating and frequently unwelcoming. Past library building design focused on constantly expanding print collections and providing enough space to house them. Although there have been many beautiful buildings, inside the building signage was poor, lighting was inadequate, and service was sometimes second rate. Interior design of many public and academic libraries left much to be desired. Today's library—the cybrary—is about creating an experience for the user in the form of something inviting that will encourage them to return by connecting them with the community.

The library today is a place for everyone. Libraries have gained popularity around the world, reflected in the enormous increase in building development in the last decade and the return of the library as an "important civic monument" (Awcock & Dungey, 1997). Whether there has been a resurgence in the use of libraries or it is the information/knowledge age that has brought clients back, libraries "have always been potent community assets at a social, political and religious level" (Schwager, 1998, p. 84).

The diverse clientele of libraries does present a problem in providing appropriate services and an attempt should be made to provide spaces that all can enjoy. For some, the library is an area for quiet reflection; for others, it is a place for group study and collaboration or social interaction. Increasingly, it is the experiences being provided by libraries to their clients that are guiding design and development. The library is an experience; it is not just a place for books, but a place that brings people together. Clients listen to CDs, look at videos, read books, communicate via e-mail, gain inspiration and ideas, prepare assignments, conduct their own learning, receive training, and in a time when community ties are breaking down, enjoy the sense of community that visiting a library brings with it. Sometimes peer pressure is the guiding influence that directs students into the library (Demas & Scherer, 2002).

Whether library managers are rebuilding a new library or looking to refurbish an old library, looking at the way clients actually use the existing services is fundamental to designing a building around the users' experiences (Williams, 2002). Many libraries undertake surveys, distribute questionnaires, and conduct focus groups to understand their community better. This is important for ongoing client service, but it is also necessary to understand the services needed before undertaking any new building development. The results of any client analysis can be included in the project brief given to the architect to help them understand the service delivery the library offers, and what design requirements will be needed (Awcock & Dungey, 1997).

SERVICE DELIVERY

Ancient libraries were erected as grand monuments or icons (i.e., recognizable edifices). Access was often restricted, books were locked away, and "customer service" was not heard of. Even today, this edifice approach remains with us and many buildings constructed in recent years resemble ancient monuments with columns and medieval fortress features. Entrances can still be difficult to find and buildings can be challenging to use. However, the traditional approach to library design has changed. Fears and predictions of the library without walls and of disappearing collections have not been realized. Small decreases in collection size have made way for computers to access electronic and digitized resources. New library services have been introduced. Beautiful library buildings are still important, but the link today is to their environment, to their accessibility, and to their focus on "function and service—not place" (Bailin & Grafstein, 2003).

Design now emphasizes self-service, includes disability concerns, and provides desks for staff–client contact, but also facilitates roving staff. Spaces for queuing and group meeting and congregating spaces are also needed. Seating is required for people with lengthy inquiries, not to mention somewhere to eat and drink. In a small library, various types of service points can be combined.

A true cybrary will replicate various in-person and in-house services online. The virtual reference collection is a group of freely available Web sites reviewed by librarians and made available on the Web site providing users with access to quality reference resources from home, laboratory, or office. Chat and/or e-mail help services are essential to offer library clients information assistance when they are outside the physical building. Some libraries have extended these services to 24/7 in collaboration with other libraries. Digitizing activities and open access archives have made what was once limited-access material more accessible both in and out of the physical walls of the library.

Some new libraries have also taken on roles that may have been previously been provided by other departments on campus, or not at all. Video-conferencing facilities and digital media centers are common features in some libraries. Conference rooms used by library staff and students can also be hired out to others.

DESIGN PRINCIPLES

Harrington (2001) discussed six design trends: self-service and operational efficiency, extreme flexibility and integration of technology, green/sustainable buildings, collaboration between public and school or college libraries, renewed interest in aesthetics, and customization of services to the local community. In any particular building project, it is essential to develop a set of design principles to be applied.

The library must be clearly visible. The exterior must be attractive and welcoming and the entrance must be easy to find. The first impression that clients have of the library must be favorable; both good and bad design will remain as lasting images. Multiple entrances should be avoided. If the library is incorporated within other buildings, then signage to the entrance needs to be obvious. Creating the library's own identity is extremely important (Jones, 1997). The content should be obvious from the outside. The use of transparent walls making the inside visible is a simple tool for marketing the library, and using natural light can provide a natural beauty and reduce the cost of lighting.

The entrance or foyer itself must be welcoming and the area near the entrance should be treated as prime real estate. Clear layout should support natural way-finding and limit the need for signage, which should be professional, positioned on the wall, or hanging at the appropriate height and location. Guidelines and standards for font, size, and presentation must be developed and signs should be directional as well as positional (i.e., indicating where one is, as well as where one wishes to go). Security near the entrance should have minimal client impact. Any inquiry desk or service point should be far enough away from the point of entry to allow users to acclimatize themselves before asking any questions.

Much attention must be paid to seating, to provide for group and individual use at carrels or tables, in individual rooms or group rooms, with specialized spaces for certain categories of user. Spatial flexibility is a must. Casual and formal spaces, quiet spaces and group spaces should be provided—with or without coffee and with or without computers. An auditorium with break-out spaces is also a requirement. Standards can be used to determine the number of seats, but the changes in use are really impacting on these standards. Couches, ottomans (couches with no backs or sides), armchairs, and bench seats are all new and popular alternatives. Getting the right combination is not always easy. Clients may not always sit on couches but will happily perch or stretch out on an ottoman. Spaces for 24-hour study with access to photocopiers and wireless zones are options that need to be considered. Wireless zones may extend beyond the walls to nearby cafes or garden areas.

Housing collections remain important. In some parts of the world, book stacks are open, but in other parts of the world closed book stacks predominate. These are, of course, expensive to service because additional staff is required to assist clients in accessing the books and journals. In Australia, most libraries have open stacks. Some libraries separate collections by format, size, age, or use. The style of shelving must be chosen—compactus, metal, or wooden. Some form of automated retrieval and collection movement may be possible for high density storage of seldom-used material. Providing and supervising appropriate security remains important and the type used will dictate design. Many libraries are ensuring that security is discrete and does not intrude on effective use.

Lighting must meet standards and needs. Up-lighting provides a soft approach. Task lighting for desks and shelving facilitates use. Natural light should be maximized. The type of lighting used will also create quiet or noisy atmospheres. The type and extent of exhibition display space must be determined—preferably located in prime real estate and easily accessible to all. Museums' approaches provide useful perspectives for libraries to consider.

Storage of chairs and equipment is frequently forgotten. Providing for book return, both when the library is open and after hours (preferably with drive-by) is essential and the facilities provided must suit both clients' and staff members' occupational health and safety as well as process requirements. Pictures and plants provide conducive atmospheres and air conditioning must meet both client and collection needs. The use of color will assist in badging and branding and way-finding, as well as making spaces attractive and conducive to particular uses.

Standards for networking must be implemented, particularly for use of wireless. Wireless is not yet "powerless." Connectivity and wiring remain topics for much investigation and accommodation. Computers can be segregated for specialized (e.g., catalogue) uses as well as all-purpose uses (e.g., accessing word processing and applications software, library resources, and the Internet). Stand-up e-mail facilities with 15-minute limits are powerful in limiting usage, which the students often enforce themselves. Housing is required for laptops to be lent, as well as facilities for plug-in laptops. Peripherals, printers, and multifunctional devices need to be physically accommodated. Projectors are required in training rooms. Large screens have been used to convey information that changes rapidly. Accommodating computers on inquiry and information desks is difficult. Clients wish to see a friendly face, not the back of an ugly computer. Some libraries have attached two screens, with one facing the staff member and one facing the client.

Design of staff spaces must focus on the combined use of open plan and individual offices, support teamwork, and network the procedures in place in each area. Ergonomic and workflow issues are important, as well as occupational health and safety. Exposing staff processes and work areas to the clients can have both positive and negative effects. Designed to increase productivity, they can leave staff feeling isolated and vulnerable (Dowler, 1996). Staff work areas and service points must be flexible and cater to the demand for new and forthcoming services (Jones, 1997).

Most library building projects involve refurbishment of facilities. They are expensive and difficult, as new building codes must often be implemented. Decisions about continuing service delivery while alterations are underway must be taken into consideration. Decanting users and collections can be expensive. Refurbishment projects can be lengthy and frequently create unforeseen problems.

Some final principles can include the use of vending machines for the supply of stationery, stamps, and discs. Maintenance costs can be reduced by segregating air conditioning areas. One-level libraries are much easier to run and they are easier for users. Once multistorey buildings are in place, then numbers of lifts and types of stairs become critical considerations.

Applying these principles throughout all the branch libraries in the one academic community, as is the case in most universities, eases use for library clients who frequent different libraries (Harrington, 2001). As university study becomes more multidisciplinary, students and staff need to use more then one library on campus for their studies and research. Adopting customer service ideas, corporate attitudes, and interior design concepts used in department stores, video shops, and other retail outlets helps to ensure that library clients can enter different branch libraries and reassuringly find the same service points and resources based on their same layout and design. Also vital is finding the "right" architect to work on a library design project. A listening ear and discerning eye are essential and excellent design results from an effective partnership.

CHALLENGES

Accommodating information and communication technologies continue to provide challenges. Should the model rely on clients bringing in their own computers for use? Most library environments have traditionally been silent or quiet zones. Many users still come to the library for a quiet, reflective place for study and reading. However, young users in particular are accustomed to noisy environments. The use and abuse of mobile phones in any social forum has become the norm. Curbing the use of phones within the library has been an uphill battle and, at times, a fruitless task. Designating areas for quiet and group use is one way around the problem. Foyers and areas generating large amounts of foot traffic can be selected as phone-friendly areas. Quiet study spaces can be located near the book stacks or on floors above the foyer in multistory libraries. "Technology-free zones" (Demas & Scherer, 2002) are essential for silent study and reading (Schwager, 1998) and the community needs to feel assured that a quiet area will be available.

CONCLUSIONS

The needs of clients are constantly changing. Developing new services and delivering resources to the clients will continue to be a real challenge. As libraries shift to cybraries, technology has been the ongoing influence over service delivery. Designing a library that provides everything for everyone is near to impossible. Finding a common ground between the technology and the books provides new opportunities and challenges: books versus bytes (Dillon, 2002).

Libraries have a long proud history. They are keepers and protectors of knowledge. They store information in varied formats, frequently in buildings designed specially to house expansive collections. They provide a sense of community among their users. As new technologies for storing and disseminating information are introduced, libraries have changed to accommodate them. Libraries still have the underlying role as a place of liberty, light, and learning, and in educational institutions libraries are facilities for learning. However, in designing modern libraries, the emphasis has moved from libraries as a place to libraries as an experience—the cybrary.

Projecting future needs and services is important. The library building needs to be flexible to accommodate a growing and changing clientele. Libraries remain important as organizers and protectors of collections that range from clay tablets to palm leaf manuscripts as well as e-books and e-journals, which may be stored locally or accessed remotely. Although the Internet has made information more widely available, there has been little reduction in print production. The bookless library remains as real as the paperless office.

The focus of building libraries in the future will be on access to learning, whether through digital networks or print collections, and as a community focal point and social identity. Many libraries are redesigning not only their buildings, but also their role in the community. Without losing their identity as a library in the classic sense as a repository of books, many new buildings are successfully using attractive features to bring people back to knowledge experiences.

REFERENCES

Awcock, F. H., & Dungey, P. (1997). Buildings for the new millennium: A study tour of recent library buildings. *Lasie, 28*(3), 34–41.

Bailin, A., & Grafstein, A. (2003). *From place to function: Academic libraries in 2012.* Retrieved December 17, 2003, from http://alpha.fdu.edu/~marcum/bailin_grafstein.doc

Boone, M. D. (2001a). Back in the USA: The Cybrarian comes home. *Library Hi Tech, 19*(2), 186–200.

Boone, M. D. (2001b). Steering the cybrary into the twenty-first century: Who is the leader? *Library Hi Tech, 19*(3), 286–289.

Boone, M. D. (2002). Penn State's new "cybrary" at Harrisburg—a talk with Dr Harold Shill. *Library Hi Tech, 20*(2), 232–236.

Bundy, A. (Ed.). (2004). *Australian and New Zealand Information Literacy Framework: principles, standards and practice* (2nd ed.). Adelaide: Australian and New Zealand Institute for Information Literacy. Retrieved June 10, 2004, from http://www.caul.edu.au/info-literacy/InfoLiteracyFramework.pdf

Council of Australian University Librarians (CAUL). (2001). *Information literacy standards.* Canberra: Council of Australian University Librarians. Retrieved June 10, 2004, from http://www.caul.edu.au/caul-doc/InfoLitStandards2001.doc

Demas, S. G., & Scherer, J. A. (2002). Esprit de place: Maintaining and designing library buildings to provide transcendent spaces. *American Libraries, 33*(4), 65–68.

Dillon, D. (2002). Turning over a new leaf. *Interior Design, 73*(5), 310–311.

Dowler, L. (1996). Our edifice at the precipice. *Library Journal, 121*(3), 118–120.

Edwards, B., & Fisher, B. (2001). *Libraries and learning resource centres.* Oxford, England: Architectural Press.

Heath, A., Kruesi, L., Lasserre, K., Todd, H., & Thorning, S. (2004, September). *Rural but not remote! Access in outback Australia. Report on the implementation of Personal Digital Assistants (PDAs) for medical students, clinical teaching staff and health librarians at the Rural Clinical Division, School of Medicine, University of Queensland, Australia.* Paper presented at the ninth European conference of Medical and Health Libraries, From Altamira Until Now: Information Transference Ways, Santander, Spain.

Harrington, D. (2001). Six trends in library design. *School Library Journal [Buyer's Guide],* 12–14.

Hughes, M., Atkins, C., & Ng, S. (2002). *Next stop digital? Defining digital markets in Australia.* Retrieved January 15, 2003, from http://www.aba.gov.au/abanews/conf/2002/papers/HughesM.pdf

Jones, D. J. (1997). Time capsules or time machines? Challenges for public library buildings. *Australian Library Journal, 46*(4), 394–403.

Jones, S., & Madden, M. (2002). *The Internet goes to college: How students are living in the future with today's technology.* Retrieved June 30, 2004, from http://www.pewinternet.org/pdfs/PIP_College_Report.pdf

Leadbeater, C. (2004). *Learning about personalisation: How can we put the learner at the heart of the education system?* Retrieved June 10, 2004, from http://www.demos.co.uk/catalogue/learningaboutpersonalisation/

McLean, N. (2003). *The M-Learning paradigm: An overview. A report prepared for the Royal Academy of Engineering and the Vodafone Group Foundation.* Retrieved June 12, 2004, from http://www.oucs.ox.ac.uk/ltg/reports/mlearning.doc

Online. (1997). *Chronicle of Higher Education 19th December, 44*(17), A22.

Online Computer Library Centre (OCLC). (2002). *OCLC white paper on the information habits of college students: How academic librarians can influence students' web-based information choices.* Retrieved June 10, 2004, from http://www5.oclc.org/downloads/community/informationhabits.pdf

Pradt-Lougee, W. (2002). *Diffuse libraries: Emergent roles for research library in the digital age.* Washington, DC: Council on Library and Information Resources. Retrieved December 12, 2003, from http://www.clir.org/pubs/reports/pub108/pub108.pdf

Schmidt, J. (2002, October). *Physical place or cyberspace? Approaches adopted by the University of Queensland Cybrary to design libraries around client use of and access to information.* Paper presented at the CONSAL XII Conference, Brunei Darussalam.

Schmidt, J., & Wilson, H. (1998, January). *Designing the real virtual library: An overview of the preparation of an upgrade of the University of Queensland Library.* Paper presented at the Victorian Association of Library Automation (VALA) ninth biennial conference, Melbourne, Australia.

Schwager, T. (1998). Mirrors and memories: How libraries connect with their communities. *Australian Library Journal, 47*(1), 83–90.

Williams, J. F. (2002). Shaping the "experience library." *American Libraries, 33*(4), 70–72.

5

Surrogation, Mediation, and Collaboration: Access to Digital Images in Cultural Heritage Institutions

Abby A. Goodrum
Ryerson University

Vision is a fundamental aspect of human thinking and engagement with the world, and image documents comprise a genre crucial to the study of culture. Images, both moving and still, form a critical information element for the humanities, sciences, education, and the arts, and the amount of information recorded and communicated pictorially rather than textually has increased dramatically with the growth of the Web.[1]

For cultural heritage institutions (defined here broadly as museums, libraries, and archives), providing intellectual access to visual information has always been a major goal. The manner in which we have provided this access reflects the scholarly milieu in which each institution exists, and the underlying institutional philosophies regarding user access, mediation, and surrogation have driven quite different approaches to image classification and control by different types of institutions. Each community concerned with providing image access creates its own system of representation and retrieval based on its understanding of the needs and tasks of their own users, and their underlying intellectual traditions. For example, the role of the curator or archivist contrasts sharply with the role of the librarian in the stage at which mediation occurs. Librarians traditionally mediate in the process of cataloguing objects and provide additional mediation through their reference services. Museum curators mediate in the process of exhibiting collections of objects and provide additional mediation through the creation of exhibition catalogues. The distinction becomes one of *connecting* users to images and associated metadata at the object level, versus the practice of *presenting* collections and associated collection level metadata to users. This is a highly simplified example of the differing locus of control exerted by these three types of institutions, but it serves to illustrate how underlying philosophies of practice have driven access to images and image information. As these institutions expand their traditional practices into the networked digital environment, visual resource collection providers can no longer ignore either the needs of other communities of users or the possibilities of wider utility or new uses for their images. This brave new world of digital image access will pose shared challenges to visual resource collection providers across institutions and has in turn driven the need for collaboration in the provision of access mechanisms to images across institutions. As the digital boundaries between these key cultural heritage institutions blur, and information flows between and among them increases, we begin to see the tantalizing possibility of creating new hybrid symbolic spaces for cultural heritage.

At the same time, general search tools on the Web, such as Google, have developed mechanisms to link users to images outside of the hidden Web of cultural heritage databases. In fact, the part of the web that is not fixed and is served dynamically "on the fly" from database content is far larger than the fixed documents that many associate with the Web. Information stored in these databases is accessible *only by query*. This is distinct from static, fixed web pages, which are documents that can be accessed directly. A significant amount of valuable information on the Web is generated from databases. It has been estimated that content on the deep Web may be 500 times larger than the fixed Web (Bergman, 2001). This is also true for nontextual files such as multimedia files, graphical files, software, and documents in nonstandard formats.

Cultural heritage providers must support the needs of users for whom these existing online tools and resources for locating images and other nontextual materials may be unfamiliar, difficult to learn, or insufficient to answer their information needs (Goodrum, Bejune, & Siocchi, 2003). Finding and selecting appropriate images on the Web is problematic due to the difficulty that users have in expressing information needs in general and image needs specifically. Moreover, finding nontextual information using textual access mechanisms presents challenges even to highly skilled searchers.

The limitations and inconsistencies of providing text-based access to images have prompted increasing interest and competition from the computer science research community in the development of automatic access mechanisms that exploit the inherent visual content of an image. This type of access is most often referred to as content-based image retrieval (CBIR). CBIR relies on image processing to define images in terms of primitive features such as shape, color, and texture that can be automatically extracted from the images themselves. Currently, these methods appear somewhat limited in their ability to assist users with higher level forms of image description and retrieval. For the foreseeable future, it seems that some form of text indexing is necessary to address the higher level semantic content of images. But CBIR technologies will continue to evolve and may pose a threat to the locus of control traditionally exerted over image collections by libraries, museums, and archives.

It is impractical to assume that a single institution will have resources for all needs, or to expect that one expert would be knowledgeable about all collections. It is also impractical to assume that the public will necessarily know how to locate appropriate collections or how to search for information. The goal is to provide "one stop—any stop" access to rich multimedia information online such that users with an information need can acquire what they need seamlessly, without having to shop the information need around to the various institutional databases separately. The question faced by cultural heritage institutions in this new visual ecology is how to respond to a growing public's demand for round-the-clock networked accessibility to multimedia collections? Moreover, how can they provide access to resources that cross institutional boundaries and disciplines? An understanding of image seeking behaviors across disciplines and institutions is increasingly necessary if multitype institutions are going to compete and collaborate for users' attention in the digital image economy. There is vast potential in collaborating across these communities, but taking the union of the disparity to form one single vision, mediation role, and representational schema may not be possible. Once users cross boundaries between specialized communities, then a way of providing access to visual resources based on the context of broad visual culture is mandatory.

An examination of the visual access literature provides little guidance in the provision of image seeking behavior, classification, and mediation across disciplines and types of institutions in a digital environment, and we have no cohesive body of research to inform this practice. Specific discipline studies of image seeking and use have been conducted in the arts, social sciences, humanities, and sciences, but little has been done to aggregate the results of these studies into a unified model of image seeking across disciplines or classification behavior across institutions. Further cross-community access is not feasible until we can position these diverse approaches to image access within the broader framework of visual culture and general image information needs and uses.

This chapter proposes a conceptual framework to examine opportunities and challenges across libraries, museums, and archives as they make their image collections available over the Web. The objective is to offer an overall account of the developing relations across digital cultural heritage institutions, and to articulate challenges created by their differing philosophies of mediation, surrogation, and access to images.

CULTURAL HERITAGE INSTITUTIONS

For the purposes of this chapter, cultural heritage institutions are defined as libraries, archives, and museums, but other institutions are often included in discussions of the cultural heritage sector, such as schools and institutions of higher learning, as well as public broadcasting institutions, historical societies, botanical gardens, and zoos. For example, the Council on Library and Information Resources (CLIR) commissioned a survey of North American-based digital cultural heritage initiatives that included "any organization or program that developed or implemented a project yielding a digital product—such as an image database, a music rights management database, scholarly e-book, or digital research tool—to be used by one or more of the sectors in the cultural or educational community" (Zorich, 2003, p. 7). This serves well to define projects that function as digital cultural heritage *initiatives,* but not necessarily operating within cultural heritage *institutions.* Initiatives are not necessarily intended for sustainability, and may be built as test projects, research proof of concept projects, or demonstrations. Institutions are relatively persistent embodiments of values and practices organized around particular goals. The distinction is important and frames much of the current discourse surrounding the definition of digital libraries, digital museums, and digital archives.

The historical functions and philosophies of service driving these institutions encompass a great deal more than providing access to collections of materials. But individual disciplines have defined digital libraries, archives, and museums differently, and there is often conflict within and among disciplines about these definitions (Arms, 2000; Borgman, 1999; Kapitzke, chap. 9, this volume; Lesk, 1997; Miksa & Doty, 1994). This chapter extends the definition of digital libraries provided by the Digital Library Federation to pertain more broadly to digital cultural heritage institutions overall. They are "organizations that provide the resources, including the specialized staff, to select, structure, offer intellectual access to, interpret, distribute, preserve the integrity of, and ensure the persistence over time of collections of digital works so that they are readily and economically available for use by a defined community or set of communities" (Digital Library Federation, http://www.diglib.org/about/ dldefinition.htm). Whereas the institutions of libraries, museums, and archives were born out of very different needs and practices, and developed different goals and audiences, the digital economy has blurred the traditional boundaries between them and is driving new collaborations with shared visions.

Although there are no cross-institutional statistics tracking the number of cultural heritage institutions with image digitization projects underway or planned, a recent survey of 85 museums in North America revealed that 57% already had a portion of their collection digitized and available online (Sayre & Wetterlund, 2004). The Art Museum Image Consortium— a group of over three dozen Member Museums, which have committed to digitize their collections and contribute them to an integrated library on an ongoing basis—now contains over 100,000 art images in its database (http://www.amico.org). Although many digitization efforts originated as independent initiatives within their own institutions, a growing number of projects are being funded by governments in Europe, Japan, Australia, and North America to link these individual projects into larger national repositories of cultural heritage. Examples include the following:

- Canada's Digital Collections: http://collections.ic.gc.ca/
- BRICKS: http://www.brickscommunity.org/
- Austrian Digital Heritage Initiative: http://www.digital-heritage.at
- Picture Australia: http://www.pictureaustralia.org
- Afghanistan Digital Library Project: http://dlib.nyu.edu/divlib/ bobst/adl/

These projects are an important step toward realizing the goal of universal access to the world's cultural heritage (UNESCO, 1995), but we are only beginning to sense how cultural heritage institutions as well as institutions of learning and culture, of trade, of civic engagement, and of entertainment will evolve in the digital environment. In order to flourish, digital cultural heritage institutions (DCHIs) will need to better understand how users seek out and interact with images in the digital environment, and will need to reconceptualize their practices in terms of mediation, surrogation, and access.

MEDIATION

Image retrieval is essentially an act of translation. Cognitive image needs must be translated into external descriptions or depictions in order to communicate these needs to other humans and to information systems.

The primary difficulty in this stems from translating a visual information need into a verbal expression. An additional challenge lies in the diversity with which images may be described by both users and by organizers of collections. To add to the dilemma, many digitized images available over the Web are not accompanied by any textual descriptions of their content, and the practice in some institutions has been to describe images at the collection level rather than the individual image level.

Historically, libraries have mediated by connecting users to images through the practices of cataloguing and reference. Museums have mediated by interpreting and presenting their collections for exhibitions and educational outreach. Instead of helping users to connect directly to objects of interest within the collection through cataloguing and reference services, the curatorial role has been to present thematic views of the collection. This constitutes a critical difference in culture and an underlying philosophical difference between the two institutions that impacts everything we do.

Among the many challenges encountered by cultural heritage institutions are the problems associated with helping users to translate visual information needs into appropriate terminology for input into information systems designed to retrieve textual information. The difficulty users often have in translating their image needs into verbal or written expressions is exemplified by the patron who states: "I can't tell you what I want, but I'll know it when I see it!" For example, the following are actual requests for images received by the Virtual Reference Desk Project at Syracuse University:

- I have a project in identifying the attached picture. The only clue I have is that it's "astronomical."
- I need to locate pictures on the Web depicting religious persecution, i.e., the inquisition, etc.
- I have been unable to find drawings of Inuit women. I need portraits, not their own artwork. I tried to find this on Google but kept getting pictures of seals and other things drawn by Inuit artists.
- I need pictures of the insides of cows.
- I am searching for a graphic depicting the rates of development in adolescents—physical, cognitive, and social development graphed versus time.
- I need educational cartoons concerning the alphabet.
- I need pictures like this one (attached).

The role of reference librarians has been one of translation, or mediating between the user's image needs and the access mechanisms that can connect the user to an appropriate image or image collection. The reference interview is an iterative process with much dialogue back and forth between librarian and patron as they work together to refine the information need. This process can be complex because patrons often have unclear information needs and little understanding about the resources available to help them. Librarians are trained in interviewing techniques to help patrons specify and communicate their needs. The goal of the interview is the disambiguation of the client's need. The librarian poses questions to understand the context of patrons' needs, their knowledge of the subject domain, their stage in the information-seeking process, and so on. Throughout the interaction, the librarian requests relevance feedback from the patron asking: "Is this what you mean?" and "More like this?" in order to refine the search and elicit increasing precision.

Reference practice in libraries grew up around bibliographic access mechanisms for texts, and an examination of the library reference practice literature provides little guidance in the provision of image mediation in a digital environment. Further, museums have not had the same tradition of reference provision as libraries. In those museums having an associated library, most reference questions are directed toward external resources such as catalogues and books rather than answered from in-house imagebases. The focus of most museum libraries has been on print resources to support the collection rather than on the collection itself. This is gradually changing as collection management systems migrate into museum libraries, but many registrars are still uncomfortable sharing deeper information about objects in the collection with users.

Educational outreach programs in museums may offer a mediating bridge between collections and access because their primary mission is to educate and support the needs of lifelong learners. Yet, preliminary studies conducted by researchers at the Information Institute of Syracuse (http://iis.syr.edu/) demonstrated that online requests for assistance in locating appropriate educational images are growing and problematic. Experts who provide visual resource mediation within the educational environment may require additional tools and training to handle questions and provide solutions to users with nontextual information needs. Patrons in this environment are diverse and demonstrate a wide range of skills and online tools to seek out and evaluate appropriate image resources. Finally, resources developed for education often ignore images as a primary source or central focus of curriculum.

Digital cultural heritage institutions are creating new audiences with digitized images and the problem is whether and how they should deal with that. Their institutional missions may not extend to offering diversity of metadata and reference services to audiences outside of their core. They may not be able to offer a level of service quality to a wider audience and "out of scope" may mean very different things in the museum reference environment than it does in the library or archival environment. This mediation practice gets at the very heart of the traditional mission differences among museums, libraries, and archives, but the distinction blurs when DCHIs make decisions about what parts of their collections to digitize and how to present those materials online. The challenge as the DCHI community moves forward will be to develop ways to leverage reference interactions and presentation practices across institutions in ways that can be reused and mined.

SURROGATION

The nature of representation is such that there exists a correspondence (mapping) from objects in the represented world to objects in the representing world such that at least some of relations in the represented world are structurally preserved in the representing world. In order for a thing to be represented of any sort, it must preserve at least some information about its referent world. (Palmer, 1978, pp. 266–267)

It is one thing to get users to describe the content of images sought, but it is quite another thing to match that expression to an existing image. Surrogates (e.g., keywords, titles, captions, or cataloguing records) function not only as attributes against which a query may be matched, but also provide support for browsing, navigation, relevance judgments, and query reformulation. In order to be effective, surrogates must convey the content of the original in such a way that users will make the same distinctions between surrogates that they would make between full documents. Effective surrogates must also provide users with a means to facilitate appropriate selection of images for a particular task.

An important factor in the successful retrieval of images is the extent to which surrogates convey the information content of the images for which they stand. Although it is generally agreed that images comprise an important source of information that is structured and utilized differently from text, access to most collections of images has been grounded on bibliographic conventions; utilizing textual surrogates for items in the collection as well as textual queries. The use of textual surrogates for the retrieval of both still and moving images has been criticized as an inadequate and subjective mechanism for conveying visual information. This has led to increasing interest in the creation of nontextual image retrieval systems that utilize primitive physical features of images in the creation of image-based surrogates. Using image-based surrogates to retrieve images is not without problems, however. Image-based surrogates are challenged by the need to differentiate between specific instantiations of an object, and objects as representations of a class or genre. This inability to represent both the general and specific nature of an image may decrease the surrogate's ability to convey adequate information for particular tasks. Given these constraints, it is unlikely that image-based surrogates will completely replace text-based representation or vice versa.

Although most retrieval systems are text based, images frequently have little or no accompanying textual information. Historically, the solution has been to develop taxonomies and thesauri that reflect the unique characteristics of a particular collection or clientele and assign terms from the controlled vocabulary to describe the subject matter of an image, the objects depicted within an image, or both. However, collections and the descriptions of their contents can vary according to factors such as collection type, curatorial approach, subject discipline, and granularity of description. In some museum collections, for example, the notion of subject access is meaningless. As a result, the cataloguing and classification of images has varied widely across collections. Libraries have tended to describe individual items such as books or journals, and classes of objects such as editions, but have only recently begun to catalogue individual images in their collections and typically have not described the collections that contain them. Museums have typically described their collections first and special properties of individual items within those collections secondarily using a hybrid approach; sometimes grouping objects together by provenance, artist, media, or historical period. Archives describe their collections based on the principles of provenance and original order. The history of the collection, its provenance in terms of who generated it, who collected it, and where it has been is more important than the history of any one object in that collection.

There are, of course, exceptions across cultural heritage institutions (e.g., descriptive methods in library special collections are more similar to those of museum practice), but on the whole there is no single descriptive method that can meet the needs of all museums, libraries, and archives. These differences make finding images across types of cultural heritage institutions difficult. The audience for a particular museum or type of museum is unique—even if the images/objects in that collection are not. It is therefore altogether appropriate that each museum be able to describe its objects in a way that best meets the needs of its users. In order to share diverse descriptions across institutions, a number of metadata initiatives have emerged.

Metadata may be descriptive, structural, administrative, or a combination of one or more of these. It can be used to control and describe objects, collections, and institutions. It supports resource discovery, use, and management of images by providing agreed on mechanisms for describing attributes of images, their creation, their owners, and their locations.

Among the most promising metadata initiatives for image description are the Dublin Core, and VRA Core metadata sets that are built on the Dublin Core. The Encoded Archival Description (EAD) metadata have been developed specifically for use in archives but have been used successfully with images in the Museums and the Online Archive of California (MOAC) project. The International Committee for Documentation of the International Council of Museums (ICOM-CIDOC, 1995) has developed a conceptual reference model (CRM) built on Dublin Core and designed to promote information exchange between museums, libraries, and archives. Mappings to the CIDOC CRM have already been created for a number of large-scale digital cultural heritage efforts from around the world.

A number of authority files exist to help standardize the description of fields such as author/artist, genre, period, and subject within the various metadata schema, including Library of Congress Subject Headings, Categories for the Description of Works of Art, and the Art and Architecture Thesaurus.

The Metadata Encoding and Transmission Standard (METS) and Synchronized Multimedia Integration Language (SMIL) are structural metadata standards providing information about the structure of a digital object and the relations between its parts, for instance, between an image and image details, or between keyframes and scenes from a video. As the number, size, and complexity of content metadata standards continues to grow, there is a need for the metadata created and maintained in one standard to be accessible via related content metadata standards. A fully specified crosswalk bridges the gap between different metadata elements and provides the ability to create and maintain one set of metadata, and to map that metadata to any number of related content metadata standards.

The primary challenge for DCHIs will be to work collaboratively to develop and implement existing image metadata consistently in order to create cross-domain access to collections, which have been historically curated within different traditions.

Despite different curatorial traditions of libraries, museums, and archives, a number of highly successful projects to share images across cultural heritage communities has started to emerge and provide examples to inform our future practice. The following are among these exemplary projects:

• Museums and the Online Archive of California (MOAC) (http:// www.bampfa.berkeley.edu/moac/). MOAC is a museum and library collaboration that, since 1998, has contributed content to an online resource of museum, archival, and library collections, made available freely by the California Digital Library. The MOAC resource has grown to over 75,000 records and images from 11 California cultural institutions.

- Colorado Digitization Project (http://www.cdpheritage.org/). Provides access to resources held in and by Colorado cultural heritage institutions—archives, historical societies, libraries, and museums. Access to resources is available through a collaborative effort to digitize photographs, maps, diaries, works of art, exhibitions, and three-dimensional artifacts.
- Voices of the Colorado Plateau (http://archive.li.suu.edu/voices/). The Voices Project is a collaborative effort uniting eight cultural heritage institutions in three states ringing the Colorado Plateau region.

One of the issues surrounding the creation of highly structured metadata stems from the consistency by which images are indexed. Studies of image indexing indicate very low levels of agreement and consistency (Markey, 1984). This issue, as well as the costs associated with manually assigning terms to images, has prompted interest in using natural language, user-generated descriptors, and automatic image-based approaches to representing image content. Although natural language approaches have performed very well for retrieval of textual information, there still remain a large number of images without accompanying text of any kind. This approach is well suited to retrieval of archival news photos and videos with an accompanying audio track or textual transcript, but does little to retrieve images that have not been formally produced with accompanying text or audio. B. O'Connor, M. O'Connor, and Abbas (1999) proposed that eliciting natural language terms and image descriptions from users seems promising, but there is no central repository from which to capture and build a searchable archive of user-generated image terms and the images to which they refer. Similarly, proposals to mine digital reference question and answer pairs as a means of generating profiles of users and objects (Lankes, 1999) may well provide user-generated image terms, rich natural language, and explicit connections between descriptions of images sought and their image solutions.

Users often request images based on features or image properties such as colors and shapes, or by requesting "more images that look like this one." This has led to the development of image-processing based solutions, often referred to as content-based image retrieval (CBIR), which rely on image processing and pattern recognition programs that retrieve primitive features such as color, texture, and shape that can be automatically extracted from the images themselves. In these systems, user queries may take the form of submitting a sketch, clicking on an exemplar image, texture, or color palette, or a combination of drawing and querying tools. For example, the Hermitage Museum (http://www.hermitage.ru/) provides users with IBM's Query by Image Content interface to search for images by drawing and positioning shapes and colors within a drawing frame.

Although promising, these approaches are still in an early phase of development for general image retrieval, and little is known about their utility for cultural heritage institutions.

But providing image "answers" is not just a matter of finding the right object in the collection (putting the issue of metadata and databases aside for a minute), it is a matter of creating a digital surrogate that can be viewed. There are significant expenses involved in digitization, description, and database creation. Further, there are different kinds of images (with different kinds of uses) in libraries, museums, and archives. For example, there are image surrogates that document objects in the collection; there are images that are part of the collection; there are things like wallpaper samples that are both images and surrogates (for something else) in the collection; and there are installations, appropriated image montages, and performance works posing additional challenges to surrogation. It is not enough to provide textual descriptions or metadata of images that exist within specific collections: Users actually want to access the images themselves and need to do so in order to make determinations about those images. Many, if not most, museums do not have readily available digital surrogates for every object in their collection.

In physical art and art historical collections, the traditional image searching pattern has been one of browsing through slides arranged by period, culture, or artist, then pulling potentially relevant images for viewing on a light box. The limiting factor in finding appropriate images in this manner is the amount of time and attention required to cull through numerous images in search of the most relevant one. The Web equivalent for this may be found in search engines and directories such as Google, which allows users to browse "shot sheets" of thumbnail images retrieved in response to a query or organized according to broad generic classes such as "celebrities." General purpose Web search engines match terms in user queries to terms appearing anywhere on the Web site where an image file appears, and present either lists of Web site surrogates, or pages of thumbnail images for browsing. Although there appears to be some weighting for terms that appear in the image's filename, in many cases the search retrieves a staggering number of images that are simply not relevant to the query. As a result, users spend large amounts of time browsing for relevant images.

A study of image search moves on the Web (Goodrum et al., 2003) indicates that approximately 60% of search moves are devoted to browsing and image inspection, whereas approximately 20% of search moves are devoted to queries and query reformulation. In this study, users of search tools that provide thumbnails viewed many more retrieved images before making a relevance judgment than users who scanned lists of textual descriptions of Web sites with potentially relevant images. The subjects in this study spent an average of 20 minutes locating an image and expressed frustration at the amount of time spent browsing nonrelevant retrieved hits.

Although browsing is an important and necessary activity in image seeking, it is clear that we have done little to "Save the time of the reader" (Ranganathan, 1957). The challenge for DCHIs here is to develop tools to aid in the presentation of image information and to make the users' search easier and more effective. We need to understand how users seek out images in the digital environment and how they make relevance judgments for digital images.

ACCESS

As the law is changing to eliminate the public good aspects of intellectual property, we are seeing a rapid increase in the commodification of information. The area of authorship and creativity will increasingly resemble the world of consumer products—intellectual property will become more bland and corporate controlled. Most individuals will find it more and more difficult to become a creator, and will settle for being merely a consumer. And diverse voices will be more and more marginalized. (Besser, 2001)

Libraries want to share content; publishers want to sell it. Museums strive to preserve culture, and artists to create it. Musicians compose and perform, but must license and collect. Users want access, regardless of where or how content is held. What all of these stakeholders (and more) share is the need to identify content and its owner, to agree on the terms and conditions of its use and reuse, and to be able to share this information in reliable ways that make it easier to find. (Bearman et al., 1999)

Assuming that we can make digitized images of our entire collections available over the Web, it is not enough to simply provide access for users to view those images. A central mission of cultural heritage institutions is the fostering of creativity within the community and wider participation in culture overall. Passive access alone is insufficient to realize this mission. The passive access afforded by mass media monopolies encourages cultural consumerism rather than the active creation of cultural expression.

DCHIs have the power to foster greater interaction and participation with visual media, but to do so they will have to overcome increasingly restrictive copyright laws. The duration of the copyright has increased dramatically over time: from 14 years in 1709, to 95 years for corporations, and 70 years after death for individuals under the 1998 Millenium Copyright Act. At the same time, content providers have shifted from *selling* their image products, to *licensing* image content to institutions. Licenses are contractual arrangements giving content providers the ability to forego rights such as *fair use* and *first sale* that have been cultural heritage institutions legal mechanism for providing access to images in their collections. For most cultural heritage institutions, tracking how images were acquired, and mapping that acquisition to applicable copyright restrictions, has become a full-time job made more complex by the myriad ways in which images have been acquired over the years.

Images in cultural heritage institutions are acquired (with or without rights to digitize or reproduce) in a number of ways. They may be purchased from creators, museums, galleries, publishers, or vendors. They may be shared through interinstitutional consortia or educational site licenses. They may come into the institution through bequests or donations. They may be created by copystand photography or scanning from published sources. In many cases, images are acquired along with provisions prohibiting sharing or exhibition outside of the primary institution. Use on an unrestricted Web site may not be covered under the fair use guidelines of the copyright act. In each case, the complexity of determining how an image was acquired, and whether the institution has the right to digitize an image in its collection and to make that image freely available over the Web, has had a chilling effect on the creation of digital cultural heritage sites.

Rights management therefore has to be considered from the start of any digitizing project. DCHIs cannot begin to service user requests for images unless they know what they can and cannot share and what constraints will be placed on sharing those images with users. The use of rights management metadata can play an important role in making users aware of who owns the rights to the images, the kinds of uses to which users are allowed to put the images, and the conditions that constrain different uses of those images. The encoded metadata might include a description of the object, details of the rights owner, and a unique registration number. The Digital Object Identifier (DOI) metadata system provides a unique identification number to digital objects, allows rights holders to link to the users of the material, and enables automated copyright management for all types of media. By clicking on a DOI, the user is connected to a central repository where the publisher maintains the object's URL. This address may contain the content itself or further information about how to obtain the content.

These efforts to map the complex network of rights ownership in digital cultural heritage institutions do little to support the fundamental need for active engagement with content in terms of appropriation, repurposing, and reuse of content. Although libraries, archives, and museums are poised to be the caretakers of digital collections, the creators of new interpretations and new cultural expressions from these collections will need mechanisms that encourage their interaction with and contribution to these collections. How will these new expressions be incorporated or linked into our existing collections in ways that will foster even more creativity? One approach to this issue has been the work of the Creative Commons (http://creativecommons.org/) (see Fitzgerald, chap. 15, this volume). Creative Commons promotes the creative reuse of intellectual and artistic work by providing a "some rights reserved" copyright in contrast to the traditional "all rights reserved." They have released a set of copyright licenses free for public use that allow creators to "dedicate their creative works to the public domain—or retain their copyright while licensing them as free for certain uses, on certain conditions."

CONCLUSIONS

The different traditions, logics, and practices of libraries, museums, and archives are changing dramatically due to the increased ability to provide access to digitized information over the Web. Digitization requires collaborative effort and we have begun to bridge the gap between these cultural heritage institutions. Yet the impact remains diffuse, with the outcomes of a multitude of digitization projects scattered across Web sites and unpublished reports. Taken in the whole, the body of image digitization work facilitated by museums, archives, and libraries constitutes an important international resource for cultural heritage. As the number of digital images on the Web increases, effectively searching and retrieving information across multiple servers, systems, and domains becomes both increasingly important and increasingly frustrating. In order to make our goal of "one stop any stop" access to distributed digital cultural heritage a reality, we will have to move beyond the creation of isolated digitization initiatives to more collaborative large-scale national and international projects with wide institutional participation. Such collaboration can only take place by paying careful attention to the mechanisms that support human image needs and uses, including search processes, metadata to support resource discovery and retrieval, and licenses that support active engagement with our content.

NOTES

1. Whereas it is common to consider "texts" as complex information bearing objects that may be comprised of words and images, as well as the structure and relationship between words and images, for the purposes of this chapter, I wish to distinguish between linguistic objects and pictorial objects. "Textual information"

and "text-based" in this context refer to word-based objects, even if stored as an image as is the case with scanned pages of text.

REFERENCES

Arms, W. Y. (2000). *Digital libraries*. Cambridge, MA: MIT Press.

Bearman, D., Miller, E., Rust, G., Trant, J., & Weibel, S. (1999). A common model to support interoperable metadata. Progress report on reconciling metadata requirements from the Dublin Core and INDECS/DOI Communities. *D-Lib Magazine, 5*(1). Retrieved January 1999 from http://www.dlib.org/dlib/january99/bearman/01bearman.html

Bergman, M. (2001). The deep web: Surfacing hidden value. *Journal of Electronic Publishing* Retrieved July 2001 from http://www.press.umich.edu/jep/07–01/bergman.html

Besser, H. (2001). *Commodification of culture harms creators*. Retrieved from http://www.gseis .ucla.edu/~howard/Copyright/ala-commons.html

Borgman, C. L. (1999). What are digital libraries? Competing visions. *Information Processing & Management, 35*(3), 227–243.

Goodrum, A., Bejune, M., & Siocchi, A. (2003). A state transition analysis of image search patterns on the Web. In E. M. Bakker et al. (Eds.), *CIVR 2003, Lecture notes in computer science* (Vol. 2728, pp. 281–290). Berlin: Springer-Verlag.

International Committee for Documentation of the International Council of Museums (ICOM-CIDOC) (1995). Retrieved from http://www.willpowerinfo.myby.co.uk/cidoc/ stand2.htm

Lankes, R. D. (1999). The virtual reference desk: Question interchange profile (White Paper, Version 1.01D). (Eric Document Reproduction Service No. 417 728). Retrieved from http://WWW.VRD.ORG/Tech/QuIP/1.01/1.01d.htm

Lesk, M. (1997). *Practical digital libraries: Books, bytes, and bucks*. San Francisco, CA: Morgan Kaufmann.

Markey, K. (1984). Interindexer consistency tests: A literature review and report of a test of consistency in indexing visual materials. *Library and Information Science Research, 6,* 155–177.

Miksa, F., & Doty, P. (1994). Intellectual realities and the digital library. In *Proceedings of Digital Libraries '94: The first annual conference on the theory and practice of digital libraries* (pp. 163–169). College Station, TX: Hypermedia Research Laboratory, Department of Computer Science, Texas A&M University.

O'Connor, B., O'Connor, M., & Abbas, J. (1999). User reactions as access mechanism: An exploration based on captions for images. *Journal of the American Society for Information Science, 50*(8), 681–697.

Palmer, S. E. (1978). Fundamental aspects of cognitive representation. In E. Rosch & B. B. Lloyd (Eds.), *Cognition and categorization* (pp. 259–303). Hillsdale, NJ: Lawrence Erlbaum Associates.

Ranganathan, S. R. (1957). *Five laws of library science*. Madras: Madras Library Association.

Sayre, S., & Wetterlund, K. (2004). *ARTstor and the K-12 education community*. A commissioned public and private report prepared for the Andrew W. Mellon Foundation. Retrieved from http://www.artstor.org/news/k_12_report.jsp

UNESCO. (1995). *Our creative diversity: A report of the World Commission on Culture and Development*. Retrieved from http://www.iccpr.org

Zorich, D. (2003). *A survey of digital cultural heritage initiatives and their sustainability concerns*. Washington, DC: Council on Library and Information Resources.

II

Arobase Knowledge

6

Next Generation Tools and Services: Supporting Dynamic Knowledge Spaces

Jane Hunter
The University of Queensland

The first generation of tools and services for digital libraries enabled resource discovery of primarily textual resources and web pages through the manual attachment of simple descriptive data, or *metadata*. The second generation of indexing tools provided support for new media types (e.g., digital images, audio, and video) and exploited the availability of automatic metadata extraction and segmentation technologies based on advances in image processing, speech recognition, and machine vision.

As digital libraries expand to include a broader range of disciplines, including the sciences (astronomy, biomedical, environmental), social sciences, and humanities, they are changing from static, formal databases to dynamic knowledge spaces. A new generation of "middleware" services is required that is capable of supporting the needs of a wide variety of users, communities, and data types. The kinds of information being created and analyzed has moved beyond books, textual documents, and scholarly publications. Complex new data types (e.g., real-time sensor data, spatial data, three-dimensional models and images, spectral analyses, tables, graphs, maps, and numerical arrays and matrices) are being generated at great expense and in vast quantities. Mechanisms are required that enable these complex, composite digital objects to be captured, indexed, interpreted, compared, assimilated, browsed, searched, retrieved, reused, and preserved.

In addition, communities of users want support for building personal digital libraries of resources and annotations that seamlessly interoperate with large formal digital libraries. There is increasing acknowledgment that libraries cannot provide access to all of the resources required by individual users or communities. Nor can they claim to present the single objective and authoritative description of resources through the metadata in their online catalogues. Digital libraries now need to support seamless interoperability between their large formal information stores and users' informal local caches that contain personalized views and personal collections of contextual information. Digital libraries also need to provide support for multiple, different, yet equally valid views or perspectives. Hence, the next generation of digital library services is enabling domain experts, scholars, and other users to attach their own interpretations, opinions, ratings, and perspectives to the increasing quantities of content being disseminated and made available through online institutional repositories. They are enabling the attachment of a rich array of secondary or contextual information (including annotations, citations, reviews, usage data, and links to related information) to primary digital sources. By enabling scholars to attach subjective, clearly attributed annotations, opinions, and hyperlinks to related resources, these tools enable the recording and sharing of new ideas, connections, and knowledge, thus encouraging scholarly communication.

The latest annotation tools and services support advanced functionality such as audiovisual or spoken annotations, threaded annotation lists and real-time collaborative annotations through videoconferencing environments. Hence, the annotations themselves become new information objects, in a variety of media formats, which in turn require management. Mechanisms are required for authenticating users who are attaching and publishing annotations and for restricting access to annotations based on the user's membership or role within a group or organization.

When such annotations or mark-up are recorded in standardized, machine readable format, using terms and concepts from a vocabulary agreed by a particular domain or discipline (an ontology), they become even more useful, with greater potential for reuse and for generating new knowledge or solutions to complex problems.

An ontology is a conceptualization of an application domain in a human understandable and machine readable form and typically defines classes of entities, relations between entities, and the axioms that apply to the entities in that domain. Ontologies provide a way of characterizing knowledge assets so that they can be reused by software agents, Semantic Web services, or other organizations to extend current knowledge bases and generate new knowledge. Combined with semantic inferencing rules, ontology-based annotations provide the basis for more advanced knowledge mining services. Methods for harmonizing ontologies from different domains is essential for multidisciplinary research. Support for managing dynamic ontologies is essential to support communities in which the knowledge is evolving.

As layers of knowledge grow, it will also be important to be able to track the source, assumptions, rules, and contextual information on which the new knowledge is based. Mechanisms are required that provide some measure of certainty, completeness, and reliability of data and metadata. Mechanisms are required to both detect and handle new, contradictory, redundant, incomplete, uncertain, or inconsistent information. Biases will hopefully be revealed through clear identification of the provenance, perspective, and intent of a digital information source plus additional services capable of analyzing and validating the attached information or annotations.

These are just some of the issues being investigated by researchers in the fields of knowledge capture and management. Clearly, the technologies required to support and manage this new view of digital libraries—as dynamic knowledge spaces that combine large formal information stores with informal local caches and personalized views and collections—are by no means readily available or simple to build.

This chapter describes some of the research being undertaken and the challenges facing digital libraries as they evolve into these new dynamic knowledge spaces. Many topics covered in this chapter were identified by an NSF Workshop on Research Directions for Digital Libraries (held in Chatham, Massachusetts, in June 2003) as key issues that digital libraries of the future need to address.

ADVANCES IN METADATA GENERATION

Metadata is the value-added information that documents the administrative, descriptive, preservation, technical, and usage history and characteristics associated with resources. It provides the underlying foundation on which digital collection management systems rely to provide fast, precise access to relevant resources across networks and between organizations. The metadata required to describe the highly heterogeneous variety of mixed-media, composite digital objects available on the Internet is infinitely more complex than simple metadata designed to enable the discovery of textual documents through a library database. The problems and costs associated with generating and exploiting such metadata are correspondingly magnified.

Metadata standards, such as Dublin Core, enable simple resource discovery of digital objects and provide a limited level of interoperability between systems and organizations. But there are still significant problems and issues that remain to be solved. Doctorow (2001) believed that the vision of an Internet in which everyone describes their goods, services, or information using concise, accurate, and common or standardized metadata that is universally understood by both machines and humans is a "pipe-dream, founded on self-delusion, nerd hubris and hysterically inflated market opportunities" (p. 1). Others have cited the popularity and efficiency of Google as an example of an extremely successful search engine that does not depend on expensive and unreliable metadata. Google combines PageRanking (in which the relative importance of a document is measured by the number of links to it) with sophisticated text-matching techniques to retrieve precise, relevant, and comprehensive search results (Brin & Page, 1998).

Some of the major disadvantages of metadata are its cost, its unreliability, its subjectivity, its lack of authentication, and its lack of interoperability with respect to syntax, semantics, vocabularies, languages, and underlying models. However, there are many researchers currently investigating strategies to overcome different aspects of these limitations in an effort to provide more efficient means of organizing content in digital libraries and on the Internet.

Because of the high cost and subjectivity associated with human-generated metadata, a large number of research initiatives are focusing on technologies to enable the automatic classification and segmentation of digital resources—that is, computer-generated metadata for textual documents, images, and audio and video resources.

Automatic Document Indexing/Classification

Automatic categorization software (Reamy, 2002) uses a wide variety of techniques to assign documents into subject categories. Techniques include statistical Bayesian analysis of the patterns of words in the document, clustering of sets of documents based on similarities, advanced vector machines that represent every word and its frequency with a vector, neural networks, sophisticated linguistic inferences, the use of preexisting sets of categories, and seeding categories with keywords. The most common method used by automatic categorization software is to scan every word in a document and analyze the frequencies of patterns of words. Based on a comparison with an existing taxonomy, the document is assigned to a particular category in the taxonomy. Other approaches use "clustering," or "taxonomy building," in which software is applied to a collection of documents (e.g., 10,000 to 100,000), searching through all the combinations of words to find clumps or clusters of documents that appear to belong together. Other systems automatically generate a summary of a document by scanning through the document and finding important sentences using rules like: The first sentence of the first paragraph is often important. Another common feature of automatic categorization is noun phrase extraction; the extracted list of noun phrases can be used to generate a catalogue of the entities covered by the collection.

Automatic categorization cannot completely replace a librarian or information architect, but it can make them more efficient and produce a better index. The software itself, without some human rules-based categorization, cannot currently achieve more than about 90% accuracy. So although it is much faster than a human categorizer, it is still not as good as a human.

Image Indexing

Images represent a key source of information in many domains and the ability to exploit them through their discovery, analysis, and integration is a challenging and significant problem. Because of the complexity and multidimensional nature of image data, manual annotation of images is slow, expensive, and predisposed to high subjectivity. Significant progress has been made in recent years on the automatic recognition of low level features within images and content-based retrieval using query-by-example (QBE) or query-by-image-content (DCSE, 2001; QBIC, 2001). These interfaces enable the user to specify the colors, textures, and shapes to search for within images.

However, comparatively little progress has been made on the machine generation of high level semantic descriptions of images. Hence, most recent research effort has focused on semantic indexing of images and the automatic recognition of real-world objects or concepts. The most common approach to image indexing involves the application of machine learning techniques to a set of manually annotated images in order to automatically label images with keywords (Adams et al., 2003; Marques & Barman, 2003).

Little and Hunter (2004) proposed an innovative, hybrid, user-assisted approach, rules-by-example (RBE), which is based on a combination of RuleML (rule markup language) and query-by-example. The RBE user interface enables domain-experts to graphically define domain-specific rules for inferring high level semantic descriptions of images from combinations of low level visual features (e.g., color, texture, shape, size of regions). The low level features are specified through examples generated from drawing tools and palettes. Using these rules, the system is able to analyze the visual features of any given image from the domain and generate semantically meaningful labels, using terms defined in the domain-specific ontology. To date, this approach has proved quite effective when applied to scientific or medical images from narrow, focused domains.

We expect that the optimum approach will involve a combination of the interactivity of RBE with the traditional machine learning black-box approach. Together, these technologies will enable faster, more adaptable, cost-effective, and accurate semantic indexing of images—maximizing their potential for discovery, reuse, integration, and processing by Semantic Web services, tools, and agents.

Speech Indexing and Retrieval

Speech recognition is increasingly being applied to the indexing and retrieval of digitized speech archives. Dragon Systems (2003) developed a system that creates a keyword index of spoken words from within volumes of recorded audio, eliminating the need to listen for hours to pinpoint information. Speech recognition systems can generate searchable text that is indexed to time code on the recorded media, so users can jump directly to the audio clip containing the specified keyword. To date, the accuracy of speech recognition systems has depended on pretraining for a particular speaker and noncontinuous, stilted speech. However, the latest speech recognition systems will work even in noisy environments, are speaker independent, work on continuous speech, and are able to separate two speakers talking at once. Dragon is also working on its own database for storing and retrieving audio indexes.

Video Indexing and Retrieval

Commercial systems, such as Virage (2003), Convera Screening Room (2003), Artesia (2003), and Pictron Media Gateway, are capable of parsing hours of video, segmenting it, and turning it into an easily searchable and browsable database. The latest video indexing systems combine a number of indexing methods, including extraction of embedded textual data (SMPTE timecode, lineup files, and closed captions), scene change detection, visual clues, and continuous speech recognition to convert spoken words into text. For example, CMU's Informedia project (Informedia, 2003) combines text, speech, image, and video recognition techniques to segment and index video archives and enable intelligent search and retrieval. Informedia also analyzes both the video and transcript to generate real-world time and location metadata. This metadata can then be used to explore archives dynamically using temporal and spatial graphical user interfaces, such as mapping interfaces or date sliders. An example of the kind of query supported is: Give me all the video content on air crashes in South America in early 2000 (Ng, Wactlar, Hauptmann, & Christel, 2003).

Current research in this field is concentrating on the problem of indexing and filtering streaming video content in real-time, rather than during a post-processing step (Mezaris, Kompatsiaris, Boulgouris, & Strinzis, 2004).

New Complex Media and Data Types

There have been some recent advances in the indexing, search, and retrieval of complex media and data types, including the following:

- Composite mixed-media objects, such as web pages containing text and images and SMIL presentations that combine images, audio, video, and text (Hunter & Little, 2001)
- Geographically and spatially indexed resources that can be searched and browsed via map interfaces (Ancona, Frew, Janée, & Valentine, 2004)
- Collections of three-dimensional objects, such as museum and archeological artefacts (Shiaw, Jacob, & Crane, 2004)

In addition, eScience applications are generating many new, highly complex data types such as real-time sensor data, spatial data, three-dimensional models and images, spectral analyses, temperature profiles, tables, graphs, maps, and numerical arrays and matrices. These are being produced in vast quantities and often in real time, at significant costs to society. Currently, significant effort is required by scientists in order to index, archive, analyze, interpret, compare, search, retrieve, and integrate these complex data types. Mechanisms are required to reduce the cost and problems associated with managing this data.

The ROADNet (2002) project on HPWREN (2001), a high performance wireless network, is a typical example of a challenging eScience application. ROADNet is essentially a large-scale observatory in California in which real-time seismic, oceanographic, hydrological, ecological, geodetic, and physical data and metadata is captured and streamed over wireless networks. Real-time numeric, audio, and video data is collected via field sensors, streamed to researchers connected to HPWREN and posted to discipline-specific servers connected over a network. This data is immediately accessible by interdisciplinary scientists to enable them to monitor and respond to environmental changes. Extraction of metadata from real-time data streams, as well as high-speed metadata fusion across multiple data sensors, are high priority research goals within applications such as ROADNet.

ADVANCES IN KNOWLEDGE CAPTURE

The research topic of knowledge capture and acquisition is not new. It began in the artificial intelligence community with attempts to develop expert systems—with limited success. The machine learning and human–computer interaction communities have been developing systems that learn how best to perform tasks by carefully monitoring how users manually accomplish tasks. In knowledge engineering, knowledge-based systems are being developed that exploit commonly occurring inference structures and domain-specific ontologies. Natural language processing is being applied to textual documents to create representations of their knowledge content. Although all of these approaches use different techniques to capture different forms of knowledge, they are related in that they all acquire information and then analyze and organize it into knowledge structures that can be used for reasoning.

This section focuses on technological advances in knowledge capture in the following specific areas:

- Annotation systems—proactive interfaces that enable users to explicitly attach their opinions, notes, critiques, and related secondary contextual information
- Tacit and communal knowledge capture
- Ontologies—a representation of the concepts, entities, relationships, and axioms that characterize an application domain
- Knowledge authentication—providing a measure of trust or certainty to data by attaching attribution, authentication, reliability, provenance, and authority metadata

Annotation Systems: Supporting Multiple Views

Knowledge, like truth, is relative to understanding. Our folk view of knowledge as being absolute comes from the same source as our folk view that truth is absolute, which is the folk theory that there is only one way to understand a situation. When that folk theory fails, and we have multiple ways of understanding, or "framing," a situation, then knowledge, like truth, becomes relative to that understanding. Likewise, when our knowledge is stable and secure, knowledge based on that understanding is stable and secure. (Lakoff, 1987, p. 300)

In *Women, Fire and Dangerous Things,* Lakoff developed a general model of cognition on the basis of semantics. He also emphasized the importance of providing and supporting multiple different views simultaneously. Different communities or individuals have different ways of understanding, contextualizing, or describing objects, events, or situations. No single view is the "correct" view. Hence, digital libraries can no longer claim to present the single objective and authoritative description of resources through the metadata in their online catalogues. They need to provide support for multiple, different, yet equally valid views or perspectives.

Consequently, the next generation of metadata tools is enabling domain experts, scholars, and other users to attach their own interpretations, opinions, ratings, and perspectives to the increasing quantities of content being disseminated and made available through online institutional repositories. They are enabling the attachment of a rich array of secondary or contextual information to primary digital sources, for example, annotations, citations, reviews, ratings, links, usage data, and related information sources.

The motivation behind annotation systems is multifold. Metadata is expensive. Libraries do not have the funding or resources to attach detailed metadata to every object in their collections. If users have the time, interest, and motivation to attach contextual information to resources that may be of value to other users, and are willing to share it with their colleagues, then annotation tools facilitating this process should be made available and proactively supported or even rewarded by digital libraries.

By enabling scholars to attach subjective, clearly attributed annotations and hyperlinks to related resources, these tools also enable the recording and sharing of new ideas, connections, and knowledge, thus encouraging scholarly communication.

The W3C's Annotea Service (W3C Annotea, 2001) and DARPA's Web Annotation Service (DARPA, 1998) are two web-based annotation systems that have been developed and made available. These systems enhance collaboration via shared annotations and bookmarks that can be attached to web documents or parts of documents. Annotations are input via simple user interfaces and stored on public annotation servers, with links to the URLs of the resources they describe. Users can search, browse, and retrieve annotations to see what their peer group thinks and respond to selected annotations through threaded annotation lists—thus providing an environment for asynchronous collaboration.

The latest annotation tools support advanced features such as audiovisual or spoken annotations (Hunter, Koopman, & Sledge, 2003) and real-time collaborative annotations through shared chatlines and videoconferencing environments (Benz & Lijding, 1998). Other annotation tools focus specifically on objects of particular media types, such as film/video and multimedia content (DSTC's FilmEd, 2003b; IBM VideoAnnEx, 2001; Ricoh MovieTool, 2002; ZGDV VIDETO, 2002), images or photographs (PAXit, 2003), and three-dimensional objects.

In many cases, the annotations themselves represent new information objects, available in a variety of media formats (i.e., text, html, audio, video), which in turn require management. Mechanisms are required for clearly documenting the source of the annotation—authenticating the users who attach and publish annotations and thus provide some measure of its credibility. Additionally, certain communities (e.g., indigenous or intelligence communities) want to be able to restrict access to annotations and stories based on membership or role within a particular community or organization. Research is currently being undertaken into defining and applying fine-grained access constraints on annotations based on user profiles (Hunter et al., 2003).

Tacit and Communal Knowledge Capture

"Knowledge," in this context, refers to the expertise, experience, and understanding of a group of people in a community or organization as well as the information artifacts (i.e., documents, reports, videos, training material, etc.) used during the execution of tasks. Tacit knowledge is what a person knows; it is derived from experience and embodies beliefs and values. Explicit knowledge is represented by some artefact such as a report or video; it has been created with the goal of communicating with another person. Because tacit knowledge is actionable knowledge, it is highly valuable. According to Nonaka and Takeuchi (1995), "The key to knowledge creation lies in the mobilisation and conversion of tacit knowledge." Consequently, this section focuses on technologies that enable tacit knowledge to be transformed into explicit knowledge so it can be shared and reused.

The most common way in which tacit knowledge is expressed and shared is through face-to-face meetings and personal interactions. Groupware is the fairly broad category of application software that enables people to work together in groups and teams by facilitating the sharing of documents and discussions, either synchronously or asynchronously. Examples of groupware include: e-mail, discussion lists, weblogs, chatlines, Wikis, whiteboards, and videoconferencing. By capturing the interactions and exchanges enabled through these technologies, in persistent forms, we are transforming tacit knowedge into explicit knowledge. By indexing and archiving these persistent forms, and providing search and browse interfaces, we are further enabling the knowledge to be shared and reused.

Hence various research groups are focusing their efforts on analyzing and structuring e-mail, discussion lists, chatlines (McArthur & Bruza, 2003), and weblogs in order to extract tacit knowledge.

Weblogging, or blogging (Reynolds, Cayzer, Dickinson & Shabajee, 2002; Sullivan, 2002), is a very successful paradigm for lightweight publishing that has grown sharply in popularity over the past few years and is being used increasingly to facilitate communication and discussion within online communities. The idea of semantic blogging is to add additional semantic structure to items shared over blog channels or RSS feeds to enable semantic search, navigation, and filtering of blogs or streaming data. Blizg (2003) and BlogChalking (2002) are two examples of weblog search engines using metadata to enable searching across weblog archives and the detection of useful connections between and among blogs.

Wikis (Wikipedia, 2004) are another relatively new technology that allows collaborative or group editing of web pages. Examples of Wikis include:

- Wikipedia—a free-content online encyclopedia in many languages, that anyone can edit through a Web browser
- Wiki@nt—a Wiki environment that supports collaborative ontology building (Bao & Honovar, 2004).

Significant research is also now being invested in archiving and indexing collaborative videoconferences and virtual meetings. Speech is being analyzed and transcribed. Agendas, minutes, notes, and annotations taken during the meeting provide additional sets of metadata that can be stored and shared. Events such as remote camera control and slide transitions are being used to segment and index the meetings for later search and browsing. The UK eScience CoAKTinG project (Bachler et al., 2004) is applying advanced knowledge technologies to enable the capture, structuring, and navigation of access grid meetings—large-scale, high performance videoconferencing for groups over broadband networks.

Other systems are capturing and exploiting tacit communal knowledge indirectly. Google's page ranking algorithm, for example, extracts communal knowledge indirectly, through the number of references or hyperlinks to the particular document. Amazon.com is another example because it allows readers to submit reviews and read other people's reviews. It also provides valuable secondary information derived from usage statistics, such as "show me the other books bought by people who purchased this book."

A common approach in the human–computing interaction (HCI) community is to extract tacit knowledge by monitoring how users perform certain tasks and measuring how successful these approaches are in order to assist new users who may be repeating the task. The "AntWorld" system, for example, assists users searching the Internet for particular information by recording feedback on page relevance from users searching for similar information (Kantor et al., 2000).

Ontologies

Ontologies provide a conceptualization of an application domain in a human understandable and machine readable form and typically define classes of entities, relations between entities, and the axioms that apply to the entities in that domain. Ontologies provide a way of characterizing knowledge assets so that they can be reused by software agents, Semantic Web services, or other organizations to extend current knowledge bases and generate new knowledge (Berners-Lee, Hendler & Lassila, 2001). Combined with semantic inferencing rules, ontology-based annotations can be used to develop advanced knowledge mining services such as automatic classification; extraction of high level semantic descriptions of resources from combinations of low level features; or the automatic assimilation of semantically related heterogeneous, mixed-media data and resources into coherent presentations or visualizations. Such graphical presentations enable the organization and interactive exploration of complex multidimensional information spaces, hopefully facilitating the detection of new patterns or relationships.

An ontology consists of a set of concepts, axioms, and relationships that describes a domain of interest. An ontology is similar to a dictionary or glossary, but with greater detail, structure, and richer relationships. It is also expressed in a formal language (e.g., OWL) that enables computers to process its content. The W3C Web Ontology Working Group (W3C WebOnt, 2003) developed the Web Ontology Language (OWL) (W3C OWL, 2003) for defining machine understandable structured web-based ontologies. Ontologies can enhance the functioning of the Web to improve the accuracy of web searches and to relate the information in a resource to the associated knowledge structures and inference rules defined in the ontology.

Upper ontologies provide a structure and a set of general concepts on which domain-specific ontologies (e.g., medical, financial, engineering, sports) can be constructed. An upper ontology is limited to concepts that are abstract and generic enough to address a broad range of domain areas at a high level. Computers utilize upper ontologies for applications such as data interoperability, information search and retrieval, automated inferencing, and natural language processing.

Multidisciplinary research will require methods for harmonizing multiple ontologies from different domains. A number of research and standards groups are working on the development of common conceptual models (or upper ontologies) to facilitate interoperability between metadata vocabularies and the integration of information from different domains. The Harmony project developed the ABC Ontology/Model (Lagoze & Hunter, 2001), which is a top level ontology to facilitate interoperability between metadata schemas within the digital library domain. The CIDOC CRM (CIDOC CRM, 2003) has been developed to facilitate information exchange in the cultural heritage and museum community. The Standard Upper Ontology (SUO, 2002) is being developed by the IEEE SUO Working Group.

Many communities are developing domain-specific or application-specific ontologies. Some examples include biomedical ontologies such as OpenGALEN (2002) and SNOMED CT (2003), and financial and sporting ontologies such as the soccer, baseball, or running ontologies in the DAML Ontology Library (2003).

A large number of research efforts are focusing on the development of tools for building and editing ontologies (Denny, 2002). These are moving toward collaborative tools such as OntoEdit (Sure et al., 2002) and built-in support for RuleML to enable the specification of inferencing rules.

As the knowledge of a community grows, the related ontology will evolve, so support for dynamic ontologies and management of ontology versioning becomes important. This is particularly relevant to the distributed development of ontologies, which is a scenario in which users in different locations are working on and editing different subcomponents of a distributed ontology (Heflin & Hendler, 2000; Klein & Noy, 2003; L. Stojanovic, Maedche, Motik, & N. Stojanovic, 2002).

Knowledge Authentication, Reliability, and Provenance

As layers of knowledge grow, it will be important to be able to track the source, assumptions, rules, and contextual information on which the new knowledge is based. The issues of trust and authentication of both the data and metadata becomes very important.

Manually generated metadata and/or annotations associated with resources cannot be assumed to be accurate or precise descriptions of those resources. The metadata and/or the web page may have been deliberately constructed or edited so as to misrepresent the content of the resource and to manipulate the behavior of the retrieval systems that use the metadata. There is an urgent need for technologies that can vouch for or authenticate metadata so that web indexing systems that crawl across the Internet developing web index databases know when the associated metadata can be trusted (Lynch, 2001a).

Various research projects are investigating methods for explicitly identifying and validating the source of metadata assertions, using technologies such as XML Signature. Search engines give higher confidence weightings to metadata signed by trusted providers and this is reflected in the retrieved search results.

The XML Signature Working Group, a joint Working Group of the IETF and W3C (W3C XML Signature, 2003), has developed an XML compliant syntax for representing signatures of web resources and procedures for computing and verifying such signatures. Such signatures can easily be applied to metadata and used by web servers and search engines to ensure metadata' authenticity and integrity. The XML Signature specification is based on Public Key Cryptography in which signed and protected data is transformed according to an algorithm parameterized by a pair of numbers—the so-called public and private keys. Public Key Infrastructure (PKI) systems provide management services for key registries. They bind users' identities to digital certificates and public–private key pairs that have been assigned and warranted by trusted third parties (Certificate Authorities).

Another approach is the Pretty Good Privacy (PGP) system (PGP, 2002) in which a "Web of Trust" is built up from an established list of known and trusted identity/key bindings. Trust is established in new unfamiliar identity/key bindings because they are cryptographically signed by one or more parties that are already trusted.

Shibboleth, a project of Internet2/MACE (2003), is developing architectures, policy structures, practical technologies, and an open source implementation to support interinstitutional sharing of web resources subject to access controls. In particular, it is developing a policy framework (Federations) that will allow interoperation within the higher education community. Shibboleth is based on a federated administration architecture in which the Identity Provider university (home to the user) provides attribute assertions about that user to the Service Provider site. A trust fabric exists between universities, allowing each site to identify the other speaker, and assign a trust level. Identity Provider sites are responsible for authenticating their users, but can use any reliable means to do this. Access control is based on the attribute assertions provided by the Identity Provider university. Shibboleth uses OpenSAML for the message and assertion formats and protocol bindings, which is based on Security Assertion Markup Language (SAML).

ADVANCES IN KNOWLEDGE MINING

Inference Engines

Once a community has formally represented their domain knowledge within an ontology, more sophisticated knowledge mining services can be built through the definition and application of inferencing and reasoning rules.

A number of research groups are currently working on the development of inferencing tools and deductive query engines that enable the deduction of new information or knowledge from assertions or metadata and ontologies expressed in formal ontology languages (RDF, DAML+OIL [DAML+OIL, 2001] or OWL). A technical report on "Ontology Storage and Querying" published recently by ICS FORTH in Crete, provides a very good survey of the current state of ontology storage and querying tools (Magkanaraki, Karvounarakis, Anh, Christophides, & Plexousakis, 2002).

The RuleML (rule markup language) Initiative is developing an XML-based markup language that permits web-based rule storage, interchange, retrieval, and invocation. Assuming a set of rules has been defined and recorded in RuleML, it can then be processed and applied to specified data using an inferencing engine. Possible inferencing engines include: Java Expert System Shell (JESS, 2004) and Mandarax, a Java RuleML engine (Mandarax, 2004). These inferencing engines are currently limited by slow processing speed, the need to convert data to in-memory RuleML facts, and the lack of native RuleML support for applying standard string and mathematical relations (e.g., greater than or equal to)—but are expected to improve with time.

Sophisticated Search Interfaces

Traditionally, web search engines have provided simple keyword search interfaces that retrieve relevant documents and present the results as a list of hyperlinks for the user to click through one at a time. Semantic web technologies are enabling more interactive, graphical, and multimedia search-and-browse interfaces that leverage semantic relations between retrieved information objects. Researchers are developing systems that can automatically retrieve and aggregate semantically related multimedia objects and generate intelligent multimedia presentations on a particular topic (André, 2000; Conlan, Wade, Bruen, & Gargan, 2000; CWI, 2000; Little, Guerts, & Hunter, 2002; Millard et al., 2003). Such automatic information aggregation tools will be extremely relevant to libraries in the future. They can automatically incorporate new content as it becomes available and will expedite the cost-effective creation of online learning objects.

eScience applications are also driving a demand for more sophisticated search interfaces that enable exploration and assimilation of large data sets using visualization, question–answering interfaces, predictive models, deduction and hypothesis testing (DeRoure et al., 2001). A new generation of search engines is emerging that can automatically retrieve, process, assimilate, and present relevant data and information. Question answering systems capable of understanding natural language queries, deriving relationships, and deducing new information from a set of facts is a key challenge.

Graphs (two- and three-dimensional), animations, virtual reality, hypermedia, maps, and combinations of these, are all being employed to visually represent and model complex knowledge bases and systems. Such interfaces are enabling interactive and collaborative data exploration, simulation steering, and hypothesis formulation. Hypotheses can be saved together with their associated provenance data or body of evidence, enabling sharing, discussion, and defense of new theories and a reduction in duplication of analytical or experimental activities (Hunter, Falkovych, & Little, 2004).

Customization and Contextualization of Results

The individualization of information, based on users' needs, context, interests, abilities, prior learning, and so on, is a major metadata-related research issue (Lynch, 2001b). Increasingly, we can expect to see systems that employ context at the individual/personal, community, and societal level to retrieve and deliver optimum information and dynamically match system capabilities to user needs to improve productivity and outcomes.

The ability to push relevant dynamically generated information to the user based on users' needs or preferences may be implemented either by explicit user input of their preferences, or learned by the system by tracking location, usage patterns, preferences, and adapting the system and interfaces accordingly. The idea is that the user can get what they want without having to ask. The following technologies are involved in recommender systems: information filtering, collaborated filtering, user profiling, machine learning, case-based retrieval, data mining, and similarity-based retrieval. User preferences typically include information such as the user's name, age, prior learning, learning style, topics of interest, language, subscriptions, device capabilities, media choice, rights broker, payment information, and so on. Manually entering this information will produce better results than system-generated preferences, but is time consuming and expensive. More advanced systems in the future will use automatic machine learning techniques to determine users' interests and preferences dynamically rather than depend on user input.

Some examples of "personalized current awareness news services" are Pointcast (2002), Financial Times Information (2003), and the eLib Newsagent project (2000). These services allow users to define their interests and then receive daily updated relevant reports. Filtering of web radio and TV broadcasts will also be possible in the future, based on users' specifications of their interests, and the embedding of standardized content descriptions, such as MPEG-7, within the video streams (Annodex, 2004; Rogers, Hunter, & Kosovic, 2002).

Other context-sensitive applications use infrared detection and transmission within buildings or GPS locators to determine where users are physically located and then beam context-sensitive data or applications to the users' PDAs or laptops (Kaine-Krolak & Novak, 1995; Marmasse & Schmandt, 2000). However, such context-sensitive applications do require location metadata to be attached to information resources in databases connected to wireless networks. Applications include the delivery of context-sensitive tour guides, plans, or field data.

CONCLUSIONS

Over the past 5 years, digital libraries have been transforming the ways in which scholarly inquiry, communication, research, and education are carried out. Shared access to vast online digital information repositories has accelerated the rate of scientific discovery, research outcomes, and scholarly productivity. But these new tools and services and this acceleration in new knowledge generation has also exacerbated the resource discovery problem. Digital information is being generated faster than our ability to organize, manage, and reuse it.

This chapter has attempted to provide an overview of some of the key digital library research issues and efforts currently underway, which are expected to improve our ability to search, discover, retrieve, and assimilate information and knowledge—regardless of media type, mode, location, discipline, or language. The topics covered here represent some of the key issues that digital libraries of the future are going to have to address. Many were identified in an NSF Workshop on Research Directions for Digital Libraries (held in Chatham, Massachusetts, in June 2003) Chatham report.

The future will continue to see a demand for systems and tools that can satisfy the requirements for storing, managing, searching, accessing, retrieving, sharing, reusing, and tracking ever-increasing amounts of digital data and information in many different formats and media types. The search and discovery engines will also be extended beyond data and information to online services, instruments (i.e., microscopes, telescopes, digital cameras, sensors), and distributed computing power needed to capture, analyze, process, and interpret the vast information and data repositories.

To date, digital library research has largely relied on the combined efforts of experts in library and information science and computer science. Future research advances are going to require a collaborative effort drawing on input across a much wider range of computing disciplines, including human–computer interaction, artificial intelligence, information retrieval, database systems, knowledge representation, machine learning, network design, computational modeling, visualization, and simulation experts.

The intellectual and technical issues associated with the development, management, and exploitation of digital libraries are far from trivial and we are still a long way from solving them. But, by adopting a coordinated

and rigorous approach to digital library research that combines expertise in library, information, and computer sciences with applications in
eScience, eLearning, and eGovernment, it will be possible to make significant progress toward semantics-based multimedia knowledge networks
that seamlessly span linguistic, cultural, geographic, and disciplinary
boundaries. Only when such infrastructure is available will the full potential of the knowledge held within digital libraries be realized and lead to
research outcomes and scientific discoveries with unimagined social and
economic benefits.

REFERENCES

Adams, B., Iyengar, G., Lin, C-Y., Naphade, M., Neti, C., Nock H., & Smith J. (2003). Semantic
    indexing of multimedia content using visual, audio and text cues. EURASIP *Journal on
    Applied Signal Processing* (Feb.).
Ancona, D., Frew, J., Janée, G., & Valentine, D. (2004, June). *Accessing the Alexandria Digital
    Library from Geographic Information Systems.* JCDL 2004, Tucson, AZ.
André, E. (2000). The generation of multimedia documents. In R. Dale, H. Moisl, & H. Somers
    (Eds.), *A handbook of natural language processing: Techniques and applications for the process-
    ing of language as text* (pp. 305–327). Marcel Dekker. Retrieved from http://www.dfki
    .de/media/papers/handbook.ps
Annodex. (2004). Retrieved from http://www.annodex.net/
Artesia. (2003). Retrieved from http://www.artesiatech.com/
Bachler, M., Buckingham Shum, S., Chen-Burger, J., Dalton, J., De Roure, D., Eisenstadt, M.,
    Komzak, J., Michaelides, D., Page, K., Potter, S., Shadbolt, N., & Tate, A. (2004, June).
    Collaborative tools in the semantic grid. Paper presented at the GGF11—The 11th Global
    Grid Forum, Honolulu, HI.
Bao, J., & Honavar, V. (2004). *Collaborative ontology building with Wiki@nt.* In *Third International
    Workshop on Evaluation of Ontology Building Tools.* Hiroshima.
Benz, H., & Lijding, M.E. (1998). Asynchronously replicated shared workspaces for a multi-
    media annotation service over Internet. *Lecture Notes in Computer Science.* Retrieved from
    http://www.informatik.uni-stuttgart.de/ipvr/vs/Publications/1998-benzEA-02.ps.gz
Berners-Lee, T., Hendler, J., & Lassila, O. (2001, May). The semantic web. *Scientific American.*
    Retrieved from http://www.scientificamerican.com/2001/0501issue/0501berners-lee
    .html
Blizg (2003). Retrieved from http://www.edifyingspectacle.org/pcstuff/archives/
    weblogging/blizg_is_a_blog_index_tha.php
BlogChalking. (2002). Retrieved from http://www.blogchalking.tk/
Brin, S., & Page, L. (1998, April). The anatomy of a large-scale hypertextual Web search
    engine. In *Proceedings of Seventh International World Wide Web Conference (WWW7)* (pp.
    107–117). Brisbane, Australia. Retrieved from http://www7.scu.edu.au/programme/
    fullpapers/1921/com1921.htm
CIDOC CRM. (2003). *CIDOC Conceptual reference model.* Retrieved from http://cidoc.ics
    .forth.gr/
Conlan, O., Wade, V., Bruen, C., & Gargan, M. (2002, May). *Multi-model, metadata driven ap-
    proach to adaptive hypermedia, services for personalized eLearning.* Paper presented at Second
    International Conference on Adaptive Hypermedia and Adaptive Web-Based Systems,
    Malaga, Spain.

Convera Screening Room. (2003). Retrieved from http://www.convera.com/Products/products_sr.asp

CWI's Semi-automatic Hypermedia Presentation Generation (Dynamo) Project. (2000). Retrieved from http://db.cwi.nl/projecten/project.php4?prjnr=74

DAML+OIL. (2001, March). *Reference description, W3C note 18*. Retrieved from http://www.w3.org/TR/daml+oil-reference

DAML Ontology Library. (2003). Retrieved from http://www.daml.org/ontologies/

DARPA Object Service Architecture Web Annotation Service. (1998). Retrieved from http://www.icc3.com/ec/architecture/webannotations.html

DCSE (Department of Computer Science and Engineering, University of Washington). (2003). Object and concept recognition for content-based image retrieval. Retrieved from http://www.cs.washington.edu/research/imagedatabase/

Denny, M. (2002, November 6). *Ontology building: A survey of editing tools*. Retrieved from http://www.xml.com/pub/a/2002/11/06/ontologies.html

De roure, D., Jennings, N., & Shadbolt, N. (2001, December). Research agenda for the semantic grid: A future e-science infrastructure, UKeS-2002-02, UK e-Science Technical Report Series, National e-Science Centre. Retrieved from http://www.nesc.ac.uk/technical_papers/DavidDeRoure.etal.SemanticGrid.pdf

Doctorow, C. (2001, August 26). Metacrap: Putting the torch to seven straw-men of the meta-utopia. Retrieved from http://www.well.com/~doctorow/metacrap.htm

Dragon Systems. (2003). Retrieved from http://www.dragonsys.com/

DSTC FilmEd. (2003b). The FilmEd Project. http://metadata.net/filmed/

Dublin Core Metadata Initiative (DCMI). (2003). Retrieved from http://www.dublincore.org/

eLib Newsagent Project. (2000). Retrieved from http://www.sbu.ac.uk/litc/newsagent/

Financial Times Information. (2003). Retrieved from http://www.info.ft.com/

Flexible interoperability for federated digital libraries. In *Proceedings of Fifth European Conference on Research and Advanced Technology for Digital Libraries (ECDL2001)*. Darmstadt, Germany. http://link.springer.de/link/service/series/0558/papers/2163/21630173.pdf

Google. (2003). Image search. Retrieved from http://images.google.com/

Heflin, J., & Hendler, J. (2000). Dynamic ontologies on the Web. In *Proceedings of the 17th National Conference on Artificial Intelligence (AAAI-2000)* (pp. 443–449). AAAI/MIT Press, Menlo Park, CA.

HPWREN. (2001). Retrieved from http://hpwren.ucsd.edu/news/011109.html

Hunter, J., & Little, S. (2001, September). *Building and indexing a distributed multimedia presentation archive using SMIL*. Paper presented at the fifth European Conference on Research and Advanced Technology for Digital Libraries, ECDL '01, Darmstadt.

Hunter, J., Koopman, B., & Sledge, J. (2003, May). *Software tools for indigenous knowledge management*. Museums on the Web, Charlotte. Retrieved from http://archive.dstc.edu.au/IRM_project/software_paper/IKM_software.pdf

Hunter, J., Falkovych, K., & Little, S. (2004, September). *Next generation search interfaces—Interactive data exploration and hypothesis testing*. Paper presented at the eighth European Conference on Digital Libraries (ECDL2004), Bath, UK.

IBM VideoAnnEx. (2001). Retrieved from http://www.research.ibm.com/VideoAnnEx/

Informedia. (2003). Retrieved from http://www.informedia.cs.cmu.edu/

Internet2. (2003). Retrieved from http://www.internet2.edu/

JESS (2004). The rule engine for the Java Platform. Retrieved from http://herzberg.ca.sandia.gov/jess/

Kaine-Krolak, M., & Novak, M. (1995). *An introduction to infrared technology: Applications in the home, classroom, workplace, and beyond . . .* Retrieved from http://trace.wisc.edu/docs/ir_intro/ir_intro.htm

Kantor, P. B., Boros, E., Melamed, B., Meñkov, V., Shapira, B., & Neu, D. J. (2000) Capturing human intelligence in the Net. *Communications of the ACM, 43*(8), 112–115.

Klein, M., & Noy, N.F. (2003). *A component-based framework for ontology evolution.* (Tech. Rep. No. IR-504), Department of Computer Science, Vrije Universiteit Amsterdam.

Lagoze, C., & Hunter, J. (2001, November). The ABC ontology and model. *Journal of Digital Information, 2*(2). Retrieved from http://jodi.ecs.soton.ac.uk/Articles/v02/i02/Lagoze/

Lakoff, G. (1987). *Women, fire, and dangerous things: What categories reveal about the mind.* Chicago: University of Chicago Press.

Little, S., & Hunter, J. (2004, November) *Rules-by-example—A novel approach to semantic indexing and querying of images.* Paper presented at the International Semantic Web Conference, 2004, Hiroshima.

Little, S., Guerts, J., & Hunter, J. (2002, September). *The dynamic generation of intelligent multimedia presentations through semantic inferencing.* ECDL 2002, Rome. Retrieved from http://archive.dstc.edu.au/maenad/ecdl2002/ecdl2002.html

Lynch, C. (2001a, January). When documents deceive: Trust and provenance as new factors for information retrieval in a tangled Web. *Journal of the American Society for Information Science, 52*(1), 12–17. Retrieved from http://www.cs.ucsd.edu/~rik/others/lynch-trust-jasis00.pdf

Lynch, C. (2001b, June). *Personalization and recommender systems in the larger context: New directions and research questions.* Paper presented at the second DELOS Network of Excellence Workshop on Personalisation and Recommender Systems in Digital Libraries, Dublin, Ireland. Retrieved from http://www.ercim.org/publication/ws-proceedings/DelNoe02/CliffordLynchAbstract.pdf

Magkanaraki, A., Karvounarakis, G., Anh, T. T., Christophides, V., & Plexousakis, D. (2002, April). *Ontology storage and querying* (Tech. Rep. No. 308). ICS FORTH, Crete. Retrieved from http://139.91.183.30:9090/RDF/publications/tr308.pdf

Mandarax. (2004). Retrieved from http://mandarax.sourceforge.net/

Marmasse, N., & Schmandt, C. (2000, September). *Location-aware information delivery with ComMotion.* Second International Symposium on Handheld and Ubiquitous Computing (HUC2K), Bristol (UK), LNCS 1927, Springer, 157-171.

Marques, O., & Barman, N. (2003, October). *Semi-automatic semantic annotation of images using machine learning techniques.* In International Semantic Web Conference, FL.

McArthur, R., & Bruza, P. D. (2003) Finding tacit knowledge in online communities. In R. M. Verburg & Jan A. De Ridder (Eds.), *Communities and technologies conference C&T2003, Workshop on knowledge sharing under distributed circumstances* (pp. 61–66). NWO-MES Press.

Mezaris, V., Kompatsiaris, I., Boulgouris, N. V., & Strintzis, M. G. (2004). Real-time compressed-domain spatiotemporal segmentation and ontologies for video indexing and retrieval. IEEE *Transactions on Circuits and Systems for Video Technology, 14*(5), 606–621.

Millard, D. E., Bailey, C. P., Brody, T. D., Dupplaw, D. P., Hall, W., Harris, S. W., Page, K. R., Power, G., & Weal, M. J. (2003). *Hyperdoc: An adaptive narrative system for dynamic multimedia presentations.* (Tech, Rep. No. ECSTR-IAM02-006). Electronics and Computer Science, University of Southampton.

NSF Workshop on Research Directions for Digital Libraries. (2003, June). *Knowledge lost in information* [Report]. (NSF Award No IIS-0331314). Chatham, MA.

Ng, D., Wactlar, H., Hauptmann, A., & Christel, M. (2003, March). *Collages as dynamic summaries of mined video content for intelligent multimedia knowledge management.* AAAI Spring Symposium Series on Intelligent Multimedia Knowledge Management, Palo Alto, CA. Retrieved from http://www-2.cs.cmu.edu/~hdw/aaai03_ng.pdf

Nonaka, I., & Takeuchi, H. (1995). The Knowledge Creating Company. Oxford, England: Oxford University Press.

Open Archives Initiative (OAI). (2003). Retrieved from http://www.openarchives.org/

OpenGALEN. (2002). Retrieved from http://www.opengalen.org/

PAXit. (2003). PAXit Image Database Software. Retrieved from http://www.paxit.com/paxit/communications.asp

PGP Pretty Good Privacy. (2002). Retrieved from http://www.rubin.ch/pgp/pgp.en.html

Pointcast. (2002). Retrieved from http://www.pointcast.com/

QBIC. (2001). IBM's Query By Image Content. Retrieved from http://wwwqbic.almaden.ibm.com/

Reamy, T. (2002, November). Auto-categorization: Coming to a library or Intranet near you! *EContent Magazine*. Retrieved from http://www.econtentmag.com/r5/2002/reamy11_02.html

Reynolds, D., Cayzer, S., Dickinson, I., & Shabajee, P. (2002). *Blogging and semantic blogging*. SWAD-Europe Deliverable12.1.1: Semantic web applications—analysis and selection. Retrieved from http://www.w3.org/2001/sw/Europe/reports/chosen_demos_rationale_report/hp-applications-selection.html#sec-appendix-blogging

Ricoh Movie Tool. (2002). Retrieved from http://www.ricoh.co.jp/src/multimedia/MovieTool/

ROADNet. (2002). Real-time observatories, applications, and data management network. Retrieved from http://roadnet.ucsd.edu/

Rogers, D., Hunter J., & Kosovic, D. (2002, March). The TV-Trawler Project. *International Journal of Imaging Systems and Technology, Special Issue on Multimedia Content Description and Video Compression*.

Shiaw, H-Y, Jacob, R. J. K., & Crane, G. R. (2004, June). *The 3D vase museum: A new approach to context in a digital library*. Tucson, AZ.

SNOMED CT. (2003). Retrieved from http://www.snomed.org/

Stojanovic, L., Maedche, A., Motik, B., & Stojanovic, N. (2002, October). User-driven ontology evolution management. In *Proceedings of the 13th European Conference on Knowledge Engineering and Knowledge Management EKAW*. Madrid, Spain.

Sullivan, A. (2002, May). The blogging revolution. *Wired*, Issue 10.05. Retrieved from http://www.wired.com/wired/archive/10.05/mustread.html?pg=2

SUO. (2002). IEEE P1600.1 Standard Upper Ontology SUO Working Group. Retrieved from http://suo.ieee.org/

Sure, Y., Erdmann, M., Angele, J., Staab, S., Studer, R., & Wenke, D. (2002, June). OntoEdit: Collaborative ontology engineering for the semantic Web. In *Proceedings of the First International Semantic Web Conference 2002 (ISWC 2002)*. Sardinia, Italy. Retrieved from http://link.springer.de/link/service/series/0558/papers/2342/23420221.pdf   Collection. http://bolder.grainger.uiuc.edu/uiLibOAIProvider/OAI.asp

Virage. (2003). Retrieved from http://www.virage.com/

W3C Annotea Web Annotation Service. (2001). Retrieved from http://annotest.w3.org/

W3C Web Ontology Language (OWL). (2003, March 31). Guide, Version 1.0, W3C Working Draft. Retrieved from http://www.w3.org/TR/owl-guide/

W3C Web Ontology (WebOnt) Working Group. (2003). Retrieved from http://www.w3.org/2001/sw/WebOnt/

W3C XML Signature Working Group. (2003). Retrieved from http://www.w3.org/Signature/

Wang, J.Z., & Li, J. (2003, September). Evaluation strategies for automatic linguistic indexing of pictures. In *Proceedings of IEEE International Conference on Image Processing (ICIP)*. Barcelona, Spain.

Wikipedia. (2004). Retrieved from http://en.wikipedia.org/wiki/Wiki

ZGDV VIDETO. (2002). ZGDV Video Description Tool. Retrieved from http://www.rostock.igd.fraunhofer.de/ZGDV/Abteilungen/zr2/Produkte/videto/index_html_en

7

Knowledge Management and Research in Cybraries

David Rooney
University of Queensland

Ursula Schneider
Karl-Frazens Universität

Cybrary is a term that implies much. Principally, it implies a library that is information technology (IT)-enabled, and that occupies some part of cyberspace in order to do more for its users than a traditional library can and wants to do. A cybrary, therefore, is no longer only a location that stores books and other print materials to be lent to borrowers. It is also a place from which information in forms other than books can be obtained. Although it is still a repository, it is now an online information service provider as well.

At a deeper level, cybrary also implies that the library, now being an online cybrary, is part of the knowledge economy or knowledge society through being a vital service provider to a critical knowledge society institution, namely, the university. In this chapter, we want to take up this knowledge economy or knowledge society positioning of cybraries in some detail because, although being an information service provider is relatively unproblematic, being a knowledge-related service provider is quite another thing. The concern is that it is not yet clear how in occupying part of cyberspace, the cybrary most sensibly contributes to knowledge.

To sensibly occupy a position relative to knowledge, the operations of a cybrary need to be informed by a theory of knowledge. More precisely, and as this chapter shows, if cybraries are to contribute to the knowledge society project by servicing groups of students, teachers, and researchers, it is imperative that their approaches to doing this are informed by an understanding of what knowledge is and how it operates sociologically. The purpose of this chapter, therefore, is to provide a conceptual framework from which a sociologically based rethinking of the library/cybrary can more usefully be done. As research (Boden, 2003) and, indeed, the theory that follows suggests, finding new ways of making representations of things (e.g., theories and models) can lead to new ways of thinking and behaving. The chapter addresses the needs of both cybrarians and cybrary researchers because both have important roles in shaping the cybrary of the future.

CYBRARIES

Before setting out a theoretical framework within which to situate a knowledge-focused cybrary, it is useful to explore what organizing or managing principles are presently associated with the cybrary concept. While acknowledging that, for good purposes, the cybrary literature is practitioner focused and theory is often only implicit in it, there is no doubt that theory can play an important role in the management of all organizations including cybraries. Boone (2001a, 2001b, 2002), for example, focused mostly on technology planning, implementation, forecasting, and managing the space that a physical library occupies. It is not hard to see that there are direct links to operations and technology management frameworks and models here. He was also concerned about organizational structures; design for collaborative and independent learning in multifaceted "gathering spaces"; content in the form of text, graphics, and sound; and interactive conferencing and video. Architecture and design, organizational design, learning, and communication theories are likely to have informed some of the thinking behind these concerns. Ensor (2000), in the preface to *The Cybrarian's Manual*, reflected that discourse on cybraries is moving to more of a sociotechnical orientation. The sociotechnical orientation draws on a significant body of technology studies theory (Bijker & Law, 1992). Other leading practitioners in the cybrary movement more clearly invoke knowledge. However, the pursuit of knowledge is inexorably linked to technology. "The world of knowledge" is accessed by an "integrated web-based way to navigate to sources of information" (Schmidt, Turnbull, & Croud, 1999, p. 1). This knowledge-technology intersection is also laced with a sense of romance. Students and researchers can be taken on a "journey" by the technology (Schmidt et al., 1999), and setting up cybrary services is like doing "fine needlework" (Cooke, Hornsby, & Todd, 2002). In other words, there are hints of technological determinism and technological utopianism, which are views that are not well supported by theory (Ellul, 1964). Moreover, there is at least an implied assumption here about a relation between technology and knowledge that is not helpful for knowledge itself. Thus, there are some unexamined and unexplained assumptions in such views. An overall assessment of the cybrary discourse, at the level of practice, is that it is a technological rather than a knowledge discourse. We argue that a technology discourse limits what cybraries can imagine and achieve in terms of a knowledge agenda. Thus, although we do not want to condemn practitioners for their undoubted enthusiasm, commitment, and good intentions, a sounder conceptual base around which to organize strategic and tactical thinking about knowledge will be useful. Such a conceptual base would enable a more effective way to think about knowledge in the context of cybraries.

DATA AND INFORMATION

To better understand the concept of knowledge, it is useful to begin by showing how it is different from data and information. Data and information are needed for knowledge to be acquired and created, but they are not knowledge. Data are unorganized "bits" (e.g., numbers and words) and are the building blocks of information. We can think of data as being raw, that is, relatively unmanipulated, unanalyzed, or uninterpreted. In other words, data are "uncolored" by human interpretive or sensemaking faculties. In this light, data are unprocessed raw materials for intellectual labor. Information, on the other hand, is data that has been organized in the form of texts, statistics, patents, and so on. Information can therefore be represented in archives and books, or transmitted through the Internet. Information is very important in knowledge-based economies because the primary economic interaction in such economies is the exchange of information (Metcalfe, 1999). But information is not knowledge, nor does it necessarily lead to knowledge. Indeed, more and more information may only lead to confusion, dissonance, or "noise" (Boulding, 1984).

Transforming data into information requires knowledge and may lead to new knowledge, but information is still not knowledge itself; to know means more than to be informed. If one knows, then one has made sense of and understood something, and has the potential to apply that knowledge in novel ways. Moreover, information can only lead to knowledge if it is contextualized with and set in a relational arrangement with other knowledge through memories, sensemaking, and understandings. In addition, knowledge requires more than organized data and more than just facts held in memory; it also consists of such things as feelings, intuitions,

predictions, inferences, beliefs, and values, and the ability to find and recognize associations between ideas. Furthermore, because sensemaking
is socially produced and reproduced (Berger & Luckmann, 1966), or is
socially justified (Fuller, 1988; Kusch, 2002), knowledge stands not only in
relation to other knowledge but to people and society. Knowledge, therefore, has highly abstract, transcendent cognitive, and social processes as
its most defining features.

The next section more clearly describes the extent to which knowledge,
or rather, knowing, is a fundamentally human and, indeed, social activity. In doing this, the discussion emphasizes how knowing is an activity
carried out by socially active people in the possession of such faculties as
intuition, imagination, creativity, memory, and so on. In doing this, our
theorization of knowledge is quite detailed and complex. We have done
this consciously even though not all readers of this book are necessarily
theoreticians. The detail we have provided allows for conceptual completeness and is useful for those who wish to position themselves to make
important fundamental contributions to the knowledge society through
cybrary management or research.

WHAT IS KNOWLEDGE?

Let us begin outlining this detailed model of knowledge by arguing that
libraries do not contain knowledge in the form of their collections, and
sophisticated information technology systems manage information and
data rather than knowledge. The knowledge found in cybraries is held by
cybrarians' and the cybraries' users. However, it is clear that libraries, in
that they contain data and information and use information technology
(IT) systems, are important for knowledge. The critical thing is how to
bring the cybraries' infrastructure and collections together with its cybrarians and users to contribute to knowledge?

Building on this preliminary discussion of knowledge, and in particular
the observations about the connectedness of knowledge, it is practical to
find ways to talk about the connections. Therefore, the discussion begins
by asserting that knowledge is a system of phenomenological qualities that
are emergent properties of interrelations that interplay with (and within)
individuals, groups, history, and places (including the physical objects in
places) (Rooney, Hearn, Mandeville, & Joseph, 2003). These interrelations
or connections and the interplays carried on within them are the generative mechanisms that create knowledge and bring about learning, and it is
on these generative mechanisms that cybrarians and cybrary researchers
can focus to develop insights and strategies for managing cybrary infrastructure and collections for knowledge.

Recent theorizing has seen organizational knowledge treated as complex, distributed systems (Chia, 1998; Hansen, 1999; Schneider, 2001; Snowden, 2000; Spender, 1996; Stacey, 2001; Tsoukas, 1996), socially distributed activity systems (Blackler, 1993, 1995; Engestrom, 1991, 1993), and shared contextual spaces (Nonaka, Toyama, & Konno, 2000; Von Krogh, Ichijo, & Nonaka, 2000). Given the focus on the interrelational aspects of knowing and the interplay between the parts as generative mechanisms, we share much in common with these approaches. However, the approach described here differs because although it covers social "structural" and phenomenological aspects of knowledge systems, it also integrates better the temporal and physical components of the system. This is important because, as Bohm (2000, p. 58) put it:

> Indeed, all man-made features of our general environment are . . . extensions of the process of thought, for their shapes, forms, and general orders of movement originate basically in thought, and are incorporated within this environment, in the activity of human work, which is guided by such thought. Vice versa, everything in the general environment has, either naturally or through human activity, a shape, form, and mode of movement, the content of which "flows in" through perception, giving rise to sense impressions which leave memory traces and thus contribute to the basis of further thought.

In other words, man-made objects, natural objects, and other features of the environment are linked to human thought and activity in a recursive flow. The material and mental elements or experience are not unrelated or juxtaposed, they are parts of the same reality. Furthermore, that Bohm speaks of a recursive flow also draws attention to time, or more precisely, to history. That is, knowing is situated in a social and historical place that contains objects and people with their own social histories who belong to cultures and places that also have histories. These historical experiences carry institutions, assumptions, stories, and so on, that influence what and how we think (David, 1994).

We want to tease out a more detailed picture of the connections, or more specifically, interrelations and interplays in knowledge systems. To do this, we will examine the social-relational and interpretive-relational contexts of knowing, the knower, the situation in which intellectual labor occurs, and the idiosyncratic processes of people enacting their knowledge.

SOCIAL-RELATIONAL CONTEXT[1]

Ideas and ideational processes are central in the interaction of human agents and social structure (Hay, 2001). In other words, social practices and structures necessarily have a conceptual dimension, and should be incorporated in a model of knowing. This means that a sociology of knowledge must account not only for the conceptual side of knowledge but also (among other things) the structures of social relations in which knowing occurs (Bhaskar, 1989). Bhaskar (1998, pp. 40–41) argued that social structures are continually reproduced or transformed by active human agents who occupy "positions," and act performing functions and tasks commensurate with those positions in the light of rules, duties, and functions, relationally. These positions can be specified in terms of the structures (e.g., hierarchies, social networks, etc.) they impose. These hierarchies, networks, relations, and positions are the social-relational context. Social-relational context, therefore, is the "architecture" of a set of interpersonal and intergroup relationships that knowers are situated in. In looking at this context, we are therefore emphasizing the connections between people and that those connections can be examined for their strength, symmetry, directionality, and so on (Scott, 2000). The structure and qualities of particular social networks, and the effects of positions, have implications for knowledge, and therefore for knowledge societies, economies, and organizations. Granovetter (1973), for instance, famously described the advantages of weak but broadly cast social connections over strong but narrowly confined social ties for facilitating the acquisition of new knowledge. Others have looked at the effects on knowledge of various social morphologies like structural holes (Walker, Kogut, & Shan, 2000).

INTERPRETIVE-RELATIONAL CONTEXT

Although social connections can be said to be structural in some way, ideas occur in a context that also has some structure, or at least order and organization, and we must also look at how those mental aspects fit a sociological explanation of knowing.

First recognize the associative nature of knowledge. Knowledge and understanding are always connected to other knowledge and understanding to form a network of ideas, memories, beliefs, and so on. Boden (2003) argued that the most creative people have excellent associative powers. That is, such people can make quite extensive (even unusual) associations between quite disparate ideas to come up with excellent new ideas. Thus, in identifying sensemaking and understanding as requiring ideas, interpretations, memories, and so on, to be linked in networks, we are highlighting what we call the interpretive-relational, or phenomenological, context that shapes or orders knowers' sensemaking frameworks. This context is not the same as the social-relational (although they overlap).

Interpretive-relational context could be perceived as an abstract terrain of distributed cognitions or distributed hermeneutics available to a defined set of interlocutors. Any social interaction related to the exchange of data and information, if knowledge is to emerge, is influenced by differences in the knowledge bases and particular mental contexts of the people involved in such an exchange (Lave & Wenger, 1991; Luhmann, 1995; Wenger, 1999, 2000). Thus, within the social exchange process, the interpretation of data and information is based on hermeneutics derived from the recipient's context (including their existing knowledge, history, and repertoire of metaphors) (Duck, 2002; Lundberg, 1974; Luria, 1976; Vygotsky, 1986). In such a process, the conversationalists create new knowledge. Importantly, this newly created knowledge need not be identical for all parties involved. That is, different people will often interpret an event differently.

Cultural systems are made up in part by theories, beliefs, values, arguments, and propositions. These things exist independently of any individual person's conscious awareness of them or of logical consistencies and inconsistencies between them (Archer, 1996, pp. 107–108). Theories, beliefs, values, propositions, and so on, being things held more or less in common in any cultural group are therefore independent of any individual, and are part of the shared mental background to social activity. Indeed, culture can be defined as a shared pattern of beliefs, and so on, that leads to relatively stable patterns of behavior of groups. It is possible to identify those beliefs, and so on, and evaluate their effects on knowledge.

Interpretive-relational context acknowledges the importance of the social production and reproduction of meaning but is not simply focused at the level of interpersonal relationships; rather, it focuses at the level of cognition and awareness, and the relations between ideas (which may transcend particular interpersonal relationships). This context, therefore, can be seen as a sociocognitive or sociophenomenological one, and importantly, also deals with intersubjectivity and intertextuality (Graham & Rooney, 2001).

It has already been pointed out that society presupposes knowledge and that a society in presupposing knowledge also presupposes the existence of ideas, theories, and ideologies. However, in having ideas, societies also have ideas about themselves and those ideas about themselves can reproduce or transform society (Bhaskar, 1998, p. 48). Therefore, knowledge held by a society about itself is by definition subjective and intersubjective. This statement raises the topic of cultural and individual self-awareness in a way that has the potential to produce reflexivity to the extent that we can acknowledge the need as groups or individuals for change or to remain the same.

In short, whereas the social-relational context is about communicating or diffusing knowledge through social network structures, influenced by position, the interpretive-relational context primarily addresses how meaning and knowledge are configured or ordered, and generated intersubjectively by their relations to other meanings and knowledge (and therefore also to culture). Thus, to reiterate, we are connecting knowledge to the networks of assumptions, values, meaning, and so forth, that make up the phenomenological background to social activity and act as an organizing force for sensemaking, intentionality, creativity, and so on. Of course, the interpretive- and social-relational contexts are not mutually exclusive, they are two different orders of the same reality and are therefore deeply connected. There are important generative mechanisms operating within and between them and they should be subject to analysis in the context of organizations contributing to knowledge.

THE KNOWER

The knower, of course, is the individual. Although we have just discussed the social-relational and interpretive-relational contexts in which individuals are less than the relationship, so to speak, we cannot escape the importance of the individual as a "doer" of things, as the base component of relationships, as a catalyst for interpersonal relationship formation, and as the possessor of the idiosyncratic mind. Therefore, "the *generative* role of agents' skills and wants, and of agents (and other social) beliefs and meanings must be recognised" (Bhaskar, 1989, p. 98, italics in original).

Even though in many cases we will be concerned with managing the contexts of knowers, we still need to be able to examine outcomes and manage at a personal level. Indeed, specific people play an important role in constituting and defining the context. Thus, the character of a group is sensitive to the type and range of personalities of which it is made.

Individuals need to be made aware of and facilitated to effectively take their place in the overall context, and to speculate, cooperate, contest, advocate, and otherwise communicate in the interest of better knowing. This also includes taking on personal responsibilities in learning, sharing knowledge, gaining general experience, being an effective communicator, being ethical, and so on. However, individuals do not operate in isolation and for our model depicting the knower as the isolated and independent decision maker is insufficient. As a minimum, we need to include social exchanges such as in dyads, teams, and so on, by introducing the possibility of more than one knower. This is different from the social- and interpretive-relational contexts that also assume more than one knower. In focusing on knowers the emphasis is shifted from sociology to a more social psychological explanation of individuals in a social setting and the generative mechanisms resulting from processes at this level. Again, it must be stressed that any analytical separation between this and other levels of analysis is an analytical, rather than a real, convenience.

THE SITUATION

Bhaskar (1989, p. 79) indicated that society "is an articulated ensemble of tendencies and powers which . . . exist only as long as they (or at least some of them) are being exercised; are exercised in the last instance via the intentional activity of human beings; and are necessarily space-time invariant." Included in our discussion of knowledge, then, is an acknowledgment that knowing occurs in a defined situation, notwithstanding the fact that the situation is in part made of the contexts already discussed. Knowledge understood in this way is said to be situated (Lave & Wenger, 1991), and situations thought of in a similar way can be said to have their own situational logic (Archer, 1996). For the purposes of this discussion, the knower's situation is defined by the time and space they occupy, and, more specifically, the time and space in which their impulse to act becomes action. Importantly, with the situation we seek to directly account for not only the personal, cognitive, sociological, and phenomenological locations and shapers of knowledge, but now also the temporal, spatial, and physical elements of knowledge systems.

The physical aspects of situations include technology, and other elements of the built environment such as buildings, and of the natural environment or geography (Burke, 2000). We acknowledge here that, at the very least, society includes not only objects but beliefs about those objects (Bhaskar, 1989, p. 101). We can go further than saying we hold beliefs about objects and also say that objects can affect our moods, attitudes, memories, and so on. Objects can, in other words, change how and what we think, learn, and do. Thus, it is also important to account for the effects of architecture, furniture, landscape, color, and so forth, on intellection. This logic explains why the spaces in which monastic contemplation and creative brainstorming take place are very different. Additionally, because the diffusion of knowledge is frequently mediated by information (e.g., text and images) stored and transmitted on various media, we should be able to explicitly include storage, diffusion, and mediating technology in our model.

Because facts are historically specific social realities, history must be acknowledged as a part of the reality of social activity (Bhaskar, 1989, 1998). Although many theorists acknowledge the passing of time, they do not specifically acknowledge historicity in social change. It is insufficient to provide only a temporal sequence at the expense of history. History is an unfolding of events in a complex context that must be understood. In this case, history is better understood as a story of what, how, and why something came to be as it is rather than a time line. Those historical unfoldings and the historiographical narratives that explain them, by virtue of their influences on knowledge, affect the future (Archer, 1995,

p. 167). How the social history of individuals and groups will predispose individuals and groups to think and act is therefore salient to knowledge. If we have some idea of how history preconditions intellectual work in given situations, then we can work with the force of history rather than against it by using knowledge of each others' histories as a basis for better understandings between people, and for drawing on the diversity of experiences in those histories to develop new insights and wisdom. Moreover, if we know what historical narratives are influencing knowledge, we are in a position to test or challenge the validity of the assumptions and beliefs reproduced in those narratives.

ENACTMENT

Collective and individual behaviors are capable of developing both relatively enduring patterns and unpredictable changes (Bhaskar, 1998), and it leads us to the final part of our model, enactment. It is the process of acting on our knowledge, intuitions, memories, and so on that we are interested in here. In looking at enactment of our knowledge, it is noticeable that we enact what we have in our minds predictably and unpredictably, intentionally and unintentionally, rationally and irrationally. Enactment, therefore, highlights more than the fact that we act on our knowledge, it brings a focus to the contradictions and paradoxes associated with the social and individual application of knowledge.

People enact their intentions in a complex world and much of this complexity is at the phenomenological level (Hearn, Rooney, & Mandeville, 2003). If we begin to explore these processes of production and reproduction at the ideational level we note, first, that enactment of the sense made of our experience and position in the world occurs more or less intentionally. The effectiveness of this intentionality depends in part on knower's conscious, intuitive, reflexive, and strategic mental powers. Knowers can be seen as strategic because in being broadly intentional they generally enact their intentions purposively to realize their goals and preferences now and in the future. Hay (2001, p. 8) argued that

> to act strategically is to project the likely consequences of different courses of action and, in turn, to judge the contours of the terrain . . . to orient potential courses of action to perceptions of the relevant strategic context and to use such an exercise as a means to select the particular course of action to be pursued. On such an understanding, the ability to formulate strategy (whether explicitly recognised as such or not) is the very condition of action.

However, knowers inevitably enact their intensions in a messy way. Therefore, Hay's comments must be qualified with his further observation that any action will likely involve both intuitive and explicit strategies; and both intuitive and explicit strategic choices are likely to also rely on incomplete or misleading information and imperfect knowledge (Hay, 2001). We must also recognize that the human mind is not a perfectly rational machine, an observation that led Simon (1955, 1991) to conclude that man is boundedly rational. Bounded rational ability is only part of limited intellectual capacity of humans. Our imperfect knowledge is not only about the shortcomings of information and data provision, it is also about having real cognitive limits to our capacity to know and understand, and the sheer scale of what is potentially knowable about the world. No matter how hard we try, we cannot know or learn everything. Inevitable outcomes of this are errors of judgment and fact, indecision, misinterpretation, and so on. It is therefore important to recognize that the messy enactment of intentionality and strategy in a model of knowledge stands in stark contrast to the fictionally rational *homo economicus*, who is not intuitive and has perfect information and knowledge. This fictional being found in standard economics, indeed that underpins much of the standard economic theory of behavior, has no place in a serious sociology of knowledge. Enactment, therefore, is the fallibly intentional and directed use of knowledge.

Further qualifying the purposive and strategic nature of enactment is the observation that people are positioned in roles that are to an extent involuntary. Different people in different parts of social systems, having different positions and roles, have different vested interests and power, and experience different rewards and frustrations. Given the extent to which those roles are involuntarily occupied, levels of commitment to the functions, duties, and so on, attached to those roles will lead to fluctuations in the playing out of roles resulting in either further unpredictability or inertial tensions in the system. Thus, vested interests need to be understood in terms of interest in maintaining the status quo and change, what positions and roles people occupy, and what is the nature of their commitment to those roles. These variables, therefore, should be considered for their effects on knowledge because positioning conditions and constrains the degree and direction of interpretive freedom, the desire to be innovative, and will condition judgements about what individuals and groups have to win or loose from change (Archer, 1995, pp. 201–203). It is obvious that these constraints on freedoms can prevent change. What is not so obvious are the tensions they create within individuals and groups, and that these tensions can be unevenly distributed causing more tensions. When enough tensions develop, dramatic change may result.

The previous points are important because they highlight that not only is the potential for change embedded in every act of social reproduction, but also in every tension. Exploring the implications of these tensions and uneven distributions, we observe that part of the messiness of enactment is that those social-relational structures and the purposes, intentions, beliefs, assumptions, proposals, and so on, of agents are not isomorphic. In other words, "each [agent and structure] possesses autonomous emergent properties which are . . . capable of independent variation and therefore of being out of phase with one another in time" (Archer, 1995, p. 66), and therefore canceling each other out in a kind of dynamic inertia. Moreover, the fallible enactment and articulation of beliefs, feelings, propositions, and so on, is also likely to lead to the uneven reproduction or transformation of our basic social assumptions within a particular situation or culture. What all this contributes to our understanding of the messiness and fallibility of knowledge is that such are the inconsistencies, incompatibilities, and tensions in societies that

> it is only in a minority of cases that an entire social system will have all [or enough of] its components (institutions, roles and distributions) aligned in terms of one emergent core complementarity or incompatibility which . . . enmeshes all agents in the same situational logic . . . [where] all material resources are mobilized in that single direction. (Archer, 1995, p. 227)

This means that change itself is likely to be unevenly distributed, incomplete, or thwarted. In a model of knowledge, it is therefore important to account for those "powers," tensions, inert forces, and isomorphic tendencies that reproduce or (unpredictably) transform knowledge, assumptions, values, and so forth.

RESEARCHING AND EVALUATING THE CYBRARY

Having set out our view of the sociology of knowledge in some detail, it should be possible for readers to better conceptualize knowledge as a social activity and how knowing can be understood in the context of specific situations, cultures, social structures, intellectual backgrounds, technologies, and so on. This means that it will be possible to make wiser and more considered decisions in the context of designing cybraries to be better contributors to knowledge. Thoughtful cybrarians and cybrary researchers will have already begun to form views about what aspects of the sociology of knowing they can already address (and what they cannot), and what they might address in the future. To assist this process we will now offer some specific suggestions and ideas. Of course, it is not possible at this stage to be definitive or complete in applying our theory to practice or research. A more complete approach will not emerge until cybrary practitioners apply their knowledge and experience to interpreting and implementing new initiatives, and until more research is done.

It is useful to summarize the main features of knowing as we see them and to identify which of those features hold the most potential for contributions by cybraries. The social-relational dimension of knowing makes it clear that we must be aware of what social networks and hierarchies exist and what the features of these structures are. Having established what these features are, we can ask questions such as: Are social networks closed or open? Are the links between members of networks strong or weak? Does communication flow more in one direction than another? And, are hierarchies rigid and oppressive in the exercise of power, or are they more open and provide enlightened leadership? Knowing answers to such questions allows us to examine and evaluate the effects of those structures on knowledge.

The interpretive-relational context acknowledges the way in which ideas belonging both to individuals and groups are ordered, and the ways in which individual and collective knowledge interrelate. We can, for example, reveal through the interpretive-relational lens the ways in which the ordering of ideas is conditioned by assumptions and beliefs to both constrain and liberate thought; and we can assess the extent to which people and groups make associations between ideas, if communication is enhanced or inhibited by the amount of redundancy in interlocutors' knowledge, and how culture (patterns of beliefs and behavior) needs to be understood, identified, and evaluated for contribution to knowledge.

We can also discipline our analyses to account for the fact that knowledge is situated and situations have their own logics. Knowing is situated in the context of social histories and the historiographical narratives and explanations histories provide. Such narratives are linked to culture, and both the intellectual constraints and novel departures that can emerge from the interplay of narratives and cultures are important for knowledge. Narratives can be identified and their assumptions and beliefs can be challenged for their validity and wisdom and contribution to situational logic. In looking at situations, we can also account for the spatial and material influences on knowing. Here we are reminded that IT, buildings, and the natural environment all have effects on the way we think and know.

When, as our theory urges, we not only focus on the macrocontextual features, but also at the level of the individual, the level of analysis moves to knowers and their idiosyncratic minds, dispositions, attitudes, motivations, and so on. Research in social psychology, cognition, memory, and even brain research can help us to understand how thinking and knowing occur within a person, including within the context of our biology.

Enactment focuses us on the messy and fallible nature of knowing. The sources of our mental fallibility can be partly attributed to the limitations placed on us in occupying positions, and performing the roles, functions, and duties associated with them. In adopting this perspective, the effects of roles, and so forth, on commitment, motivations, and narrowing of our intellectual "vision" are also brought into focus. Similarly, enactment makes us vigilant to the effects on knowledge of power, and social and psychological tensions.

The aforementioned comments about the limitations imposed by roles must be balanced against the paradoxical nature of the sociology of knowing revealed in enactment. The paradox is that knowledge systems are unpredictable and changeable even if they have enduring or restraining features. Knowers can be rational and irrational, they have bounded rationality, imperfect knowledge, and an imperfect ability to learn. Thus, whereas we tend to reproduce our assumptions and beliefs, and in doing so reproduce behaviors, the capacity for irrationality (or arationality), wrongly applying knowledge and sudden insight, and creative leaps forward guarantee the potential for unexpected change. However, change, information, innovation, and novelty need to be converted into creativity and wisdom. Understanding how to do this is a great challenge for research because both creativity and wisdom include transformative forms of knowledge and the exercise of value judgments. Cybraries may have a unique role to play here.

We are also reminded that the tensions in the system contribute to a dynamic inertia and this inertia can, through the build up of tensions, bring about radical change too. Very little research has been done on inertial dynamics in social systems.

MANAGING CYBRARIES FOR KNOWLEDGE

To come closer to an understanding of the ways our conceptual framework can be used by cybrarians, we offer some initial preliminary thoughts. It is useful to start by thinking about the situation, that is, the temporal, spatial, and material dimensions knowledge and the cybrary. Situation is an interesting concern for cybraries because one of the implications of cybraries is that space and location are no longer major limitations because cybraries, as it were, go out to their users via remote access technologies. Although it is liberating for academics or students to be able to find and retrieve resources electronically from their offices or homes, cybrarians should not forget that they can also focus on creating environments in the cybrary that better facilitate learning and knowledge creation. Meeting spaces, communication spaces, contemplative spaces, inspiring spaces, and creative spaces are all examples of task specific spaces that cybraries might provide. The design of each of these kinds of spaces might be quite different. Some ideas on how these spaces might be different include having contemplative and inspirational spaces provided through off-campus retreats in appropriate locations. Meeting and communication spaces would need to cater to the needs of temporary project work groups reaching critical phases in the life cycle of their projects. Most of these specialist spaces might be well served by the provision of expert research assistance. Assistance might arrive in the form of easily accessed analysts and analytical tools, visualization tools, data collection and input specialists, interview transcription services, literature searching and summarizing, and other services in coordination and project management for research and teaching/learning projects.

We have argued that, in the process of enacting knowledge, knowers encounter the fallibility of their capacity to know. We have also argued that overcoming fallibility is desirable and to do so requires and produces wisdom, which is a significant and socially valuable outcome. Cybraries can of course play a role in the enactment of knowledge. By providing services that put teachers, students, and researchers in touch with the community, the scope, depth, and diversity needed for wisdom is more likely obtained. Because wisdom requires a depth and scope of knowledge that is enhanced by sound ethics, balance of view, and an ability to go beyond the data and facts in an insightful and creative way (see Baltes & Staudinger, 2000; Rooney & McKenna, forthcoming, for discussions about the nature of wisdom), it requires a broadening of research and teaching horizons. Talking with a much broader community than industry and government is necessary for this to happen. Those in the community who do not have a voice in higher education and research are precisely the voices that need to be heard to help teaching and research to produce wise advice for their communities. Progress can be made in this respect if we can specify all the positions (and tasks, functions, duties) and networks of those who are included in knowledge acquisition and creation processes and who are not but should be, by accounting for the influences of power, leadership, culture, ability to influence, and so on. Wisdom may also be found in now-forgotten historical narratives and so historical debates on older versions of modern problems and ambitions should be accessible through cybraries to researchers in ways that go beyond typical literature searches and specific disciplinary treatments of issues to become histories of ideas. In the future, cybraries may well be in a position to broker or facilitate these kinds of activities.

We suggest that knowledge exists in cybraries in the cybrarians and cybrary users. Cybrary managers need to keep a focus on both groups when thinking about the future of cybraries. It is important to know who they are, what they do, what they know, what they do not know, and what they need to know. What is also essential is to be able to say how individual knowers are positioned. Defining position, role, function, and duties for cybrarians is a basic task. What we are suggesting, for example, is that what is included in a cybrarian's job description could be evaluated and improved in light of what we know about knowledge. To this end, it will be useful to ask if the tasks, duties, and commitments of cybrarians are aligned with knowledge. Do those duties include, for example, providing particular kinds of intellectual leadership and creativity facilitation roles? Is the cybrarian less a designer and provider of information services and more a provider of communication services? And to what extent do cybrarians overcome their own fallibilities in knowing?

Much of what is set out in this section suggests effects at the social-relational and social-interpretive levels of knowing. Any discussion of issues to do with position, duties, roles, tasks, and functions of cybraries and cybrarians are also addressing social networks and hierarchies. Thus, cybraries, in thinking about communication design, and design of spaces or places for knowledge creation and learning, are providing access to information and knowledge that would otherwise be difficult for researchers, teachers, and learners to obtain. This suggests that a primary motive for a knowledge-oriented cybrary is in assisting users to overcome their fallibility.

CONCLUSIONS

Databases, books, journals, and Web sites, for all their immense value to humanity, are not knowing beings. In the provision of these information artefacts, cybraries are providing an essential service to higher education and research. However, our argument is that cybraries can be more explicitly knowledge oriented and provide even more value to society. If cybraries understand the nature of the essential features of human knowledge systems, then they can begin to reconceptualize themselves as, for example, facilitators of communication and relationships, contributors to transcendent intellectual work, and contributors to wisdom through being also concerned for values and ethics (or virtue epistemology). In short, our suggestions are very much concerned with the problems associated with managing for knowledge in the face of the inevitable fallibility of our normal intellectual activities and the need to acknowledge the value of the wise application of information and knowledge—with all that wisdom implies about ethics, balance, depth, insight, and so on—should be aimed for.

NOTES

1. For a more detailed discussion of our views on the nature of knowledge see Rooney and Schneider (2005).

REFERENCES

Archer, M. S. (1995). *Realist social theory: The morphogenetic approach.* Cambridge, England: Cambridge University Press.

Archer, M. S. (1996). *Culture and agency: The place of culture in social theory* (rev. ed.). Cambridge, England: Cambridge University Press.

Baltes, P. B., & Staudinger, U. M. (2000). A metaheuristic (pragmatic) to orchestrate mind and virtue towards excellence. *American Psychologist, 55*(1), 122–136.

Berger, P., & Luckmann, T. (1966). *The social construction of reality: A treatise in the sociology of knowledge.* New York: Doubleday.

Bhaskar, R. (1989). *Reclaiming reality: A critical introduction to contemporary philosophy.* London: Verso.

Bhaskar, R. (1998). *The possibility of naturalism: A philosophical critique of the contemporary human science* (3rd ed.). London: Routledge.

Bijker, W., & Law, J. (1992). *Shaping technology/building society: Studies in sociotechnical change.* Cambridge, MA: MIT Press.

Blackler, F. (1993). Knowledge and the theory of organizations: Organizations as activity systems and the reframing of management. *Journal of Management Studies, 30*(6), 863–884.

Blackler, F. (1995). Knowledge, knowledge work and organizations: An overview and interpretations. *Organization Studies, 16*(6), 1021–1046.

Boden, M. A. (2003). *The creative mind: Myths and mechanisms* (2nd ed.). London: Routledge.

Bohm, D. (2000). *Wholeness and the implicate order.* London: Routledge.

Boone, M. D. (2001a). Back in the USA: The cybrarian comes home. *Library Hi Tech, 19*(2), 186–191.

Boone, M. D. (2001b). Steering the cybrary into the twenty-first century: Who is the leader? *Library Hi Tech, 19*(3), 286–290.

Boone, M. D. (2002). Penn State's new "cybrary" at Harrisburg: A talk with Dr Harold Shill. *Library Hi Tech, 20*(2), 232–237.

Boulding, K. E. (1984). Foreword: A note on information, knowledge and production. In M. Jussawalla & H. Ebenfield (Eds.), *Communication and information econcomics: New perspectives* (pp. vii–ix). Amsterdam: North-Holland.

Burke, P. (2000). *A social history of knowledge: From Gutenberg to Diderot.* Cambridge, England: Polity Press.

Chia, R. (1998). From complexity science to complex thinking: Organization as simple location. *Organization, 5*(3), 341–369.

Cooke, H., Hornsby, E., & Todd, H. (2002, February). *The cybrary: Seamless for the customer, fine needlework for the staff.* Paper presented at the VALA2002 "E-volving Information Futures" 11th biennial conference and Exhibition, Melbourne, Australia.

David, P. A. (1994). Why are institutions the "carriers of history"? *Structural Change and Economic Dynamics, 5*(2), 205–220.

Duck, S. (2002). Hypertext in the key of G: Three types of "history" as influences on conversational structure and flow. *Communication Theory, 12*(1), 41–62.

Ellul, J. (1964). *The technological society* (J. Wilkinson, Trans.). New York: Vintage.

Engestrom, Y. (1991). Developmental work research: Reconstructing expertise through expansive learning. In M. Nurminen & G. Weir (Eds.), *Human jobs and computer interfaces* (pp. 265–103). Amsterdam: North.

Engestrom, Y. (1993). Work as a testbed for activity theory. In S. Chaiklin & J. Lave (Eds.), *Understanding practice: Perspectives on activity and context* (pp. 65–103). Cambridge, England: Cambridge University Press.

Ensor, P. (2000). *The cybrarian's manual.* Chicago: American Library Association.

Fuller, S. (1988). *Social epistemology.* Bloomington, IN: Indiana University Press.

Graham, P., & Rooney, D. (2001). A sociolinguistic approach to applied epistemology: Examining technocratic values in global "knowledge" policy. *Social Epistemology, 15*(3), 155–169.

Granovetter, M. S. (1973). The strength of weak ties. *American Journal of Sociology, 78*(1), 1360–1380.

Hansen, M. T. (1999). The search-transfer problem: The role of weak ties in sharing knowledge across organization subunits. *Administrative Science Quarterly, 44*, 82–111.

Hay, C. (2001). What place for ideas in the structure-agency debate? Globalisation as a "process without a subject," Vol. 2003: The Web Site for Critical Realism. Retrieved from www .raggedclaws.com/criticalrealism/archive/cshay_wpisad.html

Hearn, G., Rooney, D., & Mandeville, T. (2003). Phenomenological turbulence and innovation in knowledge systems. *Prometheus, 21*(2), 231–245.

Kusch, M. (2002). *Knowledge by agreement: The program of communitarian epistemology*. Oxford, England: Oxford University Press.

Lave, J., & Wenger, E. (1991). *Situated learning: Legitimate peripheral participation*. Cambridge, England: Cambridge University Press.

Luhmann, N. (1995). *Social systems* (John Bednarz, & with Dirk Baeker, Trans.). Stanford, CA: Stanford University Press.

Lundberg, M. J. (1974). *The incomplete adult: Social class constraints on personality development*. Westport, CT: Greenwood.

Luria, A. R. (1976). *Cognitive development: Its cultural and social foundations* (M. Lopez-Morillas & L. Solotaroff, Trans.). Cambridge, MA: Harvard University Press.

Metcalfe, J. S. (1999, July 12–14). *The evolution and development of evolutionary economics: Opening remarks*. Presentation to the Self-Organisation and the Evolutionary Agenda Workshop, the University of Queensland, Australia, Department of Economics.

Nonaka, I., Toyama, R., et al. (2000). SECI, *Ba* and leadership: A unified model of dynamic knowledge creation. *Long Range Planning, 33*, 5–34.

Rooney, D., Hearn, G., Mandeville, T., & Joseph, R. (2003). *Public policy in knowledge-based economies: Foundations and frameworks*. Cheltenham, England: Edward Elgar.

Rooney, D., & McKenna, B. (forthcoming). Wise management: An evaluation of historical discourse on wisdom and ethical action.

Rooney, D., & Schneider, U. (2005). A model of the tacit, explicit and social character of knowledge. In D. Rooney, G. Hearn, & A. Ninan (Eds.), *The knowledge economy handbook*. Cheltenham, England: Edward Elgar.

Schmidt, J., Turnbull, D., & Croud, J. (1999, July). *Cybrary support for learning, teaching and research at the University of Queensland—The 1998 university of the year*. Paper presented at the 24th international conference on Improving University Learning and Teaching, Brisbane, Australia.

Schneider, U. (2001). *Die 7 todsünden im wissensmanagement: kardinaltugenden für die wissensökonomie* [The seven deadly sins of knowledge management: Cardinal virtues for the knowledge economy]. Frankfurt am Main: Frankfurter Allgemeine Buch.

Scott, J. (2000). *Social network analysis: A handbook*. London: Thousands Oaks.

Simon, H. A. (1955). A behavioural model of rational choice. *Quarterly Journal of Economics, 69*, 99–118.

Simon, H. A. (1991). Bounded rationality and organizational learning. *Organization Science, 2*, 125–134.

Snowden, M. L. (2000, June). *Modeling organizational communication and knowledge management: A systems approach to evaluation and conceptualisation*. Paper presented at the 50th annual international Communication Association Conference, Acapulco, Mexico.

Spender, J.-C. (1996). Organizational knowledge, learning and memory: Three concepts in search of a theory. *Journal of Organizational Change Management, 9*(1), 63–78.

Stacey, R. D. (2001). *Complex responsive processes in organizations: Learning and knowledge creation*. London: Routledge.

Tsoukas, H. (1996). The firm as a distributed knowledge system: A constructionist approach [Winter Special Issue]. *Strategic Management Journal, 17*, 11–25.

von Krogh, G., Ichijo, K., & Nonaka, I. (2000). *Enabling knowledge creation: How to unlock the mystery of tacit knowledge and release the power of innovation*. Oxford, England: Oxford University Press.

Vygotsky, L. (1986). *Thought and language* (T. Alex Kozulin, Trans.). Cambridge, MA: MIT Press.

Walker, G., Kogut, B., & Shan, W. (2000). Social capital, structural holes and the formation of an industry network. In E. L. Lesser (Ed.), *Knowledge and social capital: Foundations and applications* (pp. 225–254). Boston: Butterworth Heinemann.

Wenger, E. (1999). *Communities of practice: Learning, meaning and identity*. Cambridge, England: Cambridge University Press.

Wenger, E. (2000). Communities of practice and social learning systems. *Organization, 7*(2), 225–246.

8

Cybraries in Paradise: New Technologies and Ethnographic Repositories

Linda Barwick
University of Sydney

Nicholas Thieberger
University of Melbourne

Digital technologies are altering research practices surrounding creation and use of ethnographic field recordings, and the methodologies and paradigms of the disciplines centered around their interpretation. This chapter discusses some examples of our current research practices as fieldworkers in active engagement with cultural heritage communities documenting music and language in the Asia-Pacific region, and as developers and curators of the digital repository PARADISEC (the Pacific and Regional Archive for Digital Sources in Endangered Cultures: http://paradisec.org.au). We suggest a number of benefits that the use of digital technologies can bring to the recording of material from small and endangered cultures, and to its reuse by communities and researchers. We believe it is a matter of social justice as well as scientific interest that ethnographic recordings held in higher education institutions should be preserved and made accessible to future generations. We argue that, with appropriate planning and care by researchers, digitization of research recordings in audiovisual media can facilitate access by remote communities to records of their cultural heritage held in higher education institutions to a far greater extent than was possible in the analog age.

The advantages of using audio recording technology for ethnographic and scientific purposes were understood from early in the 20th century. In 1900, Léon Azoulay, the French anthropologist, was perhaps the first to point out the possibilities for systematic analysis of sound made possible by the ability to reproduce at will and in fixed detail what had hitherto been an evanescent mode of human production:

> Nor is it possible for linguistics to faithfully represent the speech of living languages even with the help of its arbitrary and totally insufficient transcriptions, made up for want of better and which no agreement has ever made uniform . . . all that of which linguistics is incapable, the phonograph from now on makes possible. (Azoulay, 1900, p. 175)

Azoulay foresaw the establishment of phonographic museums, and his own collection of 388 cylinders recorded at the Paris Universal Exposition of 1900 was to form the basis of the first French phonographic archive (Pitoëff, 1993). As predicted by Azoulay, audiovisual recordings now constitute primary data for linguistics, musicology, anthropology, oral history, and other humanities disciplines. Much publication in these areas depends on researchers' transcriptions and analysis of their own field recordings of language, music, and events.

However, we now stand at a point where the audiovisual documentary heritage created in analog recordings is reaching a crisis of format obsolescence (Council on Library and Information Resources, CLIR, 2001). It is now recognized that digitization is the only effective way to maintain access to analog audio recordings (DigiCULT Consortium, 2004; Humanities Advanced Technology and Information Institute, HATII, & National Initiative for a Networked Cultural Heritage, NINCH, 2002; National Library of Australia, NLA, 2000). This is an international problem. The technical committee of the International Association of Sound Archives has estimated that, worldwide, 100 million hours of unique analog recordings in archives need digitizing—far more than can possibly be processed in the lifetime of the dwindling number of functional analog playback machines—and this estimate does not include recordings in higher education institutions (Boston, 2003; Bradley, 2003; Schüller, 2004; Wright & Williams, 2001).

Whereas planning for digitization of recordings held in specialist audiovisual archives is relatively advanced, analog research recordings in higher education institutions face particular issues. The solitary nature of much humanities research practice and the ready availability of inexpensive consumer audio recording technologies (e.g., audiocassette) has led to the accumulation of many private research collections of important audiovisual data *held* within higher education institutions, but not necessarily *registered* with them. All too often, when researchers retire or die, their orphaned collections languish forgotten in filing cabinets or, even worse, are disposed of by relatives who do not understand their cultural significance. Furthermore, as is discussed further later, our own research institutions often have not realized the significance of these recordings, regarding them as by-products of our research, rather than integral to it.

In our research practice, we frequently confront the discrepancies and inequalities between our relatively privileged Western knowledge institutions and the remote communities with whom we collaborate. In our work, the "digital divide" (Benton Foundation Digital Divide Network Staff, 2004; Gorski, 2001; Macharia, 2004) is only too apparent, most obviously in the geographic and economic impediments to the availability of infrastructure for electronic information and communication technologies within the communities with which we work. But there is another aspect to the digital divide, one that is perhaps less obvious to the outside observer, but equally if not more significant if we wish to ensure the communication of our research results to the tradition bearers. This relates to the lack of technological development to enable discovery, description, and citation of the audiovisual media formats in which much culturally significant content is most appropriately recorded.

Western knowledge institutions and research methodologies have favored and developed formats and media that best suit text-based modes of scholarly communication. Many other societies preserve and transmit cultural knowledge instead by nontextual means, such as musical, dramatic, verbal, and visual arts. It is, therefore, no coincidence that audiovisual recordings—the primary formats in which the languages, performance traditions, and other knowledge of preliterate cultures have been captured by researchers for documentation and analysis—are of continuing interest to the communities of those recorded, indeed of more interest than the theoretical articles produced about or based on the recordings (Seeger, 2004, p. 1). This is an issue that has been poorly understood by many research institutions.

Our research institutions tend to see the preservation, indexation, and even digitization of ethnographic *texts* as part of their core business, whereas the research *recordings* on which they depend are seen as mere by-products of the research. Preservation of and access to the ethnographic articles of, say, the 1920s have been well-served by university libraries, which have pushed the development of appropriate technologies for making textual material available in digital form. Written articles of this period are easily discovered through interoperable online library catalogues; if not already available in electronic form, then texts can be digitized and distributed quickly and accurately by means of widely available copying and optical character recognition software (all the more so because they are now out of copyright); and the standardized apparatus of scholarly referencing together with the ability to cite excerpts of textual documents directly within one's own text means that researchers can easily engage with the texts and their ideas at a fine level of detail. By contrast, preservation and access to the wax cylinders of the same period has been the domain of specialist sound archives rather than university libraries. Many, if not most, ethnographic wax cylinder recordings were unpublished and thus not systematically collected or described in mainstream university library catalogues. Only specialist sound archives and a few individual collectors have the means to replay fragile wax cylinder recordings, and standardized means of describing the specialized content and citing it at a close level of granularity are only now beginning to emerge. These are impediments for researchers, but far more so for communities who now wish to regain access to their heritage in audiovisual media.

The application of digital technologies within our research practice may seem incongruous and even inequitable to those who see new technologies as exemplars of the privilege and consumerism of the developed world, complicit in globalization by providing instant access to information across regional and national boundaries. Yet, as Feld (1994) observed, the tendency to homogenize associated with globalization can be opposed by the ability of each locale—if it can afford it—to reflect on itself and its identity, using the same technologies. In fact, digital technologies are already being used by community members themselves to preserve ethnodiversity through locally made recordings, and researchers' access to the means of production and safekeeping of recordings is highly valued by many of our community collaborators.

The next three sections deal with particular instances of current practice in using digital resources in ethnographic research. The Belyuen Bangany Wangga local repository, established in the Northern Territory community of Belyuen in 2002, is an example of a local repository for digital access to audio recordings of songs from the community, a resource originally compiled for research purposes by Barwick and her collaborators. The linguistic case study discusses Thieberger's use of digital technologies in his research on the language of South Efate, from Vanuatu. Finally, we discuss the rationale and practices used in establishing a new digital repository, from our experiences in establishing PARADISEC in 2003–2004.

CASE STUDY 1: BELYUEN BANGANY WANGGA LOCAL REPOSITORY

The following case study reports on collaborative efforts by researchers and communities in the Daly region of northwest Australia to establish suitable practical platforms for digital repatriation of archival audio recordings. Barwick and her collaborators, musicologist Allan Marett and linguist Lysbeth Ford, have been centrally involved in establishing such facilities in the Daly region communities of Belyuen (formerly known as Delissaville) and Wadeye (formerly known as Port Keats) in the Northern Territory. The present case study focuses on the digital audio access workstation established at Belyuen, located on the Cox Peninsula southwest of Darwin, current population around 300. The workstation is named *Belyuen Bangany Wangga* ("Belyuen Song and Dance") in Batjamalh, the largest of the five community languages.

For centuries, Aboriginal people of the Daly region of northwestern Northern Territory have been performing their music for outsiders. Music and dance performances continue to form an integral component of ceremonial exchange and trade relationships with neighboring Indigenous groups, and musical performances for non-Indigenous people have been documented from the time of early settlement of the Darwin area. Sound recordings of such performances, dating from as early as 1942, are held in private collections, state and national sound archives, and some recordings (notably those made in the course of anthropological expeditions led by Charles Mountford and A. P. Elkin) have been published, distributed, and broadcast nationally and internationally (Elkin, 1957, 1953; Mountford, 1949). From the 1980s to the present, Marett, Barwick, and Ford have been involved in making new recordings of Belyuen singers.

Residents of Belyuen have included some of the most prolific and influential composers and singers of the public didjeridu-accompanied *wangga* song genre, also known as Nyindi-yindi. These singers include Jimmy Bunduck, George Ahmat, Tommy Burrenjuck, Bobby Lane, Jimmy Mulluk, Billy Mandji, Rusty Moreen, Colin Worambu Ferguson, Kenny Burrenjuck, Simon Moreen, David Woodie, and Roger Yarrowin. With funding from the Northern Territory Library and Information Service, a digital audio workstation *Belyuen Bangany Wangga* was established in 2002 to give local public access to archival recordings of these Belyuen singers (Barwick, 2003; Marett, 2003). The collection of some 480 Wangga songs now held in the *Belyuen Bangany Wangga* digital audio workstation represents a rich local tradition comprising many ethnographic recordings that, having been dispersed in different archives all over the world, have now returned to the home community.

Discovering Archival Recordings

During the 1990s, Barwick and her research team investigated archival holdings of recordings from the Daly region, initially in order to compare them with current musical practices in the region. It soon emerged that there was great interest in having access to these archival recordings within the community. The compilation of archival recordings made available on the *Belyuen Bangany Wangga* access workstation is the result of years of collaborative research between researchers and the community.

Some archival detective work and musicological expertise was necessary to identify early recordings as coming from the communities in question. Candidate recordings for repatriation were identified in the first instance by searching the catalogues of relevant national collections such as the Australian Institute for Aboriginal and Torres Strait Islander Studies (AIATSIS), the ABC Radio Archives, and the National Film and Sound Archive. However, initial catalogue searches did not necessarily reveal all relevant recordings. The reasons for this situation are many and complex, and our eventual success depended on close acquaintance with community members and local song styles, as well as knowledge of the historical circumstances in which early recordings were made and disseminated, and a willingness to engage with the difficult cataloguing systems of a number of different archival institutions.

The biggest impediment to discovering the recordings was that early sound recordists sometimes failed to collect the singers' names and communities of origin. For example, the recording place of the earliest recording from Belyuen, made in 1942 by ABC war correspondent Peter Hemery,[1] was deliberately omitted from the record because of the strategic importance for the Australian war effort of radar stations located near Belyuen community. Language difficulties may have prevented recordists from noting accurate information about singers, most of whom have learned English as a second language. Anthropological interest in group ownership and participation in ceremonial performances may also have contributed to the failure of anthropologists such as A. P. Elkin to record the names of individual singers (Elkin & Jones, 1958). To further complicate an already complex situation, people from these communities, especially singers, frequently traveled to other places for work or social reasons, so that the identification of the community of origin of a singer was not always known to recordists. For example, one Belyuen singer was variously recorded by four different researchers at many different locations between 1959 and 1988: at Bagot, Darwin, Mandorah, Batchelor, Katherine, Beswick, Daly River in the Northern Territory, and Kununurra in Western Australia, as well as his home community of Belyuen. Furthermore, people may be known by different names in different communities. For example, one singer, who resides occasionally at both Belyuen and Wadeye, is known by a different surname in each place.

Another impediment to identification of candidate recordings was that some old recordings—notably those made by ABC recordists in collaboration with the anthropologists C. P. Mountford in 1948 and A. P. Elkin in 1952–1953—were edited for radio broadcasts, film soundtracks, published compilations, and sometimes further disseminated on unpublished process discs and tapes to interested researchers. This has resulted in a confusing number of different instances of the same recording appearing in different archives. Further complications in identifying instances of the same recording resulted from the varying attribution of authorship of the same recording to the ABC recordist, supervising sound engineer, or anthropologist who directed the entire expedition (e.g., some recordings attributed to Charles P. Mountford were actually made by ABC sound recordist Ray Giles, supervised by journalist Colin Simpson).

Indexing the Recordings

Barwick visited the various archives holding relevant material and obtained digital audio tape (DAT) copies from the access reel-to-reel copies. She originally made cassette copies for replay in the community, but as the project developed, digital audio replayed via computer was increasingly used. Compared to audiocassettes, the digital versions of recordings were significantly easier to work with in replay, transcription, and documentation of the song because of improved audio quality, random access to individual songs, and improved ability to isolate problematic passages and where necessary slow them down for transcription. Once candidate recordings were assembled from archival resources, Barwick and her research collaborators replayed them to community members in order to identify the singers and other performers, and document contextual information about the performance, the topic and composer of each song, and where possible the song text and its translation. This information was then combined with the archival description to produce a catalogue of each song in the collection, the occasions on which it had been performed, and the recordings on which it occurred.

Designing Local Access to Archival Recordings

Until recently, there was limited infrastructure for storing sound recordings and making them accessible within the community. Belyuen school held copies of some recordings on cassette and VHS video, but there was no systematic attempt to assemble a collection. From time to time, people from the community visited Canberra to retrieve cassette copies of recordings from the AIATSIS sound archives. As the research project proceeded, Barwick and her collaborators distributed cassette copies of archival recordings to collaborators within the community on each occasion that the research team returned. However, these cassette copies tended to be shortlived. Frequently, the cassette copies obtained from archives, being third generation copies of analog originals, were relatively low fidelity and did not appeal to the ear. Both research team and community members were enthusiastic at the prospect of providing ongoing local access to recordings in digital form.

In deciding on the appropriate platform for local access, the community and researchers wanted to make the collection searchable by locally relevant categories, but also to provide information to allow the recordings to be located in the source archival collections. The components needed to be sturdy, modular, and reasonably inexpensive, using locally sustainable technologies and personnel. Community interest tended to center on particular songs and performers, so it was decided for community access to provide access at the level of the song rather than the whole recording. An iTunes database on an Apple eMac computer provided cost-effective, stable, and scriptable access that enabled individuals within the community to choose their own selection of songs.

Permissions from rights holders (i.e., institutions and/or recordists), as well as performers and their families, were sought and documented before launching the database. The community decided to restrict initial access to Belyuen itself, but at a future date it is likely that a selection of Belyuen recordings will be made publicly available through the Northern Territory Library and Information Service and/or the University of Sydney. A CD of Belyuen music, *Rak Badjalarr* (Marett, Barwick & Ford, 2001), published by AIATSIS in 2001, has made available a selection of the results of this research for the repertory of the singer Bobby Lane Lambudju (1941–1993), including archival recordings made by Alice Moyle and LaMont West. Further CDs of other Belyuen singers are planned.

CASE STUDY 2: LANGUAGE DOCUMENTATION AND THE ETHNOGRAPHIC CYBRARY

Making data available and reusable are two central foci of Thieberger's description of the indigenous language of South Efate (Central Vanuatu). The documentation of South Efate has taken into account newly emerging tools and processes that can be used to represent spoken natural language. Linguists routinely record endangered languages for which no prior documentation exists. This is vitally important work that often records language structures and knowledge of the culture and physical environment that would otherwise be lost (Maffi, 2001). However, although it is typical for the interpretation and analysis of this data to be published, the raw data is rarely made available. The data (tapes, field notes, photographs, and perhaps video) are often not properly described, catalogued, or made accessible, especially in the absence of a dedicated repository. Developments in technologies now make it possible for audio and video data to be made widely available and readily searchable, subject to intellectual property issues, the enforcement of which is also gaining more attention.

A field linguist typically engages in recording aspects of a language for analysis in a written grammar. As argued by Duranti (1997), grammars are necessarily partial documents that contain analysis of the parts of the language that are currently considered necessary to include in a style that is currently fashionable. Looking back over grammars written in the past makes one aware of how such fashions change and how difficult it can be to find information about topics not covered in the grammar. Efforts to relearn languages based on historical materials—as is becoming increasingly important to many Indigenous Australians, for example—have also highlighted the importance of a well-described broad range of language usage data that is securely archived.

There is a growing awareness of the need for a fieldworker to be recording as much information in as many contexts in the field as possible, because their recordings may well be the only documentation made of the language. A concomitant is the importance of data management for the preservation of our audio and video recordings and photographs so that they will be available for others beyond our own use of them. Himmelmann (1998) observed that documentation and description are two parts of the activity engaged in by field linguists, but that documentation has traditionally been considered a secondary task to the production of a language description. In a similar vein, Woodbury (2003) noted that language documentation has always been a part of the linguistic effort, but new technological approaches offer a way of refocusing our work. Bird and Simons (2003) discussed the technological implications of developing a dataset that will endure over time and remain accessible.

Emphasizing the documentation means that certain products of our work, such as text collections and dictionaries, become primary rather than incidental. Similarly, our concern with the reusability of our work takes on a primary focus so that the data has a use for others after we have done our analysis. Reusability is a concept from computer programming and from ecology ("Reduce, reuse, recycle"), whereby we should do a task once and then be able to address the outputs of that process rather than repeating the work involved. We need tools to enable us to work with field recordings in a way that allows their further use as archival objects. The workflow following recording includes creating citable archival files with persistent identifiers. Any annotations that we make must be clearly related to the archival files. Such annotations, from a linguistic point of view, are transcriptions, interlinearized texts, and concordances, together with broader linguistic analysis.

With appropriate tools, we can build good archival practice into our normal workflow for minimal extra effort. For example, we have tools that permit text and audio to be linked so that we can create a corpus for an otherwise unrecorded language. These annotated recordings are of far greater use than they would be as audio alone. In the South Efate data, there are currently some 20 hours of digitized field tapes that can be accessed via a textual concordance. This represents a significant part of the work done toward Thieberger's doctoral thesis (Thieberger, 2004b), and has involved preparing a dataset for analysis in a manner that will be reusable and archivable.

Audio-Text Linkage for Archival Access

It is now relatively simple to provide indexes of media files in the form of time aligned transcripts, and these are far more useful as archival material than is a tape with minimal metadata. Personal computers have been around since the mid-1980s, and it has been possible since the late-1980s to link digital audio and text by segmenting the sound into utterance-length chunks (Thieberger, 1994; Vallentine, 1992), but by the mid-1990s there was still no method for linking text and audio suitable for developing a media corpus for use in writing a dissertation. Similarly, there was no analytical tool to access all field tapes via a textual representation. Segmentation of the audio data is not a sensible option because it is too time consuming and detrimental to the very context of the utterances it is so important to preserve.

Having established a time aligned transcript—one that had a chunk of text together with a start and end point in the audio file—there was in the late-1990s no simple way of then instantiating those links, that is, of hearing the audio associated with any given textual chunk. Thieberger wrote a working tool called *Audiamus* in HyperCard that allows access to the linked data instantly via a concordance point of entry to the data. A second version of *Audiamus* has been prepared using the cross-platform software *Runtime Revolution* (Thieberger, 2004a). The data in this corpus is citable by timecode, and, in the repository established with PARADISEC, it is locatable via a universal resource identifier (URI). It will be possible to provide streaming access to the audio in this dataset in the future. This means that a URL of the following kind will be able to be resolved: <http://paradisec.org.au/NT1/NT1-98009-98009A.wav:57.4200-60.2238>. That is, a data repository can serve selected time chunks within media files linked to transcripts. By creating the data in a reusable form, it ensures that such steps are possible when the resources required are put to developing a streaming server. It is an important part of Thieberger's dissertation that all possible examples, all exemplary texts, and a representative version of the field tapes can be heard by the reader. In linguistics theses, the data is usually given as an example sentence, often with no indication of its status or provenance. In other sciences, data is provided so that claims can be tested and results can be replicated. If we believe that linguistics employs the scientific method, then accessible presentation of the data is necessary for verification. Furthermore, the transcript provides a detailed annotation of the media that will also make the archival form of far greater value than it would be as an untranscribed tape.

CASE STUDY 3: ESTABLISHING PARADISEC AS A NEW DIGITAL REPOSITORY

A major benefit of digital repositories is that they can be established without the kind of infrastructure associated with libraries in the past. PARADISEC is a collaborative cross-institutional and cross-disciplinary research resource established in 2003 by the Universities of Sydney, Melbourne, and Australian National University (joined in 2004 by University of New England), with support from the Australian Research Council's Linkage Infrastructure Equipment and Facilities scheme. The project is collaborative and cross-institutional, with our audio archiving unit in Sydney, our project manager in Melbourne, and our Web site and main data store hosted in Canberra at ANU and the Australian Partnership for Advanced Computing mass digital storage facility. We are also cross-disciplinary, with our chief investigators comprising leading linguists, musicologists, anthropologists, and computer scientists with a common concern to preserve and make accessible in digital form Australian researchers' field recordings of endangered languages and musics from the Asia-Pacific region.

Digitization of audiovisual media allows not only preservation, but also registration of these recordings. Registration in a well-managed repository can allow previously little-known, poorly described, and inaccessible recording collections to become discoverable to researchers and communities worldwide if the repository contributes metadata to global networks for discovery and access. Furthermore, digitization facilitates standardized description of recording contents through time-coded transcripts, offering the prospect of more accurate citation than possible before, and, with e-publication and appropriate digital rights management, the prospect of direct citation of primary data within research publications.

Formats and Standards

PARADISEC was initially established as a means for transferring existing field recordings to digital format, recognizing that audiotapes themselves are becoming endangered as the media deteriorate and the machines for reading them become obsolete. PARADISEC has been able to move quickly to digitize field recordings that were in a state of disrepair, and to place the data onto an accessible medium together with a metadata set adequate for describing the data. We adopt international archival standards and formats, and archive recordings using the Quadriga audio archiving system, as 24-bit 96 kilohertz Broadcast Wave Format files, which encapsulate the uncompressed linear PCM audio with summary metadata (European Broadcast Union, 1997).

Establishing a good cataloguing (metadata) set for the collection has also required conforming to international standards (see Hunter, chap. 6, this volume). In particular, metadata standards developed by the Open Language Archives Community (OLAC: http://www.language-archives .org) have been central to making our metadata conformant to the requirements of the Open Archives Initiative (OAI: http://www.openarchives .org). Adoption of these standards allows us to make endangered language material harvestable and discoverable via standard search mechanisms. Similar work in Europe by other digital endangered languages archives such as that of Dokumentation Bedrohter Sprachen (DOBES: http://www .mpi.nl/DOBES) and the Endangered Languages Archive (ELAR: http:// www.hrelp.org/archive) may also prove useful in the near future, but was not accessible during the initial period of PARADISEC's operation. In 2003, PARADISEC joined with other digital archives with similar disciplinary orientations to form the Digital Endangered Languages and Musics Archives Network (DELAMAN: http://www.delaman.org), which aims to share expertise about digital archive management, to encourage researchers to adopt international best practice, and to explore the feasibility of distributed resource management across the network.

The PARADISEC repository has been constructed by specialists in the content area represented by the collection. The consortium of researchers who successfully applied for funds and then implemented the project are fieldworkers who have recognized the need for an archive to house their recordings. The team extends into information technology areas in modeling the data to be archived and in discussing with technologists the relations between objects in the collection and how these relations can be managed in the repository. Where specialist skills are required, we have been able to buy them: for example, employing an audio preservation officer who is skilled at digitizing data from analog tape.

Archiving requires that data be in a form that allows it to be useful in the future to researchers other than the depositor. To encourage researchers to produce well-formed data, we provide training in recording techniques and in description of the data recorded. We encourage fieldworkers to build these techniques into their ordinary practice so that the recordings they produce are optimal and are able to be lodged with PARADISEC for safekeeping and persistent identification. These citable media files can then be referred to in all further analysis and can be used by others to verify the analysis (always subject to deposit and access conditions).

We have identified a number of collections of audiotapes that need to be processed, some in urgent need of treatment before they can be played due to their storage conditions, or their age, or both. We prioritize the digitization of the tapes based on a number of factors, including the immediate need that a community or a researcher may have for access to that material. For example, we knew of tapes made by an anthropologist in Papua New Guinea in the 1960s and were approached by a linguist wanting to work on the language from the same area. We accessioned the tapes into the collection and made copies available to the linguist who was then able to begin learning and analyzing the language. Similarly, recordings made by Stephen Wurm in the Reef Islands of the Solomon Islands in the 1960s will be taken back to that community by researchers working there in 2005.

In August 2004, little more than a year after commissioning the audio digitization facility, PARADISEC had identified over 3,000 hours of unique field recordings (1,466 individual items) that require digitization, representing over 150 languages from 16 different countries in the Asia-Pacific region. More collections are emerging all the time; 1,000 hours of recordings have been digitized to date, provided to depositors both on access audio CD format and via password-protected access to our online repository, where we provide the archival master and another access version in MP3 format. All items in the queue, whether or not digitized, are discoverable via the OLAC search engine (http://www.language-archives.org/tools/search/?archive=paradisec.org.au), and in 2004 we are in the process of developing a web interface to the collection.

Regional Access to Digital Archival Data

As digital ethnographic repositories are built, the metadata describing their contents can be made available via the Internet, and providing appropriate international standards are adopted and shared, searches across repositories can make metadata discoverable by the relevant research or cultural communities wherever Internet access is available. Digital data can be accessed remotely via the Internet, and copies can be made and distributed with no loss of quality, in contrast with analog data, which suffers a reduction in quality with each generation of copying. Where appropriate local facilities are available, a local repository mirroring the holdings of remote archives can be set up as a point of access and distribution of recordings, with far lower entry and infrastructure costs than a traditional archive or library.

Of course, it is crucial to observe and enforce intellectual property and moral rights in this material, but a major difficulty in establishing appropriate arrangements for reuse of field recordings is that those recorded typically live in small and perhaps remote locations. By establishing relations with national or local cultural centers, it becomes more feasible for ethnographic repositories to locate speakers or performers and their descendants. This will only be possible if there is sufficient metadata associated with a tape to allow us to locate its source—if not, for example, a speaker's name, then at least a geographical location is crucial.

Although there is a clear need to ensure safe long-term storage of ethnographic materials, it is fair to observe that access to digital data is quite uneven, especially in the region around Australia (Molnar & Meadows, 2001). In 2004, for example, the University of the South Pacific in Vanuatu had a local area network with comparatively slow access to the Internet, and the Vanuatu Kaljoral Senta had dial-up access only on individual computers. The Vanuatu National Library provided no Internet access and no public access computers (Williams, 2002). Furthermore, as Williams (1998) noted: "In all the Pacific Islands, the value of the archives and museums are not recognized as the repositories that hold and preserve the national and cultural heritage and identity of a country. These institutions are given minimal recurrent funding and are barely surviving" (p. 1). Some support for regional archives has been provided by the Pacific Manuscripts Bureau (PAMBU: http://rspas.anu.edu.au/pambu), which has microfilmed many thousands of pages of unique material, but, although copies of these films are held in various locations in the region, microfilm readers are rare and are a difficult-to-maintain technology in this context where personal computers are actually more familiar and easier to find.

Individual computer users located anywhere in the Vanuatu archipelago with a phone line can, in theory, have dial-up access, but most villages have intermittent or nonexistent electricity supply. With a basic wage of around AUD $200 per month, there is little scope for most Vanuatu residents to own computers. Nevertheless, computers are common in all government offices and local centers. For audio material, CD players are increasingly replacing cassette tape players and could be considered the current baseline technology with which to deliver archival audio material at the village level. PARADISEC has been actively working to provide appropriate support to the Vanuatu Kaljoral Senta by providing CD copies of relevant holdings in its collection, and by assisting with advice on backing up of data.

CONCLUSIONS

This chapter has presented several examples of the importance of digital technologies for the practice of ethnography, especially when working with small and endangered cultures and languages. The interaction between field recording (as in the Belyuen and South Efate examples) and the long-term storage of its products (as in the PARADISEC example) is crucial to both citability of data, and access to the data by speakers and their descendants. Indeed, we see that there is a crucial interaction between recordings made in the field with sufficient metadata for their discovery, and their subsequent location in a suitable repository. Later, this is followed by their reintroduction to their community because they are located (using web-based search mechanisms) by those recorded or their descendants.

The humanities disciplines are currently going through a major paradigm shift in methodologies and relationships with primary data. The creation of new communicative fields through technological developments has generated an increasing emphasis on teamwork and collaboration between humanities researchers, cultural heritage communities, and technological specialists who can help us to realize our aspirations and envision new ones. Humanities scholars and community bodies need to engage in the fora that decide the strategic directions of research policy and funding, to ensure that technological development understands and embraces our needs. We also need to make sure that present and future generations of humanities researchers are educated to understand and embrace a role in creating and managing resources that will contribute to the future of both our disciplines and the cultural heritage communities with which we interact.

As fieldworkers, we welcome the opportunity to use digital representations of data to facilitate access by those recorded and their descendants in a way that was not possible using analog recordings (Barwick, 2004). For this reason, we wish to ensure that our recordings are archived using the best possible methods, with sufficient descriptive material (metadata) to provide for their discovery, on media that allow the data to be migrated over time, and in sustainable institutional contexts. From a scholarly perspective, we wish to ensure that the digital data we create as part of our intellectual endeavor as ethnographers is reusable, both by ourselves and by others, first because any claims that we make based on that data must be replicable and provable by others, and second, because the effort and expense of creating a digital representation of the data should not be duplicated, but rather serve as a foundation for others to build on.

Despite the apparent gap between the consumerism of new technologies and the (cash) poverty of those recorded, we argue that, as professional ethnographers, we need to use the best current tools to do the work expected of us. As Seeger (2004, p. 1) commented: "The digital future will only be as rich as the materials supplied to the institutions distributing them. Many details will need to be worked out over time, but they all begin with the researcher."

NOTES

1. Australian Broadcasting Corporation Radio Archives Disc NAT2–3, Australian Broadcasting Corporation archives tape number 72/10/543 with commentary; 72/10/544 without commentary; AIATSIS sound archives tape A2915.

REFERENCES

Azoulay, L. (1900). L'ère nouvelle des sons et des bruits: Musées et archives phonographiques [The new age of sound and noise: Phonographic archives and museums]. *Bulletins et Memoires de la Société d'Anthropologie de Paris*, *1*(3), 172–178.

Barwick, L. (2003). The Endangered Cultures Research Group's digitisation project: using digital audio for musicological research. In C. Cole & H. Craig (Eds.), *Computing Arts 2001: Digital resources for research in the humanities* (pp. 147–159). University of Sydney: Research Institute for Humanities and Social Sciences, University of Sydney, in association with the Australian Academy of the Humanities.

Barwick, L. (2004). Turning it all upside down . . . Imagining a distributed digital audiovisual archive. *Literary and Linguistic Computing*, *19*(3), 253–263.

Benton Foundation Digital Divide Network Staff. (2004). *Digital divide basics fact sheet*. Retrieved August 14, 2004, from http://www.digitaldividenetwork.org/content/stories/index.cfm?key=168

Bird, S., & Simons, G. (2003). Seven dimensions of portability for language documentation and description. *Language*, *79*, 557–582.

Boston, G. (2003, November). *Survey of Endangered Audiovisual Carriers, 2003*. Survey conducted by George Boston, Secretary, Technical Committee of the International Association of Sound and Audiovisual Archives (IASA) with assistance from the International Council of Archives, on behalf of UNESCO's Information Society Division. Retrieved August 14, 2004, from http://portal.unesco.org/ci/ev.php?URL_ID=13437&URL_DO=DO_TOPIC&URL_SECTION=201&reload=1073385878&PHPSESSID=019c5625ccdffaf7095faf0aade5c128

Bradley, K. (2003). *Critical choices, critical decisions: Sound archiving and changing technology*. Retrieved August 14, 2004, from http://conferences.arts.usyd.edu.au/viewabstract.php?id=57&cf=2

Council on Library and Information Resources (CLIR). (2001). *Folk Heritage Collections in Crisis*. Retrieved August 14, 2004, from http://www.clir.org/pubs/reports/pub96/contents.html

DigiCULT Consortium. (2004). *DigiCULT: Technology challenges for digital culture*. Retrieved August 14, 2004, from http://www.digicult.info

Duranti, A. (1997). *Linguistic Anthropology*. New York: Cambridge University Press.

Elkin, A. P. (1953). Tribal Music of Australia [LP record]. Washington, D.C.: Folkways Records FE4439.

Elkin, A. P. (1957). Arnhem Land Volume 1: Authentic Aboriginal Songs and Dances [LP record]. Sydney: EMI (Australia) OALP7504.

Elkin, A. P., & Jones, T. (1958). *Arnhem Land Music*. Sydney: University of Sydney.

European Broadcast Union. (1997). *Specification of the Broadcast Wave Format: A format for audio data files in broadcasting*. Retrieved November 14, 2004, from http://www.ebu.ch/trev_t3285.pdf

Feld, S. (1994). From schizophonia to schismogenesis: On the discourses and commodification practices of "world music" and "world beat." In C. Keil & S. Feld (Eds.), *Music Grooves* (pp. 257–289). Chicago: Chicago University Press.

Gorski, P. (2001). *Multicultural education and the digital divide.* Retrieved August 14, 2004, from http://www.mhhe.com/socscience/education/multi/philosophy/4divide.html
Himmelmann, N. P. (1998). Documentary and descriptive linguistics. *Linguistics, 36,* 161–195.
Humanities Advanced Technology and Information Institute (HATII), & National Initiative for a Networked Cultural Heritage (NINCH). (2002). *The NINCH guide to good practice in the digital representation and management of cultural heritage materials.* Retrieved August 14, 2004, from http://www.nyu.edu/its/humanities/ninchguide/
Macharia, M. (2004). *Global digital divide: Targeting rural and economically-challenged communities.* Retrieved August 14, 2004, from *http:/www.digitaldividenetwork.org/content/stories/index.cfm?key=96*
Maffi, L. (Ed.). (2001). *On biocultural diversity: Linking language, knowledge and the environment.* Washington, D.C.: Smithsonian Institution.
Marett, A. (2003). *Sound recordings as maruy among the Aborigines of the Daly region of north-west Australia.* Retrieved from http://conferences.arts.usyd.edu.au/viewabstract.php?id=40&cf=2
Marett, A., Barwick, L., & Ford, L. (2001). *Rak Badjalarr: Wangga songs by Bobby Lane, Northern Australia* [audio compact disc]. Canberra: Aboriginal Studies Press.
Molnar, H., & Meadows, M. (2001). *Songlines to satellites: Indigenous communication in Australia, the South Pacific and Canada.* Annandale, NSW and Wellington: Pluto Press and Huia.
Mountford, C. P. (1949). American-Australian Scientific Expedition to Arnhem Land 1948 [9 78 rpm records]. Sydney: Australian Broadcasting Commission.
National Library of Australia (NLA). (2000). *National Library of Australia Digitisation Policy 2000–2004.* Retrieved August 14, 2004, from http://www.nla.gov.au/policy/digitisation.html
Pitoëff, P. (1993). Du cylindre au disque compact. Les archives sonores du Musée de l'Homme (Paris) [From wax cylinder to compact disc. The sound archives of the Musée de l'Homme (Paris)]. *Annuario degli Archivi di Etnomusicologia dell'Accademia Nazionale di Santa Cecilia, 1,* 143–149.
Schüller, D. (2004). Safeguarding the Documentary Heritage of Cultural and Linguistic Diversity. *Language Archive Newsletter, 1*(3), 9–10.
Seeger, A. (2004). *SIMS 2004 New Technology Handout.* Unpublished manuscript, Melbourne, Australia.
Thieberger, N. (1994). *Australia's Indigenous languages information stacks.* Retrieved August 14, 2004, from oai:aseda.aiatsis.gov.au:0531
Thieberger, N. (2004a). Audiamus (Version 2) [computer program]. Melbourne, Australia.
Thieberger, N. (2004b). *Topics in the grammar and documentation of South Efate, an oceanic language of Central Vanuatu.* Unpublished PhD thesis, University of Melbourne, Melbourne, Australia.
Vallentine, J. R. (1992). *Rook: A system for authoring descriptive grammars in HyperCard for the Apple Macintosh computer.* Retrieved August 14, 2004, from oai:aseda.aiatsis.gov.au:0499
Williams, E. B. (1998). *Information needs in the Pacific islands: Needs assessment for library, archive, audiovisual collection and ICT development in the Pacific islands.* Apia, Samoa: UNESCO Office for the Pacific States.
Williams, E. B. (2002). *Digital community services: Pacific libraries and archives, future prospects and responsibilities.* Suva: UNESCO.
Woodbury, A. C. (2003). Defining documentary linguistics. In P. K. Austin (Ed.), *Language documentation and description* (Vol. 1, pp. 35–51). London: Hans Rausing Endangered Languages Project.
Wright, R., & Williams, A. (2001). *PRESTO-W2-BBC-001218 archive preservation and exploitation requirements.* Retrieved August 14, 2004, from http://presto.joanneum.ac.at/Public/D2.pdf

9

Redefining Libr@ries by Rethinking Research

Cushla Kapitzke
University of Queensland

> *Symbolizing the "place" where all knowledge and non-knowledge can be found or is housed, the [libr@ry] is an enigmatic construct of both imaginary concord and very real resilience. . . . the "archive of its archives" remains haunted from the start by a specter of the past and a dream of the future.*
>
> —Trifonas (2000, pp. 116–117)

Two paradoxes of considerable import framed the conceptualization of this chapter. A key macrolevel issue was that whereas educational institutions of Western nation-states profess civic and democratic values, they remain oblivious to or complicit with government hypocrisy on the disparities of wealth and well-being created by unrestrained global capital (cf. Apple & Beane, 1999; Hertz, 2001). The second paradox, which is at a microlevel, relates specifically to libraries and the scholarly study of them. It was that, within the context of a wealth of available theoretical and methodological approaches from which researchers can draw, the extant literature on tech-nologized libraries seemed, in my view, somewhat socially disconnected, politically naïve, and theoretically impoverished.

This dearth of theoretical and methodological diversity persuaded me to quote Trifonas (2000), even though his use of the term *place* refers to

151

modern universities and not to libr@ries. His deconstruction of the modern university exposes the "irrationality" of its technoscientific rationality, and it claims that insufficient critical attention has been given to the "instrumentality" of its hegemonic power. The present chapter argues that Trifonas' indictment of unreflexive pedagogy in universities could apply similarly to the pedagogical and research practices of the modern library. Like universities, research libraries have, in some respects, remained immune to historical contextualization, critical analysis, and sociological interrogation. Yet, as Trifonas argued, libraries and their contemporary counterparts—what we call *libr@ries* (see Kapitzke & Bruce, introduction, this volume)—are "cultural artifact(s) of the principle of reason that we, as researchers, scholars, and public intellectuals, will have always already existed in" (p. 117). The aim here, then, is to render transparent the (ir)rationality of that residual past in the present and to trouble the utopian "dream" of a technocentric future.

To do this, the case is made for a critical sociology of libr@ry studies through the historicization and problematization of the object of study. Whereas the study of libraries traditionally was located within schools of library science, new media and mobile technologies have eroded the possibility of any such boundary or monopoly. The diversity of contributors' disciplinary backgrounds in this volume testifies to this shift. Because library and information "sciences" are located more commonly now in schools of information technology, business studies, communication and information sciences, and because a critical sociology of libr@ry studies would be relevant to the field of informatics, cyberculture, education, cultural heritage studies, and cultural studies, it is a potentially generative one.

Accordingly, what follows does not fit the conventional literature review.[1] Nor does it consider the future of libraries (for this, see Benton Foundation, 1998; Crawford & Gorman, 1995; Hesse & Bloch, 1995; Scammell, 1999). Instead, its focus is on what remains unwritten. The intention is to progress the endless rounds of polarized debate that have characterized the profession for two decades by changing the terms of the debate.[2] Through a metadiscursive approach the discussion notes gaps and silences and proposes some new theoretical directions. First, a brief review of the field of libr@ry studies is provided. This seeks to generate discussion, perhaps even some controversy, and to encourage researchers to consider knowledges, theories, and practices different from those that are currently dominant. To *confront* is to *complement*, and courage is needed to rethink long-standing ways of "doing" libr@ries and of "being" libr@rians. Changing times reflect and require historically apposite ways of doing this. Through a sampling of research agendas that are not so common, I aim to confront the current turbulent historical moment for

FIG. 9.1. Sculpture by Petrus Spronk outside the Victorian State Library (Melbourne, Australia) that is based on a feature of the Library's portico. Image by P. Krogdahl, copyright 2004.

libr@ries and to do to existing library and information science (LIS) literatures what the symbolism of the sculpture in Fig. 9.1 represents visually.

Recent linguistic and spatial turns in theory provide alternatives to conventional paradigms. These historically grounded approaches would understand and interpret libr@ries as manifestations of contemporary cultures, societies, economies, and polities. This is not to imply that content provided here is any more or less "truthful" or "ideological" than other work. Although the purpose is to critically examine key issues and to disrupt established research trajectories, the argument remains a situated perspective grounded in my own positionality and biases. Conscious of the discursive and political power of "naming" through categorization of self or others (Hudak & Kihn, 2001), I need to make plain that the ontological and epistemological standpoint for the following deconstruction and reconstruction of libr@ry studies is from a position of a belief in the potential of postpositivist research that is discourse oriented and socially critical. To that end, it offers some signboards for rethinking the shift to multimodal meaning spaces and texts in libr@ries.

There is a corpus of LIS literature that draws from discourse-oriented and socially critical research approaches, and is exemplified in journals like *The Progressive Librarian*. But a cursory review of mainstream literatures reveals a strong tendency toward empirical and objectivist approaches in which technology figures prominently. Whereas objectivist research is valuable and vital, there is room at the table for approaches that complement the latter through their propensity for different kinds of political analysis and social critique.[3] Indeed, exclusion of the latter altogether uses the politics of epistemology to silence contestation, diversity, equity, and change. Therefore, the argument is made that the preponderance of objectivist epistemologies and technologically determinist approaches to libr@ries in the literature presents something of a challenge for both the profession and its constituents.

SPACES OF MEANING AND MEANINGS OF SPACES

As already pointed out, the confusing array of neologisms used to denote new information spaces and services requires attention to the question of meaning. A caveat to this exercise is the unfashionability of definitions in this era of infinite linguistic *différance,* polysemy, and ambiguity. Some would say attention to meaning is a moot exercise, but it serves two purposes here: first, to inform the reader of the "commonsense" understandings of terms; and, second, to provide a basis for denaturalizing their use within the current discursive formation of libr@ry studies. How, then, are researchers and writers (re)presenting emerging information resources and services, which in turn influence how they are thought about and used?

Existing scholarship typically represents hybrid and virtual libraries, or cybraries, as "networked" or "diffuse" *libraries* (D'Angelo, 2001; Lougee, 2002; Saunders, 1999), as information *centers* and *environments* (Gorman, 2003; Von Elm & Trump, 2001), and as information *organizations* that provide learning activities in different modes (Keys, 1999). Others view them as *intelligent* or *smart technology infrastructure* in "smart buildings" (Boone, 2002; Frost & Schmidt, 1999). As is evident, *cybrary* is a hybrid term, combining the prefix *cyber* (from *cybernetics*) and the suffix *-ary* (meaning *relating to* from *library*) (see Schmidt, chap. 4, this volume, and Willinsky, chap. 10, this volume). Cybraries are represented as different from libraries because they comprise:

- hybrid spaces of physical materiality and online virtuality
- hybrid materials of print and multimodal texts
- hybrid users of face-to-face and remote location
- hybrid sociopedagogical relations of fee and free access to resources[4]

Whereas some view cybraries as a transitional stage (e.g., Oppenheim & Smithson, 1999), others consider them to be a legitimate model in their own right (Pinfield et al., 1998). The work of Champelli (2002), Ensor (2000), D. Kovacs and M. Kovacs (1997), and Ross (1997), who examined the role of the cybrarian in relation to youth, reading, and electronic information literacy in schooling and higher education contexts, are examples of the latter.

The digital library, in contrast, has no physical existence and is generally understood as a managed *collection of digital objects* accessed via a network (Arms, 2000; G. G. Chowdhury & S. Chowdhury, 2003; Hanson & Levin, 2003; Hughes & Green, 2003; Lee, 2002). Some institutions that continue to provide print materials call themselves "digital libraries." The California Digital Library at the University of California and the Digital Library of Nanyang Technological University, Singapore, are cases in point. Deegan and Tanner (2002) noted that library managers make tactical decisions to locate themselves within a digital paradigm for "strategic" reasons, namely, to improve funding possibilities. The proliferation of monographs on digital libraries—compared to hybrid or virtual libraries—signifies the literal and symbolic shift from print to electronic online formats. A reliance on private funding and subsequent pressures of accountability place commercial and economic issues foremost in this literature (cf. Boone, 2003; Elliott de Saez, 2002; Kahin & Varian, 2000). Research shows nonetheless that, despite rhetoric about cost-effectiveness, digital libraries are generally more expensive to establish and maintain than traditional libraries (Halliday & Oppenheim, 2001).

Research centers in the United States, Canada, the United Kingdom, Australia, and New Zealand have produced a substantial corpus of digital library scholarship. A foremost portal for this work is *Digital Library Research* at http://www.dlib.org/projects.html#joint. The better part of digital library research comprises manuals and case studies of hybrid and/or digital library programs and initiatives. They describe digital resource management (e.g., object modeling, cataloguing, metadata, and interoperability), digital services and functions (e.g., user interfaces and access), and administration and education (e.g., marketing, productivity, staffing, evaluation, and user education) (see Arms, 2000; Borner & Chen, 2002; Harum & Twidale, 2000; Kenney & Rieger, 2000; Nan Si, Murthy, & NetLibrary, 2003; Witten & Bainbridge, 2003). A subset of this material addresses intellectual property issues and the increasing tension between the public and private information sectors, ownership and the need to maximize access, personalized online services and the question of privacy, and the adoption of dot-com solutions to library practices (see Fitzgerald, chap. 15, this volume; Lipinski, 2002; Thomas, 2002; Wherry, 2002).

Other subsets of the literature address technical and economic mappings of national information infrastructures (NIIs) (Kahin & Wilson, 1997), the global reach and interdependence of information sectors in the public and private domains (the GII) (Borgman, 2000), and policy contexts of the GII (Nesson & Kahin, 1997). Collectively, these analyses show how libr@ries extend beyond institutional, local, and national boundaries. Like it or not, everyone is part of the GII network that comprises technical systems, nationally differentiated market forces, nation-state and international policies, industrial structures, and the communications and media sectors (Wilson, 1997).

Although information flows seem natural phenomena, like water seeping from, around, and over the texts and cultural crevices within which we operate as social beings, the specter of an emerging digital divide calls for research that provides located but politically informed analyses of these developments (cf. Bowers, 2000; Compaine, 2001; Evans & Wurster, 2000; Lax, 2001; Norris, 2001; Servon, 2002; Wyatt, Henwood, Miller, & Senker, 2000). The report of the National Science Foundation–European Union Working Group, *Future Directions for Digital Libraries Research*, confirms that most research to date comprises evaluations of experimental prototypes (Schäuble & Smeaton, 1998). Indeed, although acknowledging the cultural contexts of information, and noting the "broad military, commercial, and personalized applications" of "dynamic spatially customized data," research agendas for digital libraries remain focused on improving productivity through information access (see National Science Foundation, 2003, pp. 8–13). In summary, with exceptions like Bishop, Buttenfield, and Van House (2003), who examined digital libraries from a sociotechnical perspective, most of the foregoing research focuses on operational, organizational, and technical issues of libr@ry developments. The literature's emphasis on factualism, certainty, and control of an objective reality signifies a technocratic rationality rather than hermeneutic or emancipatory values that have more socially oriented outputs.

EPISTEMOLOGICAL STANDPOINTS

As the scientifically rationalist policies of the *No Child Left Behind Act of 2001* (Public Law 107-110) in the United States illustrate, the question of what constitutes valid and worthwhile research is a contentious one. Which aspects of libr@ries are investigated, how research questions are framed, and what methodology is used to answer those questions emerge from the researcher's epistemological viewpoint. Beliefs about the nature of meaning and the role of the mind, the self, and the body influence the ways in which knowledge is created and the value that is attributed to it. Despite the possibilities of diverse philosophical standpoints in the conduct of research, most of the foregoing corpus is positivist and deemed value free. That is, it comprises empirical research embodying an objectivist epistemology in which libr@ries exist independently of researchers and are "discerned" through "scientific" research. Methods of data collection entail observation and description, and "findings" are presented as unproblematized "fact." Because values of neutrality prevail, remarkably little critical interrogation, social explanation, ambiguity, and/or contestation of terms occurs. The question arises, then, whether the representation of libr@ries simply as physical places, undifferentiated virtual spaces, and/or informational infrastructures limits their potential as sites for teaching and learning?

Critical sociological theory would argue that libr@ries are both effects and agencies of social stasis and change. In what follows, three of many alternative theoretical and conceptual frameworks are presented for renaming, reinterpreting, and rethinking libr@ries. I do this fully cognizant that an OECD report (2003, p. 10) described educational research generally as "politicised, irrelevant, and too distant from practice." The rationale is that a good understanding of the research–practice nexus can be achieved only through a diversity of well-articulated research theories. Research is neither innocent nor disinterested. How, then, would the use of alternative theoretical paradigms conceptualize libr@ries and their social and educational effects? What ways of examining and knowing their workplaces differently would enable libr@rians to challenge positivist and technicist methods that preclude critical engagement with issues of power and politics inherent in the production and consumption of information for education?

Poststructuralist and postmodernist theories have challenged long-standing beliefs about the nature of reality (ontology) and the attainment of epistemic certainty through reason. Classical Platonic and Christian *idealism*, which sought to attain metaphysical knowledge by denying the body and privileging the mind, had long since succumbed to *dualist* epistemologies of Cartesian rationalism and scientific objectivism (Duran, 1998). Dualist theories of knowledge recognize material as well as spiritual worlds, and attribute agency to the mind through the power of the senses. The goal of dualist research—like most of the aforementioned—is neutral and "universal" knowledge. More recent *monist* theories (e.g., poststructuralism) deny the role of the knower as transcendent autonomous individual, and posit instead that reality is created in and through the material world of discourse (i.e., text). Within this way of knowing, reality and knowledge have no intrinsic, "essential" meaning because they are contingent social constructions. Recent theories using concepts of *ecology* and *complexity* have relocated the mind within the body, and resituated the body within complex biological systems and sociocultural environments. Consciousness and knowing are then embodied practices that emerge from the interaction of material and nonmaterial systems and social communities. Note that whereas poststructuralists reject universal transcendent *reason*, they are not relativists and their work does not lie outside of *rationalism*. Rather, because they view knowledge as situated and relational, their focus is on *reasons* and *rationalities*.

Debates around modernity and postmodernity have in large part subsided, and the claim is made—contentiously—that we live in a "post-theory" era (McQuillan, Purves, Macdonald, & Thomson, 1999). No single, monolithic epistemology currently holds sway, and in an effort to enrich the libr@ry paradigm, three main theoretical frameworks—poststructuralism, critical theory, and feminist theory—are discussed here. These 3 were selected because they are representative of contemporary monist and hence postpositivist approaches, and because they have considerable analytic and conceptual potential for rethinking and repracticing libr@ries.

POSTSTRUCTURALISM
AND LIBR@RY RESEARCH

Poststructuralist theorists (e.g., Derrida, Foucault) and theorists of postmodernity (e.g., Lyotard, Harvey and Jameson) provide stinging critiques of modernity and its social institutions. Their theories of text and language, knowledge and power, represent approaches that are social constructionist and/or subjectivist rather than objectivist. Key analytic concepts of this kind of research paradigm are *discourse, social practice*, and *space*.

Discourse and Social Practice

In modernist paradigms, libraries are constructed as objects (i.e., places or collections), embodying some intrinsic, essential meaning that is independent of the researcher. This status as "given" or "natural" has placed libraries and, hence, libr@ries beyond criticism. Disciplinary assumptions of social consensus and cooperation underpinning the cognitive sciences, behavioral psychology, artificial intelligence, and liberal social theory have reinforced the conception of libr@ries as neutral, autonomous places. In contrast, poststructuralist and critical sociological theories would connect the everyday events of libr@ries to wider configurations of discourse and power, economy and society. They would seek to explain how libr@ries reflect and reproduce cultural knowledges and social formations cross-generationally through, for example, text and its associated literate practice. Reality, for the most part, comprises *discourse*, or patterns of statements, rules, and routines that frame what can and cannot be thought, said, and enacted. The human subject—as *libr@rian* or *libr@ry user*—does not precede discourse, but is an effect of it. Such research looks not for origins, causes, or dominant individuals, but asks what discursive practices and techniques are used to produce and manage objects, knowledges, and human subjectivities.

The task of the discourse analyst is to disrupt common sense and the inevitability of the social world by disembedding everyday texts from their historical and social contexts. Such texts might include the content of collections; the semiotic forms of libr@ry Web sites and online catalogues; phone or face-to-face interaction between users, information technology staff, or the reference librarian; the instructional contexts of information literacy programs; the content of user feedback material; public and educational policy documents that frame information and libr@ry developments; and the semiosis of libr@ry architectural forms. Poststructuralist research would eschew instrumentalist assumptions of libr@ries as neutral conduits for information delivery, and view them instead as raced, classed, aged, and gendered social environments (see Dressman & Tettegah, chap. 3, this volume). There is an array of methods available for analyzing texts that constitute libr@ries, including deconstructionism (Derrida, 1996), sociolinguistics (Graham & Rooney, 2001; Hymes, 1996), ethnomethodology (Garfinkel & Rawls, 2002), theories of social practice (De Certeau, 1984), critical literacy (Luke, 1997; McLaren & Lankshear, 1993), social semiotics (Kress & van Leeuwen, 2001; Lemke, 1995), cultural studies (Thwaites, Davis, & Mules, 2002), and critical discourse analysis (Fairclough, 1995).

A Foucauldian analysis, for example, would chart the conditions of possibility for the emergence of libr@ries through an archeological investigation, or "dig," of text. It would look at the visible and the invisible in terms of what is said and unsaid, to show how the object of the "libr@ry" and the libr@ry "(non)user" are constituted as objects of knowledge. From a Foucauldian perspective, a libr@ry is a site for the panoptical gaze of the institution on "reader," "user," "teacher," "student/learner," and so on. Procedural and pedagogical practices of subjectification, regulation, and normalization inscribe discourses of information work on the bodies of libr@ry users through ethical conventions of quietness, obedience, tidiness, and punctuality. Three decades ago, the sociology of education showed how schools perpetuated systemic and social asymmetries of material resources and symbolic power. Research today can similarly investigate the problem of how libr@ries, as mediaries of information services, also inadvertently reproduce these asymmetries through differential access to discursive resources. As products of discourses (e.g., globalization, informationalism, managerialism, technologism, commodification, and corporatization), libr@ries perform and perpetuate certain social practices. This suggests they can productively be conceptualized as arobase spaces (see

Kapitzke & Bruce, introduction, this volume) comprising repertoires of practice with technologies of "educational" information.

The work of Bourdieu (1990, 1998) on the sociology and "logic of practice" would similarly be useful here.[5] Application of his concepts of *habitus, social field, cultural capital,* and *symbolic violence* would show how libr@ries are products of their location in social space and the practices of those who "inhabit" them. This approach would emplace libr@ries within the intersections of economic and cultural formations, class, and education. An example of such an embodied social practice is that of silent, sustained reading. A by-product of the discursive space of religious libraries (see Kapitzke, 1995), the physiology and sociality of vocalized reading was made possible by gradual changes in notation techniques for writing, such as the addition of space between words, punctuation, and line spacings (cf. Saenger, 1997).

From a poststructuralist perspective, there is no space outside of language, text, discourse, and politics. This means that libr@ries do things *to* people as well as *for* people. A focus on text and meaning emphasizes practice rather than the internal mental states of individuals (i.e., "character," "skills," or "competences"). The upshot is that, if libr@ries comprise institutional socioliterate practices—that is, selective traditions of genres, social relations, ideologies, and pedagogical events—situated within broader socioeconomic contexts, then their processes and effects are transparent and transformable. That data itself is discourse renders problematic the entire field of library and information "science." Whereas some have moved to postpositivist approaches (e.g., Budd, 2001; Day, 2000; G. P. Radford, 2003; Trosow, 2001), other recent theorizing perpetuates the objectivist assumptions of LIS (cf. Crowley, 1999; Durrance, 2003).

Space

As noted in the introductory chapter, the logics of global capitalism and communications technologies have generated arobase spaces for social interaction in online environments. These hybridized spaces are de-essentializing long-standing categories (e.g., place/placelessness, public/private, real/virtual, fixed/fluid, and broadcaster/listener) through which social relations have been understood (cf. Dodge & Kitchin, 2001). Aristotelian and Newtonian conceptions of space as static and concrete are no longer viable. Because libr@ries are not self-contained entities—indeed, they never were—research needs to explore how what goes on inside is tied to what goes on outside. The spaces of libr@ries are not absolute or passive, something to fill with books or "clients." Rather, they are relational because they are socially produced, and have meaning only through the differentiated activities of those constituting them, which may or may not include information seeking work. This approach differs from research on the physical space of libraries, most of which shows how libraries embody cultural logics, social norms, and political ideologies.[6]

Libr@rians across all educational sectors need to explore and understand how they and their clients deploy, exploit, and resist space through consideration of the following. How do new hybrids of space merge and manifest in libr@ries? What is the ratio of place-to-space in libr@ries? What cultural dynamics and dialectics are changing this ratio? To what extent do they render the geographic space of libraries placeless? How is the relation between place, identity, and community—so central previously in nurturing social and cultural capital through public, school, and university libraries—changing? How do processes of virtuality and globality affect the pedagogical relations of libr@ries? What forms do these "spaces of flows" and "flows of spaces" for learning, teaching, and researching take? What epistemic and educational values do libr@ries embody? In what ways do these learning environments constitute spaces of textuality (i.e., language, image, sound, kinesthetics, and multimodality); spaces of discourse; spaces of identity and subjectivity; spaces of social regulation; spaces of cultural inclusion and exclusion; and spaces of politics and power? What differences exist in the topologies or types of space within libr@ries? How is hierarchy and power embedded within their material and virtual spaces and the social uses of these spaces? Finally, how do libr@rians need to think differently about their workspaces as the familiar grounds of textuality and temporality, sociality and spatiality, crumble beneath them (see Boyce, chap. 2, this volume)?

With the advent of world time—that is, *live time*—during the 1980s, world timespace encroached on local times and places (J. May & Thrift, 2001). *Here and there* was dissolved; *now and then* was rendered meaningless. What does this mean for the study of libr@ries, which historically has relied so heavily on essentialist notions of place and space? What tensions and contradictions, what centrifugal and centripetal forces, are forming new spaces of time, spaces of pedagogy, spaces of disordered order? What does it mean to read and to research in a post-typographic world? Libr@rians are well placed to document multimodal literacies enabled by online media and wireless technologies both within and without the key cultural heritage institutions (see Goodrum, chap. 5, this volume). The reality is that, like Sophie in Kapitzke and Bruce's introduction, users can access the libr@ry from their bed or the beach with mobile phone or PDA. Therefore, what kinds of informal information sources do learners seek and use that erode the long-standing monopoly of libraries? When and why do they utilize listservs, chatrooms, text messaging, and blogging? How do these increasing levels of disintermediation change the political economy of scholarly publishing? What do these new economies mean for libr@ries in terms of physical versus virtual infrastructure provision? Because they remain undifferentiated in terms of focus these questions are necessary but far from sufficient. Next consider a more specialized theoretical approach, namely, that of feminism as a means of troubling the power of established paradigms.

FEMINISMS AND LIBR@RY RESEARCH

Like poststructuralists, feminists argue that Cartesian-Newtonian conceptions of reality underpinning science and technology assume a dual nature to reality and reason that is no longer tenable (Figueroa & Harding, 2003; Lather, 1991). This dualism takes the form of oppositional binarisms, examples of which are subjective knower/objective known, mind/matter, reason/emotion, public/private, male/female, rational/irrational, and order/chaos. Feminists argue that the privileging of one element over the other performs and legitimates social inequities based on gender (Harding & Hintikka, 1983; Stanley & Wise, 1995).

Whereas all seek to address the issue of "unknown women" and "unknowing research" (Bing & Reid, 1996), different feminisms (e.g., liberal, Marxist, psychoanalytic, postcolonial, and poststructuralist) focus on different constructions of gender. Questions of gender in library culture and practice were marginalized, in large part, by the profession's stand on neutrality. Research that rejects the universal human subject (*viz.*, the White, middle-class, male reified in the collections and canons of libraries) would ask, where are women in these new information environments? Which groups of women are most visible? What gave them this visibility and excluded others?

Wiegand's (1996) critical biography of Melvil Dewey, founder of the library profession in the late 19th century, links the low status of library work to Dewey's sexism and his goal of a de-skilled, compliant, clerical workforce. This raises the issue of how the shift to e-mediated forms and services has changed the cultural practice and social status of libr@ry work. Do women have equitable representation on the managerial and jurisdictional boards of national and international information organizations, programs, and initiatives? Or have the gender politics of the library profession transferred to libr@ry contexts? How do multimodal semiotic resource systems reify and perpetuate gender differences and disadvantage? How might feminist knowledges and "ways of being" do libr@ries differently? What methodologies would best suit projects that deconstruct emergent knowledges around libr@ries? These are important questions to be asked by researchers, practitioners, and theorists alike considering that the extant corpus discussed earlier offers only a singular gender-neutral, masculinist version of libr@ries that are, in large part, oblivious to the nuanced politics of gender, race, class, culture, and ethnicity.

Foundational work by Berman (1971) and more recent work by scholars like Olson (1998, 2001) challenges the legitimacy of library classification systems and their role in marginalizing and ghettoizing the languages, cultures, and histories of those without influence to construct their own powerful normalizing taxonomies. M. L. Radford and G. P. Radford (1997, 2003) similarly provided feminist explorations of the discursive construction of librarians and library users from poststructuralist and cultural studies perspectives. Their analyses of representations of libraries and librarians in popular culture examine interfaces of order and chaos, fear and power through which libraries operate. What are the implications of this work for digital environments given the overlay of anxiety that some learners experience with new technologies? Haraway's (1994) concept of the *cyborg* provides a well-known femino-Marxist response to the incursion of technologies into human bodies and, alternatively, the integration of human sensibilities into machines. Her demolition of the machine/ body dualism raises a number of questions that libr@ry literatures have not yet addressed (Hunter, chap. 6, this volume, touches on them). What other binarisms can be rethought through these ideas? For example, how do learner and teacher, librarian and user, borrowed and overdue, inside and outside, fiction and nonfiction, text producer and text consumer play out as "both/and" phenomena rather than "either/or" structures? Other common dichotomies worthy of investigation in the field are silence/ noise, high culture/low culture, canon/ephemera, nature/culture, and organization/disorganization.

If online environments are not paraspace (i.e., "other" to or separate from the physical realm of user's lives), what does this mean for the question of embodiment in both real and virtual realities? As poststructuralist and feminist work has shown, sociologies of the body also reveal the indivisibility of mind, corporeality, and experience (Shapiro, 1999; Shilling, 2003). How do libr@ry texts account for this in terms of immediacy, anonymity, and the designability of Web sites? What role do people's experiential backgrounds play in their engagement and use of these texts? If there is no libr@ry as such (i.e., no homogenous, abstracted, value-neutral libr@ry independent of the bodies, skins, senses, sensibilities, languages, discursive histories, and proclivities of users) then what kinds of social and political relations do their texts construct with reader/viewers? In what ways do masculinist biases and racialized predispositions of experiential realities transfer through computer logic, software applications, and the texts and textualities of libr@ry contexts (Balsamo, 1996; Rose, 2003)? What discursive traces do bodies leave for the mechanisms and techniques of record keeping and dataveillance deployed by libr@ries?

Postcolonial and more recent post-postcolonial theory also are rich with potential for examining intersections of body, culture, technology, politics, signs, and space.

CRITICAL THEORY AND LIBR@RY RESEARCH

Despite ongoing criticism of its focus on structure at the expense of agency, critical theory has sustained power as a means of analyzing and changing social conditions. Indeed, those disillusioned with the moral turpitude and political paralysis of *post-* theories reaffirm the value of neo-Marxian and political economic approaches to the study of social change (see Cole, 2003; Fairclough & Graham, 2002; Graham, 2000; Slott, 2002). Researchers use critical theory to examine ideological and cultural factors that reproduce social inequality. Political economy approaches, in particular, identify patterns of winners and losers of change by studying shifts in "the rules of the game" as technological convergence transforms socioeconomic structures. Critical pedagogy would assert, for example, that libr@ries are products and producers of market-driven consumer societies, and information services entail engagement with segments of capital, labor, knowledge, telecommunications, and media. Conversely, libr@ries have symbolic, economic, and material assets of their own, which they strive to serve and protect.

The language of libr@ry literature reflects this trend as librarians increasingly talk about "keeping one step ahead of competitors" and "managing relationships with competitors and customers" (see Pantry & Griffiths, 2002, p. 119). This lexicon turns learners into "clients" and "customers" who are courted as consumers through branding strategies (see Schmidt, chap. 4, this volume). The breaking of long held taboos around books and food, such as the embedding of coffee shops within libr@ry precincts, materializes this process. The sociologist, Ritzer (2000), argued that this constitutes a process of "McDonaldization" as values of efficiency, calculability, predictability, performativity, and control through technology that pervade contemporary society similarly intrude on libr@ry procedures and practices. This is an area that remains untouched by researchers.

Seminal examples of critical theoretical approaches in the LIS literature are the sociohistorical analyses of M. H. Harris, Hannah, and P. C. Harris (1998) and Birdsall (1994), who tracked library discourses from liberal progressivism to current late capitalist e-formations. Both argued that the real challenges facing the library profession are not technological but those of free market fundamentalism and neo-conservative politics. H. Schiller (1996) and D. Schiller (1999) similarly documented the implications of digital capitalism and the increasing commodification and domestication of information. They contended that, because libraries served the public interest in education and democratic participation, they were located in a liminal space between market and polity. Based on nonmarket principles of free and easy access to knowledge, libraries have been both places and institutions (Kranich, 2003).

Yet, this is not the case for libr@ries. Lyman (1996, p. 16) showed how digital libraries, for example, emanate from computerized systems and cultural contexts based on presuppositions of command and control, the market, and a "distinctly masculine" language of action "emphasizing emotional control." Are these mechanisms sufficient to serve the public interest? A growing body of critical literature on discourses of the "information society" and the close interrelation of technoculture, education, and the military/industrial complex indicates that they are not so conducive to the common good (cf. Best & Kellner, 2001; Blane, 2001; Der Derian, 2001; Pilger, 2002; Rushkoff, 2003; Saltman & Gabbard, 2003). This is an ethical issue that libr@rians have not as yet addressed, and is one that requires both theoretical and empirical testing (see Rooney & Schneider, chap. 7, this volume). Increasing trends toward privatized information necessitate a more politicized research standpoint that is not yet evident in the literature. There has always been a political economy underpinning publishing, information, and communication (see Apple, 1989; Mosco, 1996), but the General Agreement on Trade in Services (GATS) and the Agreement on Trade Related Aspects of Intellectual Property Rights (TRIPs) signed at the 1995 Uruguay Round heralds a new era. That intellectual property is now included in the regime of the World Trade Organization constitutes a significant shift in the ownership and trade of knowledge (Bettig, 1996; Drahos & Braithwaite, 2002; C. May, 2000).

The key commission here is to map the increasing dominance of the private sector on information services (Bollier, 2003). Key concerns about the erosion of the information commons include "fair use" and "first sale" concepts of copyright; intellectual property rights; the social form, scope, and impact of the "dot-commons;" anti-commons strategies on the part of business; and the interrelation of indigenous, local, and scientific knowledges (Vaidhyanathan, 2001).[7] A number of public interest groups (e.g., the Public Knowledge project of the New America Foundation and Creative Commons at the Stanford Law School) are developing a spectrum of rights as an alternative to the "all-out" copyright or "no rights reserved" dichotomy (see Bollier & Watts, 2002; Lessig, 2004). As Fitzgerald (chap. 15, this volume) notes, libr@rians are well placed to contribute to these developments and debates by way of research. This would require them to disclose powerful but tacit contradictions between professed principles and praxis, and to rethink and reoperationalize democratic values for digital information contexts.

There are many continuities within the information and communications sectors such as the expansion of NIIs, but there are also a host of new developments in terms of social movements, political activism, and economic relations (Bard & Söderqvist, 2002; Webster, 2001). Massified analyses of monolithic forms of information flow are not able to capture g/localized communications forms characterized by chaos, complexity, conversion, fluctuation, mutation, and transgression. The Greenstone Digital Library project is a case in point (see http://www.greenstone.org/cgi-bin/library). Developed in cooperation with UNESCO and the Human Info NGO, and issued under the terms of the GNU General Public License, Greenstone is open-source, multilingual software enabling nonprofessionals to build and publish digital library collections online (see Witten & Bainbridge, 2003). Research is needed to build cartographies of these marginal but socially significant archival resources. Who, for example, are the players in the field? What metaphors and metonymies compose the cultural identities and communal ideologies of these collections and communities? What hybrid forms of multimodal literacies are they affording? How is enhanced interactivity changing traditional information literacies? What effect is the fragmentation and deinstitutionalization of library economies having on educational institutions and community relationships? Which discourses are driving these new information spaces (e.g., religion, environmentalism, commercialism), and what is their impact on other dominant ideologies such as techno-economics and the traditional ethico-political value of library services?

Let me illustrate the point with a grounded example of what text-based research using a critical discourse analytic approach might look like. This method, which is taught in some library schools and also K–12 critical media literacy classes, derives from traditional evaluation practice for print reference materials that used criteria of Authority, Coverage, Bias, and so forth. For the purpose of the exercise, I have chosen a single Web site, *Infocus,* which is a service of the State Library of New South Wales (Australia) for students in their final high school year. The stated aim of the Web site is to "link people with information."[8] Three images tell the reader/viewer that "people" signifies school students because they comprise variations on a cartoon-like graphic of a blond-haired, blue-eyed adolescent sitting at a computer screen. (Which people-groups does this graphic (re)present and thereby exclude?)

Yet, it is apparent that there are more than educational goals and ideologies at play here because the most prominent signifier on the homepage is an iconic hotlink to Duke Energy International (see Fig. 9.2). The distinctive color (vivid red on a page of otherwise mostly jellybean green graphics) and its positioning (left-center to which the eyes of left-to-right

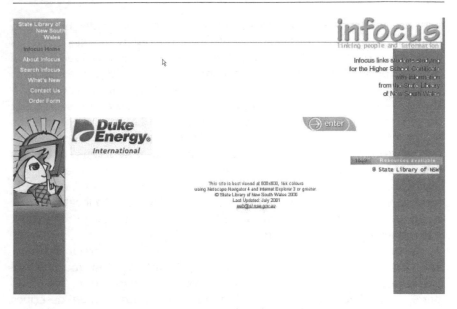

FIG. 9.2.   Homepage for Infocus Web site.

readers would fall) invite the viewer to the Web site of this transnational energy corporation. No reference is made or information provided about the legal agreement, financial arrangement, or "educational" rationale for this partnership. Hence, without any justification for its presence, *Infocus* provides Duke Energy a forum for promoting its "best" educational, environmental, and community practice to a captive audience of school students.

Conventional information literacy approaches would ask students to evaluate the site using "critical thinking" techniques. Alternatively, a critical hyperliteracies approach (cf. Kapitzke, 2003) would encourage students to ask why a "top tier gas and power marketer" and the "largest producer of natural gas liquids in the U.S." is so prominent on an information portal for Australian school students. The reader/viewer learns from Duke's Web site that the company has formed a similar "partnership" with the U.S. National Council of Teachers of Mathematics—the professional organization of over 100,000 mathematics teachers—for the purpose of "shar[ing] our technical expertise and knowledge of best practices." The reason given for this professional development initiative is that "advancements in math and science education will prepare future scientists and engineers to tackle the challenges that lie ahead."

A critical hyperliteracy pedagogy would ask what relation is established here between the text and the reader through language and image, text and whitespace? How does the text position the reader in relation to the topic, namely, to the virtues of Duke Energy, who self-portray as a caring, responsible global citizen? What evidence is provided for this self-ascription? What are these "challenges" that require more scientists and engineers? Are there more pressing issues that other kinds of professionals—perhaps environmentalists or doctors—could address, and that would be more in accordance with the image Duke presents of itself as environmentally responsible and communally sensitive? Whose interests do the proposed strategies serve, bearing in mind that the first of Duke's four charters is to: "Deliver on our financial plan and preserve the dividend of $1.10/share." How does this vision reconcile with the lackluster record of transnational energy producers in relation to local and first nation communities in majority world countries from which they extract natural resources for considerable profit?

An informed, politicized libr@rian would seek to understand discursive tension at play on a page that is called, "Changing How You Buy and Sell Energy." What does the use of the second person pronoun, "you," do here? Does the reader/viewer "sell" energy? The textual content describes how "world energy markets" have been transformed and how "market liberalization and privatization" have led to the "commoditization of energy." The nominalization of terms here (i.e., the turning of a subject/verb/object process into a single noun) hides the agency of who has privatized and commoditized energy. A hyperliteracies approach would assist students to ping the site for the IP and domain name registration information as a way of investigating who pays for and owns the site.

How transparent and honest are these dealings with the reading public, who, in this case, is most likely to be school students? Accompanying the text is an image of a tropical rainforest that is traversed by a double gas pipeline along a top-to-bottom axis of the photo.[9] Clearly, the image has been tampered with. A swathe of cloud has been crudely inserted so that the pipeline is visible only in the lower one third of the picture. Two thirds of the image, therefore, comprises lush vegetation. This brings several questions to the socially critical mind. In light of this duplicity, how much credibility can be imputed to Duke Energy's track record with respect to the social and ecological effects of its energy pipelines that traverse forests, communities, and animal habitats often with devastating consequences (see *New Internationalist*, 2003). What does the erosion of the public utilities energy sector mean for consumers, and what relation does this trend bear to the commodification of information provision for school students? Accordingly, what is the ethical responsibility of libr@rians who disregard the sociopolitical and economic ramifications of what seem to be innocuous "cross-sectoral partnerships" developed in the name of "better service" to "clients"?

STEPPING OUT

This chapter has proposed a critical sociology of libr@ry studies by disrupting the tyranny of the familiar and troubling the presuppositions of existing research. It has sought to encourage libr@ry practitioner/researchers to be skeptical of scholarship by developing a knowledge of critique through a critique of knowledge. Quite simply, it is time libr@rians became "difficult," to themselves and to others. The American Library Association's affirmation of the privacy rights of library users in response to the 2001 Patriot Act bears testimony to the residual radical and political will of the profession (see also Roberto & West, 2003). But without a politics of knowledge that turns in on itself, as well as out to the social and political worlds that give rise to it, the assertion of democratic values is largely ineffective.

To promote that agenda I have shown that, depending on the theoretical lens deployed, libr@ries can be variously conceptualized as new kinds of libraries and information centers, as technological infrastructure, as cultural communities and semiotic spaces, or as discursive formations comprising repertoires of literate practice with technologies of information and communication. Libr@ries are not innocent, homogeneous value-free entities, but comprise complex, contingent, differentiated sites for textual work. Along with quantitative approaches, interpretive qualitative methodologies and methods would show how the linguistic and literate practices of libr@ries comprise blends of institutional structure (i.e., university and/or school; public and/or private), ideological content (i.e., un/valorized curricular knowledges), discursive form (i.e., oral and/or print and/or multimodal text), social and economic relations (e.g., authorities, hierarchies, powers, resistances), and literate practices (i.e., genres, rules, and routines of use). Depending on their social, political, and economic contexts of practice, each enables and constrains different pedagogical spaces, learning outcomes, social relations, student subjectivities, and political possibilities.

Unlike conventional library research (cf. Powell, 1997), methodology has not been a focus here. Decisions about methods of data collection and analysis are lower order ones, emerging as they do from theory and epistemology, and from the kinds of questions being asked.[10] Much of the aforementioned research in the libr@ry literature remains place-bound and absolute in its perpetuation of unhelpful binaries. It is apparent, therefore, that a second generation of debate, theory, and research that includes policy and empirical studies is needed. The window of opportunity will be shortlived as local, national, and international policies, standards, and practices around information delivery via educational libr@ries stabilize and petrify. The literature shows that librarians view themselves as educational leaders beyond the confines of library walls. The reality is that, without research that is intellectually cogent, critically self-reflective, and politically informed, this will not happen. To date, libr@ry research remains haunted by the legacy of a positivist research paradigm and the dream of a technocratic, informationalized future. As theorists like Radford (2003) and Birdsall (1994) showed, LIS is poised at a liminal moment pregnant with possibility. But unless librarians understand and engage with change that is occurring in culture, economy, and education, they cannot and will not drive their own agendas.

As Trifonas (2000) argued, in the current postcritical age of military politics and the "informativizing" function of science as research in the "service of war," no discipline is beyond the power of the state and the military juggernaut. Derrida (1983, p. 11) foreshadowed the utilization of research programs—and hence educational libr@ries—in the service of "multinational military-industrial complexes of techno-economic networks." As libraries were effects of manuscript cultures and agricultural economies, so too libr@ries are progenies of an unreflective and unholy alliance of postindustrial economies and mediatized-militarized educational cultures. By both omission and commission, libr@ry practitioners and researchers are imbricated in this ebb and flow of symbolic and material forces. Like theory and practice, research is a space in which ethics and responsibility, reason and rationality compete and clash. Understanding and acknowledging one's own professional positioning and positionality is a requisite to social change. Postpositivist theories that require "getting off the fence" will help libr@ry researchers to attain this understanding (Griffiths, 1998).

NOTES

1. For a more conventional synthesis of research issues and challenges, see the special edition of *Library Trends,* 2003, *51*(4), and Wiegand and Bertot's (2003) editorial in *Library Quarterly.*

2. I use the singular iteration of the term *profession* conscious nonetheless that no such totalized entity exists except as is discursively constructed in terms like "professional association," "professional standards," and so on.

3. I acknowledge Abby Goodrum (see chap. 5, this volume) as the source of this metaphor.

4. The term *hybrid library* is used more commonly in the United Kingdom than the United States (see HyLife, 2002).

5. See, for example, Bourdieu's sociological analysis of users' attitudes to Lille University library (Bourdieu & de Saint Martin, 1994). Although still representing the library as a "place," the study demonstrates the ambiguity and multiplicities of meanings attributed to the social space of academic libraries.

6. See Van Slyck's (1995) historico-architectural analysis of Carnegie libraries 1890–1920.

7. For definitions of the terms *commons, common-pool resources,* and *common property,* see *Digital Library of the Commons,* Definitions, Retrieved August 6, 2004, from http://dlc.dlib.indiana.edu/cprdef.html

8. See http://infocus.sl.nsw.gov.au/res/home.cfm (Retrieved April6 , 2004).

9. The name of the image is "gas017."

10. The qualitative/quantitative divide is a spurious one. The real "divide" that researchers need to consider occurs at the level of epistemology. Note also that, until only two decades ago, most qualitative research was positivist like its quantitative counterpart.

REFERENCES

Apple, M. W. (1989). The political economy of text publishing. In S. de Castell, A. Luke, & C. Luke (Eds.), *Language, authority and criticism: Readings on the school textbook* (pp. 155–169). London: Falmer.

Apple, M. W., & Beane, J. A. (1999). *Democratic schools: Lessons from the chalk face.* Buckingham: Open University Press.

Arms, W. Y. (2000). *Digital libraries.* Cambridge, MA: MIT Press.

Balsamo, A. M. (1996). *Technologies of the gendered body: Reading cyborg women.* Durham, NC: Duke University Press.

Bard, A., & Söderqvist, J. (2002). *Netocracy: The new power elite and life after capitalism.* London: Reuters.

Benton Foundation. (1998). *The future's in the balance: A toolkit for libraries and communities in the digital age.* Washington, DC.

Berman, S. (1971). *Prejudices and antipathies: A tract on the LC subject heads concerning people.* Metuchen, NJ: Scarecrow.

Best, S., & Kellner, D. (2001). *The postmodern adventure: Science, technology, and cultural studies at the third millennium.* New York: Guilford.

Bettig, R. V. (1996). *Copyrighting culture: The political economy of intellectual property.* Boulder, CO: Westview.

Bing, V. M., & Reid, P. T. (1996). Unknown women and unknowing research: Consequences of color and class in feminist psychology. In N. Goldberger, J. Tarule, B. Clinchy, & M. Belenky (Eds.), Knowledge, difference, and power: Essays inspired by women's ways of knowing (pp. 175–202). New York: Basic Books.

Birdsall, W. F. (1994). *The myth of the electronic library: Librarianship and social change in America.* Westport, CT: Greenwood.

Bishop, A. P., Buttenfield, B. P., & Van House, N. (Eds.). (2003). *Digital library use: Social practice in design and evaluation.* Cambridge, MA: MIT Press.

Blane, J. V. (Ed.). (2001). *Cyberwarfare: Terror at a click.* Huntington, NY: Novinka Books.

Bollier, D. (2003). *Silent theft: The private plunder of our common wealth.* New York: Routledge.

Bollier, D., & Watts, T. (2002). *Saving the information commons: A new public interest agenda in digital media.* Washington, DC: New America Foundation.

Boone, M. D. (2002). Penn State's new "cybrary" at Harrisburg. *Library Hi Tech, 20*(2), 232–236.

Boone, M. D. (2003). Monastery to marketplace: A paradigm shift. *Library Hi Tech, 21*(3), 358–366.

Borgman, C. L. (2000). *From Gutenberg to the global information infrastructure: Access to information in the networked world.* Cambridge, MA: MIT Press.

Borner, K., & Chen, C. (2002). *Visual interfaces to digital libraries: Motivation, utilization, and socio-technical challenges.* New York: Springer.

Bourdieu, P. (1990). *The logic of practice.* Cambridge, England: Polity Press.

Bourdieu, P. (1998). *Practical reason: On the theory of action.* Cambridge, England: Polity Press.

Bourdieu, P., & de Saint Martin, M. (1994). The users of Lille University Library. In P. Bourdieu, J.-C. Passeron, & M. de Saint Martin (Eds.), *Academic discourse: Linguistic misunderstanding and professorial power* (R. Teese, Trans.; pp. 122–133). Cambridge, England: Polity Press.

Bowers, C. A. (2000). *Let them eat data: How computers affect education, cultural diversity, and the prospects of ecological sustainability.* Athens: University of Georgia Press.

Budd, J. M. (2001). *Knowledge and knowing in library and information science: A philosophical framework.* Lanham, MD: Scarecrow.

Champelli, L. (2002). *The youth cybrarian's guide to developing instructional, curriculum-related, summer reading, and recreational programs.* New York: Neal-Schuman.

Chowdhury, G. G., & Chowdhury, S. (2003). *Introduction to digital libraries.* London: Facet.

Cole, M. (2003). Might it be in the practice that it fails to succeed? A Marxist critique of claims for postmodernism and poststructuralism as forces for social change and social justice. *British Journal of Sociology of Education, 24*(4), 487–501.

Compaine, B. M. (2001). *The digital divide: Facing a crisis or creating a myth?* Cambridge, MA: MIT Press.

Crawford, W., & Gorman, M. (1995). *Future libraries: Dreams, madness and reality.* Chicago: American Library Association.

Crowley, B. (1999). Building useful theory: Tacit knowledge, practitioner reports, and culture of LIS inquiry. *Journal of Education for Library and Information Science, 40*(4), 282–295.

D'Angelo, B. J. (2001). Assembling and managing virtual libraries. *Library Technology Reports, 37*(5), 1.

Day, R. E. (2000). The "conduit metaphor" and the nature and politics of information studies. *Journal of the American Society for Information Science, 51*(9), 805–811.

De Certeau, M. D. (1984). *The practice of everyday life.* Berkeley, CA: University of California Press.

Deegan, M., & Tanner, S. (2002). *Digital futures: Strategies for the information age.* New York: Neal-Schuman.

Der Derian, J. (2001). *Virtuous war: Mapping the military–industrial–media–entertainment network.* Boulder, CO: Westview.

Derrida, J. (1983). The principle of reason: The university in the eyes of its pupils. *Diacritics, 13*(3).

Derrida, J. (1996). *Archive fever: A Freudian impression.* Chicago: University of Chicago Press.

Dodge, M., & Kitchin, R. (2001). *Mapping cyberspace.* New York: Routledge.

Drahos, P., & Braithwaite, J. (2002). *Information feudalism: Who owns the knowledge economy?* London: Earthscan.

Duran, J. (1998). *Philosophies of science/feminist theories.* Boulder, CO: Westview.

Durrance, J. C. (2003). *Crisis as opportunity: The shaping of library and information science education in the United States.* Paper presented at the 50th anniversary of the Japan Society of Library and Information Science (JSLIS). University of Michigan, Ann Arbor, MI.

Elliott de Saez, E. (2002). *Marketing concepts for libraries and information services.* London: Facet.

Ensor, P. (Ed.). (2000). The cybrarian's manual 2. Chicago: American Library Association.

Evans, P., & Wurster, T. S. (2000). *Blown to bits: How the new economics of information transforms strategy.* Boston: Harvard Business School Press.

Fairclough, N. (1995). *Critical discourse analysis: The critical study of language.* New York: Long-man.

Fairclough, N., & Graham, P. (2002). Marx and discourse analysis: Genesis of a critical method. *Estudios de Sociolingüística, 3*(1), 185–230.

Figueroa, R., & Harding, S. (2003). *Science and other cultures: Issues in philosophies of science and technology.* New York: Routledge.

Frost, D., & Schmidt, J. (1999). Setting our sites on the cybrary: Designing a library website which meets customer needs. *Lasie, 30*(4), 9–23.

Garfinkel, H., & Rawls, A. (2002). *Ethnomethodology's program: Working out Durkeim's aphorism.* Lanham, MD: Rowman & Littlefield.

Gorman, M. (2003). *The enduring library: Technology, tradition, and the quest for balance.* Chicago: American Library Association.

Graham, P. (2000). Hypercapitalism: A political economy of informational idealism. *New Media & Society, 2*(2), 131–156.

Graham, P., & Rooney, D. (2001). A sociolinguistic approach to applied epistemology: Examining technocratic values in global "knowledge" policy. *Social Epistemology, 15*(3), 155–169.

Griffiths, M. (1998). *Educational research for social justice: Getting off the fence.* Philadelphia: Open University Press.

Halliday, L., & Oppenheim, C. (2001). Economic aspects of a resource discovery network. *Journal of Documentation, 57*(2), 296–302.

Hanson, A., & Levin, B. L. (Eds.). (2003). *Building a virtual library.* Hershey, PA: Information Science.

Haraway, D. (1994). Manifesto for cyborgs: Science, technology, and socialist feminism in the 1980s. In S. Seidman (Ed.), *The postmodern turn: New perspectives on social theory* (pp. 82–115). New York: Cambridge University Press.

Harding, S., & Hintikka, M. B. (1983). *Discovering reality: Feminist perspectives on epistemology, metaphysics, methodology, and philosophy of science.* Dordrecht: Kluwer.

Harris, M. H., Hannah, S. A., & Harris, P. C. (1998). *Into the future: The foundations of library and information services in the post-industrial era* (2nd ed.). Greenwich, CT: Ablex.

Harum, S., & Twidale, M. (2000). *Successes and failures of digital libraries.* Urbana-Champaign, IL: Graduate School of Library and Information Science, University of Illinois.

Hertz, N. (2001). *The silent takeover: Global capitalism and the death of democracy.* New York: HarperCollins.

Hesse, C. A., & Bloch, R. H. (1995). *Future libraries.* Berkeley, CA: University of California Press.

Hudak, G., & Kihn, P. (Eds.). (2001). *Labeling: Pedagogy and politics.* London: Routledge.

Hughes, L., & Green, D. (2003). *Digitizing collections: Strategic issues for the information manager.* Bloomington, IN: Facet.

HyLife. (2002). *The HyLife hybrid library toolkit. Information landscapes.* Retrieved January 6, 2004, from http://hylife.unn.ac.uk/toolkit/infoland2.html

Hymes, D. H. (1996). *Ethnography, linguistics, narrative inequality: Toward an understanding of voice.* London: Taylor & Francis.

Kahin, B., & Varian, H. R. (2000). *Internet publishing and beyond: The economics of digital information and intellectual property.* Cambridge, MA: MIT Press.

Kahin, B., & Wilson, E. J. (1997). *National information infrastructure initiatives: Vision and policy design.* Cambridge, MA: MIT Press.

Kapitzke, C. (1995). *Literacy and religion.* Amsterdam: John Benjamins.

Kapitzke, C. (2003). (In)formation literacy: A positivist epistemology and a politics of (out)formation. *Educational Theory, 53*(1), 37–53.

Kenney, A. R., & Rieger, O. Y. (2000). *Moving theory into practice: Digital imaging for libraries and archives.* Mountain View, CA: Research Libraries Group.

Keys, M. (1999). The evolving virtual library: A vision, through a glass, darkly. In L. M. Saunders (Ed.), *The evolving virtual library II: Practical and philosophical perspectives* (pp. 167–181). Medford, NJ: Information Today.

Kovacs, D., & Kovacs, M. (1997). *The cybrarian's guide to developing successful Internet programs and services.* New York: Neal Schuman.

Kranich, N. (2003). Libraries: The information commons of civil society. In D. Schuler & P. Day (Eds.), *Shaping the network society: The new role of civic society in cyberspace* (pp. 279–300). Cambridge, MA: MIT Press.

Kress, G., & van Leeuwen, T. (2001). *Multimodal discourse: The modes and media of contemporary communication.* London: Arnold.

Lather, P. (1991). *Getting smart: Feminist research and pedagogy with/in the postmodern.* New York: Routledge.

Lax, S. (2001). Information, education and inequality: Is new technology the solution? In S. Lax (Ed.), *Access denied in the information age* (pp. 107–124). Basingstoke: Palgrave.

Lee, S. D. (2002). *Building an electronic resource collection: A practical guide.* London: Library Association.

Lemke, J. L. (1995). *Textual politics: Discourse and social dynamics.* London: Taylor & Francis.

Lessig, L. (2004). *Free culture: How big media uses technology and the law to lock down culture and control creativity.* New York: Penguin.

Lipinski, T. A. (2002). *Libraries, museums, and archives: Legal issues and ethical challenges in the new information era.* Lanham, MD: Scarecrow.

Lougee, W. P. (2002). *Diffuse libraries: Emergent roles for the research library in the digital age.* Washington, DC: Council on Library and Information Resources.

Luke, A. (1997). Critical approaches to literacy. In V. Edwards & D. Corson (Eds.), *Encyclopedia of language and education: Literacy* (pp. 143–153). Dordrecht: Kluwer.

Lyman, P. (1996). What is a digital library? Technology, intellectual property, and the public interest. *Daedalus, 125*(4), 1–33.

May, C. (2000). *A global political economy of intellectual property rights: The new enclosures?* New York: Routledge.

May, J., & Thrift, N. (Eds.). (2001). *Timespace: Geographies of temporality.* London: Routledge.

McLaren, P., & Lankshear, C. (1993). *Critical literacy: Politics, praxis, and the postmodern.* Albany, NY: State University of New York Press.

McQuillan, M., Purves, R., Macdonald, G. & Thomson, S. (Eds.). (1999). *Post-theory: New directions in criticism.* Edinburgh: Edinburgh University Press.

Mosco, V. (1996). *The political economy of communication: Rethinking and renewal.* London: Sage.

Nan Si, S., Murthy, V. K., & NetLibrary Inc. (2003). *Architectural issues of web-enabled electronic business.* Hershey, PA: Idea Group.

National Science Foundation. (2003). *Knowledge lost in information: Report of the NSF Workshop on Research Directions for Digital Libraries.* Chatham, MA.

Nesson, C. R., & Kahin, B. (1997). *Borders in cyberspace: Information policy and the global information infrastructure.* Cambridge, MA: MIT Press.

New Internationalist. (2003). Special Volume, Oil Pipelines. October.

Norris, P. (2001). *Digital divide? Civic engagement, information poverty, and the Internet worldwide.* Cambridge, England: Cambridge University Press.

Olson, H. A. (1998). Mapping beyond Dewey's boundaries: Constructing classificatory space for marginalized knowledge domains. In G. C. Bowker & S. L. Star (Eds.), *How classifications work: Problems and challenges in an electronic age, a special issue of Library Trends, 47*(2), 233–254.

Olson, H. A. (2001). The power to name: Representation in library catalogues. *Signs: Journal of Women in Culture and Society, 26*(3), 639–688.

Oppenheim, C., & Smithson, D. (1999). What is the hybrid library? *Journal of Information Science, 25*(2), 97–113.

Organization for Economic Cooperation and Development (OECD). (2003). *New challenges for educational research*. Paris.

Pantry, S., & Griffiths, P. (2002). *Creating a successful e-information service*. London: Facet.

Pilger, J. (2002). *The new rulers of the world*. London: Verso.

Pinfield, S., Eaton, J., Edwards, C., Russell, R., Wissenburg, A., & Wynnw, P. (1998). Realizing the hybrid library. *D-Lib Magazine*. Retrieved from http://www.dlib.org/dlib/october98/10pinfield.html

Powell, R. R. (1997). *Basic research methods for librarians* (3rd ed.). Norwood, NJ: Ablex.

Radford, G. P. (2003). Trapped in our own discursive formations: Toward an archaeology of library and information science. *Library Quarterly, 73*(1), 1–19.

Radford, M. L., & Radford, G. P. (1997). Power, knowledge, and fear: Feminism, Foucault, and the stereotype of the female librarian. *The Library Quarterly, 67*(3), 250–266.

Radford, M. L., & Radford, G. P. (2003). Librarians and party girls: Cultural studies and the meaning of librarian. *The Library Quarterly, 73*(1), 54–69.

Ritzer, G. (2000). *The McDonaldization of society*. Thousand Oaks, CA: Pine Forge Press.

Roberto, K., & West, J. (Eds.). (2003). *Revolting librarians redux: Radical librarians speak out*. Jefferson, NC: McFarland & Company.

Rose, E. (2003). *User error: Resisting computer culture*. Toronto: Between the Lines.

Ross, C. (1997). *The frugal youth cybrarian: Bargain computing for kids*. Chicago: American Library Association.

Rushkoff, D. (2003). The information arms race. In L. Strate, R. L. Jacobson, & S. Gibson (Eds.), *Communication and cyberspace: Social interaction in an electronic environment* (2nd ed.; pp. 349–359). Cresskill, NJ: Hampton.

Saenger, P. H. (1997). *Space between words: The origins of silent reading*. Stanford, CA: Stanford University Press.

Saltman, K., & Gabbard, D. A. (Eds.). (2003). *Education as enforcement: The militarization and corporatization of schools*. New York: RoutledgeFalmer.

Saunders, L. M. (1999). The virtual library: Reflections on an evolutionary process. In L. M. Saunders (Ed.), *The evolving virtual library II: Practical and philosophical perspectives* (pp. 1–13). Medford, NJ: Information Today.

Scammell, A. (1999). *i in the sky: Visions of the information future*. London: Aslib/IMI.

Schäuble, P., & Smeaton, A. F. (1998). *An international research agenda for digital libraries*. Report of the Series of Joint NSF-EU Working Groups on Future Directions for Digital Libraries Research. Retrieved December 12, 2003, from http://www.iei.pi.cnr.it/DELOS/REPORTS/Brussrep.htm

Schiller, D. (1999). *Digital capitalism: Networking the global market system*. Cambridge, MA: MIT Press.

Schiller, H. I. (1996). *Information inequality: The deepening social crisis in America*. New York: Routledge.

Servon, L. J. (2002). *Bridging the digital divide: Technology, community, and public policy*. Malden, MA: Blackwell.

Shapiro, S. B. (1999). *Pedagogy and the politics of the body: A critical praxis*. New York: Garland.

Shilling, C. (2003). *The body and social theory* (2nd ed.). Thousand Oaks, CA: Sage.

Slott, M. (2002). Does critical postmodernism help us "name the system"? *British Journal of Sociology of Education, 23*(3), 413–426.

Stanley, L., & Wise, S. (1995). *Breaking out again: Feminist ontology and epistemology* (2nd rev. ed.). New York: Routledge.

Thomas, C. F. (2002). *Libraries, the Internet, and scholarship: Tools and trends converging.* New York: Marcel Dekker.

Thwaites, T., Davis, L., & Mules, W. (2002). *Introducing cultural and media studies: A semiotic approach.* Basingstoke: Palgrave.

Trifonas, P. P. (2000). *The ethics of writing: Derrida, deconstruction, and pedagogy.* Lanhan, MD: Rowman & Littlefield.

Trosow, S. (2001). Standpoint epistemology as an alternative methodology for library and information science. *Library Quarterly, 71*(3), 360–382.

Vaidhyanathan, S. (2001). *Copyrights and copywrongs: The rise of intellectual property and how it threatens creativity.* New York: New York University Press.

Van Slyck, A. (1995). *Free to all: Carnegie libraries and American culture 1890–1920.* Chicago: University of Chicago Press.

Von Elm, C., & Trump, J. F. (2001). Maintaining the mission in the hybrid library. *Journal of Academic Librarianship, 27*(1).

Webster, F. (Ed.). (2001). *Culture and politics in the information age: A new politics?* London: Routledge.

Wherry, T. L. (2002). *The librarian's guide to intellectual property in the digital age: Copyrights, patents, and trademarks.* Chicago: American Library Association.

Wiegand, W. A. (1996). *Irrepressible reformer: A biography of Melvil Dewey.* Chicago: American Library Association.

Wiegand, W. A., & Bertot, J. C. (2003). New directions in LQ's research and editorial philosophy. *Library Quarterly, 73*(3), pp. v–ix.

Wilson, E. J., III. (1997). Introduction: The what, why, where, and how of national information initiatives. In B. Kahin & E. J. Wilson III (Eds.), *National information infrastructure initiatives: Vision and policy design* (pp. 1–23). Cambridge, MA: MIT Press.

Witten, I. H., & Bainbridge, D. I. (2003). *How to build a digital library.* San Francisco: Morgan Kaufmann.

Wyatt, S., Henwood, F., Miller, N., & Senker, P. (Eds.). (2000). *Technology and in/equality: Questioning the information society.* London: Routledge.

III

Arobase Capital

10

The Scholarly Wing
of the Public Cybrary
and the Right to Know

John Willinsky
University of British Columbia

Let us imagine that to speak of a *cybrary* is a way of moving the idea of the library into *cyberspace*. The cybrary will be enabled by existing technologies and buffeted by new knowledge economies, but it will also be shaped by the legacy of the library. The library has always been a *public* and *private* space for bringing together books, ideas, and people. In the case of the English language, this duality and its resulting tension enters very early in the history of the language. The *library* was private before it was public. In defining the word, the *Oxford English Dictionary* (*OED*) holds up Chaucer's reference to "the walles of thi lybrarye" in his book *Boethius*, circa 1374, as the first published use of the word. And yet, within 75 years of Chaucer's instance—and still before the invention of the printing press—*library* was also being used to refer to a place, as the *OED* defines the second meaning of the word: "containing a collection of books, for the use of the public or of some particular portion of it."[1] The clerical and university libraries of medieval times were the first to give library its public sense. It amounted to a limited public, to be sure, who wandered freely among those manuscripts, and such limits form the very theme of this chapter. The element that should most concern us in the ongoing formation of the cybrary, I argue, is the public scope of the scholarly pursuit of knowledge, and what can be done to expand and extend it.[2] The library is both public and private in a number of senses; there is a governed and ungoverned quality to the time spent there. What that means in terms of the cybrary is best suggested by a little more etymology on the *cyber* side of this new coinage.

Cyberspace has its origins in the creative mind of novelist William Gibson, who coined the term two decades ago in *Neuromancer* (1984): "Cyberspace. A consensual hallucination experienced by billions of legitimate operators, in every nation, by children being taught mathematical concepts . . . A graphic representation of data abstracted from every computer in the human system" (p. 51, original ellipsis). In the novel, this definition is overheard in a voice-over to a children's television program, itself a clever means of including footnote explication in the novel form. In the course of *Neuromancer*, cyberspace cowboys "jack" into "rich fields of data" on a video game high; they rustle corporate information for unsavory clients, in an age-old story of good, evil, and the making of a living (p. 5).

Even apart from Gibson's references to criminal intent, this idea of cyberspace as a *consensual hallucination* may not seem a particularly positive metaphor for thinking about libraries and literacy. And yet when you think about it, the lending library has long been home to a collective and consensual serial reading of novels among, shall we say after Gibson, *legitimate operators* of literacy. As such, it is true that the library has indeed enabled greater public participation in the hallucinatory suspension of disbelief, while permitting it to be that much more differentiated (private and ungoverned) in the choices of books to read, than is suggested by Gibson's image of students sitting in rows in their geometry class. That is, the principle at issue is that library is public in a way that affords an important degree of variation and independence, because it offers a way of pulling out, as well as plugging in.[3]

Yet as we travel deeper into the etymology of the cybrary—which I am doing by jacking in from a hotel room in Mexico City to the online edition of the *OED* at my university library—*cyber* appears to be a prefix peeled off the earlier formation, *cybernetics*, which is a term Norbert Weiner used in 1948 to name a new field of study (as well as to entitle his accompanying book): "We have decided to call the entire field of control and communication theory, whether in the machine or in the animal, by the name *Cybernetics*, which we form from the Greek χυβερνητης or *steersman*" (p. 11). Weiner's manner of lumping control and communication together, as well as grouping machine and animal—with the very ordering of terms also worth noting—managed to set the stage for Haraway's (1991) later "Cyborg Manifesto," which recognized how far we have already gone in becoming machines subject to "the informatics of domination" (p. 161). And certainly Weiner was into laying the groundwork for mechanical reasoning and self-organizing systems.[4]

Whereas Weiner drew his use of *cybernetic* from ancient Greek, somewhat more than a century before he wrote his book, André Marie Ampère used *cybernétique* in his *Essai sur la Philosophie des Sciences* of 1834 to also coin a new field of inquiry: "The future science of government should be called *'la cybernétique'*" (cited by Aström, 2001). The *cyber* prefix harbors, then, associations with control and governance. Let us choose our words carefully for, like things wished for, they may come true. Yet, Ampère lived in the very spirit of the library that I am intent on preserving in the cybrary. He did not attend school but was educated at home, taking his lessons in large measure from what was then the newly published *L'Encyclopédie*, itself forming, by text and engraving, a worldwide web of the known world, at least as envisioned by 18th-century Parisian knowledge architects, Denis Dederiot and Jean Le Rond d'Alembert. Young Ampère worked his way through *L'Encyclopédie*, from first to last volume, and was said to be able to recite entries from memory until the end of his life. Ampère went on to be a professor of mathematics, eventually with an appointment at the Collège de France, an institution given to the ungoverned pursuit of knowledge. To this day, the highly regarded faculty do not teach courses in degree programs, but rather offer a regular series of free *public* lectures or seminars around their current research.[5] Cybernetic Ampère has, then, a way of bringing us back to these themes of the governed and the open. Ampère, Gibson, and Weiner represent this cyber-urge to find the order of things through their own self-directed pursuit of ideas in public realms. Such is the originating impulse of the library. It is itself all about organizing principles, within which we cannot wait to freely wander and become lost.

Now when it comes to thinking about the library in *cyberspace*, it is easy to conjure up images of a Borgean labyrinth of endless book-filled shelves, in a fantasy of knowledge and narrative without end played against a set designed by Peter Greenaway, the great film director of book-encrusted lives.[6] And it is true that the cybrary is increasingly vast, not only in the scale of what it contains, but also in who it reaches. There is nothing quite so global in its reach, in its reconstituting the public space of the library as something accessible everywhere, if not by everyone. The huge digital divide is not about to be closed, but the Internet continues to spread not only to Internet cafés in Manila, Nairobi, Alice, and Chennai, but to rural Indian villages, remote schools in Nepal, and to government offices and university libraries around the world.

Yet, the cybrary is not fulfilling the dream of endlessly open stacks. Just as Chaucer borrowed the French word for bookseller's shop, *librairie*, in writing about Boethius' collection of books, the modern cybrary of the Web is divided between materials that are free and items that are for sale, sometimes from the same title. So although readers can browse the last

7 days of the *New York Times* for free, anything earlier, should they want the details on what took place a few weeks ago, is pay-per-view. The *New Yorker* offers readers free access to a weekly short story and cartoon, as well as a selection of reviews and articles, along with materials not available in the magazine itself; and finally—to stay with this geographical theme—the *New York Review of Books* makes close to half the articles in each free, with the rest restricted to subscribers only. (Readers interested in other perspectives on the news can as readily consult the *Japan Times*, *The Hindu*, and the *People's Daily*, and with less restricted access to the archives.) Fans of Shakespeare, Austen, and Plato do well in the cybrary with public access through the Gutenberg Project and other sites. It takes a credit card to learn more about these authors from the *Encyclopedia Britannica*, although most authors of any note have free sites dedicated to them. One can also browse through the opening pages of the latest books at Amazon.com or search for words or phrases in them, before deciding whether or not to purchase them online. The cybrary is divided in this way, not entirely a public library, by any means, and yet affording a modicum of public access and public space.

When it comes to the scholarly wing of the cybrary, things are far more sharply divided between what is public and what is closed to public view. Although the majority of academic journals have electronic editions, online access to well over 80% of this literature is restricted to subscribers, with the very high price of admission ensuring that only well-financed research libraries can provide public access to this work, if that public can make its way to the physical library and use an open terminal there. If the public wants to see what this work is about online, then there are two rather limited choices. Individuals can view the small number of open access or free online journals that are now available in almost every discipline. Or, it can turn to pay-per-view services, which the major journal publishers offer, which puts the cost of a medical research article, for example, at well over the price of a good hardback book (although the article's abstract may be free to read). Public access to this journal literature is decidedly less than one might expect of work that is largely financed by the public and for which authors and reviewers are not paid by the publishers.

By the same token, research libraries are finding their own access severely hampered by growing corporate concentration among scholarly publishers.[7] By impeding the circulation of knowledge, this knowledge economy is detrimental to the work of many researchers and students, detrimental in ways that are bound to affect the quality of knowledge itself. Restriction in access also has consequences for the public presence of research in policymaking and public life (Willinsky, 2003c). It runs counter to the interests of the researcher-authors in finding the widest possible audience for what they have learned and are keen to share with others.[8] It fails to take advantage of what this new publishing technology can contribute to the global circulation of knowledge. The good, however, is that it has given rise to a small "open access" movement among academics and librarians. They wish to use the Internet's capacity to manage and distribute journals to increase access to scholarly materials, for universities around the world, for colleges and schools, for the professions and the public generally. Advocates of open access to research are experimenting with a number of approaches that will make research free to read. Harnad (2003), for example, led the way in encouraging faculty members to deposit copies of their published articles in open access eprint archives, with free software for libraries to set up such archives readily available in open source format.[9] Meanwhile, journals are testing out a variety of economic models for providing some form of open access to their contents (Willinsky, 2003a). The focus is on using the cybrary to make this literature free to read. It places the priority in publishing on the widest possible circulation of knowledge. And it draws directly on the model and spirit of the public library, bringing it explicitly into the sphere of the cybrary, most noticeably with the Public Library of Science, which is establishing itself as a leading open access journal publisher.

Up to this point, most of the important questions about academic life in cyberspace have been about the move to online courses and degree programs, in what often amounts to a capitalization of the university's brand and a further commodification of knowledge. Whereas some see online course delivery as an extension of the human right to education, providing individuals with opportunities for personal growth and economic development, Nobel (1998) mounted a substantial critique of it as threatening to rob "faculty of their knowledge and skills, their control over their working lives, the product of their labor, and, ultimately, their means of livelihood."[10] Yet, it now seems clear that there is another side to this cyberspace tension between academe and commerce, closer to the heart of the cybrary, and no less important for what Nobel (1998) called "our once great democratic higher education system." Although only a few faculty in any given university are involved in the online development and delivery of courses, almost all faculty, whether or not they realize it, are currently caught up in shaping the scholarly side of the cybrary.

An irony here is that the self-organizing cybernetics of the Internet— with its close and controlled engineering of communication through protocols, networks, and systems—is precisely what makes open access viable for journals and archives, which can greatly expand, in turn, the intellectual scope of the *public* cybrary, and open the doors wide to this hard-won knowledge. This same technology, however, is being used by journal publishers to further privatize and commercialize the scholarly side of the cybrary. Corporate journal publishers, such as Reed Elsevier, have found they can use this technology in cyberspace to increase their share of the market by bundling their journal titles, charging per-article fees to nonsubscribers, and limiting some of the uses of journals in subscribing libraries to members.

Still, the economics of the scholarly cybrary is far from straightforward. Journal prices, for example, are not associated with journal quality as the leading journals in a field can be divided among prohibitively expensive titles—in the thousands of dollars annually—and moderately priced titles in the low hundreds (Bergstrom, 2001). That journals of the same quality can operate with such discrepancies in costs suggests how thoroughly the current state of scholarly publishing is in a state of flux. The picture is further complicated by a free online indexing service to the medical literature, PubMed (with a special MedlinePlus section designed for lay people), which is provided by the U.S. National Library of Science. PubMed serves as an elaborate catalogue, in effect, for marketing pay-per-view access to commercial publishers' articles in the life sciences, as well as providing a window on that small proportion of the literature that has been made open access. Then there is the for-profit entity, BioMed Central Inc., which has implemented—and championed—the open access business model, which it uses for over 100 titles (financed by author fees as well as institutional and national memberships). As well, many of the corporate publishers, including Reed Elsevier, have decided, through the efforts of the World Health Organization, to generously grant developing countries open access to their medical and agricultural journals.[11] The public and commercial scale of this scholarly cybrary is thoroughly entwined. But make no mistake, the corporate sector's major stake in journal publishing is only increasing, as more scholarly societies turn their journals over to them. Open access publishing has emerged as the alternative program for scholarly publishing, one that has everything to do with how the cybrary is going to be constituted across these public and private interests.

The mixed economy of the public and private cybrary is full of implications for research and public libraries. In the case of the university's serials collection, direct online access to many of the titles is rendering the library increasingly invisible to its patrons. The library licenses access to the journals, creates a portal for its patrons, and then slips into the background. Yet librarians—information scientists that they now are—understand the issues of access better than anyone on campus. As a result, many are becoming involved in the struggle over the public and intellectual quality of the cybrary. These strong advocates of alternative modes of publishing, including open access, are raising banners exhorting faculty to *declare independence* and *take back control of scholarly publishing*.[12]

The next logical step, then, is for research libraries to play a more active role in constituting the cybrary as a public space. They can do that, in my estimation, by working directly with scholarly associations to under-write and host their journals in open access formats. The research libraries could go so far as to form cooperatives that would support the journals of scholarly associations or independent editors through a system of distrib-uted journal hosting while providing financial support, which, with the eventual dropping of print editions, would be at less than current sub-scription levels. The research libraries have the technical infrastructure in place, which is currently being used to support access to the major pub-lishers' journals, among others. Librarians have the expertise in informa-tion retrieval and indexing, as well as knowing a good deal about patterns of student and faculty use of the research literature. Using open source journal management and publishing software such as Open Journal Sys-tems, the libraries could readily manage the publishing of open access journals in collaboration with associations and independent editors.[13] The institutions would remain the major beneficiaries of this support of open access journals, but it would have this bonus of global public access to a much greater portion of the scholarly side of the cybrary. It could only fur-ther the circulation of knowledge, which hardly seems to lie far outside the library's mandate, even as it changes the library's very role in the cir-culation of knowledge. One place that this active support of open access is bound to affect is the public library.

The public library is already proving a major beneficiary of the cybrary, if still considerably limited in access on its scholarly side. Access to the Internet itself appears to lead to increased numbers of people visiting their local library, at least in the United States. Internet access is now available in 95% of public libraries in the United States, up from 28% in 1996, thanks to the efforts of the Bill and Melinda Gates Foundations, matched by a cor-responding level of local support (Lohr, 2004). According to a Gates Foun-dation evaluation study, the number of visits to the library, following the installation of the Internet, increases by 30%, with the proportion of poor visitors being greater than is found in the general population (A. C. Gor-don, M. T. Gordon, Moore, Heuertz, & Evans, 2004).[14] As one patron put the benefits of having the Internet in the library, "It's rather profound . . . easy access to information . . . it expands our view of the world. We here [in a small town] are the unknowns. We become more open-minded and open to new ideas" (A. C. Gordon et al., 2004). Another said of this new access that "it gives all of us who can't get a computer for some reason [the chance] to learn just as much as those with a computer" (A. C. Gordon et al., 2004)

The Internet in these libraries is being used, above all, for e-mailing family members (52%), but patrons also used it to find information about current events (35%), do schoolwork (33%), learn about a medical problem (31%), get government information (30%), and do homework (29%) (A. C. Gordon et al., 2004). Even at the low end of this usage, with 9% of patrons using the Internet to "get information on voting issues," one can see possibilities for the social sciences contributing more to this public information sphere, if not to be read by the library patron directly, than as the research will be used by interest groups and political parties in substantiating their positions (A. C. Gordon et al., 2004). Certainly, the signs from the public's uptake of health information and related research are very encouraging, and it may yet turn out that such access can bring down health costs (Fox & Raineee, 2000).[15] As one librarian described this new level of Internet access, "It has enhanced and expanded our research capabilities for both students and general patron interest. This used to require sending them to a larger or academic library," whereas another referred to how "it's like adding a whole other wing of information onto our library, it has become indispensable to staff and patrons alike" (A. C. Gordon et al., 2004).

Now, I do not mean to suggest that I believe that providing greater public access to scholarly work is *the* requisite for living a fruitful life. Rather, I fully recognize that the work of the university is often marked by, to return to one of Foucault's (2003) lectures at the Collège de France, "the centralizing power-effects that are bound up with the institutionalization and workings of any scientific discourse organized in a society such as ours" (p. 9). True, if reinforcing this centralized power-effect were the whole of scholarly activities—and clearly it is not, given Foucault's very critique of it—then calling for a wider distribution of this knowledge would only increase its power over people. Instead, efforts to open the scholarly cybrary will create more public space for what Foucault identified as the "discursive critique," which he saw rise in the 1960s by drawing on a combination of "the buried scholarly knowledge and knowledges that are disqualified by the hierarchy of erudition and sciences . . . in which we have both a meticulous rediscovery of struggles and the raw memory of fights" (p. 8).

By going public through this new global medium, the hierarchy of erudition will be that much more open to buried knowledge and rediscovered struggles. It will be open to a new range of scholarly journals, to new proximities of critique. The risk is indeed the unorthodox approaches, with troubles arising from not being able to rely on a handful of known entities in the hierarchy of erudition. Public spaces are like that. Private ones are not. So we may well see in an open access cybrary more of what Foucault described as "playing local, discontinuous, disqualified, or non-legitimated knowledges off against the unitary theoretical instance that claims to filter them, to organize them into a hierarchy, organize them in the name of a true body of knowledge, in the name of the rights of science that is in the hands of the few" (p. 9).

This proposed openness is meant to extend the republic of science and scholarship on a global scale, making it that much more democratic, as it expands who can read this work, and expands the prospects of journals being able to operate outside the centralized power-effects. Greater access to research is only the first step in enabling more equitable participation in the circulation of knowledge by a now-global academic community. The same systems that are enabling the major journals to reduce their costs by publishing online have also been developed in noncommercial, open source formats. Software, such as Open Journals Systems, is now being used to support journal publishing across this global community, in an effort to break free of the center-periphery model endemic to scholarly publishing. It can tap into the indexing and citation systems that have, up to now, kept it invisible and devalued even within its own communities.

Yes, readers will have to be that much more discerning amid any increase in access to information, and research is underway on how to support the critical reading skills of those new to this literature (Willinsky, 2003b). But are we to restrict access to this literature on the grounds that the public is not somehow equipped to read what is known? Their right to this knowledge is inherent in its very nature as a public good. A case would have to be made that public access would reduce the contribution of this good, and it is not apparent to me how that can be done. Will nonsense be produced? Will good work be misread? Indeed. It happens all the time now, with so little open access, and it happens to such an extent that it might well be mistaken as necessary and inherent to the process of circulating knowledge. Elsewhere I have worked on a number of reasons why faculty members should take a more active role in ensuring the public scale and scope of their work. Those reasons have to do with the epistemological principles of openly circulating knowledge that is worthy of that claim, enabling it to be subjected to a thorough critique. But there are also slightly less noble principles of furthering the author's interests, as are upheld by copyright law, by increasing the readership of their work and raising the degree to which it is cited by opening access (Willinsky, 2006).

Here, however, I am guided by the history of libraries, with a focus on what it might mean to the public to make the Internet more of a public place for open learning and self-education. The ease with which we can lay our hands on scholarly work today, through the Internet, public libraries, cheap paperbacks, and secondhand bookstores, was itself the result not only of technological breakthroughs, but of people's determination to create a larger public sphere of ideas. As these Internet technologies now make open access a viable alternative for journals, so an earlier great leap forward in the public library movement was underwritten in the 19th century by new print technologies, as well as the availability of cheap paper and postal rates. Community and worker libraries took ready advantage of the reduced costs of books, magazines, and newspapers to bring a wide selection of fiction, nonfiction, and periodicals within reach of far more people than had ever had access before. *Cheap editions* is everywhere the cry of open and independent learning.[16]

Lest we forget earlier struggle for access, I would conclude with scenes from that earlier time that speak directly to what the public status of this online world of learning might mean, as we take up the legacy of this earlier struggle over the right to know, and to participate in that knowledge. Although we may think of the public library as the home of middle-class interests and manners—a well-governed and ordered space—it is built on a long-standing, if buried, struggle among the disenfranchised seeking to exercise their right to know. The library does well in housing and equipping the aspirations of its patrons, in public and private senses, and in ways that cannot be so easily governed or ordered.

A vivid picture of what public access to this larger world of ideas has taken over the last few centuries is found in Rose's *The Intellectual Life of the British Working Classes* (2002), which portrays "the vital minority of self-improving workers" and "the passionate pursuit of knowledge by proletariat autodidacts" (pp. 2, 4). Rose went back to the first miners' libraries and mutual improvement societies in the mid-18th century, and traced the efforts of individual working-class readers and writers across two centuries. These dedicated readers may not be representative of their class, in any statistical sense, but they stand as an encouraging expression of interest in the value of opening the great storehouses of academic knowledge. The "autonomous intellectual life" of the otherwise disenfranchised during that period was to give rise to the Labour Party in Great Britain which grew out of a belief that, in Rose's terms, "the politics of equality must begin by redistributing this knowledge to the governed classes" (p. 7). And whereas working-class women had far less access to even rudimentary schooling and were not always welcomed in miner's libraries or other working men's associations, they did manage to form the very successful Women's Cooperative Guild by the final decades of the 19th century, in which women presented papers on feminist themes and engaged in other forms of mutual improvement (p. 77).

Earlier in the 19th century, a radical press movement emerged in the face of repressive laws and taxations—*taxes on knowledge,* as they were called at the time. The price of access was very much an issue in those days, and the undue levy placed on inexpensive newspapers was seen as a blatant effort to restrict people's right to know. In response, Thomas Jonathan Wooler, for example, launched the *Black Dwarf,* an *unstamped* (untaxed) newspaper that made it affordable to the working class in 1817. And, for all of its critique of contemporary political practices, Wooler also included the elements of a larger learning for its curious readers, by offering extracts from Aristotle, Erasmus, Machiavelli, Locke, and others, as well as the works of poets and other writers. The *Black Dwarf* ceased publishing in 1824, but other unstamped papers continued to grow, until in 1836 there was a half-dozen that could claim a combined circulation of over 200,000 (Rose, 2002, pp. 35–36). Men and women editors, contributors, and even sellers went to jail over this freedom of the press issue, a freedom that had everything to do with maintaining both the right to criticize and the right to inexpensive access to knowledge.

It was a time when, as Lowery wrote in his autobiography from that period, that "every branch of knowledge had its public-house where its disciplines met" including those interested in music, literature, philosophy, and science (Rose, 2002, p. 38). The Spitalfields Mathematical Society, made up of weavers and other tradesmen, began meeting in the local taverns in 1717 (p. 70). Rose reported that there was also a "tradition of working class naturalists, who were meeting in pubs up until the 1920s" (p. 294). They had an impact on the research in botany, Rose noted, as works such as "William Jackson Hooker's *Muscologia Britannica* (1818) were written in accessible English because the authors depended so heavily on the contributions of plebian naturalists" (p. 224).

But then the research enterprise itself was far more of a public activity, if more largely so among the middle and upper classes, during the 19th century. For example, Endersby (2003) pointed out how "Darwin sat at the center of a web of correspondence that encircled the earth. Letters poured in every day containing answers to questions, new facts, fresh problems, seeds to plant, and an endless variety of specimens to ponder" (p. 21). Darwin corresponded with the leading men of science of the day with the letter "his primary research tool," but as Browne (2002) pointed out in her biography of him, "he hunted down anyone who could help him . . . fur-trappers, horse-breeders, society ladies, Welsh hill-farmers, zookeepers, pigeon fanciers, gardeners, asylum owners, and kennel hands" (p. 11). Making a similar point about the public contribution to research, Shippey (2003) noted the parallels between Darwin's *Origin of Species* and Grimm's *Deutsche Grammatik* ("for the humanities, the *Grammatik* had much the same effect as Darwin's Origin of Species for the life sciences"), the first volume of which appeared in 1819:

> Both works integrated literally millions of observations and sets of data, often, interestingly and significantly, recorded by people from outside the scholarly world—dog-breeders and pigeon-fanciers in the case of Darwin, dialect-speakers and old women in the case of Grimm, the despised "nurses and spinning-wives" (*Ammen und Spinnerinnen*) whom he angrily defends in his later *Deutsche Mythologie*.

There are no less impressive instances of public participation from around the world in the making of the *Oxford English Dictionary*, which began in the Victorian era and carried through to the 20th century with considerable impact on the defining of the language (Willinsky, 1994).

William Lovett was one of the leaders of the working-class sector of this earlier knowledge society. He took over as secretary in 1828 of the short-lived but promisingly entitled British Association for the Promotion of Cooperative Knowledge, having had a stormy political career that included being jailed for libeling government officials, and went on in 1841 to found the National Association for Promoting the Political and Social Improvement of the People, whose circulating libraries and teachers were funded by worker contributions (Rose, 2002, p. 36). He entitled his autobiography, which he worked on for decades, *Life and Struggles of William Lovett in His Pursuit of Bread, Knowledge and Freedom.* Lovett wrote of wishing "to establish a political school of self-instruction among them [working classes], in which they should accustom themselves to examine great social and political principles, and by their publicity and free discussion help to form a sound and healthful public opinion throughout the country" (cited by Tawney, 1964b, p. 19). He wrote that "the time has gone by for the selfish and bigoted possessors of wealth to confine the blessings of knowledge within their own narrow circle, and by every despotic artifice to block up each cranny through which intellectual light might break out upon the multitude" (cited by Rose, 2002, p. 64). Now all of that may seem a rhetoric of long ago, before public schooling, financial aid programs for colleges and other measures, and clearly the progress has been considerable. But one has only to look at the knowledge gap identified as one of the major challenges facing developing countries, to see that the blessings have not yet become universally available in ways that they reasonably could (Persaud, 2001).

These themes of self-instruction, mutual improvement, and cooperative knowledge are very much about the struggle for enfranchisement, at a time when the working classes were regarded, by those who governed, as unfit to vote or at least unfit until they were properly educated. Lovett also helped to found the London Working Men's Association, which proved to be a source of published work on workers' rights, universal suffrage education, and international politics, which drew on the work of Paine, Godwin, and Ricardo. Lovett also called for a government-supported national education system, a system that went far beyond the charity schools of the day, or the achievement score measures of today: "Imagine the honest, sober, reflecting portion of every town and village in the kingdom linked together as a band of brothers, honestly resolved to investigate all subjects connected with their interests, and to prepare their minds to combat with the errors and enemies of society" (cited by Tawney, 1964b, p. 26).

In some of those 19th-century villages and towns "learning collectives" were formed, with local libraries playing a critical role in supporting such learning (Rose, 2002, p. 67). Lovett was concerned that this education be more than, as historian R. H. Tawney put it, "a system devised by one class for the discipline of another" (p. 28). More than that, as part of this effort, Lovett arrived at the fundamental educational question: "Is it consistent with justice that the knowledge requisite to make a man acquainted with his rights and duties should be purposively withheld from him?" (p. 28). The worker association efforts at education culminated by the turn of the 19th century in the Workers Educational Association, which Tawney (1964a) captured the spirit of in this spirited and misogynous way: "Men meet and discuss. There is hesitation, curiosity, interest, eagerness for knowledge. We ought to have learned about that; can't we learn about it? We will *learn* about it, and we will find a man to help us if a man is to be found" (p. 77).[17] "Knowledge for its own sake is a better principle," was how one WEA student responded to the question of whether vocational courses should be taught (Rose, 2002, p. 285). Still, it should be noted that when Rose examined the records of worker's libraries, especially among Welsh miners, he found fiction far more popular than nonfiction, and he is happy to dispel any undue romanticization among socialists looking back, by pointing out that Karl Marx was not much read by anyone at all, although his works did figure often enough in the library holdings, serving much as they do in Diego Rivera's great murals at the National Palace in Mexico City as icons of dissent and hope (Rose, 2002, ff. 298).

Certainly, university extension, adult education, open universities, and other means of extending access to higher education, including online programs, should go hand in hand with any defense of the cybrary's public sphere. Yet even here, with such programs, the self-directed elements of this learning must be balanced against the governed aspects of such programs, to keep it from becoming one class seeking to discipline another or, in Foucault's terms, as a way of increasing the centralizing power-effects of a hierarchical erudition. The very goal of providing open access to the full body of the learning and scholarship at issue provides a check on what might otherwise be presented as a monolithic and entirely coherent understanding, when in fact it is riddled with ideas and values that are not only contested and challenged, but in need of grounding and a greater sense of connection to this very community it would otherwise educate. But then opening access would also provide a greater reason for such educational programs, as the cybrary, as public library, to go on serving people long after this or that course is completed.

Now Rose did describe how working-class interests in self-education had, by 1945, gone into a serious state of decline, and this is not meant to suggest that suddenly opening the gates to the research literature, through the never-ending cybrary, would reverse this decline, in the face of entertainment and the other time and mind absorbing enticements of our era.

But I do believe that this history demonstrates how assumed boundaries between educated and uneducated, learned and unlearned, were crossed in earlier times through developments in print technology and economics, and will be crossed again, all the more so with the support of faculty members committed to providing others with the opportunity out of a recognition of this basic right to know.

There remains much research to be done on what this new expansion in access to knowledge will mean for the public, and how that will change over time and with greater exposure to that literature. Still, before conclusive evidence on the benefits is in hand, faculty members everywhere should begin to move on this issue *now*, on the principle of the public's right to know. They should consider access and costs of the journals in which they seek to publish. They should explore how the journals with which they are associated, through professional associations or board memberships, can offer some form of open access (Willinsky, 2003a). There is no reason for faculty members to wait in posting their published work in open access Web sites and archives, or to publish their work in open access journals. This contribution will support the encyclopedic, open, and public force of the cybrary, even as it ensures the greater possible exposure or access to their work. By such means, they can begin to contribute to a cybrary that not only maintains the original spirit of the library, but greatly extends its public scale and resources.

We are withholding this research from the public domain by virtue of the choices we make in how it is published in this new online medium. The open access movement is being treated by some as a challenge to a researcher's right to pursue impact and prestige. It is being held up as a threat to the scientific system by the publishers.[18] It is being dismissed with indifference and complacency: "Hey, I have no time to worry about what this or that journal costs the library or whether it is freely available." But it makes little sense to speak of a loss of personal prestige or a threat to scholarly quality when some of the top journals in their field, from the *New England Journal of Medicine* to *Teachers College Record,* have gone with various forms of open access (while still selling subscriptions in these two cases). One's career is not being placed on the line to publish with an open access journal because open access increases readership and citation levels. And, as for complacency, it may seem in looking back to be of the most reckless and irresponsible sort, as hundreds of societies turn their journals over to corporate publishers who are contributing through their pricing policies, in effect, to a declining state of access to research on a global scale, even as the number of faculty and students continues to grow.

That leaves me, of course, with my own obvious inability, over the last few years, to place a compelling and persuasive case before an academic community otherwise entirely and deeply committed to learning, libraries, and the circulation of knowledge. What could be easier than convincing faculty members that it falls to them to shift the intellectual balance of the cybrary in favor of its long-standing *public* library legacy, which is rooted in the ancient university libraries and in the basic scholarly urge found in the unfettered pursuit of ideas? All they need to do is look up from their own work for a moment. What could be easier? What could be harder? You do have to keep your voice down, after all, in the library, even as it remains that place where the governed and ungoverned pursuit of knowledge, where the public interests and private concerns, meet.

NOTES

1. The first citation for this public use is Reginald Pecock, from the *The Repressor of Over Much Blaming of the Clergy, circa 1449,* "In caas a greet clerk wolde go into a librarie and ouer studie there a long proces of feith writun in the Bible."

2. Centuries after these initial citations that the *OED* has collected for this public sense of library, we come to how "Charitable . . . Persons have . . . erected Libraries within several Parishes and Districts," from 1708 Acts of the Privy Council, and to schemes for "free libraries," by the mid-19th century.

3. When Gibson subversively suggested that children in a geometry class are absorbed in collective illusion, it calls to mind just how closely PowerPoint slides projected on the walls of darkened rooms—whether classrooms or boardrooms—resemble one of the West's great philosophical parables. See Plato's *Republic,* Bk VII, "The Cave Allegory."

4. It may seem entirely unscholarly to raise the spectrum of coincidence in George Orwell composing his informatics dystopia, *1984*—which was the year Gibson's *Neuromancer* was published—during the same year that Weiner published his *Cybernetics,* in 1948. Weiner's choice of philosopher Leibniz as "the patron saint for cybernetics" has its own resonance with the cybrary, as Leibniz was, among many things, a librarian, who sought "to build systems of solid knowledge for promoting man's happiness" that would link together in the form of a "demonstrative Encyclopedia" (1951, p. 32; see also Willinsky, 2000, pp. 65–72).

5. For example, Foucault's lectures at the Collège de France were attended by thousands between 1971 and 1984, and are now in the process of being published. As Ewald and Fontana (2003) explained: "Professors teaching at the Collège de France . . . are under an obligation to teach for twenty-six hours a year (up to half the hours can take the form of seminars). Each year, they are required to give an account of the original research they have undertaken, which means the contents of their lectures must always be new. Anyone is free to attend the lectures and seminars; there is no enrollment, and no diplomas are required. The professors do not award any diplomas. In the vocabulary of the Collège de France, its professors do not have students, but *auditeurs* or listeners" (pp. ix–x). Foucault (2003) opened his lectures of 1976 by stating that "I do not regard our Wednesday meetings as a teaching activity, but as public reports on the work I am, in other respects, left to

get on with more or less as I see fit," and he referred to this reporting as "an absolute obligation" (p. 1).

6. On Borges, see his "The Library of Babel" (1962); on Peter Greenaway, his movie production of the Tempest, *Prospero's Books* (1991).

7. An estimate from EPS Market Monitor places ownership of the $7 billion science, technology, and medical research publishing industry at 62% of the market, with the top four players, beginning with Reed Elsevier, controlling fully half of that industry (STM Market, 2003, p. 12).

8. A recent poll of 7,400 faculty members conducted by the nonprofit Ithaka noted that the characteristic of a journal that was most desirable was wide circulation (endorsed by 87%), whereas 58% said the journal should be free, and 52% felt is should be highly selective (Kiernan, 2004, p. A34).

9. See Eprints (http://eprints.org) and DSpace (http://dpsace.org).

10. Also, see the Bryson Decision at the University of British Columbia on protecting academic freedom in online teaching contexts (2004).

11. See Health InterNetwork Access to Research Initiative (HINARI) (http://www.healthinternetwork.org/) and Access to Global Online Research in Agriculture (AGORA) (http://www.aginternetwork.org/en/).

12. See Scholarly Publishing and Academic Resources Coalition (SPARC) (http://www.arl.org/sparc/).

13. See the Public Knowledge Project, which I direct, and its Open Journal Systems, an open source journal management and publishing system, designed to be utilized with minimal technical skills and limited editorial experience, which is being used by African Journals Online and other agencies and publishers (http://pkp.ubc.ca/ojs).

14. In one county in southern Louisiana, for example, the government saw a one-quarter-cent sales tax passed in support of local libraries in 1998, which has resulted in funding for "81 computers, more staffing and a 10-fold increase in the annual book budget" (Lohr, 2004).

15. I am indebted to my colleague Stephen Carey for this entirely sensible idea.

16. Frederick Engels (1969): "And in how great a measure the English proletariat has succeeded in attaining independent education is shown especially by the fact that the epoch-making products of modern philosophical, political, and poetical literature are read by working-men almost exclusively. . . . In this respect the Socialists, especially, have done wonders for the education of the proletariat. They have translated the French materialists, Helvetius, Holbach, Diderot, etc., and disseminated them, with the best English works, in *cheap editions*" (my emphasis).

17. From its current Web site: "The Workers' Educational Association (WEA) is the UK's largest voluntary provider of adult education. Ever since it was founded in 1903, in order to support the educational needs of working men and women, the WEA has maintained its commitment to provide access to education and learning for adults from all backgrounds, and in particular those who have previously missed out on education" (http://www.wea.org.uk).

18. Association of Learned and Professional Society Publishers: "Abandoning the diversity of proven publishing models in favor of a single, untested model

could have disastrous consequences for the scientific research community. It could seriously jeopardize the flow of information today, as well as continuity of the archival record of scientific progress that is so important to our society tomorrow" (Publisher's Associations' Statement, 2003).

REFERENCES

Ampere, A. M. (1834–43). *Essai sur la philosophie des sciences ou Eposition analytique d'une classification nouvelle de toute les connaissances humaines.* Paris: Bahelier.

Aström, K. J. (2001). *For cyber freaks.* Lund, Sweden: Lund Institute of Technology. Retrieved August 21, 2005, from http://www.control.lth.se/news/cyber.html

Bergstrom, T. C. (2001). Free labor for costly journals? *Journal of Economic Perspectives* 15(4), 183–198. Retrieved September 27, 2003, from http://www.econ.ucsb.edu/~tedb/Journals/jeprevised.pdf

Borges, J. L. (1962). The library of Babel. In *Labyrinths: Selected stories and other writings* (pp. 51–58). New York: New Directions.

Browne, J. (2002). *Charles Darwin: The power of place. Volume II of a biography.* Princeton, NJ: Princeton University Press.

Endersby, J. (2003, November 21). Kew gooseberries. *Times Literacy Supplement,* 3–4.

Engels, F. (1969). *The condition of the working class in England.* Moscow: Panther. Retrieved on August 21, 2005 http://www.marxists.org/archive/marx/works/1845/condition-working-class/ (Original work published 1845)

Ewald, F., & Fontana, A. (2003). Foreword. In M. Foucault, *Society must be defended: Lectures at the Collège de France, 1975–1976* (pp. ix–xiv). (D. Macey, Trans.). New York: Picador.

Foucault, M. (2003). *Society must be defended: Lectures at the Collège de France, 1975–1976.* (D. Macey, Trans.). New York: Picador.

Fox, S., & Raineee, L. (2000). *The online health care revolution: How the Web helps Americans take better care of themselves.* Washington, DC: Pew Internet and American Life Project. Retrieved September 28, 2003, from http://www.pewinternet.org/reports/toc.asp?Report=26

Gibson, W. (1984). *Neuromancer.* New York: Ace.

Gordon, A. C., Gordon, M. T., Moore, E. J. Heuertz, L., & Evans, D. J. (2004). *Legacy of Gates foundation's U.S. library program: Impacts of public access computing positive, widespread.* Los Angeles, CA: Multimedia. Retrieved on August 21, 2005 http://www.pacp.net/LJ Online.pdf

Harnad, S. (2003). Electronic preprints and postprints. *Encyclopedia of library and information science.* New York: Marcel Dekker. Retrieved September 28, 2003, from http://www.ecs.soton.ac.uk/~harnad/Temp/eprints.htm

Haraway, D. J. (1991). *Simians, cyborgs and women: The reinvention of nature.* New York: Routledge.

Kiernan, V. (2004, April 30). Professors are unhappy with limitations of online resources, survey finds. *Chronicle of Higher Education,* p. A34.

Leibniz, G. W. (1951). Precepts for advancing the sciences and arts. In P. P. Wiener (Ed.), *Leibniz: Selections* (pp. 29–46). New York: Scribners. (Original work published 1680)

Lohr, J. (2004, April 22). Libraries wired and reborn. *New York Times.* Retrieved on August 21, 2005 http://tech2.nytimes.com/mem/technology/techreview.html?res=9C0CE4D7163A F931A1575C0A9629C8B63

Noble, D. F. (1998). Digital diploma mills: The automation of higher education. *First Monday.* Retrieved on August 21, 2005 http://www.firstmonday.dk/issues/issue3_1/noble/

Persaud, A. (2001). The knowledge gap. *Foreign Affairs, 80*(2), 107–117.

Publisher Associations' Statement on open archives. (2003). *Scholarly Communications Report,* 7(11), 8.

Rose, J. (2002). *The intellectual life of the British working class.* New Haven, CT: Yale University Press.

Shippey, T. (2003, November 7). Grimm's law. *Times Literary Supplement,* p. 14.

STM Market. (2003). Slow growth but profitable according to EPS. *Scholarly Communications Report,* 7(11), 8, 12.

Tawney, R. H. (1964a). An experiment in democratic education. In R. Hinden (Ed.), *The radical tradition: Twelve essays on politics, education and literature* (pp. 70–81). New York: Pantheon.

Tawney, R. H. (1964b). William Lovett. In R. Hinden (Ed.), *The radical tradition: Twelve essays on politics, education and literature* (pp. 15–31). New York: Pantheon.

Wiener, N. (1948). *Cybernetics, or control and communication in the animal and the machine.* Cambridge, MA: MIT Press.

Willinsky, J. (1994). *Empire of words: The reign of the OED.* Princeton, NJ: Princeton University Press.

Willinsky, J. (2000). *If only we knew: Increasing the public value of social science research.* New York: Routledge.

Willinsky, J. (2003a). The nine flavors of open access publishing. *Postgraduate Journal of Medicine, 49*(3), 263–267. Retrieved on August 21, 2005 http://pkp.ubc.ca/publications/index.html.

Willinsky, J. (2003b). Open access: Reading (research) in the age of information. In C. M. Fairbanks, J. Worthy, B. Maloch, J. V. Hoffman, & D. L. Schallert (Eds.), *51st national reading conference yearbook* (pp. 32–46). Oak Creek, WI: National Reading Conference.

Willinsky, J. (2003c). Scholarly associations and the economic viability of open access publishing. *Journal of Digital Information, 4*(2). Retrieved on August 21, 2005 http://jodi.ecs.soton.ac.uk/Articles/v04/i02/Willinsky/

Willinsky J. (2006). *The access principle: The case for open access to research and scholarship.* Cambridge, MA: MIT Press.

11

The Politics and Philosophy of E-Text: Use Value, Sign Value, and Exchange Value in the Transition From Print to Digital Media

Timothy W. Luke
Virginia Polytechnic Institute

This chapter examines the politics of knowledge and the cultures of information in contemporary scholarly communication, because they are being transformed into digital modes of communication from a print-based regime of scholarship and knowledge accumulation. As these changes unfold, the work of libraries and librarians must adapt to these transformations. Whereas some are, many are not, inasmuch as the practices of print have provided implicitly the standards used by scholars and society to judge the quality, utility, and durability of knowledge. Although print literacy is not lost in the online environment with electronic media, digitalization changes what documents are, who can create them, how information is generated, why it is valued, where it is accumulated, and when it is used.

Given this transition to e-text, the cybrary, cyberschooling, and cyborganization all are new sites for scholarly practice to develop. And, in these new formations, the conventional understandings of how scholarship is done, where teaching is conducted, and what archives are generated in the knowledge creation, circulation, and collection processes are shifting significantly. This chapter reevaluates these shifts, while asking how scholars, schools, and societies are perhaps changing their conceptions of how knowledge is valorized in use, by location, or through exchange. In addition to reflecting about these developments in general, it also will consider how they have worked in particular at the Center for Digital Discourse and Culture (CDCC), as well as the Virginia Tech Cyberschool at Virginia Polytechnic Institute and State University in Blacksburg, Virginia, over the past decade.

Although Baudrillard's work on hyperreality rarely addresses it, the Internet plainly constitutes a domain that is, ironically, cause and effect, map and territory, material and hyperreal. Its creation marked a peculiar moment in time, whose communicative necessities shaped an artifact with multiple potentialities. Once the changing terrain of Cold War geopolitics lessened the salience of the Internet's original purposes, those capabilities became immensely more useful in the fast-changing flows of the post-Cold War era. A device designed in the 1960s to actuate reliable communications in thermonuclear attack environments became in the 1990s a utility to enable cheap, rapid, and multimedia communication environments potentially or eventually, for anyone anytime anywhere. Larger changes in the global economy allowed digital communicative capabilities to become accessible to the multitudes. This digital hyperreality opened to anyone online 24/7, and practically to almost all places with reliable connectivity. The Internet, like mass advertising, television, or consumer goods, is now another concrete expression of those globalizing transformations. It is not the ultimate cause of change in all of its complexity, but cybrarians need to ask much bigger questions here about text, where it is stored, who uses it, what use occurs, and how constant technological disruptions affect their collections.

Older notions of fixed, stable, enduring national publics inside of stable states and cohesive societies tied to print are breaking down. Aggregating centralized authority in state governments, allocating material wealth inside of and between territorial regimes was a political project that went awry in the 20th century. Some librarians have continued driving forward while staring too long into the rearview mirror; yet, their sense of direction here is rooted in concepts drawn from traditional print practices, which are quaint anachronisms that few forces in the economy or society now strongly support. Here, as Baudrillard (2004) suggested, "the social which, in its time, was a fine idea, has assumed concrete form, has substituted itself for the political and it is now itself swallowed up by the cultural. What an unhappy fate the book has met with—and sociology with it. . . . How can you go on doing your own thing in your own little discipline as though nothing had happened" (p. 56). Many cybrarians see the wisdom of this insight, and they are trying to open disciplinary boundaries by exploring the possibilities of e-text.

With digitalization, as Baudrillard anticipated in *For a Critique of the Political Economy of the Sign* (1981), all of the objective shapes, semiotic syntax, and collective rhetoric of marketable goods "refer to social objectives and to a social logic. They speak to us not so much of the user and of technical practices, as of social pretension and resignation, of social mobility and inertia, of acculturation and enculturation, of stratification and of social classification" (p. 38). Thus, digitalization permits consumer goods and services, especially as they intertwine with consumption in social, political, and economic exchange, to mediate the political economy of the sign and its culture of consumption more virtually. Cybrarians recognize that digital objects as such need to be interrogated to discover new modes of utility, mobility, and survivability for text as bits. Indeed, they are vital for cybraries to advance as serviceable cultural institutions.

The characteristics of a digital library, as Levy (2001) observed, are still ambivalent, conflicted, and unfixed. All of these qualities follow from the tug-of-war between its probable users, custodians, and architects to articulate what the cybrary will be, and then what it will do:

> For some groups, most notably librarians, the phrase refers most directly to *institutions that oversee digital collections,* while for other professions, primarily computer and information scientists, it refers to *digital collections,* without regard to the institutional settings, (if any) in which they might be managed. (Notice that the phrase "software library" means a collection of computer programs or routines, and makes no reference to an institution.) *Digital library,* it seems to me, draws much of its power from this ambiguity: it provides a name for collections of digital materials that invokes the aura of the modern library and its social mission (library) as social institution. But it does so without actually making any commitments to the public good (library as collection). (Levy, 2001, p. 135)

This general effort to define a digital library seems at odds with itself. Not all print libraries are public institutions or devoted to the public good: Many are closed archives, private subscription operations, or collections of texts accessible to few, if any, ordinary users. A cybrary could easily be both, or organized in a manner that both ends would be served. The cybrary could be, and in fact would be, a social institution that would assemble and oversee digital collections with their own operational provenance as well as offer access to collections held at many other widely distributed locales.

Nonetheless, the ambiguity Levy ascribed to the digital library is an attribute that invites further consideration in the creation of cybraries for informationalizing economies and societies. In particular, what social missions will cybraries serve, and which commitments will they have to public, private, and general interests?

Online digital documents, unlike print ones, are fluid concretions of *kanban* content, or clusters of bits pulled together "just-in-time" on demand for communication. Any single document sits as coded elements in discretely deactivated, disconnected, distended arrays, awaiting assembly into representational objects. Calling it up for use online pulls together its bits just-in-time to be viewed, printed, or stored again. What actually becomes taken as addressing its delimited URL creates the representation of digital documentation? Like print libraries, the cybrary requires a vast industrial ecology to create, nurture, and sustain its collections. Digital documents do not yet have the institutionalized stability of codex books, or the embedded and professional expectations of brick-and-mortar libraries trailing long with them. They can acquire it, but it is taking, and will continue to take, time to draw up the conventions of collaboration, co-invention, and cooperation to realize the full utility of cybraries to function.

The digitalization of documents has come about only recently. Yet, the technological ability to make documents essentially digital objects has existed for 25 to 30 years (Negroponte, 1995). The 1990s was a context that combined increasing costs of print documents, decreasing ability to pay for print objects, and an unprecedented opportunity to circulate documents in fairly stable forms over the Web, which pushed longer standing technological possibility into the realm of ordinary technical practice. Even though e-texts, e-tickets, e-memos, e-dissertations, e-dossiers, e-portfolios, and so on, are first sold as being the same as print only electronic, all of the significant differences soon show themselves, and bring along new, unanticipated changes in discursive and cultural practices (Cairncross, 1997). The increasing costs of print documents come from corporate consolidation and the proliferation of many important, but small circulation, titles. Although there is a willingness to pay for print's relative permanence, the ability of many individuals, organizations, and universities to pay is no longer there due to less disposable income and disinvestments in public goods. With the World Wide Web—a quick and efficient mode of distribution, archiving, and use—digital documents become a feasible alternative to print, even though e-texts have their own special drawbacks for cybraries to manage.

INFORMATION SOCIETY: THE CYBRARY AND HYPERREALITY

During the late 20th century, Baudrillard argued that advanced capitalist society underwent an implosive reversal in the circulation of power between the masses and their organized institutions. Once, as Baudrillard (1983a) claimed, "capital only had to produce goods; consumption ran by itself. Today it is necessary to produce consumers, to produce demand, and this production is infinitely more costly than that of goods" (p. 27). As individual desires, however, are now formed abstractly as bits around prepackaged needs that serve as productive forces, the social lifeworld evolves into even more fluid aggregates of atomized individuals, whose roles mediate the packaged encoding of their desires in the corporate marketplace. Schmidt (see chap. 4, this volume) anticipates this development in her exploration of new library designs for new library patrons. Cybraries need to consider how much individual subjects "are only episodic conductors of meaning, for in the main, and profoundly, we *form a mass*, living most of the time in panic or haphazardly, above and beyond any meaning" (Baudrillard, 1983b, p. 11).

Today's posthistorical social mass, therefore, is perhaps neither a subject nor an object. It bears no necessary relation to any historical social referent—a class, a nation, a folk, or the proletariat. Instead, its activities and their records often could be no more than a statistical cluster of coincident activities whose main traces appear in market analyses, social surveys, opinion polls, and now web page downloads. The silent majorities of the masses perhaps are no longer representable in materialist political terms or concretely identifiable in realistic social terms. The once ordinarily assumed "ontological givens" taken for granted by epistemic realism essentially evaporate, according to Baudrillard, in the blackholes of cyberspace. The complex codes of media in the global market set the outer boundaries of the social mass "at the point of convergence of all the media waves which depict it" (Baudrillard, 1983a, p. 30). Thus, cybraries must consider how to document records, traces, or activities of social formations whose layers essentially are a complex simulation of reality, designed specifically to sustain the fragile cycles of political, economic, and cultural reproduction, in which signs of the real—like virtual worlds—take the place of reality itself.

Modernity itself transmutates with these digital developments in advanced capitalist exchange as cultural life becomes more entwined within informational modes of production (Luke, 1989, pp. 2–16). If simulation, rather than representation, constitutes the dominant organizing principle of this new era, then what cybraries collect and catalogue must change. Therefore, in Baudrillard's vision of today's new world order, the modern nation-state, industrial economy, liberal democracy, and enlightenment culture all slip away under "a political economy of the sign." Cybraries need to look into "the very heart of the economic mode of domination," and ask how it reinvents (or reproduces) the logic and the strategy of signs, of castes, of segregation, and of discrimination; how it reinstates the feudal logic of personal relations or even that of the gift exchange and of reciprocity, or of agonistic exchange—in order simultaneously "to thwart and crown the 'modern' socio-economic logic of class" (Baudrillard, 1981, p. 38).

In the last analysis, Baudrillard overstated his claims when he envisioned a "society" where agents who are regarded as individuals now conform to "a logic of simulation which has nothing to do with a logic of facts and an order of reasons" (Baudrillard, 1988, p. 175). These claims do not support Jameson's (1991) demand to look at the rare, the unusual, and interesting, "for shifts and irrevocable changes in the *representation* of things and of the way they change" (p. ix). E-textuality could be such a point of investigation, but e-texts are often print documents that use bits to fuse their symbolic imaginaries with sophisticated material design and complex process engineering. The effects of e-text may follow from "concealing that reality no more exists outside than inside the bounds of the artificial perimeter" (Baudrillard, 1983b, p. 26). In this account, the virtual exists as a viral force, and "the hyperreality" of e-textuality is *real*. The bits and bytes of e-textuality, then, anchor a new international order where the *cultural* and the *economic* "collapse back into each other and say the same thing" (Jameson, 1991, p. xxi). When all is said and done in e-textuality, the operative semiotic principles of this informational order are those of simulation rather than preindustrial counterfeit or industrial mechanical reproduction. Digital texts can no longer be seen as "the maps," "the doubles," "the mirrors," or "the concepts" of any terrain metaphorically regarded as "the real." On the contrary, in the virtual world, all abstract frames of the real effectively function as simulations, and these simulations are what must be regarded as hyperreal materials to be captured, catalogued, and circulated. For Baudrillard (1983b), "simulation is no longer that of a territory, a referential being or a substance. It is the generation by models of a real without origin or a reality: a hyperreal. The territory no longer precedes the map, nor survives it. Henceforth, it is the map that precedes the territory—PRECESSION OF SIMULACRA—it is the map that engenders the territory" (p. 25). In e-textuality of hyperspace, something very important has disappeared; but, at the same time, an important new reality appears. On the one hand, then, as ineluctable nonidentity of map and terrain can emerge; one sees that, on the other hand, e-textuality can sublate and surpass print textuality.

Cybraries, then, will accumulate digital copies of existing analogue materials, ranging across a wide spectrum from ancient manuscripts and traditional print documents to contemporary cinematic and televisual works, as well as entire new varieties of e-texts rooted in digital knowledge production. Still, these networks of scholarly communication, and the new audiences for such knowledge consumption, guarantee that cybrarians will always have difficulty staying ahead of the waves of change thrown forth by digitalization.

Many "born-digital" documents may never be all collected, archived, and used, but those that have been judged to have some significant cultural, aesthetic, historical, or social significance must be sought after by cybrarians. Of course, many "original analogue" texts, whether print, film, or music, have been lost over time due to inattention to the impermanence of their initial media of expression, prejudice about their long-term worth, or the incompressible overload of information that comes along with any new medium of knowledge creation. Recognizing these trends from the outset, cybrarians need to be actively engaged in gathering, assessing, and preserving the flood of digital documents that hide in the inaccessible realms of the "hidden web" or "dark Internet" that evade access, as Hunter (see chap. 6, this volume) suggests, in machine-readable material forms. And, just as they must preserve the bits, cybraries also should be aware of the attendant need to acquire (and keep operational) whatever special hardware systems or software packages that might be required to keep the bits they accumulate useful for their patrons. The performativity of cybrarian labor requires these actions (Lyotard, 1984).

One example of such e-texts at the Center for Digital Discourse and Culture is the Digital Fordism site. Originally based on a 2000 archive tied to an *Organization & Environment* article, this online analysis of the Fordist and post-Fordist mode of production in Ford Motor Company automotive products was as an intertextual node between an expanded and elaborated journal article, other writings on Fordism/post-Fordism/Sloanism, and additional reference sites on the changing forms of labor. From its inception, it also was imagined as a prototypical example of a "research e-dition" from an electronic point-of-publication to anchor new scholarly communities. Since 2000, it has attracted considerable interest and use. Hits and page downloads from the beginning were respectable, and a major expansion and upgrade in 2003 only added to its robust levels of use. In 2000, it typically came up on Google in the top 10 out of 4,200 "Fordism" URLs. Since then, it has basically kept that top 10 to 15 position, depending on the time of year as well as the year searched. In 2002, it still was coming in at the top 10 to 15 out of around 7,800 "Fordism" sites; in late August 2004, it logged in at 6 out of 27,800 and, in late august 2005, it came in at 11 and 12 out of 67,900 "Fordism" sites. The site itself contains the original Fordism materials, as well as a respectable archive of over 58 other major studies of Fordism in several languages that are used now on this site with the original author's permission to "reprint" here. The nature of use, circulation, or impact here is difficult to compare to print, but it indicates a high level of visitation and use on the World Wide Web that has opened up the arcane topics of Fordism to a diverse global constituency.

"Blogs" are another case in point. Some regard them as the digital drivel of self-important individuals that will soon go the way of mimeo broadsheets, whereas others see them as a significant new Internet communication medium. Either way, their absorption of discursive energies at this point in history should prompt cybraries to collect their content, link to their sources, and catalogue their various streams of analysis. Yet, because of their number, variety, and quality, few—if any—are systematically tracked or collected. For some period of time, and for a considerable number of daily net users who write and read blogs, a whole dimension of digital discourse is being produced, circulated, and consumed, but with little attention to its collection, interpretation, or presentation. Of course, with close to 10,000 new blogs starting each day (Battelle, 2004, p. 62), this task is daunting. Nonetheless, cybraries must be attentive to such new media as well as being committed to incorporating them into new digital libraries for posterity: Some will be electronic ephemera, but others surely will remain documents of some significance from this particular period in history.

As with automobiles when they were called "horseless carriages," digitalization at this juncture mostly still looks backward, producing electronic books and journals as "e-texts." Many are simply facsimile copies of their long-running print formats, pushed into PDF images. Consequently, their organization, look, feel, or application closely parallels their paper print editions. Because the professional sign value of publishing in paper journals persists, those who do publish electronically, as well as those who editorially gatekeep online, mostly wish to sustain these symbolic links of achievement and authority.

Yet, all of these bundled scholarly practices carry into e-textuality material constraints from the paper print world that no longer persist. Space— understood as yearly issue numbers, volumes per decade, total pages available—was defined by the cost of other physical materials. Online issues can be longer or shorter, volumes more or less frequent; pages available per issue or page length per article are less meaningful for e-text. Also, the binding of many research studies into an issue can be undone, allowing unbound or unbundled articles to appear alone, circulate singly, or be hyperlinked to other relevant pieces in other issues, other publications or other media through digitalized institutional repositories, virtual journals assembling pieces from many different repositories, or free floating one-off digital publications. Such pieces can be reviewed as before, but now circulate on their own more directly, rapidly, and forcefully. And, cybraries need to accommodate these e-texts in their "collections."

Such materially enabled practices begin to reconfigure scholarly communication through e-texts almost immediately. Articles can be preprinted, para-printed, or post-printed as e-text on their own, no longer gathering dust until editors have the 8 to 10 other pieces needed for an issue. As entries in an e-print archive or discrete e-textual objects with their own unique URL, each article also can be subjected to alternative assessments of its actual quality, utility, or veracity by tracking quite easily the rapidity of downloads, number of users, types of written reactions, applications in other research all hyperlinked together as supportive scholarly struts in bigger rhetorical struggles. Thus, the balance of e-textual valorization might shift from the supply side—who accepted it, published the piece, and edited its findings—in professional organizations or prestigious outlets. Instead, demand side indicators of trustworthiness, quality, or impact would become available to tally for career advancements. Unbundled e-texts also easily could assemble their own accompanying convoys of commentary, which electronic publications can link to the discrete analytical paper or build an attendant directory with line-by-line correspondences in multimedia cross-links through text, data, and images in support of, or in opposition to, the rhetorical claims of the unbundled discursive e-textual object.

Experiments like this go back to Ginsparg's Los Alamos "pre-print" archive in 1991, which has been emulated by comparable enterprises in many fields of medicine, some areas of the humanities, certain specialties in psychology, or many research programs in computer science. Likewise, many para-print or post-print services like Northern Light or Lexus-Nexus also begin to catalogue such unbundled e-texts for one-off sales separate from the remainder of the journal issue. Many cybraries are not dealing with these disparate forms of e-textual circulation and accumulation. Here, once again, rather than some bureaucratically chosen expert being empowered to manage a pre-publication peer review process to assess the quality of research, one might see more and more unvetted pieces appearing as e-texts, but then continuously put under strict scrutiny to assess who is using what, how often, to what end, with which effects, where, and why. Editing such scholarly discourses in the unbundled domain of scholarship, therefore, might become more like copyediting as quality assessment is gauged by demand side indicators (perhaps wrongly) instead of supply side screens (and perhaps wrongly) as many more scholars produce publications.

Yet, this rising output reflects the need for more people to place their papers online (even if they float forever or only at first as an e-print); the reality of fewer scholarly organizations being able to publish a wide range of papers quickly and effectively (even if their periodicals are meant to just appear in print on time); the growing disregard for official peer review by bureaucratic scientific formations usually organized by discipline or geographic region (even if these factors once constituted value-adding pre-screening functions); and the unwillingness of many print formations to invest in publishing and archiving new information. Publishers can see this unbundling of discourse into e-print forms as disruptive, but it basically shifts around work and responsibility rather than wholly destroying it. Quality control here in unbundled e-textual discourses would not necessarily disappear, but so too would real quality not automatically be presumed simply because a work is a product of such-and-such press.

"No name" systems of e-text serving could transmit, archive, and interconnect scholarly products of equal, or greater, quality than those of "big name" presses. Many have spent time and money reading the output of such major outlets, wondering why they bothered. And, many others find gems of discovery in the e-textuality arising from e-print and e-book domains that antiquated publishing practices, old boy networks, or clashing paradigmatic assumptions kept out of print. Hence, with e-textuality, the unbundled paper, chapter, or review plainly opens more scholarly texts to greater readership far more rapidly in support of academic communication. Quality, utility, and veracity in scholarship will migrate around in the production, consumption, circulation, and accumulation cycles, but they will not necessarily disappear completely.

For scholars, the unbundling of their discursive contributions to learned discourse as e-text will have an influence on their professional identities, career courses, and salary potentials. Still, this impact already has been prefigured by the flexibilization of their labor and hollowing out of their disciplinary units. Performativity of e-textual pieces in use instead of the prestige of print pieces due to sites of placement could become the new sine qua non of quality. In turn, highly performative pieces may well attract analytical accompaniments, fellow travelers, critical commentary, or joint producers in order to share the new symbolic wealth of status and reputation just as great sacrifices are made now to place the right manuscripts in the right print periodical or press in order to be seen with equally so endowed significant scholars, even though little or none of the print product might be actually utilized, proven true, or accepted as quality on its own merits.

In most academic disciplines today, e-texts are appreciated for their low cost, ease of transport, relative accessibility, and rapid roll-out qualities. All of these attributes of electronic texts make them useful media for scholarly communication, especially for conference paper production, project draft refinement, tight deadline work, and rapid exchanges with less developed countries. Yet, at the same time, appreciation in use is not the same thing as valorization by professions, associations, or even governments. For many scholarly societies, no study is real until it is fixed in final form on paper in print. Until trees die to preserve knowledge in print-era journals, books, reports, or archives, the only scholarly text in most disciplines with any true worth is one preserved on paper. Some of this reaction is unthinking tradition, some of it is technophobia, some of it is backlash against rapidly obsolescent digital software–hardware versioning, and some of it is trust in the tested simplicity so characteristic of print's relative stability, security, and survivability.

Scholarly discourse has been gradually entrenched in print artifacts since the 15th century, but it became more common, consistent, and complex only in the 19th century with the establishment of most disciplines' professional scholarly societies, the expansion of universities and colleges, the elaboration of multinational print media, and the extrusion of more and more paper as cost-effective pulp replaced older vellum or parchment archives. Such cheap print production allowed scholarly communication to pretend that professional research results, artistic works, or scholarly writing projects could be committed "for the ages" to print.

The finality of print on paper, the high cost of correcting printed pages, the juried authority mobilized to vet manuscripts as worthy of "going into print," and the special literacies required for effective scholarly writing and reading all collaborated to close the scholarly production of research in national, disciplinary, monophone, specialized, and university-based discourses. Once scholarly careers were based on producing articles, reports, studies, or books for such print-based communication systems via the "publish-or-perish" criteria for job-getting, position-keeping, salary-increasing, and status-enhancing purposes, print-based scholarly communication could not be easily disentangled from disciplinary development as such. The arrival of viable forms of digital documents in the 1970s with the e-text generation begins to change these practices, but the changes are slow, uneven, discontinuous, and hard-fought despite the many merits of digital documents. Plainly, the print artifacts themselves (i.e., books, journals, monographs, or reports) are potent presences in many people's lives as things. Arrayed on office shelves, exhibited in departmental display cases, pinned up on hallway bulletin broads, and hawked at professional meetings, the print artifact communicates a great deal before it is ever, or really never, read. This materiality is thus far not an attribute of e-text documents, and the machinic mediations of electronic texts rarely substitute as well for scholars and their audiences.

Digitalization's real-time assemblages of various digital objects to replicate texts, images, graphics, or all together in e-text permit various bundlings of such objects to remain together as such or become untied in ways that open the scholarly text to modes of use, reception, or production that print essentially makes impossible. At this juncture, the PDF application basically reproduces the ways that print documents look in an electronic form. This application makes some sense at this uncertain conjuncture of different media systems, because PDF brings a print logic into electronic environments. Nonetheless, it also is a rearview mirror approach

to scholarly communication that pushes discourse ahead while its participants look into the rearview mirrors at print rather than scanning ahead
out through the windshield for all the merits of e-text.

CYBRARIES AS DIGITAL INSTITUTIONS

Universities, like most social institutions, must embed their practices in
specific technologies and cultures simply in order to provide their outcomes of teaching, research, and service. At the highest levels of sophis-
tication in any given society, thousands of people must master particular forms of literacy and share certain cultural meanings, and this effect
has been maintained through print processes for decades. Digital e-texts
represent a major change in the everyday technologies that many people
must use to perform their work at universities, and the culture of print
once used to operate in predigital environments will not necessarily mesh
well with e-textual operations. Online education represents a major cultural transformation in university technocultures, but, as this analysis
suggests, it is only one part of many larger social shifts toward digital discourses, documents, and disciplines as print is supplanted by code in the
generation, circulation, and utilization of information (Deibert, 1997).

Discussions of e-text frequently get ensnared in crass economic calcu-
lations about how to get more academic content out faster, cheaper, and
better. Although such debates have merit, they miss the bigger questions
about investments in institution-building implied by the introduction of
e-text into scholarly communication. Likewise, a decision to use this technology here and now rather than later will lock literacy, communication,
and archiving down for cybraries in a manner that creates clear cultural
preferences, economic realities, and political forms for individual values and collective goals (Luke, 1989). These decisions about cybraries are
quite central to the workings of contemporary economies and societies,
and they need to be considered very seriously.

Without being as apocalyptic about e-texts as Birkerts (1994), the process of digitalization itself, apart from commodification, does bring some
fundamental transformation in many settled forms of everyday activity at
libraries. With the advent of computer-mediated communication, through
e-textuality, he argued that "the primary human relations—to space, time,
nature, and to other people—have been subjected to a warping pressure
that is something new under the sun. . . . We have created the technology
that now only enables us to change our basic nature, but that is making
such change all but inevitable" (p. 15). Cybraries must manage this move
from printed matter to digital bits to accumulate, circulate, and manipulate stores of knowledge. As Turkle (1997, p. 17) noted, different "interface

values" are embedded in every medium, and those carried by print inculcate a special measured, linear, introspective type of consciousness that has anchored our understandings of higher education for several centuries.

Inasmuch as cybraries become tied totally into digital discourses, documents, and disciplines, they might supplant libraries of print with e-text. Should this development take place, a certain erasure of experience could indeed occur. Again, Birkerts (1994) believed that "our entire collective subjective history—the soul of our societal body—is encoded in print. . . . If a person turns from print—finding it too slow, too hard, irrelevant to the excitements of the present—then what happens to that person's sense of culture and continuity?" (p. 20). He recognized, of course, that his worries and warnings are overdetermined questions, leaving no one an effective path for pulling one strand out of his question at a time for easy analysis. One is left instead to judge between the possibilities of profound loss and immeasurable gain as e-textuality spreads. Birkert's anxieties about how everything will change unalterably when it is run through electronic circuitries lead him to believe that things mostly will turn out for the worse. One also must admit, however, that everything will not remain necessarily the same for cybraries. Along the fractures of the machinic fault line between silicon and paper, what is new and different in cybraries must be anticipated and found before any possible negative fallout disrupts the workings of universities in society.

In a marketplace that mostly militates against anticipating the nature, direction, and impact of digital change, cybraries need to anticipate the first, second, and third order implications of digital textuality on the practices of cybrarianship. The information banks filled with print since the 15th century are being put into question by electronic documents but will not disappear. Despite the fact that many proponents of e-text believe computers will be the only mode of generating and storing text, the realties are more complex. Accepting diverse modes of discourse and multiple forms of text must be conceded before the unintended consequences of e-textuality disable the positive side of print media as cybraries arise out of these transformations. Who will build cybraries, how they will be built, why they must be built, and where they might be built, are all questions whose answers will reshape academic life and the larger societies that cybraries serve in the years to come.

ACKNOWLEDGMENT

Part of this chapter was originally presented at the "Learning On Line '98: Building the Virtual University" conference, Hotel Roanoke, Roanoke, VA, June 18–21, 1998.

REFERENCES

Battelle, J. (2004). Why blogs mean business. *Business 2.0, 5*(1, January/February), 62.

Baudrillard, J. (1981). *For a critique of the political economy of the sign*. St. Louis: Telos Press.

Baudrillard, J. (1983a). *In the shadow of the silent majorities*. New York: Semiotext(e).

Baudrillard, J. (1983b). *Simulations*. New York: Semiotext(e).

Baudrillard, J. (1988). *America* (C. Turner, Trans.). New York: Verso.

Baudrillard, J. (2004). *Fragments: Conversations with Francois L'Yvonnet*. London: Routledge.

Birkerts, S. (1994). *The Gutenberg elegies: The fate of reading in an electronic age*. New York: Fawcett.

Cairncross, F. (1997). *The death of distance: How the communications revolution will change our lives*. Boston: Harvard Business School Press.

Deibert, R. J. (1997). *Parchment, printing, and hypermedia: Communication in world order transformation*. New York: Columbia University Press.

Jameson, F. (1991). *Postmodernism, or the cultural logic of late capitalism*. Durham, NC: Duke University Press.

Levy, D. M. (2001). *Scrolling forward: Making sense of documents in the digital age*. New York: Arcade Publishing.

Luke, T. (1989). *Screens of power: Ideology, domination, and resistance in informational society*. Urbana: University of Illinois Press.

Lyotard, J.-F. (1984). *The postmodern condition: A report on knowledge*. Minneapolis: University of Minnesota Press.

Negroponte, N. (1995). *Being digital*. New York: Knopf.

Turkle, S. (1997). *Life on the screen: Identity in the age of the Internet*. New York: Touchstone.

12

Alternatives to Pay-for-View: The Case for Open Access to Historical Research and Scholarship

Mark Lawrence Kornbluh
Michigan State University

Melanie Shell-Weiss
Johns Hopkins University

Paul Turnbull
Griffith University

This chapter makes the case for establishing open historical resource networks. It argues that historical scholarship is a cultural resource and the benefits to be gained from its free and wide circulation outweigh what historians stand to gain from allowing their work to be locked within pay-for-access online publication systems. Historians would do well to follow the lead of the growing number of scientific research communities who have opted to share information openly, not just between researchers, but also with the many constituencies that stand to benefit from free and open access to high quality information. And historical societies should follow the lead of libraries, museums, and other cultural institutions that are developing freely available online knowledge repositories for all to use.

H-NET: HUMANITIES AND SOCIAL SCIENCES ONLINE

Our perspective is shaped by nearly a decade of work with H-Net: Humanities and Social Sciences On-Line. H-Net is an international inter-disciplinary society of scholars and teachers dedicated to developing the educational and research potential of the Internet. The edited discussion networks and their companion Web sites publish peer-reviewed essays, multimedia materials, syllabi, and discussion for colleagues and the inter-ested public.

Since its founding in 1993, H-Net has strived to foster cross-cultural understanding of the historical experiences and cultural traditions of humanity. This has involved creating and managing a robust communi-cation infrastructure that enables communities with common interests—ranging in diversity from Middle Eastern gender studies to urban his-tory to the history of Florida—to overcome traditional barriers to debate and to exchange scholarly information. At the end of 2001, some 120,000 researchers, teachers, librarians, archivists, and educated readers world-wide are members of one or more of over 140 H-Net discussion networks. The conversations of these networks are not only distributed to members by Listserv software after scholarly assessment, but are made freely avail-able by H-Net through the World Wide Web. We are the world's largest, free online publisher of historical knowledge, and as such stand at odds with what we regard as a disturbing and unproductive trend over the past decade: the locking up of online historical research and scholarship in commercial "pay-for-view" systems.

THE INTERNET AND THE DEMOCRATIZATION OF KNOWLEDGE

At the outset, we should make it clear that the H-Net community has always seen networked communication and online publication as tools to democratize access to historical knowledge and other humanities resources. For us, much of the attraction of the Internet is its ability to bridge distance and to network a wider international community of schol-ars, teachers, and students. We acknowledge, as analysts such as Bruce (2000) pointed out, that in developing nations there are significant costs associated with Internet access, arising from factors such as the need to ensure scholars and educators have adequate software and technical sup-port. It is also critical not to underestimate the costs to be incurred in ensuring that networked communication does not contribute to the ero-sion of cultural and linguistic diversity (Bruce, 2000). Nonetheless, our experience over the past decade has been that the playing field can be substantially leveled, and the entire humanities community can benefit from dialogue encompassing more diverse perspectives.[1]

The potential inherent in networked communications is particularly poignant when taking a comparative international perspective. In most of the world, humanities scholars live and work in societies that have not enjoyed anything like the levels of support for their endeavors that scholars in advanced industrial economies such as the United States and Australia take for granted. For many members of H-Net's Africa networks, for example, the legacies of colonialism include poor and often highly selective access to print-based information resources. It is hard to overemphasize the inaccessibility of books and journals for most African scholars and students. The main library at the University of Ghana in Accra scarcely contains a single humanities journal published outside the country since 1950. Given their low GNP, comparatively weak and erratic economic growth, pressing social needs, unequal exchange rates, and the worsening economics of conventional print-based communications, universities, and governments in countries such as Mali or Ethiopia will not be able to afford to narrow this gap in the foreseeable future. Virtually overnight, however, Internet access can address the vast inequalities of access to scholarship and fulfill the challenging task of enriching the knowledge resource base of scholars and teachers in these countries and others with similar histories of disadvantage. A scholar in Accra who never got to see print journals and had scarce contact with colleagues outside his country can now browse through rich online resources and communicate instantly worldwide.

In July 2000, the leaders of the G8 nations agreed on the Okinawa Charter on the Global Information Society (Dot Force, 2000). Underlying this charter is the recognition that advances in information and communication technology provide a unique opportunity to support both economic development and democratization around the world. As the G8 leaders declared, they are committed "to the principle of inclusion: everyone, everywhere should be able to participate in and no one should be excluded from the benefits of the global information society. . . . Above all this Charter represents a call to all, in both public and private sectors to bridge the international information and knowledge divide" (Dot Force, 2000, article 3, 5). Admittedly, within the governments of the G8, nations adhere to various policies that run counter to this principle. However, the evolution of thinking about the economics of technological innovation within government policy circles of G8 nations since the early 1980s has been firmly grounded in the idea that the free and rapid circulation of specialist knowledge is a necessary prerequisite for economic growth (Lundvall, 2004). And our experience has been that it has been possible to convince various government agencies and private foundations in the G8 nations to assist countries that were left out of print-based networks to gain access to the increasingly global information society (see footnote 1).

Our experience within H-Net in working with scholars and teachers from around the world, including many of the poorest nations, has convinced us that access to scholarship and teaching materials is precisely what our colleagues most desire. They recognize that the Internet provides a unique opportunity to provide knowledge and information that they cannot and will never be able to get through print publication. Access to scholarship on the Internet thus has revolutionary potential for these scholars, their students, and their nations.

Equally important, we believe that networked communication has significant political and cultural implications for industrialized nations as well. Many of H-Net's most committed participants come from universities and communities remote from the largest libraries and best funded universities. With the near universal spread of access to the Internet in the United States, open knowledge networks are as available to the student in Fairbanks, the professor in Lubeck, and the lawyer in Duluth, as they are to those at Harvard and Berkeley. Many scholars in elite institutions within North America, Europe, and Asia continue to pursue traditional modes of peer interaction and debate, limiting engagement with the Internet to private e-mail and electronic versions of print journals. However, an increasing number of faculty in elite institutions are active participants in open knowledge ventures such as H-Net, whereas more than 40 learned societies and peak scholarly bodies around the world now endorse H-Net's mission to promote the open, global dissemination of scholarly knowledge.

Not only does the Internet narrow the gap between elite institutions and other universities and colleges, but it also offers an opportunity to bridge the chasm that has increasingly divided academics from the broader society in the post-World War II culture of expertise and specialization. With networked communication, ivory-covered walls are increasingly permeable. Knowledge and resources that are clustered within the university are readily extended to their host communities and to the world. Scholarship stands to benefit from this re-engagement. For history and the humanities, which have declined in influence within both the university and society over the past half-century, this broadening is particularly important. As Lindt (2002) of the Coalition for Networked Information argued, "Democratizing access will be essential to the viability of the humanities and to the character of this society as a democratic nation."

OPEN-KNOWLEDGE NETWORKS

Scholarly knowledge is first and foremost a cultural resource. The worth to be derived from its free circulation far outweighs any private or communal benefit that might accrue from this knowledge being treated as a commodity in conventional economic terms. To take full advantage of the potential of the Internet, the history community should embrace open access to scholarly communication and online publication of information. Scholarly societies, including H-Net, can play a critical role in providing cultural resources for scholars, students, and citizens in many nations. Free and open access to these cultural resources vastly increases their value.

There is nothing new or particularly radical about this belief, as Lessig (2004, pp. 85–94) reminded us in tracing the centrality of the concept of fair use in creativity and innovation since the early 18th century. Lessig reminded us that since the Enlightenment there has been a long tradition of intellectuals and scientists not patenting their ideas because, to quote Benjamin Franklin, "we enjoy great advantages from the invention of others, we should be glad of an opportunity to serve others by any invention of ours, and this we should do freely and generously" (Marx, 1987, p. 39). Franklin's reasoning about the social benefits owing to the free circulation of knowledge indeed seem remarkably prescient in the light of contemporary thinking about economic innovation. In the view of many policy analysts, the success of economic development in the postindustrial or "informational" economy largely hinges on the capacity of governments, industries, and university-based research communities to promote innovation through the rapid widespread dissemination and uptake of specialist knowledge.

The dissemination of new knowledge is furthermore enhanced by providing free or publicly subsidized access to, and ensuring the integrity of, existing knowledge. Indeed, some analysts go further and argue that successful innovation—given the myriad new uncertainties of the contemporary world—depends on open, democratic assessment of the social and cultural implications of how new knowledge is used by industry and government. For example, the recent New Zealand government report, *Knowledge, Innovation and Creativity*, stresses that innovation and creativity are complex social processes that can best be fostered through reflective engagement between humanists and scientists (New Zealand Ministry, 2000). This emphasis has been supported by organizations like the American Council of Learned Societies, who make free access to and creation of "a significant mass of digitized networked information in the humanities and arts" central to "enrich[ing] a sense of community, foster[ing] intellectual collaboration, preserv[ing] cultural information, and improv[ing] the quality of teaching and learning" (Pavliscak, Ross, & Henry 1997).

Bringing Historians and Historical Scholarship Online

During H-Net's first years, like many early adaptors of the new communication technologies, much attention was focused on proselytizing about the virtues of networked communication. In 1993, few humanities scholars used e-mail and the potential of the World Wide Web as a platform for creating and disseminating complex multimedia information resources was only beginning to be explored. For much of the first decade of H-Net, workshops were held around the world teaching historians how to use the Internet. We sponsored affiliated sessions at the AHA each year to demonstrate the potential of networked communication. Amidst the cacophony of voices, especially from elite institutions and more established scholars about the frivolity of electronic "chat," H-Net grew exponentially.

The debate over the potential of the Internet and networked communication for scholars and teachers seems like ancient history. Washed away in the worldwide euphoria of IT development in the 1990s and buried under an avalanche of invaluable online resources developed by libraries, museums, and other cultural institutions, scarcely an objection is made today to the usefulness of electronic communication. Elite universities have leapfrogged into the lead in developing online resources; even the most staid and established scholars today incorporate e-mail and online research into their professional lives.

The issue is no longer one of whether or not the history community will embrace the Internet, but rather what type of knowledge networks we will build and who will use them. Unfortunately, as more scholarly societies overcome their initial skepticism about integrating networked communication into scholarly practice, most have chosen to transfer their print-based pay-for-access practices to the online world. In contrast to libraries, museums, and other cultural institutions worldwide, which are building vast online freely accessible cultural repositories, our scholarly societies are locking up historical research within commercial distribution channels. Scholarly societies are choosing either to give their online content to commercial publishers to sell back to our scholarly community, or publishing online themselves but limiting access to those who take out membership in the society. Strikingly, it is not only current issues of journals that are being locked behind fee-based systems, but access to back issues also are included within these commercial licensing systems. These are frequently available only with subscriptions to current issues or at additional cost.

Believing that only pay-for-view systems ensure that colleagues and students can secure online access to high quality, well-organized scholarly materials, many institutions and individuals have surrendered this knowledge, and accepted that it would only become available to others at a price. In short, they have assumed that the best way to translate historical practice into the networked environment is to replicate the relationship they have with commercial publishers in the networked environment. Understandably, commercial publishers and their supporters have encouraged this migration path, arguing that fee-based access will allow for the creation of "value-added" services such as online indexes, dynamic searching, and access to back issues of journals.

We, however, firmly believe that locking up online historical scholarship behind closed database walls and subscription services is short-sighted, and overlooks alternatives with greater benefits for both researchers and those with whom they seek to share their insights into the richness and complexity of the past. If the historical community continues to structure its scholarly publication and communication along the commercial nexus born of print scholarship, then we will miss out on the enormous opportunities afforded by the revolution in networked communication.

THE IRRATIONALITY OF THE COMMERCIAL MODEL FOR HISTORICAL SCHOLARSHIP IN A NETWORKED ENVIRONMENT

For many reasons, it makes little or no sense for historians to look to commercial publication of scholarly knowledge. The outcomes of historical research are cultural resources. They are highly specialized intellectual products, created through time-consuming, wide-ranging, and often expensive processes of investigation and reflection.

Judged by conventional economic criteria—as publishers must judge it—historical research is a commodity with limited value beyond a small and highly specialized market. Its worth in conventional economic terms derives from the low cost by which they can be obtained and the willingness of a small specialist audience to buy it, or as is more often the case, persuading the libraries serving them to buy it. In other words, researchers give away their intellectual property—often produced at high public cost—to commercial publishers who then sell it back to our institutions, which often rely heavily on public funding.

The economics of pay-for-view access to online historical scholarship are in the words of a former president of the United States, "voodoo" economics. Authors of history articles do not get paid for their intellectual property—nor, for that matter, do the overwhelming majority of those who write history monographs, nor are their colleagues who serve as peer reviewers compensated for their intellectual labor. Indeed, outside of a handful of editors at the most prestigious journals, journal editors are not paid by their journal. The cost of their intellectual work, like that of authors and reviewers, is subsidized by themselves and by their universities. It is in the interest of all whose intellectual work goes into producing historical scholarship to have that work as widely distributed as possible.

In the print media, where paper and postage cost money, each additional copy of a journal or book had a real cost associated with it. Commercial publishers with wide distribution networks offered the best opportunity to distribute print scholarship and thereby serve the interests of the entire historical community. Ironically, the opposite is true for online scholarship. Digitization, mark-up, and online delivery costs are largely fixed (given the size of the audience for historical scholarship and the cost of servers) regardless of use. It is far more costly for scholarly societies and commercial publishers to run subscription management systems and limit access to online content than it would be for them to make their online journals freely accessible to all.

Naturally, those entrusted with managing scholarly societies for the history community are fearful that they will lose their financial base if they give away their publications. Who would pay for membership, they wonder, if their journals are freely available? In effect, they are using the intellectual labor of their member authors, reviews, and editors to support the society. Such expropriation was rational when the print journals of scholarly societies offered academics the best route for wide distribution of their intellectual work. That is no longer the case. Authors, reviewers, and editors are not having their interests served by scholarly societies that limit access to scholarship to those who can pay or work at institutions that pay for access. In the long run, it is not a viable strategy for scholarly societies to base their financial future and institutional existence on limiting access to the intellectual work of their own members. Such strategy not only is not in the best interests of their members, but it also undermines the entire history profession.

MARGINALIZING HISTORICAL SCHOLARSHIP

Almost all of the major history journals in the world are now available online through commercial publishers, content aggregators such as EBSCO and Gale, and/or independent ventures, such as the history cooperative. Virtually all of this scholarship is gated, however. It is sold as a commodity and delivered through proprietary gateways. Universities throughout Africa have gained access to the Internet, but our professional history journals are no more accessible in Accra than they were 20 years ago as we have locked them behind economic gates. (Our back journals, many of which have been long digitized by JSTORE, remain unavailable as well, a decade after being digitized.) The same is true for much of this country. Access to online historical scholarship in journals is limited to researchers, students, and the public who pay for that access, or work and study in institutions that pay for that access.

The economic hurdle for access to historical journals is severe, but it is not the only problem with this system. Equally problematic is the decision to gate off this scholarship from the larger Internet and the searching tools that students, researchers, and the general public are using to uncover and navigate their way through online resources. Much research still needs to be done on how we find content on the World Wide Web, but existing studies show that people prefer searching for information by using one of several highly sophisticated and free of charge commercial search engines. Teachers and researchers may also consult commercial products (but even then we postulate that they would vastly prefer free online tools), but students tend to be conscious of the limitations on their time and will usually go no further than discovering and using free online resources (Jones, 2002, p. 13).

In countries with high levels of networked access, high school and undergraduate students are disposed to access and use free online information to complete assessable research and writing tasks. Why should we expect otherwise when we are now teaching students in the higher levels of education for whom the World Wide Web has been part of the fabric of everyday life from their first days of schooling? When faced with writing a paper on some historical question, students may go to the library. But, rather than first consulting online catalogues of the library's holdings, they are likely to use one of the more commercial sophisticated search engines such as google.com to find full text information. With the diffusion of the Internet into homes throughout the United States, the general public also increasingly has access to this powerful research tool. Thus, when they want to look something up, they go through Yahoo, Google, AOL, or another search engine to discover free online resources (for a critical perspective on what search engines do and do not provide, see Fabos, chap. 13, this volume).

In many instances, searching via google.com or similar engines leads to high quality online resources offered by libraries, museums, and art galleries. One can also find the growing number of excellent resources created with limited funds and, still in many cases, little professional recognition by university researchers and history teachers. However, for every one good resource discovered this way, one also finds many created by enthusiastic amateurs containing factual inaccuracies or offering dubious interpretations of events. Increasingly, commercial entities are moving in as well. The Discovery Channel, the History Channel, the History Place, and hundreds of more specialized online ventures are setting themselves up to be major doorways to delivering historical content online. Needless to say, regardless of the value of these individual sites, the concerns of professional historians are not their paramount interest.

There will doubtless be those that argue that this is precisely why we need online ventures between historical societies and commercial publishers. But although there is no question that commercial ventures can guarantee provision of high quality resources, we would do well to question whether students accustomed to finding information quickly and at no cost beyond those of connectivity will prefer commercial resources, especially when those resources are highly selective in what they offer, are often cumbersome to use, and in many instances are only usable within on-campus networks. Try as we might to convince them otherwise, the engrained preference of students and the public is for free online resources. If we circumscribe what is freely and conveniently available to them by commercializing historical knowledge then we risk leaving them outside the walls of pay-for-view systems imagining the past in inaccurate and trivial ways.

The appetite for historical content online is vast and growing. So is the amount of historical content online. Gated access and pay-for-view systems marginalize our profession from this interest, however. To take but one relevant example, both back issues and current issues of the *American Historical Review* (*AHR*) are digitized and available online. For the first time in history, the technology exists and the product exists for students, scholars, and the general public worldwide to easily and rapidly find out what the best historians in this country have written about any given history topic. But, unfortunately, the *AHR* is now gated off from the rest of the Internet. As a result, searching through commercial search engines leads to the Discovery Channel rather than to articles and reviews by professional historians. Certainly, an enormous opportunity is being missed here.

FREE AND OPEN ACCESS
TO SCIENTIFIC RESEARCH

Outside of the humanities, a very different model is emerging for distribution of scholarship online. We believe it is important for historians to take note of this model and consider how we might adopt it to our needs. In the physical and natural sciences, an increasing number of communities have established pre-print servers giving access to copies of papers either under review by leading print journals, or that have been accepted for publication. Given the nature and costs of experimental work in the sciences, the virtues of pre-print servers have long been apparent. They provide access to research results and (often) associated data weeks or months before appearance in print form. In many communities, print-based versions of papers are now less a means of disseminating research outcomes than archival artifacts charting the development of research in a field, and recording the professional contribution of the authors.

Among scientific research communities that have embraced networked communication, a number have gone as far as to establish e-journals, thus transferring the entire process of submitting, peer reviewing, and disseminating the outcomes of research. In some instances, the decision to go digital has occurred with the coalescence of new fields of research, notably in areas of the biomedical sciences and information technology. However, an increasing number of established communities are exploring a fully electronic publication cycle.

What is also noteworthy is that research communities are not simply opting for networked publication but, in many instances, are establishing servers in collaboration with research libraries to make what they publish freely available to colleagues and other interested researchers. To serve this information, many are using open source programming and shared standards for the encoding and description of knowledge information. Much effort has also been devoted to creating search and retrieval programming to enhance discovery of knowledge that may reside on one of a large number of such servers located in libraries throughout the world. The Open Archives Initiative (OAI), funded by university and library coalitions and the U.S. National Science Foundation, has established common protocols for paper servers as a first step towards comprehensively networked research repositories (see http://www.openarchives.org/).

To a large extent, this shift has occurred because researchers in various scientific fields have seen the economics of conventional publication evolve to the point that it now works against their interests. Since the mid-1990s, the cost of print journals in many fields of scientific inquiry has risen steeply while university and research center operating budgets have remained static or have declined in real terms. As the 2004 British Parliament's Select Committee on Science and Technology found:

> The average price of an academic journal rose by 58% between 1998 and 2003, compared to a UK retail price index increase of 11% over the same period. For the different period between 1990 and 2000, Blackwell's Periodical Price Indexes show an increase in average journal price of 184.3% in medical journals and 178.3% in science and technology journals. The Chartered Institute of Library and Information Professionals (CILIP) reported that "between 1996–97 and 2000–01 the information resource budget of UK university libraries has decreased by 29% in real terms, while the average journal price over the same time period increased by 41%. The proportion of university library information resource expenditure on journals has increased from 47% to 52%, but this increase has failed to maintain the actual number of journal subscriptions." Although all these statistics refer to different periods of time, a clear pattern emerges of increasing prices against decreasing library budgets. (Great Britain Parliament 2004)

In many instances, the move to commercially produced electronic editions of journals has not brought reductions in the costs of subscription, nor have enhancements such as online indexes and access to digital archives justified increases in subscription costs (C. T. Bergstrom & T. C. Bergstrom, 2002; Willinsky, 2003). Journal editors and reviewers continue to contribute their time freely in return for peer recognition.

Importantly, the migration of research communities to free online modes of publication has not simply been a reaction to the costs of commercially produced journals rising beyond what researchers and librarians are prepared to pay. The decision of scientists to augment or replace commercial publication with free online access is also motivated by wider philosophical and ethical considerations. Even more than humanists, scientists appreciate the interconnectedness of scholarly research and the economic and social importance of rapid and widespread circulation of knowledge in the postindustrial or "informational" economy (UNESCO World Conference on Science, 1999).

THE POTENTIAL OF NETWORKED SCHOLARLY RESEARCH

We are conscious that there are significant differences between research in the sciences and history. It is certainly true that traditional historical research has centered on writing books, whereas scientific research revolves around the production of what are often highly technical papers that are less discrete entities than parts of an evolving dialogue about a particular problem among a large number of researchers. Indeed, it is worth recalling that hypertext mark-up language (HTML) came about because of the desire of high energy physicists to aggregate, digest, and respond to rapid advances in the knowledge of their community.

However, it is worth pursuing the contrast a little further. Reviewing discussions among historians about the potential of electronic publication over the past 3 or so years, it strikes us that this has largely been a conversation about replicating the form and function of specialist books and learned articles in the online environment. It is a conversation that betrays nostalgia for tangible printed forms and does not look forward to the potential benefits that networked information, collaborative research, and hypermedia can offer.

Historical societies and commercial publishers engaged in pay-for-view publication generally think of electronic publication as something to be produced in much the same way as print-based books or articles. In other words, an electronic resource is something produced retrospectively after the completion of a research project as one of a number of publishing formats. Published scholarship is individual pieces of work that can be licensed and sold separate from other pieces of scholarship.

The popularity of H-Net, in contrast, demonstrates the hunger of scholars for a more interactive, iterative process of research, teaching, and publication. The rapidity of communication, the ease of online publication, and the ability to build connections in scholarly work with hypertext provide new opportunities for scholarly collaboration and the development of new forms of scholarship, which are not isolated pieces of individual work, but rather are built on connections to sources and other scholarship (on the innovative potential of hypertext in history, see especially Darnton, 1999).

It is more useful, however, to think about conventional print-based books, articles, and their electronic surrogates as destined to become increasingly interconnected with new forms of research outcomes that exploit the hypertextual, visual, and sonic possibilities of networked communication. There is no reason why historians should not continue to publish in traditional print-based genres, but the future of these genres is very likely to be one in which they will be disseminated electronically and will be interconnected in new and diverse ways with online research that employs hypermedia to do things that are either poorly done or impossible to do in print-based media.

The catch, of course, is that to build these connections, online resources have to be open and freely available. Links to other work, examination of visual and audio sources, and statistical analysis across databases is not possible when scholarship is gated by economic boundaries. The pay-for-view system that drastically limits access to historical scholarship is also holding back the development of more interactive, iterative, networked research and publication.

THE PROMISE AND IMPLICATIONS OF HYPERMEDIA

For scholars interested in moving beyond text and working with images, sound, and video, an open networked environment is essential. Hypermedia demands a very different relation between research processes and outcomes than conventional print-based publications. Hypermedia is created by editing and analyzing sources created during the research process—video, animation, and audio recordings—in addition to incorporating digital copies of more conventional kinds of textual and graphic materials. This contrasts markedly with the conventional process of publishing in the humanities and social sciences, where appraising and incorporating evidence in the form of writing results in a text. Working with hypermedia involves constructing key elements of the final product during the earliest stages of the research process. Indeed, this is beneficial to the research process by requiring that analytical and interrogative work be done from the outset. Researchers, moreover, must be aware of the need to communicate with their intended audience, to ensure communication through good information design, which in turn adds a further analytical dimension to the research process. In short, whereas such considerations should be present irrespective of the communication medium, in hypermedia it is an essential dimension to research.

What attracts younger scholars to working in networked hypermedia is the potential to facilitate more dialogic modes of scholarly conversation, in which research results are presented, discussed, and perhaps challenged by incorporation or connection with new hypermedia artifacts. This is especially true of researchers working cross-culturally with indigenous knowledge custodians and ethnic communities whose aspirations have not been well-served by more traditional forms of scholarly inquiry and publication (on the particular challenges of working with indigenous Australian peoples on digital archiving of ethnographic information, see Barwick & Thieberger, chap. 8, this volume). However, for this potential of hypermedia to be realized, there is a need for shared technical processes and protocols for creating seamless exchange and interconnection of online resources within highly structured and contextualized web spaces. As recently argued by McCarthy, one of Australia's leading researchers in the field of heritage informatics:

> The key principles or functional requirements of web object publication . . . are citability, coherence, communicability and endurance. Adherence to these principles will not only enable the building of connectedness at the micro level but will enable the building of larger scale structures and architectures based on the concepts of scale-free complex networks. (McCarthy & Evans, 2002)

The critical point is that these networks are emerging. So too are the technical processes and protocols for ensuring the translation of the critical assumptions and practices of disciplines such as history into the networked environment. Much essential work has been done within library and museum circles over several years on resolving key problems relating to the exchange and description of scholarly knowledge in digital forms. Indeed, much of this work is of direct benefit to historians wanting to work in hypermedia because personnel within museums and libraries have very similar intellectual objectives to historians. From long immersion in print culture and the creation of complex bibliographical resources, they know the importance of ensuring citability, coherence, communicability, and endurance in the networked environment. Like historians, they are concerned to ensure that the digital surrogates of cultural objects and information they create embody standards that will allow future generations to determine who created a particular resource and the assumptions they employed in doing so. Libraries and museums have, moreover, built on international cooperative links established over many years to implement open standards and create software tools using open source programming for creating structured and conceptualized online resources. Thanks to library- and museum-based research, historians already have much of what they need to ensure the translation into the digital realm of the kinds of editorial procedures and standards which, in the world of print, have traditionally enabled historical inquiry.

A HISTORICAL PERSPECTIVE
ON THE TRANSFORMATION
OF SCHOLARLY PUBLISHING

It is not surprising that historians often look to the past to help understand the changes wrought by the revolution in communication technology. It is, therefore, not uncommon to find what we are experiencing compared to the development of print-based modes of communication in European scholarly communities through the course of the 16th and 17th centuries. However, comparisons drawn between contemporary and past experiences of technological change have generally relied on a problematic interpretation of the relationships that existed between scholars, publishers, and readers from the Reformation to the era of the scientific revolution. As Johns (1998) argued, the way these relationships have been understood, notably in Eisenstein's (1983) highly influential work on the press as an agent of cultural change, has tended to overemphasize the transformational power of print technology—that is, its capacity to create networks, which functioned so as to produce widespread conformity in intellectual practices and products. Johns suggested that the mistake has been to see the medium as the message, in the sense of being not just an agent of change, but new processes and criteria for determining scholarly knowledge. Hence the book has been seen as an artifact that, in displacing the cultural premium traditionally given to oral recitation, has radically changed human cognition—a view that seems implicit in works such as Birkerts' (1994) *Gutenberg Elegies*.

However, as Johns persuasively argued of the 17th-century London book trade, print-based communication did not permit the imposition of consensus as to what constituted scientific truth, or agreement as to the criteria by which truth was most certain to be established. Seventeenth-century English natural philosophers found themselves entangled in new and often antagonistic relations between different learned societies, publishers, booksellers, and readers. This complex sphere of interaction was in turn subject to the influence of wider cultural forces in operation in the highly volatile religious and political climate of the 17th century.

One could argue that we are experiencing a similar predicament. The Scholarly Publishing and Academic Resources Coalition (SPARC) sees much of the current uncertainty about the future of scholarly communications as stemming from the shift away from the traditional nexus between paper journals and libraries controlling all the various functions of scholarly communication: registration, certification, and distribution of new ideas, and importantly, the archiving of intellectual activity (Crow, 2002, pp. 7–15). SPARC views the disruption of the status quo by pre-print servers as a healthy development, in that it promises to accelerate the distribution of new ideas and greatly increases access to new scholarship. What is happening is in part a "decomposition," breaking scholarly communication into various component parts in contrast to the print-based system where journals and libraries link the system together (Crow, 2002, pp. 29–30).

It could further be argued that, like the turmoil characterizing scientific communication in 17th-century Britain, much of the debate about the strengths and weaknesses of networked communication is similarly entangled within wider cultural considerations of the outcomes of this process of "decomposition."

From the perspective of historians, the breaking of the traditional nexus between print journals and libraries serves to remind us of the provisional and shifting nature of the production of historical knowledge. We in H-Net find this, in many respects, an exciting development that raises interesting questions about how online historical scholarship may evolve. For others, "decomposition" raises fears about what the future holds, and we suspect figures strongly in the decision of historical societies to opt for pay-for-view systems. It is understandable that entrenched assumptions and practices should inform how new technologies might best be used.

However, we believe that the interests of historians and their readers are best served by taking advantage of the robust and inexpensive means of free online publication developed by scientific communities and librarians. Unlike commercial online publication systems, these tools and the protocols for information management they embody have been designed from the premise that scholarly knowledge is a cultural resource and, like other kinds of cultural resources, its value derives from generating insight and creativity through free circulation. Further, the work done thus far in creating tools for open publication gives historians not only cheap and effective means of sharing their knowledge, but the tools by which to build the kinds of structured and contextualized web resources that will truly facilitate the evolution of historical scholarship in the networked environment.

NOTES

1. See, for example, the logs of H-Net's African discussion networks, which can be accessed through http://www.h-net.org/lists; and the Web sites of associated projects serving community and educational needs in developing nations at http://matrix.msu.edu/projects.php

REFERENCES

Bergstrom C. T., & Berstrom, T. C. (2002). *Electronic subscriptions to scientific journals: A boon for whom?* Retrieved October 25, 2004, from http://octavia.zoology.washington.edu/publishing/boon.pdf

Birkerts, S. (1994). *The Gutenberg elegies: The fate of reading in an electronic age.* London: Faber & Faber.

Bruce, B. C. (2000). Access points on the digital river. *Journal of Adolescent & Adult Literacy, 44*(3), 262–268. Retrieved October 25, 2004, from http://www.readingonline.org/electronic/elec_index.asp?HREF=/electronic/jaal/11–00_Column/index.html

Crow, R. (2002). *The case for institutional repositories: A SPARCS position paper.* Retrieved October 23, 2004, from http://www.arl.org/sparc/IR/IR_Final_Release_102.pdf

Darnton, R. (1999). The new age of the book. *New York Review of Books, 46*(5), 5–7.

Dot Force. (2000). *Okinawa Charter on the global information society.* Retrieved October 23, 2004, from http://www.mofa.go.jp/policy/economy/summit/2000/documents/charter.html

Eisenstein, E. (1983). *The printing revolution in early modern Europe.* Cambridge, England: Cambridge University Press.

Great Britain Parliament House of Commons Science and Technology Committee. (2004). *Tenth report: Scientific publications: Free for all?* Retrieved October 25, 2004, from http://www.publications.parliament.uk/pa/cm200304/cmselect/cmsctech/399/39907.htm#a16

Johns, A. (1998). *The nature of the book: Print and knowledge in the making.* Chicago: Chicago University Press.

Jones, S. (2002). *The Internet goes to college: How students are living in the future with today's technology.* Pew Internet and American Life Project Report 71, Retrieved October 23, 2004, from http://www.pewinternet.org/PPF/r/71/report_display.asp

Lessig, L. (2004). *Free culture: How big media uses technology and the law to lock down culture and control creativity.* New York: Penguin. Also retrieved October 27, 2004, from http://free-culture.org/

Lindt, G. (2002). The implications of electronic information for the sociology of knowledge. *Technology, scholarship and the humanities: The implications of electronic information.* Coalition for Networked Information Working Group Reports. Retrieved October 23, 2004, from http://www.cni.org/docs/tsh/wgroups.html

Lundvall, B. (2004). Introduction to technological infrastructure and international competitiveness by Christopher Freeman. *Industrial and Corporate Change, 13*, 531–539.

Marx, L. (1987). Does improved technology mean progress? *Technology Review* (January), 33–41.

McCarthy, G., & Evans, J. (2002). The open resource scholarly network: New collaborative partnerships between academics, libraries, archives and museums. *VALA 2002 Conference Proceedings.* Retrieved October 24, 2004, from http://www.vala.org.au/vala2002/2002pdf/15McCEva.pdf

Pavliscak, P., Ross, S., & Henry, C. (1997). *Information technology in humanities scholarship: Achievements, prospects, and challenges—the United States focus.* American Council of Learned Societies, Occasional Paper Series, No. 37. Retrieved October 23, 2004, from http://www.acls.org/op37.htm

New Zealand Ministry of Research, Science & Technology. (2000). *Knowledge, innovation, and creativity: Designing a knowledge society for a small, democratic country.* Retrieved October 24, 2004, from http://www.morst.gov.nz/publications/humanz/Humanz.htm

UNESCO World Conference on Science. (1999). *Declaration on science and the use of scientific knowledge.* Retrieved October 25, 2004, from http://www.unesco.org/science/wcs/eng/declaration_e.htm

Willinsky, S. (2003). Scholarly associations and the economic viability of open access publishing. *Journal of Digital Information, 4*(2). Retrieved October 25, 2004, from http://jodi.ecs.soton.ac.uk/Articles/v04/i02/Willinsky/

13

Search Engine Anatomy: The Industry and Its Commercial Structure

Bettina Fabos
Miami University of Ohio

> *It is vitally important for business people to understand how search engines work, and how to use them. . . . Search is how your business, whatever it is, will market itself.*
> —The business section of *The Age*, Melbourne, Australia
> (2003, November 4)

The topic of search engine enterprise—discussed relentlessly in the business world—has somehow slipped under the radar of librarians, educators, most academics, and the news media (save for the business section). Even as search engines become increasingly reconditioned to serve free enterprise, and now address people as *consumers* rather than *users*, the industry has been particularly good at sustaining four prevalent myths about their services:

1. Search engines are impartial information tools.
2. Search engines search the entire Web, gleaning the most relevant results.
3. Search engines vary greatly, thus offering choice and a competitive marketplace.

4. Search engines are the only place to go for relevant information on the Web.

Yet, if we do not acknowledge the commercial nature of search engines and believe that search engines are looking after users' best interests, then it is easy to fall prey to these myths.

Indeed, these myths can be easily debunked (although the search industry certainly does not want that to happen). Search engines are not impartial or reliable. Most information they organize is, quite intentionally, commercial. Users wade through veritable strip malls of search engine results, often blaming themselves for not using better searching skills to get better results. The truth about search engines is that no knowledge of advanced searching practices (e.g., Boolean terminology and understanding the subtle differences between individual search engines) will change the main focus of commercial search engines, which is to connect consumers to their advertisers. Moreover, because most "search engines"—which are later distinguished as "search portals"—are fed by an extremely small number of increasingly consolidating search providers, all of which mimic each others' algorithm strategies, the notion of choice between search engines is almost moot.

What is so unnerving about these four myths is the extent to which users believe them, using search engines as the main gateway to all web information (Griffiths & Brophy, 2005), and the extent to which the search engine industry benefits from this ignorance. Consequently, rather than spending time learning about search engine technology, advanced searching skills, Boolean terminology, the differences between search engines, or web page evaluation skills, it is much more important to understand the industry itself—and the economic and political forces that control it—if one wants to be a truly knowledgeable user of the Web. This chapter, or "anatomy lesson," is thus an attempt to bring the discussion of the Web's evolving commercial structure into the sphere of educators, academics, and others located on the periphery of the information technology business world. That there are alternatives to search engines (as this book clearly attests) is the answer to a more democratic and relevant Web. The challenge for all of us, then, is to first understand the way our information tools are shaped by economic forces, and second, to learn that there are alternatives to excessively commercialized web services on which we have come to rely.

ANATOMY LESSON 1:
SEARCH INDUSTRY STRUCTURE

Search engines were once considered a failed business idea because they were only a conduit to other pages. In other words, they lacked stickiness; no one stayed long enough to see the advertising. In response to this crisis, search engine portals tried to develop new services to attract and retain users. For example, AltaVista spent millions to develop new portal content that it hoped would make it a comprehensive web portal for not only searches, but other activities such as news, travel, and shopping. Google resisted such efforts, and insisted instead on focusing on being the best-syndicated search engine provider, with the most relevant search results. However, analysts mocked Google for its seeming lack of a means to make money from its singular mission of search excellence.

Then, search engine portals began experimenting with sponsored links—a list of two or three paying sites that appear above the actual search results. Because sponsored links are so highly targeted (they directly relate to the search terms that users type in), they became enormously profitable. A small company dealing with specialized golf equipment, for example, could sponsor a link that accompanied a user's search on golf, directly targeting the golfer. Oftentimes because users did not know the difference between sponsored and actual searches, they were clicking sponsored links from 12% to 17% of the time (Waters, 2003), far in excess of the less than 1% banner ad click-through rate today (Harvey, 2003b). And, every time a user clicked on a sponsored link, the search engine earned money. Not surprisingly, search engine services barely distinguished between the sponsored and nonsponsored categories in order to generate as many click-throughs as possible.

First, start with a little dissection. To understand the search engine industry and its gradual and quiet commercialization, it is necessary to distinguish between the four facets of the search engine industry: directories, search engine providers, search engine portals, and *commercial* search providers. The four areas of the search engine industry have their own completely separate functions. Certain companies, like Google, may perform all the functions within a single company; other companies contract out to smaller ones, which each perform a singular function, and are merged to form the basis of what most people consider to be a "search engine."

Directories

Often mistaken for search engines, directories are nothing more than comparatively small databases that may or may not feed a search engine. Directories predate search engines. Librarians began cataloguing Web sites in the early 1990s, but it was Yahoo! who developed the first commercial directory in 1994 by hiring numerous editors to compile Web pages and place them into logical categories. The directory was steadily growing as individuals, organizations, and companies submitted sites for Yahoo! employees to review and (hopefully) add to a category. As the largest directory on the Web, Yahoo! became instantly recognized as the place to look for information. Yahoo!'s initial income came from banner advertising, but also from individuals, organizations, and (mostly) companies who paid Yahoo! for "express submissions" to the Yahoo! Directory (a recurring annual fee of $299 by 2004). Other online directories followed Yahoo!'s model, like the Australian-based directory Looksmart, which launched in 1996. Another significant directory (especially to the search engine industry) is the Open Directory Project, which was launched in 1998. This enormous noncommercial endeavor, constructed entirely by a global army of volunteers (or, as they are referred to, "net-citizens"), is by far the largest directory on the Web and continues to grow in size every day.

Directories have become an important component to the search industry in that they provide massive lists of indexed pages to feed search engine providers (more on these later). The Open Directory Project is the most significant directory to this end for two reasons: It is the largest directory on the Web, and it has licensed its content for open content distribution. This means that any search engine provider can draw on the Open Directory Project as it conducts its searches. Search engine providers all claim to have amassed their own proprietary web page databases through which they conduct their searches, but the Open Directory Project makes up a large portion of each of these databases (Fine Brand, 2003). Yahoo!'s directory has also been an important database that feeds the company's larger search portal, and the MSN portal has long relied on Looksmart's directory to distinguish its search results from other search services (although that relationship ended in 2004).

Search Engine Providers

Search engine providers are the tools that actually do most (but not all) of the searching. Sometimes referred to as "algorithmic search engines," or "crawler-based search engines," search engine providers license highly complicated crawling software to search the Web. Search engine provider companies have all got their start in a similar way: Various very smart teams of computer engineers first put their heads together and came up with a unique mathematical formula, or algorithm, for determining web page relevance. They then obtained venture capital to amass a database containing billions of web pages, and through extensive automated text indexing tools, built a "proprietary web index"—the bigger the better. Search engine providers then began to syndicate their service to other search portals (what are commonly thought of as "search engines"). Because the job of creating and updating these web search algorithms, and then amassing and managing (i.e., updating, cleansing) these web indexes is so huge, there are actually only a handful of search engine providers in existence. At the time of this writing, the most prominent search engine providers can be counted on one hand: AltaVista, Inktomi, Google, AlltheWeb, and Teoma. The finite number of search engine providers is one reason why search results from different "search engines" are so similar—they are powered by the same provider.

AltaVista and Inktomi are the oldest existing search engine providers, both emerging in 1995.[1] The AltaVista algorithm was developed by scientists at the Digital Equipment Corporation in Palo Alto, California, and the Inktomi algorithm was created by a computer science professor and his graduate student at Berkeley. The reason that AltaVista is better known than Inktomi is that AltaVista developed its own branded search portal (while also syndicating its services elsewhere); Inktomi opted to just syndicate, with Yahoo! and MSN being its first major customers. Google arrived in 1998, bringing a new kind of searching standard to the industry. Created by Larry Page and Sergey Brin, two grad students at Stanford, Google's formula became instantly recognized as *better*. Whereas AltaVista and Inktomi had based web page relevance on keywords (the greater number of keywords on a page, the more relevant), Google based relevance on links (the number of links that point to a given web page, the more relevant). Google became the most sought-after search engine provider as a result of its superior algorithm (e.g., Yahoo! dumped Inktomi for Google in 2000), and initially made half its revenue from selling its search technology and access to its massive web index, to various Web sites (Harvey, 2003a). The search engine provider became an overnight success as a branded search portal as well.

Two more search engine providers emerged after Google. AlltheWeb was created by a group of scientists at the Norwegian University of Science and Technology in 1999, and became hugely popular throughout Europe. Finally, Teoma was born in a Rutgers University computer lab in 2000. There are other, smaller search engine providers, such as Wisenut, and numerous specialty search engines (e.g., focusing on medieval or ancient topics, or the Chinese language), but the reality of the small world of search engine providers is that it is getting even smaller. By 2004, three search engine providers—AltaVista, Inktomi, and AlltheWeb—had all merged under the Yahoo! umbrella (more details later), leaving just three main search engines providers—Google, the Yahoo! group, and Teoma— to power nearly all the searches on the Web.[2] Therefore, the myth that there are many search engines to choose from, each with varying algorithms, is simply untrue.

Search Engine Portals

Yahoo!, Excite, MSN, AOL, Google, Ask Jeeves, and Lycos are all search portals. They are Web sites that offer a search toolbar, which is powered by a syndicated search engine provider (most often one of the top five). For example, at the time of this writing, the portals Netscape, AOL, Go, Google, and thousands of smaller, specific-purpose portals (e.g., ESPN. com, Amazon.com, Walmart.com, Mamamedia.com) are all powered by Google. The search portal Lycos is powered by AlltheWeb; Amazon.com and eBay are powered by Inktomi; AskJeeves is powered by Teoma; and Hotbot is powered by four search engine providers—Google, AlltheWeb, Inktomi, and Teoma. Again, these different relations explain why some search engine services (e.g., Google and AOL) have more similar results than others at a given point and time: They are powered by the same search engine provider.

To complicate the matter of partnerships, a few search portals such as Yahoo! and MSN, integrate directory listings alongside an algorithmic database. In other words, the Yahoo! search portal draws listings from its own Yahoo! Directory in addition to the results provided by Inktomi; MSN, until recently, was drawing listings from the Looksmart Directory and the Inktomi search engine provider. Not surprisingly, whichever search engine provider or directory a search portal decides to partner with, it is a big deal for that company. For example, Yahoo! vaulted Inktomi's profile in 1998 from a relatively unknown search engine provider to a significant player when it chose to outsource its searching technology to the company; then Yahoo! devastated Inktomi when it switched to Google in 2000. In a strategic move, Yahoo! then bought the diminished Inktomi outright in 2003, and now is in the business of syndicating Inktomi's technology.

Which brings us to another complication: Some branded portals—the new Yahoo!, Google, and AlltheWeb—also syndicate their own search engine provider. Yahoo! and Google are now in intense competition, not only for portal prominence, but for search engine provider prominence.

Commercial Search Providers

Commercial search providers build and manage indexes of web pages (like search engine providers), provide an algorithm for searching these indexes (like search engine providers), and then syndicate this service to search portals (also like search engine providers). The main difference is that the indexes of commercial search providers are all advertisers who pay to be there. To date, every major search portal combines both algorithmic and commercial searches, which are conducted side by side; key words are used to identify both relevant web pages and relevant advertisers. Typically, commercial search results appear in separate locations on the search result list (top, bottom, side) as "sponsored listings" or "featured sites," but many times with as little demarcation as possible between the sponsored and nonsponsored listings so as to inspire more

click-throughs. For example, in 2004, AlltheWeb used a nearly impercep-
tible thin grey line to separate the first three sponsored links from "the
rest"; AltaVista used a large font size, so the first four sponsored listings
took up the entire page—a user had to scroll down to get to the nonsponsored results. And MSN listed sponsored sites ahead of the regular search
results, but employed the same consecutive numbering system. In other
words, if there are three sponsored matches, then the first nonpaid match
began as number four.

The company GoTo.com (now called Overture) has been instrumen-
tal in activating the commercial search business, and now provides commercial results to the majority of search portals on the Web. GoTo began
as a search portal in its own right, relying on Inktomi for its algorithmic searches and banner advertising for its income. However, in 1998,
the company began a new income-generating scheme: It brazenly auc-
tioned off placement within the portal's "impartial" search engine result
list itself. The higher an advertiser's bid, the higher the Web site appeared
in GoTo's search result list; GoTo's search results were effectively stacked
with paying customers. Although the move caused considerable controversy among consumer advocates (and within the industry), advertisers
were delighted.

High placement within a search result list is important for two reasons. First, users trust this list because they believe it prioritizes relevant Web sites according to the key terms entered. Second, users typically do not tend to look beyond the first two or three pages in a search
result list, believing that the first two pages are the most relevant (Lasica,
2001). Recalling the four myths introduced at the beginning of this chapter, search engines are less impartial than people typically think. Another
GoTo breakthrough was its "Pay-For-Performance™" strategy, whereby
advertisers paid GoTo *only* if a user clicked on a sponsored link. By 2000,
the company began to syndicate its commercial search services to other
search portals (AOL being its first major customer). Because portals kept
a portion of the "Pay-For-Performance" revenue every time a user clicked
on one of GoTo's paid placements, search portals were as happy as advertisers. Banner advertising had become increasingly ineffective, and finally
there was a way, through search itself, to make money. One Lycos executive justified the practice this way: "We thought long and hard and decided
it doesn't matter if we are paid for a link, so long as the results are what the
user wants. . . . The industry has trained users to avoid anything that looks
commercial. By calling them paid listings, it hurts the user" (Lasica, 2001,
p. 2). Indeed, the growing justification among Internet industry folk was
that people generally use the Web for commercial purposes anyway. They
use the Web to find flower delivery services or to purchase a barbecue
grill.

Toward the end of 2000, GoTo renamed itself Overture, disbanded the GoTo search portal, and concentrated solely on its new role as a syndicated commercial search provider. By 2002, Overture had signed up 80,000 advertisers (Overture, 2003a) and was distributing its for-profit search results to tens of thousands of web portals across the Internet, including MSN, Yahoo!, Lycos, AltaVista, HotBot, Netscape, AOL, Infospace, Fast, and ESPN.com. These Web sites retained their algorithmic search provider (e.g., Google), but cross-listed this database with Overture's growing index of sponsored web links. Yahoo!, for example, mixed its Yahoo Directory results with Google's algorithmic results and Overture's Pay-For-Performance sponsorship results, although it is not exactly clear whether the sponsored pages were always restricted to the "sponsored" section, or slipped down into the regular web results. Because search portal companies are not obliged to disclose exactly where the commercial influence lies in a given search result list—in the sponsored listings above a search result list (Kopytoff, 2003), or within the result list itself, revealing their mode of user deception has not been common practice. MSN, which had mixed the Looksmart Directory results with Inktomi's algorithmic results and Overture's pay-per-click sponsorship results, has been purportedly following the GoTo.com model by stacking its result pages (Fine Brand, 2003). Before AltaVista became a Yahoo! subsidiary, AltaVista experimented with selling its search results to the highest bidder independently of Overture (Fine Brand, 2003; Hansell, 1999). Back to the four myths, search engines are not impartial.

Regardless of visible above-the-line sponsorship or invisible within-the-list sponsorship, the advent of commercial search providers has meant that a search within a search portal is more likely to be heavily commercialized. In a single quarter of 2002, Overture facilitated 563 million "paid introductions" (click-throughs) and made $126 million, compared to Google's approximately $15 million in revenue for its main business of running nonpaid searches (Overture, 2003b). But Google was not about to stand by and watch. Google responded to Overture's success by amassing its own index of commercial sites and creating the "AdWords" program. AdWords essentially combines Overture's auction system of selling key words and placement to the highest bidder with an algorithm that factors relevance, or the ad's click-through rate, into placement. Advertisers pay only when users click on their AdWord link. In addition, Google also established a more expensive sponsored links option for links appearing above, rather than on the side, of the search result list. Significantly, Google took the higher road by promising to never place sponsored links within the company's objective search results. Such company integrity, however, may be irrelevant, or, at worst, it may be a convenient marketing tool. Already, plenty of other channels have evolved to undermine

Google's promise of integrity. For this discussion, we need another anatomy lesson.

ANATOMY LESSON 2: THE CRAFTY CRAFT OF SEARCH ENGINE SPONSORSHIP

First, a slight review is in order. As we've seen, search results on any commercial search portal are already skewed toward commerce due to a number of basic payment practices.

• Commercial directories charge a recurring annual fee for an express submission (in Yahoo!'s case, $299), which ensures a continued listing once a submission is approved. The Looksmart Directory, as of 2002, accepts *only* paid submissions from commercial sites to its directory. These enterprising strategies indirectly benefit well-endowed and for-profit sites that can afford elite treatment and positioning within a directory.

• Commercial search providers have instituted pay-for-placement deals designed to directly benefit commercial sites. The higher an organization bids on a key word, the higher they are listed in the search portal.

Yet these developments are just the beginning of an evolving and commercially innovative search industry.

Paid Inclusion

In 2001, Inktomi introduced a new variable that would serve commerce—and the search engine industry—extraordinarily well: *paid inclusion*. Paid inclusion means that customers who pay a flat fee are guaranteed to be included in every search completed by the Inktomi search engine. Search engines do not search the entire Web, only parts (here, another myth is deflated). With paid inclusion, paying sites would always be incorporated into the searchable index (unlike many other sites, which simply slip away as algorithms are updated). Although paid inclusion does not guarantee the Web site's rank within the search results, it does guarantee inclusion, somewhere, each time a search is conducted. For niche topics especially, this bodes well for the advertiser. As Gaither (2003) explained, "Internet companies have realized that, if someone is hunting for information on a topic like mesothelioma, the person is ripe for specialized advertising" (p. F1).

Inktomi's model was soon copied by every major search engine provider save Google, meaning that by 2002, Inktomi, AlltheWeb, Teoma, and AltaVista were all offering paid inclusion as part of their overall syndicated package. As the practice of paid inclusion exploded, advice about paid inclusion practices appeared as unproblematic common sense in countless business newsletters and magazines by 2003:

> The key to success is finding the words that will drive traffic to your site—and, more important, convert those potential customers into sales. [Martin Child, Overture's managing director for Northern Europe] says generic terms such as travel may generate a large number of leads but many of those will be wasted if your firm offers only a niche service. "'Travel' may not convert as well as 'Icelandic expedition,'" he says—even though there would be far fewer searches that use the latter, much less expensive term. Bunis recommends a mix of generic and specific descriptions of your business. (Durman, 2003, p. 16)

With such a profitable commercial system, search engine providers were finally seen as money-makers in their own right, and as such came to be regarded more as lucrative properties rather than services for mere syndication. By early 2003, Yahoo! had acquired Inktomi ($235 million) and Overture had scooped up both AlltheWeb ($70 million) and AltaVista ($140 million). "The paid-inclusion model is really icing on the cake," said Yahoo! Chief Financial Officer Sue Decker in 2003. "That alone really justifies the price of the transaction" (Reuters, 2003). A few months later, Yahoo! then acquired Overture.

As surely as paid inclusion is lucrative to search engine providers, there is also a noteworthy fringe benefit to advertisers investing in paid inclusion: Part of the flat fee involves advice on how to write advertisers' listings so as to further enhance their position. "Since [commercial search engines] alone understand how the algorithms inside their search engine 'black boxes' work," Waters (2003) observed that "they generally know how to game the system, though it is a power they claim to use responsibly" (p. 30). In other words, even if paying sites did not pay for prominent placement directly, at least they got the tools to figure out how to get there. As advisory material from an online marketing firm called the Web Search Workshop related in 2004, these new "opportunities" could get their clients' Web sites "more (and faster) exposure in a crowded market": "There is some dissatisfaction that these paid services are now opening up a gap between those websites able or willing to pay and therefore changing the balance of search results being offered. However, this trend for providing a paid alternative in return for privileges is likely to stay and probably increase in the future" (The Web, 2004, p. 1).

For good reason, there was heady jubilation within the search industry and in business circles over the Web's commercial viability via search engine listings. Results had become so commercially skewed, however, that consumer advocacy groups were increasingly alarmed. A campaign, initiated by the media watchdog group Commercial Alert, led to a Federal Trade Commission (FTC) investigation into the practice of undisclosed, paid search results within search portals. Completed in June 2002, the study reported (not surprisingly) that the Web's largest search engines did not reveal the preferred treatment they accorded to sponsors. The FTC's response was typical in terms of the current political climate: a gentle rebuke and a call for self-regulation. The rebuke however, did *seem* to be effective: It led to more differentiation between sponsored sites and "non-paid" sites. For example, Yahoo!, AskJeeves, Lycos, and numerous other portals began stressing the "objectivity" of their web results by using bold red headings to demarcate a sponsored link from a nonsponsored link. These distinctions, however, more or less veiled the incursions of paid inclusion, which had surreptitiously become the industry norm.

Search Engine Marketers (SEMs)

Only one search engine provider/portal has resisted both pay-for-placement and paid inclusion. Google has taken an admirable stance on search engine integrity since its inception and, although it has rigorously pushed its AdWords program, which matches sponsored sites to key words within a search, the company has widely publicized its refusal to allow any direct commercial influence in its search result lists. This is not to say, however, that Google's result lists are free from market influence. One of the most significant developments just outside of (but directly affecting) the search engine industry has been the rise of search engine marketing. This mini-industry exists to influence placement within the databases of search engine providers and maximize the overall visibility of any client's Web site. The search engine optimization (SEO) market, which offers "positioning" and "advisory & marketing" services to its clients, is flourishing. These small SEO companies (or SEMs) try to guarantee prominent listings for their clients. Although most business organizations know the four necessary steps toward Web site visibility (a subscription to Google's AdWords, Overture, Yahoo!'s Directory, and a submission to the Open Directory Project), SEMs aggressively act on their behalf.

Most SEMs are especially focused on Google, a sort of Holy Grail for SEMs. Google is the most popular search portal/search engine provider (conducting 83% of all searches in 2003; Hindman, Tsioustsiouliklis, & Johnson, 2003), yet it is a tough nut to crack for SEMs, because it does not give anyone access to its algorithm. In fact, one of the most typical promotional statements appearing on these companies' Web sites concerns the ability to decode the patterns behind Google's objective search results. "We understand the 'spidering' schedule that Google employs," says Morevisibility.com. "By submitting at the appropriate intervals, we are able to systematically deep-penetrate the Google database" (More-Visibility, 2003). Meanwhile, as Harvey (2003b) reported, "so many small companies have sprung up in this field that Google engineers spend much of their time tweaking its search criteria in order not to fall prey to them" (p. 32).

Because Google's PageRank algorithm strategy is partially based on the number of links pointing to a site (ostensibly making it more "popular," and therefore more worthwhile to most web searchers), SEMs have become especially savvy to the linking game, working with their clients to increase the number of links leading to their clients' Web sites. We hear about this practice in popular culture: For example, pranksters and political activists turned official Web sites for 2004 Democratic nominee John Kerry and President George W. Bush into the top listings for search terms like "waffle" or "miserable failure." This strategy is called "Google bombing" in the mainstream media, and is considered a harmless novelty. Meanwhile, enterprising SEMs (who we don't tend to hear about) use the term "horizontal marketing," and do anything they can to increase linkage for paying clients. This includes specializing in particular areas such as health and insurance-related sites to better shape web rings of reciprocal links. Blogrolling is another common way SEMs have generated more links: By applying the popular software supplied by Blogrolling.com, a user can add links to a blogpage with one easy click, which in turn more easily leads to link-farming, the practice of creating Web sites with nothing but links. As Walker (2005) explained in her helpful analysis of the link economy: "There is a black market for links. You can pay dollars or kroner or yen to buy links to your site from link farms, circles of sites with nothing but links. There is also a common law perception of link prostitution or link slutting: shamelessly selling one's own integrity for links" (p. 527).

Because Google's market success is dependent on its perceived credibility (the company's motto is "Don't Do Evil"), Google has heavily discouraged link-farming, and has punished link-farming companies and their clients with lower search results. One such firm, the Oklahoma City-based SearchKing, which had practiced link-farming and was "punished" by Google, filed a federal lawsuit against Google in 2002. However, Google won the case in 2003 on the grounds that it has First Amendment rights to present its search results in any order it sees fit (Kopytoff, 2003). Although the SearchKing vs. Google case pitted one commercial company's interests against another, the case has some interesting implications for any future efforts to decommercialize search engine result lists. Like the landmark *Midwest Video* case in 1979, which entitled cable companies to pick and choose which channels to carry and escape Federal Communication Commission (FCC) regulation, this case allows search engine providers to escape any rules that would force them to disclose why some content (namely, commercial content) appears more heavily concentrated than others. Of course, these developments may bode well for Internet consumers (as they are now universally referred to in the search industry), but not so well for Internet users with noncommercial tasks.

Because of Google's aggressive actions toward link-farms and its win against SearchKing, link-farms have become more risky than worthwhile. Meanwhile, as SEMs continue to be punished and are, as a consequence, losing a successful marketing tool, Google has emerged a winner on two counts. First, the company can continue to boast about its commitment to search engine integrity. Second, with the demise of link-farming, advertisers have become increasingly dependent on Google's very successful AdWords program (Goodman, 2003). They have also become increasingly dependent on reciprocal linking as a necessary marketing tool. In this regard, Google is doing a fine job to accelerate this trend, which in the business world is referred to as contextual linking.

Contextual Links

As it stands, link-farms have never been nearly as effective at influencing Google's ranking system as singular links from a highly prominent Web site. A link, for example, to the used pick-up truck company Bronco Graveyard (broncograveyard.com) that appears on the home page of the popular trucking magazine *Truckin'* (truckin.com) can do a world of good in terms of enhancing Bronco Graveyard's visibility; a link on the popular Tennis.com Web site to the less known raquetdepot.com also helps increase the small Web site's "popularity," and thus its ranking on regular search results. Called "contextual links," they are links to other sites that match the context of the main Web site. Today, users can click on contextual links at the bottom of nearly every online article in a commercial publication. But, small as they are, they are effective far beyond the advertising spot on a given page; the act of linking is also an act of endorsement, and consequently increases the company's PageRank standing in Google search results. As Walker (2005) explained, "The economy of links is not product oriented. It is service oriented, and the service is the link. The link is an action rather than an item; an event rather than a metaphor" (p. 526).

Contextual links are, not surprisingly, highly valued, with commercial online publications quickly jumping into the contextual link business by giving advertisers the option to buy links on their home page, as Tennis. com does through its "Tennis Magazine MarketPlace Program." Although SEMs have worked hard to establish reciprocal links between smaller sites, it turns out that it is the more well-connected and powerful search engine companies, Google and Yahoo!/Overture, that are the most busy broker-ing contextual link deals through their massive index of advertisers.

Google introduced its AdSense program in 2003, and Yahoo! introduced Content Match a month later (Acohido, 2003). Both programs broker con-textual links on content Web sites. Yahoo!, for example, supplies spon-sored links to CNN.com and Wall Street Journal.com. Google supplies sponsored links to *U.S. News & World Report*, the Weather Channel, and ABC.com (Mangalindan, 2003). Its purchase of Sprinks in 2003 (a pay-per-click advertising network owned by media conglomerate Primedia), and a resulting relationship with Primedia (which, among other media products, owns the largest number of niche magazines, all of which have an online presence), will allow Google to supply contextual links to all these pub-lications. Google's drive to plant more and more contextual links among prominent pages across the Web, a process that increases the prominence of all these commercial pages within the Google PageRank system, actu-ally undermines the company's line about search engine result integrity.

With Yahoo! increasingly mirroring Google's PageRank system, and with such prescribed contextual linking in place, the search results of both search engine provider/portals are now nearly indistinguishable, especially in terms of their promotion of the most prominent sites (with which they have advertising relationships). Again, the myth about search engine variance is discredited. As Hindman et al. (2003) observed, "All modern search engine algorithms—including those radically different from Google's PageRank—tend to return these most connected sites first" (p. 27). These authors have also observed that the Web, via search engines, now operates much like traditional media, with heavily concentrated oli-gopolies serving as gatekeepers for entry into the rest of the community.

With these developments, both Google and Yahoo! are also becoming more general online ad agencies than search engines, and like ad agen-cies, they increasingly measure "ad" performance and collect consumer data. Consequently, both measure the results of ads (what the industry now euphemistically terms "customizes") by tracking the clickstream data, cookies, pixel tags, and contact/personally identifying information of search engine users. Whereas Yahoo!/Overture relies on the large, web-based company called Doubleclick for this purpose, Google relies on its new subsidiary, Kaltix, which is a start-up company that has developed profile-tailoring software to better target individual users by tracking their choices on the Web; Google purchased Kaltix in October 2003 (Man-galindan, 2003). As Mangalindan observed, "By gathering more data on each Google user, the reasoning goes, the search engine would know that a search for 'apple' is one for fruit rather than computers" (p. B1). Both Yahoo! and Google are also working toward providing successful geo-location functions to their marketing toolkits (Oct. 18). These ad services identify users' specific locations, and thus enable local advertisers to use search engines as a marketing strategy.

Interestingly, Google defines these local business opportunities in terms of greater democracy. In 2003, Google's director of product management argued that her company enabled democracy because anyone, even small advertisers, could advertise via Google (Mangalindan, 2003). Accordingly, in the world of search (as spoken by representatives from the "search engine of integrity"), the notion of online democracy no longer has anything to do with regular users (i.e., the democracy of ideas) but applies only to the advertising world (i.e., the democracy of the marketplace). The word "relevancy" has also come to have new meaning in the world of search business-speak. Rather than attempting to deliver the most relevant information to users, the task is now for search engines to deliver the most relevant consumer information to consumers (Jan. 6). As Crowe (2003, p. 29) stated in the *Australian Financial Review*, "Keeping advertisers happy with their paid searches is now the most important objective for the big search companies."

In 5 short years, an industry study revealed that the pay-per-click market had grown from under $100 million a year to a multibillion industry in 2003, and included these startling statistics: Forty-two percent of those who bought from online retail sites arrived via search engines (Schacther, 2003). So successful was search engine sponsorship that rates increased by 50% in 2003 alone, revealing that "the adoption of the internet as an advertising vehicle by traditional advertisers is truly taking place" (Hansell, 2003b, p. 32). Industry reports also pointed to search engine sponsorship as an increasing, rather than diminishing trend: The business analyst group Bancorp Piper Jaffray projected that the search industry would swell to $7 billion by 2007 (Oct. 11).

ANATOMY LESSON 3: GOOGLE, YAHOO!, AND THE PREDATORY GOALS OF MICROSOFT

Three main companies, all American-based, dominate the search industry: Google, Yahoo!, and Microsoft. Google has been involved in search technology from its inception (1998), syndicating its search engine provider services and becoming a favorite search portal among users. Yahoo!, which began as a directory and search portal (outsourcing to Inktomi, and then Google, for its search technology), became a dominant player with its purchase of Inktomi and then Overture (which in turn had just purchased AltaVista and AlltheWeb) in 2003. Since these acquisitions, Yahoo! has been in direct competition with Google for search portal prominence. Yet Microsoft, with its powerful MSN portal, is on the horizon as the most dominant player of all. As CEO Bill Gates said, "we will catch them," setting the date for summer 2005 (Feb. 1; Markoff, 2004).

The Google/Yahoo! Rivalry

In 2000, Yahoo! hired Google to conduct the searches on its search portal, giving the company "its first big break" (Hansell, 2003a). By 2003, however, Google and Yahoo! had become the fiercest competitors. To understand the extent of this rivalry, it is helpful to look at the major acquisitions each company made prior, during, and just after 2003:

October 2001: Overture achieves profitability, with "outstanding financial results," establishing search as a key business strategy

May 2001: Inktomi introduces "paid inclusion"

October 2002: Google launches AdWords program, begins head-on competition with Overture

December 2002: Google launches the Froogle shopping tool

March 2003: Yahoo! enters the search engine provider business, acquiring Inktomi (and dumping Google)

April 2003: Overture acquires AlltheWeb and AltaVista

April 2003: Google acquires Applied Semantics (an online advertising software co.)

May 2003: Google launches its AdSense program

June 2003: Overture introduces Content Match, directly competing with AdSense

September 2003: Yahoo! expands Yahoo! Shopping (using Inktomi technology), to compete with Froogle

September 2003: Google acquires Kaltix (online profiling and marketing company)

October 2003: Yahoo acquires Overture (which includes AltaVista and AlltheWeb)

October 2003: Yahoo! introduces SmartSort (which helps users quickly narrow a search for certain products)

October 2003: Yahoo! acquires 3721 Network Software (Chinese letter search engine)

March 2004: Yahoo! acquires Kelkoo, Europe's leading online comparison shopping service

March 2004: Yahoo!/Overture introduces Site Match (a controversial combination of paid inclusion and pay-per-click)

March 2004: Google introduces Google Local, allowing advertisers to connect with local users

The end result of this run of acquisitions, which mostly occurred during 2003, meant that two rival search engine companies provide the searching functions (both commercial and algorithmic) to nearly every search portal on the Web. The one remaining search engine provider, Teoma (owned by Ask Jeeves) is considered a ripe prospect for acquisition (Savitz, 2003). Google itself has been preyed on by the software giant, Microsoft. Indeed, apart from the Google/Yahoo! rivalry, Microsoft emerged as the third dominant player by the end of 2003.

Microsoft Makes a Move

Microsoft's moves on Google were not surprising given the company's nearly limitless resources and stated ambitions in content acquisition. As early as 1995, Gates was talking about going "well beyond simply providing a pipe for bits" (1995, pp. 241–242). Microsoft, in Dawson and Foster's (1998) words, is "interested in moving up 'the economic food chain' from the delivery and distribution of bits at the bottom to computer applications and services and content at the top. Such companies want to own the bits, not simply deliver them" (p. 60). However, when Google denied the partnership or takeover opportunity at the end of 2003, Microsoft turned to Plan B. For most of 2003, MSN was still relying on Inktomi to power its algorithmic searches, Overture to power its commercial searches, and Looksmart as a fortifying directory. In other words, MSN was deeply dependent on subsidiaries owned by Yahoo! But by October (after the Google talks unraveled; Teather, 2003), MSN had ditched Looksmart and had started work on its own search engine platform, resolving to drop Inktomi and Overture sometime after 2005, when it would roll out its "Google-killer" search engine algorithm (Bazeley, 2004). In other words, Microsoft had begun to amass a proprietary index of sites from which to conduct searches and was hiring hundreds of engineers to work on web-searching algorithms to top Google. By 2005, 25% of MSN's hugely prestigious Beijing lab focused solely on search, and the company had more than 500 engineers and marketers perfecting the MSN serach-based advertising system. With the Encarta Encyclopedia in its arsenal for factual query results, the MSN search engine was growing in use at a rate faster than Google. Moreover, the software company planned to integrate its search technology *directly into its Windows operating system* under a project code-named "Longhorn" in 2006 (Peterson, 2005).

For anyone familiar with Microsoft's history of annihilating the competition, this strategy seems hauntingly familiar to Microsoft's triumph over Netscape in the web browser business. "Today we are number one in email, we are number one in messenger. Our ambition is to be number one in search," Sharon Babyle, the general manager of MSN's consumer

Internet service, said at the end of November 2003 (Conners, 2003). During
the run-up to Google's public offering, which finally occurred in August
2004, Microsoft was working hard to destabilize Google and snag Google
employees (Markoff, 2004). Given Google's subsequent release of its new
desktop computer search software (Google Desktop Search), which allows
users to search their desktops far more efficiently than Microsoft (Bazeley, 2004), it is clear that, if anything, Google will put up a good fight. But,
now that Google's future requires the company to attend to the demands
of shareholders, many analysts are forecasting damage to Google's search
integrity. As the opening sentence of a story in *Wired* plainly said, "The
world's biggest, best-loved search engine owes its success to supreme
technology and a simple rule: Don't be evil. Now the geek icon is finding
that moral compromise is just the cost of doing big business" (McHugh,
2003). For starters, the Google Desktop Search program increases the company's ability to target users with personalized advertising. Likewise, the
company's Gmail program, introduced in March 2004, examines the content of individual e-mails and sends users' marketing information back
to company headquarters. Moral compromise and commercial intrusions into Google's search listings will certainly continue as Microsoft and
Yahoo! continue the onslaught.

CONCLUSIONS

Despite the considerable implications of search engine commercialization for knowledge access, the topic has not gained much attention in academic and library spheres. One reason for this lack of attention is good
public relations: The search engine industry continues to highlight "integrity," "relevance," and "objectivity" as a mantra, meanwhile stealthily
undermining Internet users' faith in search technology. Another reason
is the general silence in the U.S. mass media when it comes to any criticism of commercialism (because the mass media themselves are major
participants in advertising-supported commercial media culture). Consequently, the four myths about search engine services resound: They are
impartial, they are all-inclusive, they vary greatly, and they are the most
reliable place to go for relevant online information.

We educators, for the most part, buy into these myths; we continue
to have a largely optimistic outlook on search engines as helpful and
trustworthy educational and research tools. Despite its heavy commercialism, the Web's potential as a place for online scholarship and diversity is still evident—when the right search terms are used—and positive
experiences can certainly outweigh negative experiences, for now, anyway. Moreover, educators and librarians have heavily promoted individ-

ual skills (advanced searching techniques, web page evaluation skills) as a way to cope with excessive commercialism. Although it may feel empowering to teach or possess these skills, a wholesale critique of the commercial web structure remains sidelined (Fabos, 2004).

Fortunately, researchers in economics, political science, communication studies, applied physics, and computer science have begun to scrutinize the structural components of the Web against the framework of democracy and knowledge access. Introna and Nissenbaum (2000), for example, examined search engines' current trajectory as market-driven information tools and questioned the future of the Web as a public good. They argued that "if search engines systematically highlight Web sites with popular appeal and mainstream commercial purpose, as well as Web sites backed by entrenched economic powers, they amplify these presences on the Web at the expense of others" (p. 28).

Hindman et al. (2003) were also concerned with the increasing concentration (and visibility) of heavily linked sites. They analyzed the hyperlinks surrounding political Web sites (measuring link structure on a massive scale), and concluded that the number of highly visible sites is small, and the visibility drop-off is rapid. They called this organizational structure "googlearchy" (the rule of the most heavily linked), and suggested that the Web is more like the current corporate mass media, with top-down control of limited content, rather than a diverse platform of ideas.

Gerhart (2004) researched a residual effect of Web site consolidation: the way search engines inherently suppress controversy. In her study, which tracked search engine results about five controversial topics, Gerhart found that three out of five were buried by commercial sites, and concluded that significant amounts of controversial material are unattainable via search engines. In her words, controversy is important because:

> controversies often express the richness and depth of a topic. Controversies dramatize change. Controversies may make a critical difference in life-altering decisions. Scientists, journalists, and intelligence analysts are professionally required to address multiple perspectives, facts, authorities, and opinions on topics. Search engines may significantly decrease their productivity or conceal incompetence if controversies are overly difficult to investigate. (p. 4)

According to Gerhart, unless a controversy has already been recently highlighted in the mainstream media, or unless a searcher is already aware that a controversy about a particular topic already exists (and can type the appropriate keywords), controversial topics are largely invisible. Walker (2005), another scholar researching the implications of a link-driven online economy, eloquently summarized the mainstreaming of web content this way: "We are participants in this power structure whether we like it or not. We can criticize it, reflect upon it, approve of it or try to subvert it. We must not ignore it. This standardization of links and their value will shape what the future finds. It defines what can be found. It defines knowledge" (p. 528). Indeed, all of this research is important, because it goes beyond the net result of search engine result lists (what librarians and most educators are typically concerned with) and addresses the complex and economically charged structure of the Web that affects all search results regardless of how well one crafts an individual search.

As people habitually turn to commercial search engines to navigate a commercial environment, they are unaware of the increasing difficulties to locate content that is not commercial. They are unaware of the misleading motives of the Internet navigation tools they use, and of the constant efforts among for-profit enterprise to bend the Internet toward their ends. McChesney (1999), who has been on the forefront of discussions about media concentration, is another researcher who touched on the Internet as the latest in a long line of commercial media that have been colonized by corporate power, turning a so-called democratic medium into one wholly controlled by big media oligopolies. "Despite its much ballyhooed 'openness,'" he wrote, "to the extent that it becomes a viable mass medium, it will likely be dominated by the usual corporate suspects" (p. 183).

Today, the Internet is an oligopoly, with Google, Yahoo!, and Microsoft as the three companies controlling most of the Internet's information flow. These companies are capable of bringing good things to the web search environment, and will do their best to appear as if they put the interests of users first, rolling out new plans to make search experiences more worthwhile and exposing "the invisible web." For example, Google has begun to digitize vast holdings of books from libraries such as Stanford, Oxford, and New York Public Library and include this wealth of information in its database (although copyright issues have thwarted this "philanthropic" endeavor). In March 2004, Yahoo! initiated its "Content Acquisition Program," part of which involves content partnerships with organizations like the Library of Congress, National Public Radio, the New York Public Library (owner of Project Gutenberg), the National Science Digital Library, and Michigan's OAIster digital archive. These considerable archives will supply "premiere" (i.e., educational) listings on the Yahoo! search result list. And as Microsoft's search engine becomes a significant player, the company will more than likely make well-publicized efforts to improve its database with rich, noncommercial archives. As with television, there has to be some decent content to drive the ads—that is the basis of how commercial mass media operates in the United States.

Regardless of these seemingly good intentions, however, the myths surrounding search engines must be debunked. Commercial search engines will always be educationally compromised; they will always give advertisers premium treatment in their services. The other part of Yahoo!'s "Content Acquisition Program," for example, involves Site Match, a more vigorous paid inclusion program refreshed every 48 hours, which allows web-heavy companies more control over which of their pages are frequently indexed. The creation of Yahoo!'s Site Match also marks a change in the paid inclusion payment model. Now, a finder's fee is involved beyond the original flat fee: Any time a user clicks on a commercial link, whether it is on page 1 or page 20 on the search results page, advertisers pay the search engine a small listing fee—naturally giving search engines more incentive to get users into the "click-through" mentality.

If we want to go beyond a mainstream, commercialized, sponsored online information repository, then we need to turn to a different structure that offers a more inclusive, democratic information environment. We need to discredit the final myth: that search engines are the only place to go for relevant online information. Some places to start are the nonprofit world of subject gateways (e.g., The National Science Digital Library, INFOMINE, OAIster, or the Resource Discovery Network), issue networking sites such as Govcom.org, or the collaborative environments of wiki pages (e.g., wikipedia.org; disinfopedia.org), where people, not corporations, make the significant choices about the information—controversial and diverse—that is accessible online.

NOTES

1. Both Lycos and WebCrawler, which emerged in 1994, pre-date AltaVista and Inktomi, but stopped developing their algorithms in favor of outsourcing search services from AlltheWeb (Lycos) or multiple search engine providers (Webcrawler).

2. Teoma was purchased by Internet conglomerate InterActive Corp. in 2005.

REFERENCES

Acohido, B. (2003, November 17). Simplifying the info hunt. *USA Today*, p. 11E.
Bazeley, M. (2004, October 15). Google rolls our search software. *San Jose Mercury News*, p. B2.
Conners, E. (2003, November 25). Microsoft in search of top spot. *Australian Financial Review*, p. 32.
Crowe, D. (2003, October 18). In search of a profit engine. *Australian Financial Review*, p. 29.
Dawson, M., & Foster, J. B. (1998). Virtual capitalism. In R. McChesney, E. M. Wood, & J. B. Foster (Eds.), *Capitalism and the information age: The political economy of the global communication revolution* (pp. 51–68). New York: Monthly Review Press.
Durman, P. (2003, November 9). Customers clicking with online adverts. *Sunday Times* (London), p. 16.

Fabos, B. (2005). *Wrong turn on the information superhighway: Education and the commercialization of the internet.* New York: Teacher's College Press.

Fine Brand Media Inc. (2003). *A brief history of search engine marketing on the Web.* Retrieved March 7, 2004, from http://www.finebrand.com/ideacenter/search-engine-optimization/abriefhistory-2.cfm

Gaither, C. (2003, February 23). Searching for dollars as banner market flags, net giants pin hopes on revenue from targeted ads related to specific queries. *The Boston Globe,* p. F1.

Gates, B. (1995). *The road ahead.* New York: Viking.

Gerhart, S. L. (2004, January). Do web search engines suppress controversy? *First Monday,* 9(1). Retrieved January 23, 2004, from http://firstmonday.org/issues/issue9_1gerhart/index.html.

Goodman, A. (2003). Cracking Google's new algorithm. *WebProNews.* Retrieved from http://www.webpronews.com/ebusiness/smallbusiness/wpn-2-20031203CrackingGooglesNewAlgorithm.html

Griffiths, J. T., & Brophy, P. (2005, Spring). Student searching behavior and the Web: Use of academic resources and Google. *Library Trends, 53*(4), 539–554.

Hansell, S. (1999, April 15). Altavista invites advertisers to pay for top ranking. *New York Times,* p. C2.

Hansell, S. (2003a, April 7). Yahoo plans improvements in effort to regain lost ground. *New York Times,* p. 2.

Hansell, S. (2003b, October 9). Yahoo's resurgent profit is led by strong advertising. *New York Times,* p. C7.

Harvey, F. (2003a, January 15). Online ads await click-through to profitability: Questions have been raised about whether the medium works, but analysts are optimistic. *Financial Times,* FT Report, p. 1.

Harvey, F. (2003b, March 4). Putting a price on results: Recent acquisitions suggest the sponsored search sector is a bright spot in a gloomy market. *Financial Times,* p. 32.

Hindman, M., Tsioutsiouliklis, K., & Johnson, J. (2003). "Googlearchy": How a few heavily-linked sites dominate politics on the Web. Retrieved April 10, 2004, from www.princeton.edu/~mhindman/googlearchy--hindman.pdf

Introna, L., & Nissenbaum, H. (2000). Shaping the Web: Why the politics of search engines matters. *Information Society, 16*(3), 186–189. Retrieved from http://www-us.ebsco.com/online/Reader.asp (if your library is subscribed).

Kopytoff, V. (2003, November 9). Google's future looking good; Bulked-up search firm beats up rivals. *San Francisco Chronicle,* p. I1.

Lasica, J. D. (2001, July 23). Search engines and editorial integrity. *Online Journalism Review.* Retrieved December 12, 2001, from http://www.ojr.org/ojr/technology/1017778969.php

Mangalindan, M. (2003, October 16). Seeking growth, search engine Google acts like ad agency. *Wall Street Journal,* p. B1.

Markoff, J. (2003, October 31). Microsoft and Google: Partners or rivals? *New York Times,* p. C1.

Markoff, J. (2004, February 1). The coming search wars. *New York Times,* sect. 3, p. 1.

McChesney, R. (1999). *Rich media, poor democracy: Communication politics in dubious times.* Urbana: University of Illinois Press.

McHugh, J. (2003, January). Google vs. Evil. *Wired Magazine, 11*(1). Retrieved March 20, 2004, from http://www.wired.com/wired/archive/11.01/googgle_pr.html

MoreVisibility platform three: E-commerce initiative. (2003). More visibility.com. Retrieved April 18, 2003, from http://www.morevisibility.com/serices_three.html

Overture. (2003a, February 25). Overture to acquire web search unit of Fast Search & Transfer—FAST. Press release; Overture, Inc. Retrieved April 18, 2003, from http://www

.corporate-ir.net/ireye/ir_site.zhtml?ticker=OVER&script=410&layout=0&item_id=
385605

Overture. (2003b). *Vision: Corporate overview*. Overture, Inc. Retrieved May 25, 2003, from
http://www.content.overture.com/d/Usm/about/company/vision.jhtml

Peterson, K. (2005, May 2). Microsoft learns to crawl. *Seattle Times*. Retrieved August 18, 2005,
from http://archives.seattletimes.nwsource.com

Reuters. (2003, December 24). Yahoo! to buy software maker. *Los Angeles Times*, sect. 3, p. 2.

Savitz, E. (2003, October 30). Why are Jeeves shares so high? *Toronto Star*, p. K07.

Schachter, K. (2003, December 5). The pay-per-click Internet market grows into multi-billion
dollar business. *Dolan Media Newswires*.

Teather, D. (2003, November 1). Microsoft runs search for a way to take over Internet giant
Google. *The Guardian*, p. 1.

The Web Search WorkShop. (2004). *Materials: Paying for search engine and directory listings*.
Retrieved March 21, 2004, from http://www.websearchworkshop.co.uk/paying.htm

Walker, J. (2005, Spring). Links and power: The political economy of linking on the Web.
Library Trends, 53(4), 524–529.

Waters, R. (2003, March 12). Search industry scours scrap heap for bargains. *Financial Times*,
p. 30.

14

Monopoly, Monopsony, and the Value of Culture in a Digital Age: An Axiology of Two Multimedia Resource Repositories

Phil Graham

INTRODUCTION

My argument here has formed over more than twenty years of experience in various aspects of the culture industries. The central assertion on which I base my argument is that mass mediated culture has lowered the default value of cultural materials to zero; that is to say unless people's words, dances, songs, music, movies, or scripts are bought, promoted, and distributed through the key institutions of mass mediated culture, they are generally considered to be of no financial worth. One key factor in misrecognising or overlooking this outcome is that studies in political economy of communication in particular, and critical media studies more generally, have tended to regard the major corporate persons who comprise the global culture industry as monopolies (Bagdikian, 1997; McChesney, 2000). However such a view is "consumption-sided" to some large extent, focusing on the effects that industry structures and practices have upon cultural "consumers," and therefore cannot recognise that having a small group of organisations as the largest buyers of cultural materials in a global media system has serious implications for the character and value of culture. This perspective, in which monopolies are seen from the view of producers, is called monopsony: one buyer, many sellers. This perspective provides a far reaching and very different view of cultural axiology than can be derived from monopoly-based perspectives.

However, new media always provide new opportunities, and the perplexing, contrary axiology of mass mediated culture provides interesting potentials in the emergent media environment comprised of networked digital technologies. With ever expanding technological facility to store, retrieve, reconfigure, and redistribute literally mountains of cultural "junk" (the bulk of which is neither poor quality nor essentially useless); with ever increasing amounts of multimedia material being produced; and with copyright being exercised ever more strenuously by the "official" industries of mass culture, the opportunity, if not the impetus, exists for more people to participate in the development of local and global culture by exercising different choices than those typically made within the confines of the culture industries. Such an opportunity can be realised by making high-quality, yet ostensibly worthless cultural "junk" widely available. That is what ACRO and CCCI are designed to do: provide open access to high-quality multimedia materials under new and flexible licensing regimes, such as those developed by Creative Commons (*www. creativecommons.org*) and AESharenet (*http://www.aesharenet.com.au/FfE/*). These licenses are designed to allow people to re-use existing materials without fear of breaching intellectual property, and for intellectual property owners to express the kinds of digital rights they wish to extend in order to allow their works to be shared as a continual and ongoing part of creativity and culture (Lessig, 2004).

The axiological "wager" made by the developers and funders of ACRO and CCCI is that providing widespread, open access to rich media resources will (a) add value to "junk" material by promoting the adaptive repurposing of those materials; (b) provide the basis for developing new content forms suited to new media environments, especially in the emerging context of broadband networks; (c) promote new authorial and technological literacies; and, (d) entail new conceptions about the value of cultural materials, and about the expectations that people have about being able to consciously and actively participate in the production of their cultures.

The rationale for doing so is straightforward:

> The essential task of all sound economic activity is to produce a state in which creation will be a common fact in all experience: in which no group will be denied, by reasons of toil or deficient education, their share in the cultural life of the community, up to the limits of their personal capacity. Unless we socialize creation, unless we make production subservient to education, a mechanized system of production, however efficient, will only

harden into a servile byzantine formality, enriched by bread and circuses. (Mumford, 1934/1962, p. 430)

Mumford's words were indeed prescient. The global culture industries have become servile and byzantine systems redolent of bread and circuses, and designed to provide mass distractions for special interests (Postman, 1985; Graham & Luke, 2003). Bill Hayton, Europe Editor of BBC's World Service makes the following observation in respect of the global news gathering and distribution practices, emphasising one way in which the logic of current media practices tend towards homogeneity:

> There are two main news footage agencies—Reuters and APTN (AP having bought the third, WTN some years ago). You might have thought that this would double the amount of available material but it doesn't. Since neither agency wants to miss pictures which the other one can offer its subscribers exclusively, they follow each other around! This is exacerbated by the Eurovision system in Europe whereby public service broadcasters exchange material. This allows the agencies to send their pictures back to London (where they are both based) for free—they don't have to pay for their own satellite time. If the agencies both have the same pictures then they get what's known as a "common" which means that APTN feeds their pictures and Reuters has access to them (or vice versa). Another incentive for both agencies to get the same shots rather than seek an alternative view! (Bill Hayton, Europe Editor, Newsroom, BBC World Service, email correspondence, August 26 2004).

Again we see the devaluation of cultural production in such a shift; its cheapening to the lowest possible price; and the resultant lack of creativity, novelty, and difference that occurs as a consequence. While it would be anachronistic to wish for a return to the "village pump" model of news-telling, it is worth drawing the analogy to emphasize the participative way in which new information—*news*—has been historically introduced into cultures, and to foreground the cultural function of "news" more generally.

News is a unique and influential form of "ritual" drama for cultures; "a portrayal of the contending forces in the world" that positions people within the "dramatic action" portrayed by what we call news; "a presentation of reality that gives life an overall form, order, and tone" (Carey, 1989, p. 20–21). Briefly, news is "a form of culture" that was commercialized during the eighteenth century, its impetus at the time being a middle-class desire to "do away with the epic, heroic, and traditional in favor of the unique, original, novel, new—news" (1989, p. 21). It is an early precursor of mass mediated cultures and its progress towards an ironic lack of novelty, diversity, and creativity in its historical development typifies the progress of mass culture more generally. The hero is back. The

Old Testament tradition of revenge has re-emerged as a staple theme of the monopsony's culture. The epic struggle between good and evil has once again taken centre stage. In this respect, the historical trajectory of the culture industry is an example of what Horkheimer and Adorno (1947/1998) named the *Dialectic of Enlightenment*, the contradictory historical oscillation between *ratio* and *mythos* in culture.

To explain these apparently typical phenomena that pertain to massified, commercialized systems of cultural production, I rely on the following assumptions: Cultures extend as far in time and space as the systems of technologies and practices that mediate them permit, and so they rely for their existence on these systems (Innis, 1951a, 1951b). New patterns of mediation produce new cultural interactions and new ways of extending, reinforcing, and otherwise transforming the character of any culture that is touched by these new patterns (Silverstone, 1999). Cultures are primarily axiological, which is to say our cultures are identifiable as such because of the unique patterns of evaluation that its members have developed over many years; by the way the members of a culture express themselves; and by the choices they make in doing so. New media systems, especially those that span larger and larger geographical spaces, therefore tend to promote axiological conflicts and (sometimes) syntheses. During such moments in history, cultural axiologies change quickly, and at numerous levels, as exemplified by the strong globalising movements of the 1990s and the rapid cultural fragmentation that followed early in the twenty-first century (Graham & Luke, 2003). Therefore to understand the ways in which new media environments—in this case the development and use of digital repositories—might affect cultures, an axiological approach is necessary. An approach based in political economy of communication is therefore implicated because it is concerned primarily with how communication figures in the production of values and the distribution and exercise of power (Graham, in press).

POLITICAL ECONOMY OF COMMUNICATION AND THE VALUE OF CULTURE

The term "media monopoly" is most often used in political economy of communication to describe the role of mass media in supporting the kinds of political economic environments that developed during the twentieth century (Bagdikian, 1997; McChesney & Foster, 2003; Smythe, 1981):

> For a long time now it has been widely understood within economics that under the capitalism of giant firms, corporations no longer compete primarily through price competition. They engage instead in what economists call

"monopolistic competition." This consists chiefly of attempts to create monopoly positions for a particular brand, making it possible for corporations to charge more for the branded product while also expanding their market share. (McChesney & Foster, 2004, p. 1)

This particular conception of "monopoly capitalism" is developed by Dallas Smythe (1981) and is a communication-oriented derivative of V.I. Lenin's theory of imperialism (Lenin, 1916). To summarise in Lenin's words:

> ... the principal stages in the history of monopolies are the following: 1) 1860–70, the highest stage, the apex of development of free competition; monopoly is in the barely discernible, embryonic stage. 2) After the crisis of 1873, a lengthy period of development of cartels; but they are still the exception. They are not yet durable. They are still a transitory phenomenon. 3) The boom at the end of the nineteenth century and the crisis of 1900–03. Cartels become one of the foundations of the whole of economic life. Capitalism has been transformed into imperialism. (Lenin, 1916)

Smythe shows the role that mass media plays in the extension of monopoly capitalism, which he defines as the form of global political economy in which a "relatively few giant monopoly corporations" engage in the "deliberate collusive avoidance of price competition" (1981, p. 11). For Smythe, mass media practices are essential to the development and maintenance of mass societies and monopoly capitalism. The most obvious example in this respect is advertising because it is designed to generate the "necessity for consumers to buy new products" based on "stylistic" obsolescence through the "calculated manipulation of public tastes" (1981, p. 11).

McChesney (1999) argues that any understanding of how media ownership in monopoly capitalism inhibits the capacity of citizens to attain a "democratic genuinely egalitarian participatory democracy" must include studies of how a system-wide propaganda that favors the system itself is maintained. Yet perspectives focused on consumption effects cannot comprehend how a self-sustaining systemic propaganda is achieved for the same reasons that one cannot derive the character of a political economic system by focusing solely on how staple foods affect different individuals or groups. Understanding how people *produce* is a necessary part of understanding the political economic character of a culture (Marx, 1976/1981):

> ... the capitalist process of production is a historically specific form of the *social production process* in general. This last is both a production process of the material conditions of existence for human life, and a process, proceeding in specific economic and historical relations of production, that produces and reproduces these relations of production themselves, and with them the

bearers of this process, the material conditions of existence and their mutual relationships. (1976/1981, p. 957)

If relations of production are definitive of a political economic system, then providing new ways for people to participate and relate in production is the key to changing political economic and cultural environments.

Even while taking the radical and edifying step of identifying that audiences in mass mediated societies perform a kind of productive labor, to do so, Dallas Smythe (1981) had to presuppose production of the materials on which audiences perform their labor: the products bought and sponsored by the cultural monopsony. The argument for a theory of audience labor runs as follows: the first task of a commercial media venture in mass mediated societies is to produce an audience of consumers. Media corporations are therefore assumed to be a primary producer of mass culture and mass cultural groups, *pace* Horkheimer and Adorno (1947/1998). Audiences, in turn, are media corporations' commodities and are sold to advertisers. Smythe's theory of audience labor identifies a key fallacy in most consumption-sided media studies:

> It is easy to see why conventional, bourgeois theory about communication is idealist. The entire literature—bourgeois and Marxist alike—about mass communications has defined their principle product of the mass media as "messages," "information," "images," "meaning," "entertainment," "education," "orientation," "manipulation," etc. *All* these concepts are subjective mental entities; all deal with superficial appearances, divorced from real life processes. The concepts of entertainment, education, orientation, and manipulation do not even refer to any aspects of mass media content but to its *effects*, or *purpose*. (Smythe, 1981, p. 23)

No analysis, according to Smythe, had addressed the role of "Consciousness Industry from the standpoint of its historical materialist role in making monopoly capitalism function through demand management" because none "take account of how the mass media under monopoly capitalism produce audiences to market commodities, candidates, and issues to themselves" (1981, p. 25).

Still, even while recognising that any moment of labor is also moment at which values are created, that consumption is part of production, that any meaning making processes require interaction, and that elements of culture had become commodified, Smythe's most radical of perspectives cannot entirely grasp the political economic implications of mass culture because any audience-based theory is necessarily one-sided. Further, it results in sharp conceptual divisions between the producers of cultural material, its consumers, and that mythical entity called "The Media" through which official culture presently flows. Rather than being monolithic in any sense, the bulk of what is called "The Media" is in fact comprised of an unruly group of more or less itinerant workers who specialise in symbolic artisanship of one kind or another. The organisations involved in production tend to be small and loosely allied (Vecchio, Hearn & Southey, 1992), and must constantly seek favor from advertisers, broadcasters, and media corporations in order that their wares are bought for distribution. The most "visible" part of cultural production—its numerous instantiations in magazines, films, books, music, newspapers, and so on—is the "final product", which is branded, broadcast, and otherwise deployed by media corporations in order to produce audiences for sale to advertisers.

MAKING CULTURE

The force, falsehood, and consequences of conceptually dividing "audiences" and "The Media" become most evident when one considers the entirety of what is meant by culture. The myriad elements of any given culture emerge from the history-bound interactions of *all* people who associate and live through the cultures they continuously help to make and remake (Carey, 1989). Yet a miniscule percentage of human cultural activity is included in "official culture," by which I mean the materials commodified, bought, and distributed by the small group of corporations who "own" the global culture monoposony: Viacom, General Electric, Disney, Time Warner, Vivendi Universal, Bertelsmann, and News Corp (Free Press, 2004). By excluding the mass of people and their cultural products from official culture, the monopsony has achieved a total devaluation of culture, if only because it is in its interests to continuously lower costs. Because the monopsony is the only significant purchaser of cultural materials, and because the global pool of human culture is so rich with cultural products, the monopsony also has the power to devalue culture to the maximum possible extent. The production of *worthlessness* is the essence of monopsony.

Long before the radio was successfully deployed as the first instantaneous mass medium, the participatory character of culture had been diminishing for centuries, due largely to the influence of industrialisation and technologisation. Diminishing participation in music is a case in point well noted by Lewis Mumford:

> The workshop song, the street cries of the tinker, the dustman, the pedlar, the flower vendor, the chanties of the sailor hauling the ropes, the traditional songs of the field, the wine-press, the taproom were slowly dying out during this period. Labor was orchestrated by the number of revolutions per minute, rather than by the the the rhythm of song or chant or tattoo . . . No one any

longer thought of asking the servants to come to the living room to take part in a madrigal or ballad. What happened to poetry had happened likewise to pure music. (1934/1962, p. 343).

Music became, like every other industrial "occupation," specialised and relegated to the rarified realms of expertise. Those people living with the effects of cultural monospony typically do not sing or dance in public. Cultural vibrancy requires widespread participation, experience, and education in the Arts:

> Art . . . cannot become a language, and hence an experience, unless it is practiced. To the man [sic] who plays, a mechanical reproduction of music may mean much, since he already has the experience to assimilate. But where reproduction becomes the norm, the few music makers will grow more isolate and sterile, and the ability to experience music will disappear. The same is true with cinema, dance, and even sport. (Waldo Frank, cited in Mumford, 1934/1962, p. 343)

But under the influence of industrialisation, culture, like nature, appears as an alien force to be conquered, mastered, codified, objectified, disciplined, and deployed in the pursuit of profit.

The waning of Arts faculties in universities, and the corollary appearance of Creative Industries faculties in their place, is another indicator of the impact that monopsony has on culture: whether made by mind, mouth, or gesture, culture must enter the monopsony before it realises cultural worth. This is confirmed in the frenzy of intellectual and policy activity focused on the concept of "the creative industries" and their increasing value to society (DEST, 2002; National Office for the Information Economy, 2002). Such activities are most usually concerned with developing policies and curricula designed for the monopsony, and with how universities and other organs of education can best tailor their wares to the monopsony's structures and practices. Yet the state of monopsony is the reason why the majority of people educated as visual artists, dancers, musicians, film makers, photographers, and writers rarely get to ply their trade as lifelong professionals, something that does not typically happen to other professional trainees. It is also, in part, why Arts faculties have been continuously devalued during 25 years of free market ideology. The simultaneous marketisation and devaluation of the Arts in universities, and of universities more generally, is at least in part an effect of a functioning global cultural monopsony. The practices of the burgeoning academic "industry" exemplify the practices of cultural producers in a monopsony: academics write research papers and manuscripts and submit them to publishers in the hope that they will be accepted, even though an acceptance will usually bring little or no direct financial reward. Prior to being accepted through official channels, academic work is considered to have little or no "official" status as knowledge. The same is true for producers of music, film, dance, and theatre. To exacerbate the problems that cultural monopsony poses for the development of participatory culture, the axiology of its goods is inverse to that of every other kind of industrial commodity.

CULTURAL AXIOLOGY IN CONDITIONS OF MONOPSONY

The axiology of mass culture does not apply to more tangible commodities such as footwear and furniture. As shoes and chairs are used over and over, they typically become worth less with time (except in very rare circumstances, most of which are related to the culture industries). Conversely, when cultural materials are consumed *en masse* their worth increases, and the more the commodities of mass culture are used, the more they become valued as significant parts of the cultures in which they are used. While this is definitely an effect of monopsony, it is an interesting and worthwhile point to note. The present axiology of mass culture is in place because most cultural materials that people produce never become part of official culture. Even within the formally recognised sectors of the culture industries, many times more material is produced than is ever experienced by the monoposony's audience-commodities. A 60-second advertisement, for example, can take as long as two years to produce and involve the work of many hundreds of people. Even a low-budget, 90-second promotional video takes a minimum of three hours to shoot, even longer to edit, thereby producing at least almost three full hours of supposedly "waste" material.

Add to the "waste" produced by mass culture the practically infinite amount of cultural production that continuously occurs throughout humanity, but which is never recognised as culture, and the extent to which the state of monopsony impedes participatory culture can be seen to be enormous. Billions of hours of conversations, dances, songs, ceremonies, audio recordings, and videos; acres of writing, diaries, photographs, and paintings are all regarded as worthless because they do not realise a price within the cultural monopsony. The axiology of cultural production is counterintuitive in an industrialised, allegedly capitalist world. More than a century of experiments on people by management researchers has been oriented towards efficiency and productivity, towards less wasted effort in the production of commodities and the management of work. Yet the cultural monopsony seemingly thrives on the opposite: the production of waste by rendering the greatest proportion of cultural productions, *including its own*, worthless.

Yet there is hope in this bleak assessment. The cultural monopsony first established its purchasing power based on the expense of its production processes. To participate in mass culture meant to participate in a system that relied on massive amounts of equipment and teams of experts sometimes comprised of hundreds of people. Today, though, the cost of production for cultural products favored by the monopsonies has dropped to almost zero, and a single person may make an entire feature. The means of distribution are also cheaper and far more widely accessible than ever before.

RECLAIMING CULTURAL PRODUCTION AND REHUMANISING CULTURE

As someone informed by Marx's approach to political economy, a production perspective is a primary focus for analysis. I do not, however, believe automatically or dogmatically that widespread ownership of the means of production for cultural materials will necessarily translate into a powerful movement, or even to a self-consciously participatory culture. The widespread ownership or access to means of production is a necessary but not a sufficient condition. Currently a monopsony situation regulates distribution. That is largely because its products get mistaken for culture more generally. But cultural production processes have changed radically over the last 20 years largely due to rapid advances in production technologies and their corollary cheapening. These advances have greatly increased the number of people who have access to the means of cultural production. For example, to record a broadcast quality album in 1980, the cost of professional studio hire in Australia was around $2000 per day. Add to this the cost of a producer, an engineer, several session musicians, the exorbitant cost of 2-inch tape (an industry standard at the time), and the cost of recording a single song to broadcast quality could easily run to about $4000, and that would have been a relatively inexpensive recording. From 1980, through to the early 1990s, broadcast-quality studios could cost many millions of dollars to build.

Today however, professional quality audio recordings can be produced on personal computers at a cost that is fast approaching zero. Quite sophisticated software can be accessed legally without paying money (see *www.sourceforge.net*). The same goes for video production software, with Avid's DV program now available for free download (see Avid's website: *www.avid.com*). Similarly, Digidesign's Protools program is also available for free download (*www.digidesign.com*). Many other open source video editing and audio production programs are available for no cost on the

World Wide Web. I use the Digidesign and Avid programs as examples because they have been industry standard digital production tools for some time. And even while the free versions of these programs come with some restrictions and less features than their paid-for versions, broadcast quality productions can still be made with these programs.

The low cost of the means of production for multimedia content has given rise to an entirely new class of cultural producers who would not previously have had the opportunity to be thus engaged. These include students, non-professional artists and producers, and professional artists who would previously have been required to buy or hire facilities that cost many thousands of dollars. In addition, high-quality audio and video recording equipment has made its way to the "consumer" market, turning cultural "consumers" more self-consciously into producers of culture. At the same time, the business model is changing for the monopsony, along with the character of cultural labor.

THE CHANGING COMPOSITION OF CULTURAL LABOR AND ITS POTENTIAL EFFECTS FOR MONOPSONY

Smythe's "free lunch" approach to mass culture, the process I described above in which culture industries provide content that can bring the audience commodity into being to raise advertising revenues, entails a form of labor Smythe calls "consciousness labor," the same kind of labor that all learning entails:

> Consciousness is the total awareness of life which people have. It includes their understanding of themselves as individuals and of their relations with other individuals in a variety of forms of organization, as well as with their natural environment. Consciousness is a dynamic process. It grows and decays with the interaction of doing (or practice) and cognition over the life cycle of the individual in the family and other social formations. It draws on emotions, ideas, instincts, memory and all the other sensory apparatus. (Smythe, 1981, pp. 270–271)

The free lunch model is, however, undermined by new media trends. One marker of this change, and of its extent, is the fact that for the first time since the inception of mass mediated societies, consumers now spend more on media in the US than do advertisers:

> In a milestone that signals a fundamental shift in the economics of the media industry, consumers now spend more money on media than advertisers do.

The shift, which occurred during 2003, but is just now coming to light via a report released Monday by investment banker Veronis Suhler Stevenson (VSS), reflects that advertising no longer is the primary business model for most media content, consumers are. (Mandese, 2004)

The trend, according to the report, is as follows:

Sources of Communications Industry Revenues

	Advertising	Marketing Services	Consumer End-User	Institutional End-User
2002	$170.4 bil	$134.8 bil	$167.5 bil	$147.2 bil
2003	$175.8 bil	$141.0 bil	$178.4 bil	$153.1 bil
2004	$188.5 bil	$148.1 bil	$191.3 bil	$161.8 bil
2005	$198.4 bil	$156.4 bil	$204.2 bil	$171.8 bil
2006	$211.7 bil	$165.8 bil	$218.0 bil	$183.0 bil
2007	$223.8 bil	$176.4 bil	$232.8 bil	$194.2 bil
2008	$241.1 bil	$187.4 bil	$248.7 bil	$207.1 bil

Source: Veronis Suhler Stevenson's 2004 Communications Industry Forecast & Report, PQ Media as cited in Mandese (2004).

This trend toward an increased percentage of revenues from "consumers," and a decreasing percentage of revenues from advertisers, portends fundamental changes in the character of the monopsony and its basic business model:

In 1998, the current base year of VSS' 2004 report, ad-supported media accounted for nearly two-thirds (63.6 percent) of the time consumers spend with media. By 2003, advertising's share of consumer time had eroded to 56.4 percent and by 2008, VSS predicts it will dwindle to just 54.1 percent. Given the fact that time spent with consumer-supported media is growing at more than twice the rate of ad-supported media, it is conceivable that advertising could become a minority of the time consumers spend with media within a decade. (Mandese, 2004)

What this means is that the whole impetus for the way twentieth century media monopsonies developed is being eroded. With the emergence of electronic mass media, the first move towards monopsony was for the early culture industries to provide free programming and the technologies to disseminate those "programs." This is how the first mass audiences were called into being by the architects of mass culture. The culture industries learned how to produce "audiences" for sale through the production of content. Now, however, advertising is retreating as the main source of the monopsony's revenue becomes the group formerly understood as "audience": its members have become the monopsony's main *clients*.

MEANS OF PRODUCTION ARE NOT ENOUGH

The free and inexpensive means of production and distribution are not enough by themselves to effect any massive change in the composition and structure of cultural production. The one similarity between the mass culture industries and other mass industrial forms is that both require raw materials: the presence of a steel mill, railroads, and trucks do not guarantee that steel will be successfully produced and distributed. Access to resources in the form of iron ore, as well as labor and expertise, is necessary. Similarly with the production of cultural materials, legal access to cultural labor, expertise, and raw materials is essential. In this respect, "open content" repositories oriented towards cultural production processes have a unique role to play in providing legal access to "raw" cultural materials, and in providing an essential part of the means for producing participatory culture.

From the perspective of political economy, it is the distinction between production and "consumption" oriented digital repositories that foregrounds the first major functional split in digital repository types. Consumption oriented repositories, archetypically digital libraries and museums, are geared towards the preservation and dissemination of more or less "official" knowledge, an undoubtedly important task. These repositories are organised largely along the lines of their non-digital historical counterparts in so far as their role is to maintain digital artifacts of materials that are considered to be of historical, cultural, and social significance. Their historical precedents can be traced to ancient Greece. Production repositories, on the other hand, are oriented towards providing resources that can be used and reused. Their historical precedents are fairly recent: "stock" sound effects, footage, photographic, and music libraries. Their primary purpose is to provide cultural producers with raw materials suitable for repurposing in the production of new cultural materials.

The difference between consumption and production oriented digital repositories is analagous to the differences between reading and writing. They require different literacies, different skills, and different attitudes towards the medium at hand. Their underpinning assumptions are entirely different: teaching people to write presupposes an innate ability for them to produce new meanings, to be creative. Teaching people to read begins with the assumption that people have an innate ability to comprehend. Creativity is not part of that presupposition, except in so far as it extends to a more or less novel understanding of texts. The same holds true for production and consumption repositories. Consumption repositories are designed to allow people to comprehend the past and its relevance for the present and, perhaps, the future. Production repositories are designed to provide people with resources for the production of new cultural materials (see, for example, American Broadcasting Corporation, 2004). Both types of repositories are, I believe, essential to the development of a participatory digital culture. But each requires different approaches to collection, design, architecture, and access. Successful design for each requires an understanding of the different axiological underpinnings of the functions they are designed for.

IMPLICATIONS OF MONOPSONY
FOR PARTICIPATORY CULTURE

In the context of monopsony, cultural products are assumed to be fairly much alike and exist to promote themselves and the monopsonies of which they are part. The result for audiences is the "freedom to choose what is always the same" (Horkheimer & Adorno, 1947/1998, p. 167). That is a function of mass culture being mistakenly subject to the same axiologies as other industrial goods: the values of predictability, replicability, and homogeneity—the production of mass culture is essentially a risk averse endeavor and is inherently conservative in its approach to buying cultural products. The myriad elements of culture, no matter how mundane or elaborate, are assumed to be worth nothing "at birth" by the monopsony, unless of course they are born within, or later bought by, the media monopsony.

WORTHLESSNESS AND FREEDOM

The promotion of widespread cultural worthlessness by the media monopsony has a potentially positive side: since cultural production is generally considered to be of little or no value, there is no disincentive for people to distribute their production free of charge. Paradoxically, the most successful products in new media environments are, *prima facie*, "free" (see, for example, www.jibjab.com). That is, they obtain cultural and economic value by being distributed free of cost. Consequently struggle over control of the means of distribution have become the focal point for all those concerned about the ownership of "official" culture. This is realised in the struggle over intellectual property regimes (Lessig, 2004) and, more dramatically, in the seizure of independent media servers from *Rackspace* (BBC, 2004).

The "free" model is not at all new to multimedia producers. Every time an advertising agency pitches to win a new client, every time a musician submits work for a movie, or a moviemaker develops a pilot—just as academics submit academic articles for review—the authors are "giving away" something in the hope that an organ of the monopsony will buy it. The new media environment has done at least three things in respect of the monopsony: it has (1) emphasised the "free" and social character of creative labor; (2) it foregrounds the "worthlessness" of creative labor in a system of monopsony; and (3) it has multiplied the potential number of buyers, producers, and sellers in the market for cultural products, thereby threatening the stability of the monopsony. A major potential of open content repositories is that of a new media system that provides the myriad producers of culture a new space for conversation, cultural recombination, and participatory culture unmediated by the axiology of cultural monopsony (see also Barwick & Thieberger, this volume; Kornbluh et al., this volume; Willinsky, this volume).

CHALLENGES AND OPPORTUNITIES FOR DIGITAL PRODUCTION REPOSITORIES

Thus far, I have outlined the axiological underpinnings of ACRO and CCCI: the set of contradictory value systems in play in the current climate. First, there is the inherent impetus of monopsony to drive the value of cultural production towards zero in order to keep its costs down. Second, there is the inverse commercial axiology of mass culture: the fact that its most "consumed" products (which are of course never really consumed) are its most valuable goods, with unused materials being considered as "junk." Third, I have outlined a political economic view—that of monopsony—that provides a very different view of the culture industries than is available through the lens of monopoly capitalism: both views are necessary if we are to understand the political economic character, and hence the axiological underpinnings, of mass culture.

What remains is to identify the character and potentialities of the cultural production systems that production repositories such as ACRO and CCCI might engender, and the perils they might present. ACRO and CCCI are designed explicitly to provide open access to high quality cultural resources that can be used legally in the production of new materials. Like the means of production and distribution, the provision of resources is no guarantee of success in achieving a participatory official culture. All three are necessary, but even combined, they are not sufficient conditions. Most importantly in the achievement of participatory culture, people need to know how to read *and* write with new multimedia resources and tools; they must learn to make meanings with them and, most importantly, be given permission to make music, videos, and other forms of art within new media environments. New literacies are an essential part of this, and an axiological change in the structure of mass culture will rely on multimedia and information literacies becoming part of curricula from the earliest ages. Given the current lack of novelty in the global system of "official" culture, understanding how to read and write multimedia has become a political, cultural, and economic imperative, if only to show people how easily sounds and images are manipulated in the digital environment.

There is of course the danger inherent in such an approach of turning education systems into a massive training grounds for cultural labor in a global monopsony—all new systems must be built upon the foundations of their predecessors. In much the same way that the monopsony has served up audiences for sale to advertisers, the proposed approach to participatory culture put forward here could conceivably be appropriated as a system for turning out armies of skilled producers for the existing monopsony, thereby further degrading potentials for culture to be rehumanised, revalued, and redistributed.

There is also a double-edged sword in the business models that such a system might promote. On the one hand, we see examples such as the Prelinger Archive housed in the Internet Archive (*www.archive.org*). Rick Prelinger owns roughly 48,000 films and runs a stock footage archive. With some initial reticence, he put 1,000 of these online with open access to anybody with an Internet connection. The result was that his sales skyrocketed (Prelinger, 2004): no free lunch, just free samples, a model used to great success in the Internet by the pornography industry (Legon, 2003). Another example is the jibjab.com political satire featuring caricatures of President G.W. Bush and Senator John Kerry, and cleverly reworded version of Woodie Guthrie's *This Land is Your Land*. The parody was propagated through emails and "drew an impressive 10.4 million unique visitors in July, more than three times the 3.3 million Americans who collectively visited JohnKerry.com and GeorgeWBush.com" (Center for Media Research, 2004). JibJab has since become part of the monopsony by being appropriated and absorbed by the system. That is a function of the corporatist pattern of buying, rather than fostering and creating, innovative ideas (Saul, 1997).

Another challenge for participatory culture is that of creating virtual communities of a "human scale" (Mumford, 1934/1962). That is to say, it is all well and good to promote mass participation in the production of a global media environment, but it is entirely another to foster conversations and communities that are of a size that can give meaning to participation—a digital, multimediated Tower of Babel is not a desirable outcome, and weaving the local into the global, as well as providing forums for developing global communities of interest, are problems not easily solved. Conversely, such an approach to fostering participatory culture also needs to recognise the potentials of a global balkanisation of interests in which cultures and communities become closed off from, or hostile towards, each other. These are just a few of the problems that face open content production repositories oriented towards participatory culture beyond those shared by digital repositories more generally (accessibility, useable metadata, format versioning, common standards and protocols, and so on).

Finally, the axiological virtues of participatory culture require some qualifications. Any reader of my previous work will know that I am far from being a techno-utopian. Yet I am convinced that there is, indeed *must be*, a profound cultural shift inherent in our new media environments. This shift may be either positive or negative. If it is to happen in a positive way it must, I believe, be based on an axiology of humanistic principles and aims: unqualified respect for persons; aspirations to the production of beauty and vibrancy in culture; a spirit of understanding and cooperation between people from diverse backgrounds, cultures, and countries; the full development of human faculties; and the betterment of the lot of peoples in general, which naturally includes access to resources, means of production, and means of distribution. The global cultural monopsony has turned itself inside out at almost every significant level, and despite the bleak political environment of the early twenty-first century, the potential now exists for a transformation in global culture. It will be a slow and fraught process, but it may be that it is possible, if not necessary, for people to engage in the production of culture in a self-conscious way. That is to say, people must take responsibility and respond to their obligations in respect of the cultural landscape they help make, especially in current circumstances.

REFERENCES

American Broadcasting Corporation (ABC) (2004). *Production libraries.* Available online at http://www.abcradio.com/index.cfm?bay=content.view&catid=72&cpid=131: Accessed October 8, 2004.

Bagdikian, B.H. (1997). *The media monopoly (5th Edn.).* Boston, MA: Beacon Press.

British Broadcasting Corporation (BBC) (2004). *US seizes independent media sites.* Available online at http://news.bbc.co.uk/1/hi/technology/3732718.stm. Accessed October 11, 2004.

Carey, J. (1989). *Communication as culture: Essays on media and society.* London: Routledge.

Center for Media Research (2004, October 11). *JibJab parody reaches three times as many as Kerry plus Bush.* New York: MediaPost. Available online at: http://www.centerformedia research.com/cfmr_brief.cfm?fnl=040830 Accessed October 11, 2004.

Department of Education, Science & Training (DEST). (2002). *Frontier technologies for building and transforming Australian Industries: Stimulating the growth of world-class Australian industries using innovative technologies developed from cutting–edge research.* Canberra: Commonwealth of Australia (http://www.dest.gov.au/priorities/transforming_industries .htm). Accessed February, 2003.

Free Press. (2004). *Who owns the media?* Available online at: http://www.freepress.net/ownership/. (Retreived August 2004).

Graham, P. (in press). Issues in political economy. In Alan Alabarran et al. (Eds.) *Handbook of Media Management Economics*. New York: Erlbaum.

Graham, P., & Luke, A. (2003). Militarising the body politic. New media as weapons of mass instruction. *Body & Society, 9*(4), 149–168.

Horkheimer, M., & Adorno, T. W. (1947/1998). *The dialectic of enlightenment* (J. Cumming, Trans.). New York: Continuum.

Innis, H.A. (1951a). *The Bias of communication.* Toronto: Toronto University Press.

Innis, H.A. (1951b). Industrialism and cultural values. *The American Economic Review, 41*(2), 201–209.

Legon, J. (2003, December 11). *Sex sells, especially to web surfers.* Cable Network News. Available online at http://www.cnn.com/2003/TECH/internet/12/10/porn.business/. Accessed June 12, 2004.

Lenin, V.I. (1916). Imperialism, the highest stage of capitalism: A popular outline. Available online at http://www.fordham.edu/halsall/mod/1916lenin-imperialism.html. Accessed July 14, 2004. Modern History Sourcebook. New York: Fordham University.

Lessig, L. (2004). *Free Culture: How big media uses technology and the law to lock down culture and control creativity.* New York: Penguin Press.

Mandese, J. (2004, August 3). Consumers Outspend Advertisers on Media. *Media Daily News.* New York: MediaPost. Available online at: *http://www.mediapost.com/dtls_dsp_news.cfm?newsID=262413.* Accessed August 10, 2003.

Marx, K. (1976/1981). *Capital: A critique of political economy* (Vol. 1), (B. Fowkes, Trans.). London: Penguin.

McChesney, R.W. (2000). The political economy of communication and the future of the field. *Media, Culture & Society, 22*(1), 109–116.

McChesney, R.W. (1999). Noam Chomsky and the struggle against neoliberalism. *Monthly Review, 50*(11), 40–48.

McChesney, R.W., & Foster, J. B. (2003). The commercial tidal wave. *Monthly Review, 54,* 10.

Mumford, L. (1934/1962). *Technics and civilization.* New York: Harcourt Brace & World.

National Office for the Information Economy. (2002). *Creative Industries Cluster Study: Stage One Report.* Canberra: NOIE, DCITA, Commonwealth of Australia.

Postman, N. (1985). *Amusing ourselves to death: Public discourse in the age of show business.* New York: Viking.

Prelinger, R. (2004). *Rick Prelinger.* Interview with Creative Commons. Stanford, CA. Available online at: http://creativecommons.org/getcontent/features/rick. Accessed September 21, 2004.

Saul, J. R. (1997). *The unconscious civilization.* Ringwood, Vic.: Penguin.

Silverstone, R. (1999). *Why study the media?* London: Sage.

Smythe, D. (1981). *Dependency road: Communications, capitalism, consciousness, and Canada.* New Jersey: Ablex.

Vecchio, R. P., Hearn, G., & Southey, G. (1992). *Organisational behaviour: Life at work in Australia.* Sydney: Harcourt Brace Jovanovich.

15

Structuring Open Access to Knowledge: The Creative Commons Story

Brian Fitzgerald
Queensland University of Technology

Over the last 10 years we have realized the following:

- We now possess an amazing capacity to negotiate digital content through networked computers—any person of any age can do it globally at little cost.
- Copyright law is being fiercely defended as copyright owners fear cyber anarchists or digital libertarians will loot their property— the owners will pursue a strategy that a group of Harvard Law professors have labeled as a quest for "total control."
- Social and technological innovation is being threatened by focusing solely on the exclusive rights of the copyright owners.
- A significant amount of copyright material lies inactive with little hope of use because many perceive it is too difficult or expensive to negotiate access to it.
- Government and public institutions hold vast quantities of copyright material that is owned through the Crown on behalf of their citizens, which could be more effectively "licensed out" through open content user protocols to the benefit of all.

In light of this, there should be little surprise to learn that many people throughout the world have been working on developing ways in which copyright content can be made more negotiable—accessible and active in the name of creativity, education, and innovation—while still respecting copyright law. This is the story of open content licensing or access, and the Creative Commons (CC) is but one chapter in that story.

WHAT IS OPEN ACCESS?

Copyright embodies a set of exclusive legal rights (limited in time) that grant the content creator, for example, the author of a book, control over their creative outputs. Without these legal rights such as authorizing reproduction of a book, the content owner would find it hard to protect their value or intangible intellectual property. Others could simply reproduce the book and sell it more cheaply in the marketplace. Therefore, copyright provides the reward of individual legal rights as incentive for creators to produce outputs that will, in the broader sense, benefit the community. In recent times, greater focus has been placed on whether these individual legal rights or copyrights over all kinds of creative content—particularly digital content—can be utilized to provide greater access to content. This is where the notion of Creative Commons and open access enter the picture.

The fundamental idea of Creative Commons is that copyright owners are asked to use the power of their copyright ownership to structure open access and reusability in preference to the closure and total control of economic exploitation. The Creative Commons plays on the label we see on all our digital entertainment products—"all rights reserved"—to declare that only some rights will be reserved to the copyright owner. Copyright owners may want such a system for the following reasons:

1. Ideologically and financially, this may be acceptable—the most compelling example is government where information is ultimately owned by and for the people—but it will not suit everyone, and should be understood as only one of a variety of models for information management and distribution.
2. Open contenting one version of your material such as a draft (E Print) or a chapter, may in fact be a strategy for enhancing the commercialized version of your content.
3. A wish to share with others for creative and educational purposes.
4. Publicity—what the free and open software movement calls "egoboo" or reputation within the open community, which in some cases will be exploited commercially down the track.
5. Negotiability—through technologically implemented generic protocols that can be utilized with the click of a mouse.

6. "What is junk to one may be gold to another"—the idea that the off-cuts or digital junk of one person may be the building blocks of knowledge and creative genius for another.

To fully understand open access, we really need to start with the notion of free and open source software. The powerful insight that Richard Stallman and his associates at the Free Software Foundation discovered was that if you want to structure open access to knowledge, then you must leverage off or use as a platform your intellectual property rights. Stallman's genius was in understanding and implementing the ethic that if you want to create a community of information or creative commons you need to be able to control the way the information is used once it leaves your hands. The regulation of this downstream activity was achieved by claiming an intellectual property right (copyright in the software code) at the source and then structuring its downstream usage through a license known as the GNU General Public Licence (GPL). This was not a simple "giving away" of information, but rather a strategic mechanism for ensuring the information stayed "free" (as in "free speech," not price) (A. Fitzgerald & B. Fitzgerald, 2004).

In the classic free software scenario embodied in the GNU GPL software source code is distributed in a manner that is open and free, allowing software developers (usually many hundreds, known broadly as the "hacker community") further down the line to modify and improve on the initial software product. The initial distributor of the code controls its presentation and further dissemination through copyright and contract law (contractual software license). As a consequence, the down-the-line developer and modifier is required to make source code of any derivative work that they distribute available for all to see. In this process, copyright law is used to create a "copyleft" effect as opposed to a "copyright" effect by mandating that code should be open and free for all to use in innovation and development of software. By way of contrast, in a proprietary or closed distribution model source code is not released and can only be ascertained through decompilation or reverse engineering (B. Fitzgerald & Bassett, 2001).

The free and open source model for software development has formed the basis of the open content movement. As already explained, the context for this is the underutilization of significant amounts of digital content and the "cut-and-paste negotiability" of digital networked environments. Through modalities such as "digital repositories or conservancies" like the Australian Creative Resources Archive (ACRA), or merely distributed networks of information open content, licensing projects such as the Creative Commons will facilitate access to digital commons content for the purpose of reutilization and further innovation with a minimum of legal knowledge and transactional and physical effort. Taking digital content from the commons, as under the free and open source software model, may carry obligations such as attributing the author of the digital content or sharing any derivative product back to the commons. In these open content projects, owners of intellectual property rights manage and control their rights at the source to structure open access downstream.

WHAT IS THE CREATIVE COMMONS?

Creative commons is a social philosophy backed by a worldwide movement designed to facilitate greater access to content, especially digital content. Creativecommons.org is a Web site and a not-for-profit corporation based at Stanford University Law School sponsored by the Center for the Public Domain, the MacArthur Foundation, and the Hewlett Foundation. The Creative Commons concept was given worldwide impetus through the release of Lessig's *The Future of Ideas: The Fate of the Commons in a Connected World* (2001) and is further reinforced by *Free Culture: How Big Media Uses Technology and the Law to Lock Down Culture and Control Creativity* (2004). In February 2004, Queensland University of Technology (QUT) became the Australian institutional affiliate for the project, and over the last few months has worked closely with Blake Dawson Waldron (BDW) Lawyers to set up the platform for the project in Australia (see http:// creativecommons.org/projects/international/au).

Creative Commons aims to build a distributed information commons by encouraging copyright owners to license use of their material through open content licensing protocols and thereby promote better identification, negotiation, and reutilization of content for the purposes of creativity and innovation. As the project highlights, the use of an effective identification or labeling scheme and an easy to understand and implement legal framework is vital to furthering this purpose. This is done by establishing generic protocols or license terms for the open distribution of content that can be attached to content with a minimum of fuss under a CC label. In short, the idea is to ask copyright owners—where willing—to "license out" or distribute their material on the basis of four protocols designed to enhance reusability and build out the information commons.

THE PHILOSOPHY

Creative Commons represents a new approach to information management supported by a technologically aware movement. The philosophy is a product of 21st-century culture, including the vast digital landscape that we increasingly inhabit. Two themes, recently the subject of popular discussion, provide context for this project. They are the notions of free culture and the creative class.

Free Culture

Free culture, as outlined by Lessig (2004), calls for open access to and reuse of content, or in essence a commons. It builds on the "cut-and-paste" negotiability that the digital environment provides and asks for a greater ability to negotiate and exchange content in the name of creativity and innovation.

Creative Class

The other theme that gives context to this project is the increasing significance of creative activity to social, cultural, and economic prosperity. Florida (2002), speaking in Brisbane in March 2004, reminded us that the "creative class" and "creative places" build innovation and economic success. These "creatives" employ modalities to foster creativity and free culture, and creative commons are no doubt part of that story. Florida remarked that "as we have seen, diverse and open communities have compelling advantages in stimulating creativity, generating innovations and increasing wealth and economic growth" (p. 323).

THE MOVEMENT

This philosophy that calls for open access to and greater negotiability of content is backed by a movement that is employing new age modalities to meet its goals. The hallmark of open content licensing is easy to use licenses that have low transaction costs and are nondiscriminatory in nature; in other words, they can be employed by everyone with a minimum of effort, simply by clicking a button.

Through the Creative Commons project, a copyright owner of content—be it text, music, or film—can place that material in the commons subject to a Creative Commons license. The license will provide that anyone can use the content subject to one or a number of the following conditions: attribution, no commercial use, share what is created with the work by giving it back to the commons, or verbatim copying only. The license can be presented in common, legal, or digital code language—by simply going to creativecommons.org and choosing a license online. This is then linked to the work that you wish to give or license out through the commons. Creativecommons.org reports that in its first year of operation over one million objects were placed under a Creative Commons license—in ways that have further promoted creativity, innovation, and education.

Like the free software movement, Creative Commons uses intellectual property rights as the platform on which to structure downstream user rights. By claiming copyright in the content that will go into the commons the owner can determine how that content can be used downstream, for example, to further develop the commons. However, unlike the "copy left" free software licenses, Creative Commons does not *require* utilization of material in the commons to carry with it an obligation to share further innovations back to the commons; this is only one of four conditions, known as "share and share alike," the copyright owner might employ.

The following are four key protocols of the Creative Commons:

- **Attribution:** Other people may use, modify, and distribute the content, as long as they give the original author credit.

- **Noncommercial:** Other people may use, modify, and distribute the content, but for noncommercial purposes only.

- **No derivatives:** Other people may use and distribute the content, but cannot modify it to create derivative works.

- **Share alike:** Other people may modify the content and distribute derivatives, but only on the condition that the derivatives are made available to other people on the same license terms. This term cannot be used with the **No Derivatives** term, because it applies only to derivative works.

"PORTING": THE AUSTRALIAN CC PROJECT

The first role of the Australian Creative Commons project team (QUT Deputy Vice-Chancellor Tom Cochrane, Ian Oi from BDW Lawyers in Sydney, and myself) has been to draft and publicize an Australian version of the Creative Commons licenses, tailored to meet the needs of the Australian legal system. An unknowing adoption of the U.S. version of the CC licenses would miss subtle differences in copyright terminology, consumer law, and moral rights protection between the two countries. Known as International Creative Commons, or *i*Commons, and coordinated by Christiane Asschenfeldt, this process of "porting," or translating, the base license to each national jurisdiction is well under way and will see momentum for the commons continue to grow.

WHY GOVERNMENTS NEED TO UNDERSTAND OPEN CONTENT LICENSING (OCL)

Australia is currently debating the extent to which the Crown (equating to government) should own copyright in vast amounts of content such as legislation and court judgments (CLRC, 2004, *Crown Copyright Inquiry* clrc.gov.au). This has been a common inquiry throughout Commonwealth countries in recent years. By way of contrast, the U.S. government does not own copyright in legislation and judgments (Section 105 *Copyright Act 1976*).

Ten years ago, the question would have been simply whether the Crown should or should not have copyright? Many advocating for the Crown to not have copyright would have been seeking open access to information. Today, however, we know more about the intricacies of open content licensing. It is arguable that a broader and more robust information commons can be developed by leveraging off Crown copyright rather than merely "giving away" material.

If the Crown is to have the capacity to strategically manage information either in a closed manner for maximum economic reward or in an open fashion for maximum public access, then Crown copyright should remain. The copyright becomes the key tool in managing downstream usage—open or closed. A proposal that the Crown does not have any rights to copyright material would in effect reduce the ability of the Crown to structure user rights and otherwise manage information.

Once it is acknowledged that Crown copyright should remain and the scope of that copyright is properly determined (itself an issue for significant debate), the question then becomes what kind of material should be available for open access, and in what way should open content licensing be used to structure that access. To this end, in its final report the Australian Copyright Law Review Committee (CLRC) should engage with and evaluate the significance of open content "licensing out" models in achieving open access. In doing so, it should also evaluate how such licensing models could be employed to facilitate open access to Crown copyright.

For a system of open content licensing to prosper in government, policy on information management needs to be clearly articulated in accord with core democratic principles and, where necessary, legislatively reinforced. In other words, if the Crown is to retain copyright its obligation (as fiduciary of the people?) to license out certain kinds of information in an open manner should be articulated, at least at the level of principle. If Crown copyright is to remain, then the CLRC should provide guidance on the principles on which this copyright material should be available for access—when and on what conditions should it be available? The spectrum seems to run from copyright material that will only ever be commercially available through to copyright material that must be subject to open content licensing to ensure the broadest possible access to that information. The approach taken in the European Union *Directive on the Re-Use of Public Sector Information* 2003/98/EC and that contemplated in the United Kingdom (CLRC, 2004, pp. 44–45) appears to reflect the philosophy that government copyright should remain, and what becomes important is the management of that information downstream.

THE ROLE OF LIBR@RIES IN THE CREATIVE COMMONS

Libr@ries and universities will play a key role in implementing the philosophy of projects such as Creative Commons. A key function of libr@aries is information management; libr@ries are in the business of acquiring or locating information and organizing that information for use by their consumers. It will be through libr@ries engaging with and utilizing open content through and for their consumers that the notion of the information commons will multiply.

Some have questioned how such a distributed project as Creative Commons can succeed. The power is in the network that is created and social branding that occurs. The project managers in the Creative Commons are many: the licensing projects, repositories, or conservancies of digital content, and the institutional users within the knowledge industries such as libr@aries.

At the most fundamental level, libr@ries will connect users to the Creative Commons by cataloguing open content and its whereabouts (see, e.g., the Creative Commons search engine http://creativecommons.org/getcontent/): the content that can be accessed, reutilized, and for what purposes. A core task of any reputable libr@ry will be informing its users of the protocols, projects, and repositories of the open content world. Understanding open content protocols will be critical to the acquisition and development of knowledge in the digital environment. Libr@ries, along with introductory university courses on information management and retrieval, will facilitate this task. Libr@ries will not only direct people to distributed open content, but many will become repositories or conservancies collecting and managing open content within their institution or jurisdiction.

The interesting challenge in all of this will be as to how libr@ries respond and adapt to a distributed network of open content in which they will be critical agents. Moving the openness of being able to read and reutilize content in a physical library to the virtual worlds of the digital environment where the right to read is inherently an act of reproduction will to some small extent depend on the power of open content and the information commons. If libr@ries are to be effective, then the "total control" of digital content by copyright owners must be balanced by other more social models of information management that allow for further innovation and creativity.

THE FUTURE

The more we cultivate the Creative Commons, the more we are learning about an endless array of possibilities. Much effort is now being put into spreading the word throughout the creative (including education) industries and informing people about what open content licensing means— socially and legally—and what benefits it might bring. There will no doubt be criticism from key institutional players in the copyright world, but the challenge will be to show them that Creative Commons does not mean the death of copyright but rather a realignment or shift in the way people think about, create, and share creative content. Creative Commons and the open content movement are predicated on copyright to leverage and structure open access.

Like free and open source software, the Creative Commons project has a grassroots appeal that promises to revolutionize some areas of information management particularly in the public sector. Where creative product is intimately involved with commercial exploitation, there could be some difficulty in obtaining the appropriate permissions (called "clearing rights") to contribute material to the commons. In many instances, the commercializing agent of a creative product (e.g., the publisher of a book) will be the copyright owner and the creator may well be powerless over what can be contributed. Not everyone will want to contribute to the commons, but we should not give up on convincing them of the value of openness.

It is opportune that we have been able to map out the boundaries of the Creative Commons project in this volume on new approaches to libraries and knowledge management because there is little doubt that libr@ries will be critical players of the information commons. The Creative Commons story is very much about harnessing the power and value of the immense discursive capacity of networked digital content. It is a story that is just beginning; but what an exciting story it promises to be.

ACKNOWLEDGMENTS

I owe thanks to Ian Oi, Tom Cochrane, Cushla Kapitzke, and Cheranne Bartlett for their support with this project.

REFERENCES

Copyright Law Review Committee (CLRC). (2004). *Crown Copyright Issues Paper.* Retrieved November 1, 2004, from www.law.gov.au/clrc

Fitzgerald, A., & Fitzgerald, B. (2004). *Intellectual property in principle.* Sydney: LBC/Thomson.

Fitzgerald, B., & Bassett, G. (2001). Legal issues relating to free and open source software. *Journal of Law and Information Science, 12*(2), 159–214.

Florida, R. (2002). *The rise of the creative class: And how it's transforming work, leisure, community, and everyday life.* New York: Basic Books.

Lessig, L. (2001). *The future of ideas: The fate of the commons in a connected world.* New York: Random House.

Lessig, L. (2004). *Free culture: How big media uses technology and the law to lock down culture and control creativity.* New York: Penguin Press.

16

The Arobase in the Library—
The Libr@ry in Society

Bertram C. Bruce
University of Illionis, Urbana-Champaign

Cushla Kapitzke
University of Queensland

Contributors to this collection have sought to understand current practices and future implications of changing technologies for libraries through accounts that have been analytical, critical, and at times visionary. While maintaining a focus on present conditions and future possibilities, we nonetheless turn back the calendar a century in order to shed light on the issues of today. Although involving different technologies of information and communication, the following historical cameo, *Mato's fez*, provides a useful contrast to explore issues of arobase place and space, the implications of the arobase for knowledge and the library, and the meaning of arobase capital as discussed in the book. We draw from the narrative of *Mato's fez* here because it enables us to ground the analysis materially and to link the past with the present and the future.

Mato's fez
by Cushla Kapitzke

Just a few days before leaving for Paris in September 2004 to complete the present chapter, I stumbled on a book given to me some time ago.

FIG. 16.1.   Executive of the Dalmatian Peasants Party 1904. Mato
Drvenica, middle row 2nd from right. Josip Smodlaka, middle row
3rd from right. Yele Drvenica's brother, Machune Yerenich, back
row 3rd from right.

Written by a relative and entitled *An Australian Saga: Dedicated to
Multi-Racial Australia* (Darveniza, 1986), the book celebrates Australia's multicultural history through a biographical narrative of
the emigration and settlement in Australia of my paternal fore-
bears. As I casually thumbed the pages, a photograph caught my
attention and caused me to read with some interest the contents of
the book recounting the life story of my great-grandfather, Mato.

The photograph in question portrayed three rows of men and
was captioned, "The executive of the Dalmatian Peasants Party
1904" (see Fig. 16.1).

Its quaint mix of Byzantine backdrop and period costume
belied the affinities that I—a participant of postmodernity—soon
discovered I had with the young man, Mato, in the tasseled tar-
boosh. As I read the story of his life, it became apparent that the
photo's old-world charm masked some extraordinary historical
continuities and biographical parallels. I had known Mato only
through family stories of him as an ascetic, eccentric old man
who, although a farmer, loved books and wrote poetry. But as I
read this partial and possibly embellished version of events documented by one of his sons, what surprised me was not the differences of our lives and labors, but their similarities. This, despite
our separation in time and space by a century and several conti-
nents.

Mato's life story began in the village of Trnovica near the walled city of Dubrovnik in Croatia, the former Yugoslavia. The technology of reading was central to its unfolding. Like many accounts of literacy and its unforeseen effects, Mato's narrative was embedded within a context of religious belief and practice (cf. Kapitzke, 1995). Described as "intellectual," and "deeply religious" Mato persuaded the priest to teach him the Cyrillic alphabet. Because the Serbo-Croat language is phonetic, "the youngster was able to achieve literacy without further instruction," and "not content learning himself, . . . [Mato] helped his peers to become literate" (Darveniza, 1986, p. 10). When the priest realized that Mato was "dedicated to learning," the lessons quickly stopped, allegedly because "a literate peasant may prove difficult to 'keep in his place'" (p. 10). But once the proverbial floodgates of knowing and knowledge are opened, they cannot easily be closed.

As Mato grew, it was evident that he had little aptitude for peasant farming, so his parents apprenticed him to a bread baker in Dubrovnik. There he met Josip Smodlaka, a lawyer involved in the Slav Liberation Movement seeking freedom from the "yoke" of the Austro-Hungarian empire, which ruled Dalmatia at the time. Josip, Mato, and their compatriots founded the Dalmatian Peasants Party in 1889, and—in an act that is unusual for a committee either now or then—made a visual record of their political commitment through the new technology of photography.

On returning to Trnovica with newfound political zeal, Mato started classes to teach reading and writing. While his father and wife "tilled the soil, planted, harvested the grain and vegetables, milked cows, goats and sheared the sheep," Mato established a school that was attended by children during the day and adults at night. Despite the fact that "the church censured and proscribed" the classes, the village eventually "boasted a 60% literacy [rate]" (p. 13). Peasants from neighboring villages began attending the school and, although the role played by Mato is not made clear, other "self taught schools" were opened "far afield in Dalmatia and via Medkovic to Mostar and into Bosnia-Herzegovina."

In the ongoing struggle for political freedom, and despite a "speech impediment," Mato became a "spellbinding orator." Speeches he wrote were printed as far afield as "the Croat, Slovene, Serb, and Czechoslovak presses of the Americas" (p. 29). Traveling widely throughout the region, he wore a red felt fez in Muslim areas like Bosnia-Herzegovina to highlight the reality for him that "their common ethnic bond transcended religious beliefs" (p. 28). These activities—considered heretical by

the church and treasonable by the state—led to his arraignment
in 1907 before the Bishop of Dubrovnik where he was indicted as
an "apostate who was furthering the interest of the Muslim faith
and denigrating Christianity." Wearing his customary fez, Mato
"disdained the charge and attacked His Eminence, asserting that
the Catholic Hierarchy, down the ages, had supported the oppres-
sors of the Slavs, be they the Turks, Christian Austro-Hungarian
[Empire] or the Napoleonic French" (pp. 30–31).

By this time, Mato was in danger of imprisonment or assassina-
tion from the "security forces," so his influential friend and men-
tor, Dr. Smodlaka, arranged for him to leave the country. In 1909,
he left his "beloved Dalmatia" and sailed with Yele—very pregnant at the time with their ninth child—for Australia.

Mato's story seems at first far removed from the realm of the Internet, digital libraries, multimedia, metadata, and other topics of this book.
The photograph, in particular, harkens to a forgotten time in which sub-
jugated peasants were fighting for access to the written word. And yet,
in its own way, the tale exemplifies the complex interplay of technology,
values, social practices, politics, time, and space that are in the chapters of
this book.

The new signifiers and technologies for Mato were the alphabet, the
printing press, the camera, and even the red felt fez—which, Cushla's
parents subsequently informed her, he was still wearing some 40 years
later in the heat of far northern Australia. The affordances and limits of
these tools shaped his story and were in turn shaped by the actions of
participants, just as digital media are mutually constituted by the cultural
and literacy practices of today. As is the case for electronic technologies,
at no point was Mato's use of these tools a neutral act, independent of the
religious, cultural, and political forces of the time. The point here is not to
suggest that nothing ever changes, but rather to highlight that the story
of libraries today is part of a larger narrative in which literacy proceeds
through appropriation and adaptation of new technologies, always situated in particular historical and social circumstances.

Mato's fez thus also causes us to reflect on the role of place in libraries.
For Mato and his compatriots, the unfolding of literacy was intimately
tied to the material realities of life in Trnovica and to the political forces of
the day (e.g., those represented by the parish priest and the colonial forces
of imperial Austria). On the other hand, there was also a reaching beyond
that local reality through the distribution of political pamphlets, or a markedly politicized photograph representing the deepest longings for cultural

self-determination and political freedom. Literacy itself helped to connect the peasants with the world beyond their isolated villages, both to learn about the views of others and to share their own. The technology of literacy helped shape whether, when, and how Mato and others could step out of their local realities and be who they were and wanted to be. This brings us to reconsider a basic aspect of the changing world of libr@ries, namely, the place/space distinction evident in Mato's story, as well as explicitly or implicitly in every chapter of our book.

PLACE AND SPACE

Much of the discourse about libraries proceeds as if there were a clear and stable distinction between place and space. On the one hand, those who valorize the traditional library speak about the intrinsic worth of having books one can see, touch, and smell. They speak of large print and talking books for the visually impaired, and books that can be chewed and tasted for small children. They emphasize the crucial role of human reference librarians who help turn anonymous and confusing sources into friendly and useful information. They understand the many ways in which library architecture, furniture, and layout shapes the user's experience. Such people tend to describe digital resources as lacking embodiment, that grounding in *placeness* with all its rich connotations.

Conversely, those who valorize online and virtual spaces tend to focus on the limitations of place. They point out that a resource formerly available in one location can now be easily accessed around the world. They tend to use words like "anywhere," "anytime," and "freedom" to emphasize the *spaceness* of the digital realm, which is freed from the constraints of everyday time and place. This place–space dichotomy provides useful fodder for rhetorical explorations, and does indeed capture something important about what we are all experiencing. We believe, however, that it is ultimately limiting as an analytical construct, and in this section, explore some reasons why.

The photograph of the Dalmatian Peasant Party Executive expresses what many feel about the traditional library. The image portrays a group of men with cultural affinities that are expressed in traditional dress. Their presence together in a single place and time signifies a commitment to one another and to a common cause. Their project of literacy acquisition is part and parcel of their social, cultural, and political grounding. For many librarians, teachers, and ordinary citizens today, the library is similarly conceived as a place-bound institution serving a real, geographically defined community. Places within the library also serve specific well-defined needs and community groups. The children's corner, for example, has books on low shelves, a volunteer who reads stories, comfortable chairs set low to the ground, decorations, stuffed animals, and a variety of other material elements that reflect and constitute its human and service-oriented mission. The grounding of the library and parts of the library as place is seen as a strength by those who believe in that mission. Conversely, those who see the library as a warm and friendly place question the cold abstractness of digital resources.

And yet the library of today, even one with limited computer access, already has multiple opportunities to stretch beyond its place. Modern libraries participate in interlibrary loan programs through which patrons can access materials from distant locations. Many libraries offer mobile programs that extend services beyond the confines of the library building. Increasingly, as catalogues are placed online and made accessible to patrons through online public access catalogues, the interaction with physical resources such as books, maps, photographs, and so on, is mediated by computers. Libraries with Internet access now bring the space of the digital realm within the place of the library. In short, the conception of the library as completely bound within one physical location misconstrues how it already participates in the virtual realm. This is one of our motivations for placing the arobase within the word *library*—to signify that the virtual realm exists not as an alternative to library but as an integral part of it.

At the same time, discourses around cybraries, digital libraries, and virtual libraries express another important aspect of our modern experience. Today a child with Internet access can search vast digital repositories located around the world, acquire real-time images of other places through webcams, use telescopes and other instruments to extend the senses and create an impression of being able to move freely through time and space, and employ new communication modalities to speak with others far away. These affordances of digital technologies lessen some of the constraints of earlier ways of organizing knowledge and communicating. For many, they suggest a qualitative shift, namely, from place-bound regimes of knowledge to entirely new knowledge spaces. This shift is seen as fundamental for both epistemology and literacy.

However, this place–space dichotomy breaks down when viewed from a space perspective as well. As long as humans have bodies, their interaction with new digital spaces exists in real times and places. The material conditions of use dramatically affect one's "digital experience." How crowded is the library or Internet café? What is the ambient lighting? How noisy is it? How expensive is it, which might influence how long one stays online and what is achieved? Does one even have the necessary physical components (e.g., the electrical supply, the appropriate plugs and cables) to connect? Even when we consider wi-fi and long-life batteries, no one has yet shown a way to escape the physicality required to connect a living, breathing human to cyberspace.

Furthermore, digital resources themselves are highly tied to place (e.g., the production of images of real places is entirely dependent on place-bound technologies such as a lens on a mountaintop or telescopes in outer space). A webcam may display a cityscape to users around the world but the quality of its image cannot escape the local weather conditions. Digital collections in humanities can be excellent resources for scholars of all ages, yet it must be remembered that the specific items in any collection derive from documents once scanned or typed into a computer in real physical locations. Access to these and other digital resources is contingent on organizational affiliations, financial resources, equipment maintenance, and a host of other social and economic factors that themselves are inevitably tied to concrete places.

Indeed, we might go further and say that the attempt to view digital resources as somehow entirely free of place may be one of the most serious hindrances to their effective use. For example, some current digital library programs focus almost entirely on the collection and organization of digital documents, acting as if the construction of a superior digital library in and of itself will address the needs of users. What such projects often overlook to their own eventual detriment is that every use of the library will necessarily be situated in a particular time and place. As a result, the digital library will be but a part of a larger information ecology (Bruce & Hogan, 1998; Nardi & O'Day, 1999).

That information ecology often includes other digital documents, physical documents, and people who serve as helpers, critics, and so on. The failure to take the larger information ecology into account means that design decisions may preclude or hamper access by some individuals or entire communities, who unfortunately are often those groups already seriously underserved. For example, the otherwise excellent National Science Digital Library, which Jane Hunter discusses (chap. 6), has almost all of its resources in the English language. Not only does that limitation fly in the face of the rhetoric we often hear about global cyberspace. Even in the context of the United States, this limitation seriously diminishes its usefulness and charter in a culturally diverse nation with millions of non-English speakers.

THE AROBASE IN THE LIBRARY: LESSONS FOR NOW AND THE FUTURE

What then does the Dalmatian Peasants Party of 1904 have to tell us about the Internet, digital collections, and multimedia today? There are a number of important lessons that can be learned by integrating the story with the chapters of this book. These pertain to the nonautonomy of literacy technologies, their impact on society, their modes of effect, the lived experience of users, and the construction of knowledge.

First, the operations and effects of technology are not autonomous. Technologies are developed by real human actors operating in established social relations to address everyday social problems; they are grounded in social practice. For Mato and his compatriots, this is evident as we consider the technology of the alphabet, which was the tool to enable literacy. As a forbidden object, the alphabet participated in the distribution of social and political power within Dalmatia at that time. The means of access to the alphabet in books, pamphlets, newspapers, and so on, were no mere technical features but instead highly valenced social practices. We can only speculate as to how different alphabets or different means of using an alphabet might have affected social practices at that time. What we can say is that the description of the alphabet as a technology, its modes of access, its distribution and control are inseparable from a discussion of the political events of that time. Thus it, like the camera, must be viewed as part of a system of social relations, and not as a discrete entity.

The theme of nonautonomous technology pervades nearly every chapter of this book. For example, Fabos (chap. 13) asks us to look at the familiar search engine technology in terms of the commercial interests that ultimately shape the order and forms of presentation of search results. She makes a convincing case for the idea that web-based search tools are not neutral mechanisms for information retrieval but rather reflect the power of capital and business. Graham (chap. 14) shows how a monopsony (single buyer) of media content turns technologies that could promote diverse lines of communication into technologies that promote a single point of view. The ACRO project he describes represents a counter to the monopsony of media content. It does so, not by making the technology autonomous—an impossibility—but by making the technology attuned to a broader set of social interests. Chapters by Barwick and Thieburger (chap. 8) and by Kornbluh, Shell-Weiss, and Turnbull (chap. 12) similarly address the autonomy issue. They show how the organization, representation, and distribution of scholarly knowledge is not independent of the economic and social processes of publishers, professional organizations, and scholarly communities. Their calls for more open scholarly communication (echoed by Willinsky, chap. 10), are, as in Graham's case, calls to organize the production and distribution of knowledge in line with more democratic ideals, rather than to disconnect it from social relations.

Second, the story of the Dalmatian Peasants Party reminds us that new technologies are already having and will continue to have a significant impact on libraries, scholarship, communities, workplaces, and democratic institutions. The camera used to photograph the Dalmatian Executive Committee was not simply a device to produce black and white representations of a visual field. It was a crucial means for establishing the presence, importance, and legitimacy of a newly established political party. It participated in the making of a social history, the ramifications of which continue to this day in places far removed from Dalmatia. Both the power and the limitations of the photographic technology of 1904 were deeply implicated in the act of constructing the Executive's sense of identity and history.

In chapter 1, Burbules talks about the significant impact that virtual spaces can have on libraries, and he examines dimensions of which their use can build on to extend the traditional library. In her discussion of digital libraries, Hunter (chap. 6) continues this theme showing a range of ways in which digital repositories extend the possibilities for scholarship and education. Chapters by Boyce (chap. 2) and Schmidt (chap. 4) explore in concrete ways the impact that new technologies have on libraries in educational contexts.

Third, the effects of new technologies are nondeterministic and nonlinear. Rather than a highly predictable one-step process, the incorporation of new technologies into social practices typically leads to changes in those practices, which in turn shape the use of those technologies leading to further changes in social relations and social practices. There is a continual reformulation of the larger system and the technologies infused within it. The introduction of alphabetic literacy was far more than simply an immediate solution to a simple problem. When Mato learned the alphabet, he established a school that led to many others over time throughout the region. There were both positive and negative consequences. As the people became literate, they began to challenge the church and were excommunicated. Reverberations continue a century later as young people in Dalmatia utilize their alphabetic and multimodal literacies when they learn about and through the Internet.

While acknowledging the impact of technology, Dressman and Tettegah argue that technological change is far from immediate and total. Their case studies show that the effects of technology are mediated by the social backgrounds, values, and approaches to information literacy within school library programs.

Fourth, virtual spaces are not realms separate from the lived, embodied experiences of users. Instead, they are implicated in complex ways with the physical spaces and material conditions of human existence. Thus, libr@ries need to be understood in relation to the grounded material worlds of users. The representation of experience through alphabetic writing might well be considered a precursor to the virtual world we ascribe to computers today. The church and the state did not forbid literacy because

they saw it as a world distinct from the farms and marketplaces of Dalmatia in 1904. True, much of the church's ecclesiastical power derived from
its ability to stand independently of time and space. However, their fear of
literacy, although reprehensible, was nonetheless rational. They knew that
the written word provided power over the world, as Freire (1999) argued
much later. The same kinds of issues recur today in libr@ries that allow
communication independent of time and place, and yet are also deeply
grounded in social, cultural, and economic realities.

Kapitzke (chap. 9) develops this idea in her analysis of the field of
library studies, showing the need for new theoretical and empirical
directions to take account of both the material conditions of life and the
(im)possibilities of digital tools. Boyce (chap. 2) shows how student and
teacher conceptions of literacy in school libraries are tied not only to the
act of reading but also to the occasions and locations of reading. This is a
key issue for educational libraries as they consider such mundane things
as which room should house the computers and which should be "reading rooms."

Fifth, because the effects of new technologies are pervasive and recursive in the sense defined earlier, we need to reexamine issues such as the
nature of knowledge, and of knowledge production and distribution.
Mato's story highlights for us that representing knowledge with different media can be important. For all the value one might place on the ordinary experience of these Dalmatian peasants and the articulation of their
experience through oral discourse, the lack of written literacy posed an
obstacle to their empowerment. Mato's speeches in written form could be
made accessible to many more people throughout the region and around
the world than if they had remained in oral form. Print literacy enabled
the peasants to extend and better reflect on their own condition and
understanding of it. Thus, the very nature of knowledge in the community changed through incorporation of new technologies, and was a consequence that the authorities feared and resisted.

Barwick and Thieberger (chap. 8) show this point in their chapter on
digital repositories for ethnography. The very act of digitizing cultural
resources calls for significant efforts in such things as identifying the per-
former of recorded music, which had not been done prior to the digital
repository. Thus, the new tools and media not only enhance access but
have effects on the construction of knowledge. For example, they call
for commitments about the identity of people as represented in the corpus, dates, places, names of songs, and other elements that had been left
open in earlier media. It is worth noting here the interesting contradiction
that digital technologies are often conceived as free-flowing, virtual, and
transcending time and space. Their use typically requires an encoding of
knowledge into categories, which can be productive for a discipline of

study while simultaneously limiting future possibilities (Bowker & Star, 1999). Rooney and Schneider (chap. 7) similarly remind us that although technologies have an impact on the nature of knowledge, knowledge does not exist in technologies but in the libr@ries and their users. Their exploration of knowledge is in terms of the social and interpretive relations within and among the people involved.

POLITICAL ECONOMY OF NEW TECHNOLOGIES

New technologies cannot be separated from the economic conditions that define their development and use. Accordingly, it is vital today to examine the political economy of new technologies and not view them as mere technical artifacts or devices somehow free from the relations of ownership, control, power, and political interest. For the Austro-Hungarian Empire of Mato's time, the control over knowledge was both a consequence of the concentration of power and an enabling condition for it. Thus, as we seek to understand Mato's story, we cannot focus on the acquisition of literacy merely as an individual, psychological process, but instead must conceive it within a historical analysis of the distribution and organization of cultural capital within society. Those who were permitted to read and write acquired the symbolic and social capital that comes with being known as literate: which is the knowledge to access and utilize literacy and the knowledge that could be acquired and distributed through enhanced communication.

The relation between capital and knowledge is considered in several chapters. Fitzgerald (chap. 15) addresses ownership and access issues in his discussion of a Creative Commons. Issues of open access to knowledge and open production of new knowledge recur in the chapters by Graham (chap. 14), Willinsky (chap. 10), Hunter (chap. 6), Kornbluh, Shell-Weiss, and Turnbull (chap. 12), and others. They call for a new approach to knowledge creation, consistent with Benkler's (2002) model for the free software movement. Benkler saw the emergence of a new mode of production in the digitally networked environment, one that he called "commons-based peer-production," to distinguish it from property- or contract-based models of firms and markets. That model frames technology as a system in which members of diverse communities have the potential not only to access knowledge resources but to create them as well.

Mato's story is one grounded in a particular historical moment, yet the lessons from his story are relevant today. They point to the vital importance of every citizen having a voice, of being able to learn and to contribute intellectually, free of oppression. Freedom to access knowledge has been a cardinal principle of librarianship, one that is highly contested in the current technological moment. New technologies promise to increase our capacity to access knowledge, but at the same time it threatens to shut down that access (Lessig, 2004). New technologies are not only about access to preexisting knowledge. As so many of the authors in this book have indicated, they also offer the possibility of two-way communication in which all citizens, like Mato, are able to write and create as well as view and read.

The possibility of expanding meaning making to ever larger communities—to the very young and the very old, to speakers of diverse languages and participants in diverse cultures, to people in every location on earth, and people from all races and classes—is the most profound potential of the new technologies. The wonders of search engines, digital repositories, multimedia, hyperlinks, real-time data acquisition, high speed computing, and mobile and ubiquitous computing have meaning only as they shape social relations.

In his introduction to Freire's *Pedagogy of the Oppressed* (1999), Shaull wrote:

> There is no such thing as a neutral education process. Education either functions as an instrument that is used to facilitate the integration of the younger generation into the logic of the present system and bring about conformity to it, or it becomes 'the practice of freedom,' the means by which men and women deal critically and creatively with reality and discover how to participate in the transformation of their world. (p. 16)

If our view of libr@ries, education, and political structures is that they should "communicate the logic of the present system and bring about conformity to it," then the new technologies can help us achieve that goal, and libr@ries will become ever more constrained and compatible with dominant political and economic power. If, on the other hand, we seek what Shaull and Freire called "the practice of freedom," then the new technologies and the new library may look very different. We have the capacity now to create libr@ries that dramatically expand the possibilities for creating, finding, accessing, and distributing knowledge. Those new possibilities suggest significantly expanded roles for libr@ries in democratic societies. In the final analysis, the construction of new libraries is not a task for the technician alone, but instead requires the deepest examination of our human needs, values, capacities, conflicts, dreams, and desires.

LIBR@RIES AS *PARRHESIASTES*

The chapters herein have shown how new developments around libr@ries are unfolding out of and yet have enfolded within themselves the social, cultural, and symbolic forces and discourses of late modernity. We believe that, notwithstanding the accelerating commodification of human life and knowledge, growing public and community advocacy on the issue provides reason for optimism. As Borgman (2000) noted, however, there is no room for complacency because the increasing invisibility of libraries within national and global information infrastructures renders them increasingly vulnerable.

Yet, despite the complexities and vulnerabilities of the human condition at the current historical moment, we take heart that, irrespective of creed, class, or culture, most people seek hope and a future. For millennia, libraries have connected learners and learning communities of the past and the present with the future. This role is now seriously unsettled as the hype of technological innovation and the need for professional relevance in a rapidly changing world distracts many from what we believe is core library business: namely, the provision of information and knowledge for critical participation in open, strongly democratic societies.

We therefore close with a challenge for you, reader and (re)writer of this, our message. In a relatively unknown text, Foucault (2001) provided a typically elegant archeological analysis of the obscure concept, *parrhesia*. In what might surprise those who reject Foucault's work for its epistemological relativism, he defined the important social figure of the *parrhesiastes* in Greek literature as one who tells "the unvarnished truth." This vital social practice is "a kind of verbal activity where the speaker has a specific relation to truth through frankness, a certain relationship to his [or her] own life through danger, a certain type of relation to himself or other people through criticism (self-criticism or criticism of other people), and a specific relation to moral law through freedom and duty" (p. 19).

Like Mato's courage in speaking the truth as he saw it to his Bishop, the *parrhesiastic* citizen of Greek democratic culture "uses his [or her] freedom and chooses frankness instead of persuasion, truth instead of falsehood or silence, the risk of death instead of life and security, criticism instead of flattery, and moral duty instead of self-interest and moral apathy" (p. 20). We feel that these words have especial potency in the social and political climate of today. The catch here is that Foucault used the term not to establish truth, but to problematize it: that is, to expose practices and "games of truth" that position and shut down social spaces of insight, understanding, and empathy.

We hope this collection will assist those who see themselves as socially responsible brokers of knowledge—as *parrhesiastic*, "truth-telling" libr@ry workers—to reflect on the politicization of knowledge and their professional selves by asking questions such as the following. To what degree am "I" speaking, and in what ways are social agendas speaking through me? Which power relations and effects does my discursive practice reproduce, and which ones does it revamp and/or restore? Do these information discourses, services, and practices cut new ground with hard-hitting questions, or do they recycle pat answers and a compliant politics through the endless play of worthless words? Considering that we are all different, all variously enabled and disabled, how do new libr@ry services and practices generate openness and a space for complexity—and confrontation, if necessary—within dialogues that are safe, but also disconcerting, disturbing, and difficult? Within that context, we hope you find the ideas herein to be useful, a touch edifying, and a tad troubling.

REFERENCES

Benkler, Y. (2002). Coase's penguin, or, Linux and the nature of the firm. *Yale Law Journal, 112*(3), 369–447.

Borgman, C. L. (2000). *From Gutenberg to the global information infrastructure: Access to information in the networked world.* Cambridge, MA: MIT Press.

Bowker, G. C., & Star, S. L. (1999). *Sorting things out: Classification and its consequences.* Cambridge, MA: MIT Press.

Bruce, B. C., & Hogan, M. P. (1998). The disappearance of technology: Toward an ecological model of literacy. In D. Reinking, M. McKenna, L. Labbo, & R. Kieffer (Eds.), *Handbook of literacy and technology: Transformations in a post-typographic world* (pp. 269–281). Mahwah, NJ: Lawrence Erlbaum Associates.

Darveniza, Z. (1986). *An Australian saga: Dedicated to multi-racial Australia.* Marrickville, NSW: Southwood.

Foucault, M. (2001). *Fearless speech* (J. Pearson, Ed.). Los Angeles, CA: Semiotext(e).

Freire, P. (1999). *Pedagogy of the oppressed.* New York: Continuum.

Kapitzke, C. (1995). *Literacy and religion.* Amsterdam: John Benjamins.

Lessig, L. (2004). *Free culture: How big media uses technology and the law to lock down culture and control creativity.* New York: Penguin.

Nardi, B. A., & O'Day, V. L. (1999). *Information ecologies: Using technology with heart.* Cambridge, MA: MIT Press.

Author Index

A

Abbas, J., *83*
Acohido, B., 242
Adams, B., *95*
Adorno, T. W., *xl, 256, 256, 266*
American Broadcasting Corporation (ABC), 266
American Educational Research Association (AERA), xl
Ampere, A. M., 181
Ancona, D., *97*
André, E., 105
Angele, J., 103
Anh, T. T., *105*
Annodex, 106
Apple, M. W., xl, *151*, 165
Archer, M. S., 119, 121, 123, 124
Arms, W. Y., 76, 155
Aronowitz, S., *xl*
Artesia., 96
Aström, K. J., 181
Atkins, C., 61
Awcock, F. H., *65, 66*
Azoulay, L., 134

B

Bachler, M., *101*
Bagdikian, B. H., 253, 256
Bailey, C. P. 105

Bailin, A., *66*
Bainbridge, D. I., *155, 166*
Baker, N., xl
Bakhtin, M. M., xxix
Balsamo, A. M., 163
Baltes, P. B., *127*
Bao, J., *101*
Barabási, A-L., x
Barber, B. R., xl
Bard, A., *166*
Barman, N., 95
Barwick, L., 137, *140*, 147
Bassett, G., *273*
Battelle, J., 204
Baudrillard, J., 198, 199, 201, 202
Baym, N., 42
Bazeley, M., 245, 246
Beane, J. A., *151*
Bearman, D., 85
Bejune, M., 74, 84
Benkler, Y., xlxii, 91
Bentley, A. F., xxxi
Benton Foundation Digital Divide Network Staff, 135
Benton Foundation, 152
Benz, H., *99*
Berger, P., *116*
Bergman, M., 74
Bergstrom, C. T., *222*
Bergstrom, T. C., 183, *222*
Berman, S., 163
Berners-Lee, T., *102*

Berstein, J. M., *xl*
Bertot, J. C., *170*
Besser, H., 85
Best, S., *165*
Bettig, R. V., 165
Bhaskar, R., 118, 119, 120, 121, 122
Bibliothèque Nationale de France, xxviii
Bidum, C., *31*
Bijker, W., *114*
Bing, V. M., *162*
Bird, S., *141*
Birdsall, W. F., xxviii, 164, 170
Birkerts, S., 208, 209, 225
Bishop, A. P., *156*
Blackler, F., 117
Blane, J. V., 165
Blizg, 101
Bloch, R. H., *152*
BlogChalking, 101
Boden, M. A., 114, 118
Boekema, F., xxvi
Bohm, D., 117
Bollier, D., xxxiii, xli, 165, *165*
Boone, M. D., 64, 114, 154, 155
Borges, J. L., 194
Borgman, C. L., 76, 156, 293
Borner, K., 155
Boros, E., *101*
Boston, G., 134
Boulding, K. E., 115
Boulgouris, N. V., 97
Bourdieu, P., xxix, 160, *170*
Bousquet, M., xl
Bowers, C. A., 156
Bowker, G. C., *291*
Bowker, G. C., *xxxvi*
Bradley, K., 134
Braithwaite, J., *165*
Brawne, M., 32
Brin, S., *94*
British Broadcasting Corporation (BBC), 255, 266
Brody, T. D., 105
Brophy, P., 230
Browne, J., 189
Bruce, B. C., xxxvii, 212, *287*
Bruen, C., *105*
Bruza, P. D., 100
Buckingham Shum, S., *101*
Budd, J. M., 160
Bundy, A., 19, 62

Burbules, N. C., 3–15
Burke, P., 121
Buttenfield, B. P., *156*

C

Cairncross, F., 200
Capra, F., x, xi
Carey, J., 255, 259
Castells, M., xi, 20, 31, 33
Cayzer, S., *100*
Center for Media Research, 268
Champelli, L., 155
Chen, C., *155*
Chen-Burger, J., *101*
Chia, R., 117
Chomsky, N., xl
Chowdhury, G. G., *155*
Chowdhury, S., *155*
Christel, M., *97*
Christophides, V., *105*
CIDOC CRM, 102
Clément, C., xxxii
Cole, M., 164
Compaine, B. M., 156
Conlan, O., *105*
Conners, E., 246
Convera Screening Room, 96
Cooke, H., *114*
Cooper, M., xlii
Cope, B., *21, 28*
Copyright Law Review Committee (CLRC), 277, 278
Council of Australian University Librarians (CAUL), 62
Council on Library and Information Resources (CLIR), 134
Crane, G. R., *97*
Crang, M., *xxxi*
Crawford, W., *152*
Creative Industries Report, 259
Crossiant, J., *xxxiii*
Croud, J., *114*
Crow, R., 226
Crowe, D., 243
Crowley, B., 160
Curtin, P., *xxxvii*
CWI's Semi-automatic Hypermedia Presentation Generation (Dynamo) Project, 105

D

D'Angelo, B. J., 154
Dalton, J., *101*
DAML Ontology Library, 103
DAML+OIL, 104
Darnton, R., 223
DARPA Object Service Architecture Web
    Annotation Service, 99
Darveniza, Z., 282, 283
David, P. A., 117
Davis, L., *159*
Dawson, M., *245*
Day, R. E., 160
DCSE (Department of Computer Science
    and Engineering, University of
    Washington), 95
De Certeau, M. D., 25,159
De Roure, D., *101, 105*
de Saint Martin, M., *170*
Deegan, M., *155*
Deibert, R. J., 208
Deleuze, G., xxxi
Demas, S. G., *66, 70*
Denny, M., 103
Department of Education, Science &
    Training (DEST), 260
Der Derian, J., 165
Derrida, J., 170
Di Chiro, G., *xxxiii*
Dickinson, I., *100*
DigiCULT Consortium, 134
Dillon, D., 70
Doctorow, C., 94
Dodge, M., *xxxiv, 160*
Dot Force, 213
Doty, P., *76*
Douglas, A., 42
Dowler, L., 69
Dragon Systems, 96
Drahos, P., *165*
Dressman, M., 19, 24, 25, 26, 41, 53
DSTC FilmEd, 99
Dublin Core Metadata Initiative (DCMI), 94
Duck, S., 119
Dungey, P., *65, 66*
Dupplaw, D. P., 105
Duran, J., 157
Duranti, A., 141
Durman, P., 238
Durrance, J. C., 160

E

Eaton, J., *155*
Education Queensland, xxxix
Edwards, B., *60*
Edwards, C., *155*
Eglash, R., *xxxiii*
Eisenstadt, M., *101*
Eisentein, E., 225
eLib Newsagent Project, 106
Elkin, A. P., 137, *138*
Elliot de Saez, E., 155
Ellul, J., 115
Endersby, J., 189
Engels, F., 194
Engestrom, Y., 117
Ensor, P., 114, 155
Erdmann, M., 103
European Broadcast Union, 144
Evans, D. J., *185, 186*
Evans, J., 225
Evans, P., *xxxvi, 156*
Ewald, F., *193*

F

Fabos, B., 247
Fairclough, N., xxix, 159, *164*
Falkovych, K., *106*
Feld, S., 136
Fenwick, S., 19
Figueroa, R., *162*
Financial Times Information, 106
Fine Brand Media Inc., 232, 236
Fisher, B., *60*
Fitzgerald, A. 273
Fitzgerald, B. 273
Florida, R., 275
Fontana, A., *193*
Ford, L., *140*
Foster, J. B., *245, 256*
Foucault, M., xiii, xxix, 25, 37, 46, 53, 186,
    193, 293
Fouché, R., *xxxiii*
Fox, S., *186*
Frechette, J. D., xxxvii
Free Press, 259
Freire, P., 290, 292
Frew, J., *97*
Frost, D., *154*
Fuller, S., 116

G

Gabbard, D. A., *165*
Gaither, C., 237
Garfinkel, H., *159*
Gargan, M., *105*
Garrison D., 38, 42, 46
Gates, B., 245
Gerhart, S. L., 247
Gibson, W., 180
Giddens, A., xxxxvii
Goodrum, A., 74, 84, 241
Goodson, I., *xxxvii*
Google, 94
Gordon, A. C., *185, 186*
Gordon, M. D., *185, 186*
Gorman, M., *152*, 154
Gorski, P., 135
Grafstein, A., *66*
Graham, P., *119, 159*, 164, *164, 255*, 256, *256*
Granovetter, M. S., 118
Great Britain Parliament House of
      Commons Science and Technology
      Committee, 221
Green, B., 25, *31*
Green, D., *155*
Griffiths, J. T., *230*
Griffiths, M., 170
Griffiths, P., *164*
Guerts, J., *105*

H

Hall, W., 105
Halleck, D. D., xl
Halliday, L., *155*
Hannah, S. A., *164*
Hansell, S., 236, 244
Hansen, M. T., 117
Hanson, A., *155*
Haraway, D., xxxi, 163, 180
Harding, S., *162*
Harnad, S., 183
Harrington, D., 67, 69
Harris, M. H., *164*
Harris, P. C., *164*
Harris, S. W., 105
Harum, S., *155*
Harvey, D., xl
Harvey, F., 231, 233, 240
Hauptmann, A., *97*

Hay, C., 117, 122, 123
Hearn, G., *116, 122, 259*
Heath, A., *60*
Heflin, J., *103*
Hendler, J., *102, 103*
Henry, C., *215*
Henwood, F., *156*
Herron, S., xxviii
Hertz, N., 151
Hesse, C. A., *152*
Heuertz, L., *185, 186*
Himmelmann, N. P., 141
Hindman, M., *239, 242, 247*
Hintikka, M. B., *162*
Hodge, R., *17, 33*
Hogan, M. P., *287*
Holloway, S. L., *xxxvii*
Honavar, V., *101*
Horkheimer, M., *256, 258, 266*
Hornsby, E., *114*
HPWREN, 97
Hudak, G., *153*
Hughes, L., *155*
Hughes, M., 61
Humanities Advanced Technology and
      Information Institute (HATII), *134*
Hunter, J., *95, 97, 99, 102, 105, 106*
HyLife, 170
Hymes, D. H., *159*

I

IBM VideoAnnEx, 99
Ichijo, K., *117*
Informedia, 96
Innis, H. A., 256
International Committee for Documentation
      of the International Council of
      Museums (ICOM-CIDOC), 82
Internet2, 104
Introna, L., *247*
Iyengar, G., *95*

J

Jacob, R. J. K., *97*
Jameson, F., 202
Janée, G., *97*
Jennings, N., *105*
JESS, 105

Johns, A., 225
Johnson, J., *239, 242, 247*
Johnson-Eilola, J., 21, *21*, 27, *27, 29*
Johnston, R., xxxvi
Jones, D. J., 63, 67, 69
Jones, S., 61, 219
Jones, T., *138*
Joseph, R., *116*

K

Kahin, B., *155, 156*
Kaine-Krolak, M., *106*
Kalantzis, M., *21, 28*
Kantor, P. B., *101*
Kapitzke, C., ix, xxxvi, 32, 160, 167, 283
Karvounarakis, G., *105*
Kellner, D., xxxix, *165*
Kenney, A. R., *155*
Keys, M., 154
Kiernan, V., 194
Kihn, P., *153*
Kitchin, R., *xxxiv, 160*
Klein, M., *103*
Knobel, M., *xxxvii*
Knorr Cetina, K., *x*
Kogut, B., *118*
Kompatsiaris, I., 97
Komzak, J., *101*
Koopman, B., *99, 100*
Kopytoff, V., 236, 240
Kosovic, D., *106*
Kovacs, D., *155*
Kovacs, M., *155*
Kranich, N., xli, 165
Kress, G., *17,* 22, 27, *33, 159*
Kruesi, L., *60*
Kusch, M., 116

L

Lagoze, C., *102*
Lakoff, G., 98
Lanham, R. A., 25
Lankes, R. D., 83
Lankshear, C., *xxxvii, 159*
Lash, S., xl
Lasica, J. D., 235
Lassere, K., *60*
Lassila, O., *102*

Lather, P., 162
Latour, B., xxxi
Lave, J., *119, 121*
Law, J., *114*
Lax, S., 156
Le 'pataphysicien Net, xxviii
Le dictionaire encyclopédique de la langue française du XXIe siècle, xxviii
Leadbeater, C., 60
Lee, S. D., 155
Lefebvre, H., xxxi
Legon, J., 268
Lemke, J. L., 159
Lenin, V. I., 257
Lesk, M., 76
Lessig, L., xli, 165, 215, 254, 266, 274, 275, 292
Levin, B. L., *155*
Levy, D. M., 199
Liebman, M., *25, 27*
Lijding, M. E., *99*
Lin, C-Y., *95*
Lindt, G., 214
Lipinski, T. A., 155
Little, S., *95, 97, 105, 106*
Livingstone, S. M., xxxvii
Lohr, J., 185, 194
Lougee, W. P., 154
Luckmann, T., *116*
Luhmann, N., 119
Luke, A., 32, 159, *255, 256*
Luke, C., xxxvii
Luke, T., 201, 208
Lundberg, M. J., 119
Lundvall, B., 213
Luria, A. R., 119
Lyman, P., 165
Lynch, C., 103, 106
Lyotard, J. F., 203

M

Macdonald, G., *158*
Macharia, M., 134
Madden, M., 61
Maedche, A., *103*
Maffi, L., 140
Magkanaraki, A., *105*
Mandarax, 105
Mandese, J., 264
Mandeville, T., *116, 122*

Mangalindan, M., 242, 243
Mangan, J. M., *xxxvii*
Marett, A., 137, *140*
Markey, K., 83
Markoff, J., *xxxiii*, 244, 246
Marmasse, N., *106*
Marques, O., 95
Marx, K, 257
Marx, L., 215
Massey, D., 32
May, C., xlii, *161*, 165
May, J., *xxxi*
McArthur, R., 100
McCarthy, G., *225*
McChesney, R., *xlii*, 248, 253, *256*, 257
McDermott, R., *xxxvi*
McHugh, J., 246
McKenna, B., *127*
McLaren, P., *159*
McLean, J., xxxvii
McLean, N., 60
McQuillan, M., *158*
Meadows, M., *146*
Melamed, B., *101*
Meñkov, V., *101*
Metcalfe, J. S., 115
Mezaris, V., 97
Michaelides, D., *101*
Miksa, F., *76*
Millard, D. E., *105*
Miller, E., 85
Miller, N., *156*
Molnar, H., *146*
Moore, E. J., *185*, *186*
Moore, N., xli
*MoreVisibility platform three: E-commerce
     initiative*, 240
Mosco, V., 165
Motik, B., *103*
Mountford, C. P., 137
Mules, W., *159*
Mumford, L., 255, 259, 260, 268
Munt, S. R., xxxi
Murthy, V. K., *155*

N

Nan Si, S., *155*
Naphade, M., *95*
Nardi, B. A., *287*

Nardini, R. F., xxviii
National Initiative for a Networked
     Cultural Heritage (NINCH), *134*
National Library of Australia (NLA), 134
National Office for the Information
     Economy, 260
National Science Foundation, 156
Negroponte, N., 200
Nesson, C. R., *156*
Neti, C., *95*
NetLibrary Inc, *155*
Neu, D. J., *101*
New Internationalist, 168
New London Group, 21
New Zealand Ministry of Research, Science
     & Technology, 215
Ng, D., *97*
Ng, S., 61
Nissenbaum, H., *247*
Noble, D. F., xl, 183
Nock, H., *95*
Nonaka, I., *100.*, *117*
Norris, P., 156
Novak, M., *106*
Noy, N. F., *103*
NSF Workshop on Research Directions for
     Digital Libraries, 107

O

O'Connor, B., *83*
O'Connor, M., *83*
O'Day, V. L., *287*
Olson, H. A., 163
Online Computer Library Centre, 65
Online, 63
OpenGALEN, 103
Oppenheim, C., *154*, *155*
Organisation for Economic Cooperation
     and Development, xlii, 157
Overture, 236

P

Page, K., *101*, 105
Page, L., *94*
Palmer, S. E., 80
Pantry, S., *164*
Parish, H., 54

Paulston, R. G., *25, 27*
Pavliscak, P., *215*
PAXit, 99
Persaud, A., 190
Peters, M., *xxxvii*
Peterson, K., 245
PGP Pretty Good Privacy, 104
Pilger, J., 165
Pinfield, S., *155*
Pitoëff, P., 134
Plexousakis, D., *105*
Pointcast, 106
Poster, M., *xl*
Postman, N., 255
Potter, S., *101*
Powell, R. R. 169
Power, G., 105
Pradt-Lougee, W., 61
Prelinger, R., 268
Publisher Associations' Statement on open
    archives, 195
Purves, R., *158*

Q

QBIC, 95
Quinion, M., xxviii

R

Radford, G. P., *xxviii*, 160, *163*, 176
Radford, M. L., *xxviii, 163*
Raineee, L., *186*
Ranganathan, S. R., 85
Rawls, A., *159*
Reamy, T., 94
Reger, O. Y. 155
Reid, P. T., *162*
Reinking, D., 23
Reuters, 238
Reynolds, D., *100*
Ricoh Movie Tool, 99
Ritzer, G., 164
ROADNet, 97
Roberto, K., *169*
Robins, K., *xxx, xl*
Rogers, D., *106*
Rooney, D., *116, 119, 122, 127, 128, 159*
Rose, C., 155

Rose, E., *163*
Rose, J., 188, 189, 190, 191
Ross, S., *215*
Rushkoff, D., 165
Russell, R., *155*
Rust, G., 85

S

Saenger, P. H., 160
Saltman, K., *165*
Saul, J. R., 268
Saunders, L. M., 154
Savitz, E., 245
Sayre, S., *77*
Scammell, A., 152
Schachter, K., 243
Schatzki, T. R., *x*
Schäuble, P., *156*
Scherer, J. A., *66, 70*
Schiller, D., *xlii*, 164
Schiller, H. I., *xl*, 164
Schilling, C., 163
Schimdt, J., 63, 64, *114, 154*
Schmandt, C., 106
Schneider, U., 117, *128*
Schüller, D., 134
Schwager, T., 66
Scott, J., 118
Seeger, A., 135, 147
Senker, P., *156*
Servon, L. J., 156
Shabajee, P., *100*
Shadbolt, N., *101, 105*
Shan, W., *118*
Shapira, B., *101*
Shapiro, C., *xxxvi*
Shapiro, S. B., 163
Shiaw, H-Y., *97*
Shippey, T., 189
Silverstone, R., 256
Simon, B., xl
Simon, H. A., 123
Simons, G., *141*
Siocchi, A., 74, 84
Sledge, J., *99, 100*
Slott, M., 164
Smeaton, A. F., *156*
Smith, J., 95
Smith, R., *xxxvii*

Smithson, D., *154*
Smythe, D., 256, 257, 258, 263
SNOMED CT, 103
Snowden, M. L., 117
Snyder, W., *xxxvi*
Söderqvist, J., *166*
Soja, E. W., 25, 33
Southey, G., *259*
Spender, J-C., 117
Staab, S., 103
Stacey, R. D., 117
Stanley, L., *162*
Star, S. L., *xxxvi*, 291
Staudinger, U. M., *127*
STM Market, 194
Stojanovic, L., *103*
Stojanovic, N., *103*
Strintzis, M. G., 97
Studer, R., 103
Sullivan, A., 100
SUO, 102
Sure, Y., 103

T

Takeuchi, H., *100*
Tallmo, K. E., xxviii
Tanner, S., *155*
Tate, A., *101*
Tawney, R. H., 190 191
Taylor, J., ix
Teather, D., 245
The Web Search Workshop, 238
Thieberger, N., 142
Thomas, C. F., 155
Thomson, S., *158*
Thorning, S., 60
Thrift, N., *xxxi*, *161*
Thwaites, T., *159*
Todd, H., *60*, *114*
Toyama, R., *117*
Trant, J., 85
Trifonas, P. P., 151, 170
Trosow, S., 160
Trump, J. F., *154*
Tsioutsiouliklis, K., *239*, *242*, *247*
Tsoukas, H., 117
Turkle, S., 208
Turnbull, D., *114*
Twidale, M., *155*

U

UNESCO, 77
UNESCO, World Conference on Science,
    222

V

Vaidhyanathan, S., xlii, 165
Valentine, D., *97*
Valentine, G., *xxxvii*
Vallentine, J. R., 142
Van House, N., *156*
van Leeuwen, T., *159*
Van Slyck, A., 171
Varian, H. R., *xxxvi*, *155*
Vecchio, R. P., *259*
Virage, 96
Von Elm, C., *154*
von Krogh, G., *117*
Von Savigny, E., *x*
Vygotsky, L., 119

W

W3C Annotea Web Annotation Service, 99
W3C Web Ontology (WebOnt) Working
    Group, 102
W3C Web Ontology Language (OWL), 102
W3C XML Signature Working Group, 103
Wactlar, H., *97*
Wade, V., *105*
Walker, G., *118*
Walker, J., 240, 241, 247
Waters, R., 231, 238
Watts, T., *165*
Weal, M. J., 105
Webster, F., *xxx*, *xl*, 166
Weibel, S., 85
Wenger, E., *xxxvi*, 119, *119*, *121*
Wenke, D., 103
West, J., *169*
Wetterlund, K., *77*
Wherry, T. L., 155
Wiegand, W. A., 162, *170*
Wiener, N., 180, 181
Wikipedia, 101
Williams, A., *134*

Williams, E. B., 146
Williams, J. F., 65, 66
Willinsky, J., 182, 183, 187, 190, 192, 193
Willinsky, S., 222
Wilson, E. J., *155*, 156
Wilson, H., 64
Wise, S., *162*
Wisner, W. H., xl
Wissenburg, A., *155*
Witten, I. H., *155, 166*
Woobury, A. C., 141

Wright, R., *134*
Wurster, T. S., *xxxvi, 156*
Wyatt, E., *xxxiii*
Wyatt, S., *156*
Wysocki, A., *21, 27, 29*

Z

ZGDV VIDETO, 99
Zorich, D., 76

Subject Index

A

Access, 85–87
Appropriating technology, xxxiii
Architecture, xxxiv, 7–10
   enclosure / exclusion, 9
   interaction / isolation, 8
   movement / stasis, 8
   publicity / privacy, 9
   visibility / hiddenness, 9
Archival access, 142–143
Archival recordings, 137–140
   designing local assess to, 139–140
   indexing, 139
Archives, 73, 82
Arobase, xi, xiv, xxvi, xxviii, 281, 287–291
   capital, xiv, xl–xliv
   knowledge, xiv, xxxvi-xl, xxviii
   space, xi, xiv, xxviii-xxxvi, 281
   place, 281
Australian Creative Resources Archive
   (ACRA), xliv

B

Blogs, 204

C

Canadian Center for Cultural Innovation
   (CCCI), xliv

Card catalogue, 42, 45, 53, 58, *See also*
   Dewey's system
Case study, 25–33, 136
Communication, 25–33
   two modes of, 25–33
Consensual hallucination, 180
Consumers, 229
Context, 117–120
   interpretive relational, 118–119, 125
   social relational, 117–118
Contextuality, 28
Copyleft effect, 273, *See also* Copyright
   effect
Copyright, xliv, 85–86
   law, 271–273
   owner, 271–272
   material, 271–272
   effect, 273
Copyright Law Review Committee (CLRC),
   277–278, *See also* Open Content
   Licensing
Creative Commons, 272–274, 276, 278–279,
   291
   publicity, 272
   negotiability, 272
   attribution, 276
   noncommercial, 276
   no derivatives, 276
   share alike, 276
Critical discourse analytic approach, 166
Critical theory, 164–168
Crown Copyright Inquiry, 277
Cultural axiology, 261–262

Cultural conflict, 24
Cultural freedom, 266–267
Cultural heritage initiatives, 76, *See also*
    Cultural heritage institutions
Cultural heritage institutions, 73–74, 76–77
Cultural labor, 263–264
Cultural production, 262–263
Cultural transition, 33
Cultural worthlessness, 266–267
Culture, 256
    making, 259–261
    participatory, 266
    rehumanizing, 262–263
    value of, 256–259
Cybernetics, 180
Cyberspace, 179–181
Cybertechnology, 39, 47–52, 54–55
Cybrary, xxvi, 63–65, 113–115, 154, 181–182,
    202, 208–209
    management, 126–128
    researching and evaluating, 124–126

D

Data, 115–116
Data collection, 50
Dewey Decimal Classification System,
    38–39, 53
Digital institutions, 208–209
Digital Millennium Copyright Act (DCMA),
    xli
Digital repository, 143–146, 273–274, 287,
    290, *See also* PARADISEC
    formats and standards, 143–145
    regional access, 145–146
Discourse, x, xxiv, xxx
    scholarly, 207
Dominant image, xxxi
Dualist epistemology, 157

E

Ecology, x
Enactment, 122–124, 125–127
Epistemological standpoints, 156–158
Epistemologies, xxxvii–xxxviii
    digital, xxxvii
    ethics or virtue, xxxviii
E-text, 197, 202–203

F

Feminism, 162–164
Foucauldian analysis, 159–160
Free software movement, 275–276, 291

G

Gender, 42, 45
Global information infrastructures, ix
Grammar, 141

H

Historical scholarship, 217–218
    commercial model for, 217–218
    marginalizing, 218–220
H-net, 212, 223
Hypermedia, 223–225
Hyperreality, 198, 200–208

I

Ibiblio, xxxii–xxxiii, *See also* online library
Idealism, 157
Image, 77–80
    retrieval, 77–80
    search, 80–85
Information, 115–116
Information literacy, 62–63
Information society, 200–208, 215
Informational utility, ix-x
Internet, 212

K

Knowledge, xxxviii, 11, 13–14, 116–117,
    125–126
    democratization of, 212–214
    fugitive, xxxix
    illegal, xxxix
    management, xxxviii, 113
    practice, 10–13
Knowledge capture, 98–104
    annotation systems, 98–100
    knowledge authentications, reliability
        and provenance, 103–104

ontologies, 101–103
  tacit and communal, 100–101
Knowledge mining, 104–107
  inference engines, 104–105
  customization and contextualizations of
    results, 106–107
  sophisticated search interfaces, 105–106

L

Language documentation, 140–142
Learning collectives, 190–191
Legitimate operators of literacy, 180
Library, xxxii, xxxiv, 285–287
  clients, 61–63
  design, 17, 24, 30–33, 57, 64, 67–70
  digital, xxxiv, *See also* Cybrary, 91–93, 107,
    155–156, 199
  experience, 65–66
  history of, 187–189
  hybrid, 63, *See also* Cybrary
  online, xxxii
  print-based, xxxix
  private, 179
  program, 41
  public, 19–21, 38, 179, 185
  research library, 183–185
  school, 18–21, 24, 31, 37, 39, 45–47
  service delivery, 57, 66–67
  library technology, 288–291
  libr@ry, xii, xiv, xxvi–xxx, xxxvii–xxxviii,
    152–154, 158, 165, 278–279, 292–294
  libr@ry studies, 152
  critical sociology of, 152
Library and information science (LIS)
    literature, 153–154
Library research, 158–162, 169
  discourse and social practice, 158–160
  space, 160–162
Liminality, 25
  spatial, 32
Literacy
  print, 25
  readings, 25–30

M

Mapping, 6–7, 9
  Maps, xxxiv, *See also* Mapping

Mass culture, 263–264
  free lunch model, 263–264
Meaning, 154–156
  spaces of, 154–156
Mediation, 77–80
Metadata, 91
Metadata generation, 93–98
  automatic document Indexing/classifica-
    tion, 94–95
  image indexing, 95–96
  new complex media and data types, 97
  speech indexing and retrieval, 96
  video indexing and retrieval, 96–97
Microsoft, 243–246
  Google/Yahoo! Rivalry, 244–245
  makes a move, 245–246
  predatory goals of, 243–246
Mobility, 5
Monist theories, 157
Monopoly capitalism, 257
Monopsony, xliv, 254, 261–264, 266
Mueseum, 73, 79, 82
Multiliteracies, 21
Multimedia response repositories, 253

N

Network, x–xii
  biological, x
  historical resource, 211
  open-knowledge, 214–215
  social, x
Networked scholarly research, 222–223
News, 255

O

Online digital documents, 200
Online Public Access Catalogues (OPACs), 58
Ontology, x, xxxviii, 92–93, 101–103
  a materialist social, x
Open access, 272–274, 291
Open Content Licensing (OCL), 277–278

P

PARADISEC, 143–146
Parrhesiastes, 292–294

Peer-to-peer sharing (P2P), xxxvii
Philosophy, 274–275
    Free culture, 275
    Creative class, 275
Place, xxvi, xxxv, 3, 5–10, 151–154, 284,
        85–287
    knowledge, 3, 10–13
    virtual, 12, 14
Porting, 276
Postmodernist, 21–24
Poststructuralism, 158
Power, xii
Production respository, 265
    digital, 267
Project Guttenburg, xxxii

R

Rhizome, xxxi
Rhythm, xxxi
    metaphors of, xxxii

S

Scholarly publishing, 225–227
Scientific research, 220–222
Search engine, 229–230, 246–249
Search engine sponsorship, 237–243
    paid inclusion, 237–239
    search engine marketers (SEMs), 239–241
    Contextual links, 241–243
Search industry structure, 230–237
    directories, 231–232
    search engine provider, 232–233
    search engine portals, 233–234
    commercial search provider, 234–237,
        248

Security, 59
Semiotic coding, 27–30
Signature specification, 103–104
Social class background, 41–45
Social logics of textual surfaces, 27–30
Social relationships, 27–30, 32
Social spatiality, 18–22, 24–25
Software development, 273–274
Space, xxvi, xxix, xxxi, 3–10, 26, 31, 126–127,
        285–287, *See also* Place
    digital, 23
    family of, 32
    interface, 22–23
    knowledge, 3, 10–13, 91
    liminal, 25, *See* Liminality
    meanings of, 154–156
    sexualization of, xxxii
    virtual, 4, 12, 14, 30, 289
Spatial relations, 28
Structuration, xxxiv
Subjectivity, 27–30
Surrogation, 80–85
Switchers, xiii

T

Teaching and learning environment, 59–61
Technolocks, xli, *See also* DCMA
Text, xxix, xxx
    print, 21
Time, xxxi
    social, xxxii

W

Wikis, 101
World Wide Web, 51–53, 56